THE DIARIES OF KATHLEEN LYNN

THE DIARIES OF KATHLEEN LYNN
A Life Revealed Through Personal Writing

To Mary — with best wishes, Mary (handwritten)

MARY McAULIFFE and HARRIET WHEELOCK

(signatures)

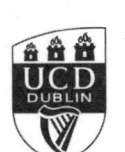

UNIVERSITY COLLEGE DUBLIN PRESS
PREAS CHOLÁISTE OLLSCOILE BHAILE ÁTHA CLIATH
2023

First published 2023
by University College Dublin Press
UCD Humanities Institute, Room H103,
Belfield,
Dublin 4

www.ucdpress.ie

ISBN 978-19-1-08200-18

CIP data available from the British Library

UCD Press and the editors kindly acknowledge the Royal College of Physicians of Ireland funding in support of this publication.

Typeset in Dublin by Gough Typesetting Limited
Text design by Lyn Davies
Printed in England on acid-free paper by
CPI Antony Rowe, Chippenham, Wiltshire

Dedicated to Madeleine ffrench-Mullen (1880–1944)
Revolutionary comrade and life partner of Dr Kathleen Lynn

Contents

Acknowledgements

The publication of Dr Kathleen Lynn's diaries has been under contemplation since 1992, when the diaries were first donated to the Royal College of Physicians of Ireland (RCPI). This publication would not have been possible without the ongoing support of the Members and Fellows of the College, especially Dr Michael Scott, Dr Paul Darragh and Professor Brendan Kelly, successive Dun's Librarians. Also, the members of the RCPI Library and Heritage Committee and Professor Mary Horgan, RCPI President 2017–23.

Thanks must go to Margaret Connolly for her herculean work in transcribing the diaries, without whose work this book would not have been possible. Thanks also to the late Margaret Ó hÓgartaigh who played an important role in bringing the life of Dr Kathleen Lynn to public knowledge. To Canon Richard 'Billy' Wynne and his son Stephen Wynne, for their generosity in donating Dr Kathleen Lynn's diaries to RCPI.

To Maura Tierney, National University of Ireland, Susan Leyden, Royal College of Surgeons in Ireland, and Selina Collard, UCD Archives, for their help in locating information on Lynn's medical education. To the staff in the Irish Military Archives and the Dublin Diocesan Archives whose help has been invaluable. A special thanks to the UCD Press team, Noelle and Órla, Fiachra, Shane, Jane and Sebastian. We would also like to thank our peer reviewers whose feedback and encouragement was so helpful in finishing this project. Also, Pauline O'Hare and Dr Anne Freeman for their invaluable proofreading.

Personally (Mary McAuliffe), I would like to thank my colleagues in the Women's History Association of Ireland (WHAI) and in Gender Studies in UCD. Many thanks for the engaging conversations on revolutionary women and their afterlives with Professor Caitríona Beaumont, Dr Leeann Lane, Dr Margaret Ward, Dr Fionnuala Walsh, Professor Lindsey Earner-Byrne and all on the Afterlives Project. Thanks for all her support to Dr Sinéad Kennedy, as well much gratitude to my ever-supportive family and, as always, thanks to Julie Valois for her constant love and support.

Personally (Harriet Wheelock), I would like to thank my colleagues, past and present, in RCPI. Thanks to my parents Jane Harvey and John Wheelock, and my brother Daniel, for their ongoing and unfailing support.

Mary McAuliffe and Harriet Wheelock
October 2023

Foreword

My Kathleen Lynn may not be the same as yours. That's all right – hers was a broad church. My Kathleen Lynn is at least partly fictional. I've been asked to introduce this volume because she features as a central character in my 2020 novel set in a Dublin hospital's maternity/fever unit during the Great Flu, *The Pull of the Stars*. For my purposes, Lynn is the archetypal good doctor, witty, analytical and compassionate, working on a vaccine in the lab when she's not striding from ward to ward to battle with Death for each patient.

For other readers, Lynn will be primarily a revolutionary – of the socialist, suffragist, anti-imperialist, or hard-core Irish Republican kind, depending on which of the threads of her commitment you follow. A political and medical campaigner and reformer, a TD and councillor, a hospital founder and administrator… Nor should we forget that Lynn was an Anglo-Irish Protestant, a minister's daughter, and a zealous Christian to the end, even if she climbed out of the comfortable social niche of her upbringing when she chose to embrace radicalism.

Lynn also embraced her fellow radicals. She was a great friend to many – her lifelong loyalty to an alcoholic comrade comes across touchingly in these pages. She was the passionate partner for three decades of Madeleine ffrench-Mullen. Lynn described the couple with discreet understatement as a 'great team' in all things; perhaps their most lasting legacy was the small, ecumenical miracle that was St Ultan's Infant's Hospital. (In a tiny link which thrills me inordinately, my mother's diary includes a reminder to bring me there for my TB vaccine in 1970.)

Judging from this rich collection of excerpts, the Kathleen Lynn diaries – close to a million words written over four key decades in the formation of Ireland (1916–55), often consulted by scholars but not published till now – are an astonishment. From her first entry in 1916, they bristle with an energetic intelligence, a hunger for change: 'Thank God Ireland is alive & throbbing.' Lynn as social commentator is opinionated, rueful, funny and heartfelt. Her countless references to her beloved 'M ffM' add up to one of the best accounts we have of a long same-sex partnership. Mostly she jotted down their work, meetings and travels, relieved by moments of domestic respite or fun with friends or their dog Bran, but sometimes absence prompted an eloquent declaration of what 'barren wilderness' life could be without Madeleine.

A.G.O.W., all goes on well, Lynn wrote repeatedly, despite how many reasons she had for crushing disappointment, as the vote for women and freedom for Ireland failed to bring in the new and just world she'd worked for. *D.G., deo gratias*, Lynn kept adding, determinedly thankful for everything from a good meeting to a release of prisoners, a sunrise, to the serene expression on a dead friend's face. She noted that her hunger-striking comrade Thomas Ashe died 'with my finger on his pulse', and what the phrase evokes for me is that Lynn would always keep her finger on the pulse of life in its smallest, most personal details as well as its grander historical movements.

There are many Kathleen Lynns; she squeezed so much into her 81 years. *Alive & throbbing*, indeed, as long as breath was in her, and the world was better for the marks she left on it, which is only one reason why the long-overdue publication of a selection of Kathleen Lynn journals is a cause for what she would have called a loud *hip hip DG*.

Emma Donoghue
September 2023

PART 1: INTRODUCTION

THE DIARIES OF KATHLEEN LYNN
REVEALING HISTORY THROUGH PERSONAL WRITING

INTRODUCTION

In March 1916, Kathleen Lynn, who was then 42 years old, began keeping a diary. At that stage of her life, she was a qualified medical professional, a seasoned political activist, and already engaged in what would be a lifelong personal relationship with fellow activist Madeleine ffrench-Mullen. She would continue to keep the daily diary, with very few interruptions, until close to her death in 1955. As a historical source it is very important for Irish women's history as it covers her involvement in many momentous events in early-to-mid-twentieth-century Irish history: the 1916 Rising, the War of Independence, the Civil War, and the formative three and a half decades of the Irish Free State, 1922–55. More importantly, the diaries allow us to hear Kathleen Lynn's own voice as she speaks about her activism, her network of close female comrades and friends, and her relationship with ffrench-Mullen. They reveal her intimate thoughts, feelings and emotions, as she navigated her way through her public and private life, as well as her responses to local, national, and global politics and events. Diaries and personal texts are often written in a uniquely individual style, seen clearly in the Lynn diaries, revealing 'intimate and private matters, such as loves, dreams, worries and friendships, and offer a highly subjective interpretation of events'.[1]

These diaries demonstrate how Lynn negotiated her own conflicting identities, her journey from moderate to radical politics, her work as a doctor, her activism, her politics and personal life. In 1916, she was about to become involved in one of the most significant events in early-twentieth-century Irish history, when she began to record both what was happening and her responses to it. It was common that women, especially those involved in activism, began diaries during periods of great change, such as during revolution, when they felt they were 'part of history and wished to record their experiences for posterity'.[2] The fact that Lynn begins her diaries on scraps of paper, which she later transferred into notebooks, indicates that she felt she was part of something meaningful which deserved to be recorded. Without records, like those Lynn created, we would know much less of Irish women's participation in these histories, because much of what is known of the suffrage and revolutionary women is mediated through gendered archives that shaped the male centric, hegemonic narrative of most revolutionary and post-revolutionary histories. Despite, however, the male subjectivity of institutionalised archives, there are surviving memoirs, letters, documents and diaries by revolutionary women, whose eyewitness accounts give

---

1. June Purvis, 'Using primary sources when researching women's history from a feminist perspective', *Women's History Review*, 1992, p. 294.
2. Ibid., p. 294.

a gendered, complicated, and nuanced understanding of their experiences of the period. Scholars have used sources such as Lynn's 'to overcome and challenge the gendered and racialised boundaries of the archive, to literally tell different histories'.[3] They can reveal how women activists negotiated societal customs and expectations, challenged attitudes, broke through gendered boundaries to, like Lynn, live a life less ordinary, outside of the expected norms of marriage, motherhood, and domesticity.

While diaries written by women who lived during the revolutionary period and on into the Irish Free State are few, Lynn was not the only one in her friendship network to keep a diary. Rosamond Jacob was also a daily diarist and both women feature in each other's diaries.[4] Unlike Lynn, Jacob began her diary as a child, well before her involvement in cultural, suffrage and nationalist organisations, allowing the reader to follow 'her developing sense of self identity as an Irish nationalist and her growing feminist consciousness'.[5] Lynn, on the other hand, began her diary in March 1916, with her first full entry on St Patrick's Day, 17 March which read, 'Went to Irish Service at S. Andrew's, saw Volunteer Parade in street and heard bands. Thank God Ireland is alive & throbbing'.[6] Lynn's already established militancy is visible; she was delighted to see the Irish Volunteers parading on Ireland's National Day and that Ireland was 'alive & throbbing' with patriotic nationalism. The question must be asked, however, how the daughter of a conservative Protestant clergyman, from a unionist background, an ostensibly respectable and successful female doctor, then in her 40s, found herself actively involved in fomenting revolution against the British Crown? The historian must also consider what the diary meant to Lynn: she began it as her life was taking a dramatic and radical turn and is indicative of an awareness and self-knowledge of the importance of what was happening and what she was part of. Her diaries allow her to record emotions, ideas, events, people and places that are central to her identity as a revolutionary, a feminist, a socialist, and as a doctor.

THE KATHLEEN LYNN DIARIES

As well as being a fascinating insight into Lynn's life, her diaries are also an extraordinary archival item, created in a way completely unique to Lynn. The 39 years covered by the diaries are compressed into just four volumes. Rather than the standard daily or weekly diary layout, Lynn uses a double page spread for each day of the year. Within each double page spread a printed line is used to record one year: the first line is the year 1916, the next 1917, and so on. With such limited space she compresses several lines of script into each printed line. Combined with the use of numerous abbreviations, code names and her doctor's typically bad handwriting, the diaries are a compact block of cramped and difficult-to-decipher text. While Lynn never records why she started the diaries, it is obvious that the events of 1916 were the catalyst. Her diary entries for the days and weeks following Easter

3. Jane Freeland and Christina von Hodenberg, 'Archiving, exhibiting, and curating the history of feminisms in the global twentieth century: an introduction', *Women's History Review*, 2023, p. 2.
4. See Leeann Lane, *Rosamond Jacob: Third Person Singular* (Dublin, 2010).
5. Ibid., p. 14.
6. Kathleen Lynn Diaries (henceforth KLD), 17 March 1916. Lynn's diaries are held in the Royal College of Physicians (RCPI) Archive, IE RCPI/KL, 1916–55.

Monday 1916 were originally written in blue pencil on scraps of paper, presumably all that she had to hand while in jail.[7] Entries in the diaries continue to be sporadic and short until the end of 1918, often just noting key events, such as on 25 September 1917; 'Thomas Ashe died in Mater with my finger on his pulse'.[8] From 1919, however, until a few months before her death, in September 1955, she kept a diary, almost daily, resulting in a record of her life stretching to over 900,000 words.

At some point, between 1916 and 1919, Lynn transferred her initial rough diary entries into two volumes, the first covering entries from January to June and the second from July to December. In 2023 when these volumes were being prepared for digitisation the paper and cloth covers were removed to reveal the original bindings. The volumes are bound in blue leather, with gold decorative tooling, with the lettering 'On Sea & Land by W R Wynne', on the spine. Probably dating from the second half of the nineteenth century, the covers would have been an expensive, custom order.[9] W. R. Wynne was certainly a relative of Lynn's, and was probably her uncle, Willoughby Robert Wynne (1843–87), a judge who died at sea when returning to Ireland from a posting in the Straits Settlement (now Malaysia). It seems most likely that the volumes were originally commissioned to contain an autobiography by W. R. Wynne but remained unused in the Wynne family until taken by Lynn to record a very different life. The reuse of the books would also have had the added benefit of disguising the diaries, as they could have sat openly on a bookshelf giving no hint of their content. This would have been very important during police or military raids on her home, during the War of Independence, Civil War and in the 1930s when important papers were often taken. In contrast to the fine bindings of the first volumes, the two later volumes, containing the years 1937 to 1955, are plain hardbound notebooks from Healy's of Dublin.

A reading of the diary entries gives an insight into the rhythm of Lynn's life, one brimming with activity, energy, and deep commitment to her beliefs. Despite the limitations on length of entries set by her unique format, Lynn manages to cram a huge amount into an entry. In four short lines she reflects the breadth of her interests, from politics to gardening, her patients to the weather, her family to the benefits of fresh air and sunshine. Her religious life comes across strongly, most entries starting with a reference to her attendance at a morning church service, and she notes key dates in the liturgical calendar. Most likely because of the format used to write her diaries, she has a tendency towards comparison with and reflection on what had happened in previous years, something that becomes increasingly common as she ages. The second last diary entry, written on 24 April 1955, recalls the events of 39 years earlier '2 A.E. 8 a.m. R.mines. Then 11.30 Commemoration Service. S. Mary's very nice, tho' not over many there. A beautiful day like 1916 was.'[10] Preserved within the pages of the diaries are ephemeral items which also reflect the things that were of importance to her: newspaper cuttings about St Ultan's Hospital, to which she devoted her working life, her 1927 election handbill, a lock of her dog Bran's hair and,

---

7. These are preserved with the diaries, KL/2/1 (1–6), RCPI Archives.
8. KLD, 25 September 1917.
9. Interview with Tom Duffy of Duffy Bindery, 11 May 2023.
10. KLD, 24 April 1955.

perhaps most poignantly, a four-leaf clover given to her by Madeleine ffrench-Mullen in 1922.

The diaries give a deep insight into the life of a professional woman in the first decades of the Irish Free State. They demonstrate the revolutionary, socialist, and feminist fervour of the pre-1922 radical women, what motivated them and the work they did for women, workers, and Ireland. They also shed a light on the difficult road forged by these radical political women in the new Free State: a free state that still viewed women through the constraining lens of marriage, motherhood, and domesticity, where women like Lynn were regarded, and often treated, as threats to the establishment. Lynn's diaries give interesting insights into the supportive networks of professional, political, and activist women who worked together for social and political change long after the revolution was over. The diaries also vividly demonstrate the number of women who had an impact on medical care in the first decades of the Irish Free State, but whose legacies are often overlooked or forgotten. They cover her medical work, showing her devotion to her patients, often working long and late into the night. They demonstrate her commitment to better housing and education for all, particularly those caught in the vicious cycle of poverty in the Dublin slums. They give a revealing insight into her private life and thinking, revealing a woman fully engaged with the world. The most sustaining relationship was with 'M ffM' – Madeleine ffrench-Mullen – her partner of many years. She was also supported and sustained by her paternal Lynn family, her maternal Wynne family and a close network of friends. They also show a woman fully committed to her faith, with near daily attendance at Church of Ireland services. She was a lover of the outdoors, the diaries show her firm belief in the health efficacy of fresh air, sunbathes and swims. Few political women who lived through the Irish revolutionary period and the early decades of the Irish Free State have left behind as substantial a record as Kathleen Lynn.

Following Lynn's death her diaries were preserved by her maternal cousin, Canon Richard 'Billy' Wynne, and, in 1997, Canon Wynne and his son Stephen donated the diaries to the Royal College of Physicians of Ireland (RCPI). They wanted them to be housed with the records of her life's work at St Ultan's Hospital, which had been transferred to RCPI following the closure of the hospital in 1984. The following year RCPI appointed archivist Margaret Connolly to undertake the task of deciphering and transcribing Lynn's writing. She described the task as being akin to unpicking stitches in knitting, untangling one stitch at a time. Connolly recalled that, as she worked, she became familiar with Lynn's handwriting and the structure of the entries. As she was, however, focusing so intently on making out individual words, she didn't gain much of a sense of the overall narrative of the diaries.[11] From the start, RCPI had wanted to publish the diaries in some format, but initial enquiries with publishers were disheartening, one responding with a short-sightedness rooted in a dismissal of the female voice: 'There is little here for the historian to get *his* [our emphasis] teeth into – no original insights, no privileged observation of events, just a corroborative commentary on materials already well known'.[12] Despite this negative assessment, the diaries have consistently been the single most consulted item in

11. Interview with Margaret Connolly, 10 May 2023.
12. Letter dated 3 September 1998, ACC/1997/2 Documentation File, Royal College of Physicians of Ireland.

RCPI's archive collections, accessed and studied by researchers from around the world. This publication of selected extracts from her diaries serves in part to readdress issues created by past archival and publishing practices which have, in many cases, marginalised or silenced the voices and histories of women.

The task of editing the 900,000 words of Lynn's diaries into a manageable quantity for publication was a daunting one. We decided early on that we would not edit or shorten the entries, as we felt this would result in the loss of Lynn's unique voice. The style of her entries – short, packed with activities, friends and opinions – reflect her busy and varied life and we did not want to lose this. Instead, we selected whole entries for inclusion or exclusion. As we worked through the entire transcript, we brought our backgrounds in gender, social, revolutionary and political history and the history of medicine to the selection of entries. This process was repeated, and refined, four times to provide what is a representative sample of Lynn's words and life. In keeping with the decision to preserve Lynn's voice as far as possible we have not attempted to 'correct' or standardise her spelling and grammar. The text retains Lynn's staccato style, her idiosyncratic spelling and her codenames for friends. In some instances Lynn's handwriting has defied transcription. These places are indicated using [ ] to show either gaps or our best guess at what Lynn wrote. We have provided a glossary to Lynn's diaries to help identify the sometimes bewildering array of individuals who formed the medical, political and friendship networks across her long life. Also, where possible, we provide context to the events Lynn mentions and comments on in her diaries. It has not been possible to identify all the names and events: some have, unfortunately, slipped through the cracks of history. Any error in the transcription of Lynn's diaries are the editors alone and can be corrected in future editions. For those who wish to engage with the original diaries and tackle Lynn's handwriting themselves, the original diaries have been digitised and made available on the RCPI Heritage Centre website – heritage.rcpi.ie/ Projects/Dr-Kathleen-Lynn.

KATHLEEN LYNN, 1874–1916

Kathleen Florence Lynn was born in January 1874 in Mullafarry, near Killala, Co. Mayo, the second daughter of Robert Lynn, a Church of Ireland clergyman, and his wife Catherine (née Wynne) of Drumcliffe, Co. Sligo. She had two sisters, Anne Elizabeth 'Nan' (*b.* 1873), Emily Muriel, known as Muriel (*b.* 1876), and a brother John (*b.* 1877), all of whom feature in her diaries. The family were of the Anglo-Irish Protestant upper middle class. Her maternal family, the Wynnes, were descended from planters who were granted lands in Sligo in the 1670s. Among the senior branches of the family were the Earls of Hazelwood. Owen Wynne (1843–1910), a second cousin to Lynn, married Stella (1846–87), a daughter of Sir Robert Gore Booth, and aunt of Constance Markievicz (née Gore Booth), of Lissadell in Co. Sligo. This connected two Protestant radical revolutionary women, Lynn and Markievicz, by class, social standing and marriage, long before they became comrades in arms. On the paternal side, the Lynns were doctors and clergymen. Robert Lynn, the son of a doctor, took his degree in divinity in Trinity College Dublin. The family moved to Mullafarry when he was appointed rector of Ballysakeery in the early 1870s. In 1882, when Kathleen was eight years old, the family moved to Shrule in Longford where her father took over at Ballymahon parish. A growing reputation as a clergyman then won Reverend Lynn a prestigious appointment in the gift of Lord Ardilaun (of the Guinness family) at St Marys in Cong, Co. Mayo in 1886.[13]

By the time the family moved to the well-appointed rectory in Cong, Kathleen was preparing to leave home for school in Dublin. However, important aspects of her character were influenced by her childhood in Mayo and Longford. Her mother, Catherine was involved, like most women of her class, in charitable good works, which, as she later acknowledged, made the young Kathleen aware of the extreme levels of poverty and deprivation in Mayo.[14] The western seaboard areas had seen enormous depopulation after the Great Famine (1845–50) with much of the remaining population surviving on small farms of mountain, bog and bad land. The local economy was often one of subsistence, with families surviving on the potato crop, a few cattle or pigs, and wages from seasonal migration to Scotland or England. Most were tenant farming families, and any fall in prices for cattle or cash crops, as happened in the late 1870s, impacted their livelihoods, ability to pay rent and to feed themselves. While the Lynn family were, because of their class and social standing, insulated from the deprivations of hunger and poverty faced by many of their less fortunate neighbours, they cannot have been unaware of what was happening around them. Mullafarry was an impoverished place, most of its population living in poverty, and, as Lynn later recalled, the sight of this had an impact on her as a young girl.[15] While Shrule in Longford had better land and was more prosperous, it was here that she encountered the local doctor, Dr Francis Smartt, who, much to her admiration, was 'able to ease the distress of the local people'.[16] Smartt was related to the Lynn family and, as she recalled, he was a 'fount of help and hope, and so I decided to become a doctor'.[17] Aged 16 she was sent to school in England and Germany, beginning a lifelong love of the German language, people, and culture. By the time she was 17, in 1891, she had left home to enrol in Alexandra College in Dublin. Cong would, from then on, be a place she visited while Dublin would be her home for the rest of her life.

Alexandra College was founded in 1866 by Anne Jellicoe who was among several pioneering women educationalists most of whom were part of the suffrage and reform movements in Britain and Ireland from the 1850s. These women sought to 'address the issues of middle-class women's access to education and career opportunities' and develop routes for women to all levels of education.[18] Alexandra was the first university-style institution for women in Ireland and had a broad curriculum which included 'English language and literature, mathematics, history, natural science, geography, Latin, mental and moral philosophy, music, drawing, and callisthenics'.[19] Jellicoe, however, had greater

---

13. Medb Ruane, 'Kathleen Lynn (1874–1955)' in Mary Cullen and Maria Luddy (eds), *Female Activists: Irish Women and Social Change 1900–1960* (Dublin, 2001), p. 62.
14. Ibid., p. 62.
15. Ibid., p. 62.
16. Margaret Ó hÓgartaigh, *Kathleen Lynn: Irishwoman, Patriot, Doctor* (Dublin, 2006), p. 7.
17. Ruane, 'Kathleen Lynn', p. 62. One of Dr Smartt's daughters, Elizabeth 'Lizzie' remained close to Lynn and appears in the diaries.
18. Gillian McLelland and Diana Hadden, *Pioneering Women: Riddel Hall and Queen's University Belfast* (Belfast, 2005), p. 9.
19. Ibid.

ambitions for women's education: one of the major contributions she made through Alexandra was to 'open University education and public examinations to women', as it became the first educational institution for girls in Ireland 'that aspired to University education for its pupils'.[20] By 1869 she had persuaded Trinity College Dublin to set up examinations for women so that 'female students could be examined in university subjects and thereby display their academic ability'.[21] By 1879, the Intermediate Education Act allowed girls to take examinations at secondary level, soon followed by the Royal University Ireland Act, providing for the formation of a new University in Ireland, which could grant degrees to women and men. For ambitious students like Kathleen Lynn, there was now a path forward for tertiary training and education.

Lynn was an excellent student, achieving high marks in many courses including 'arithmetic, geography, Latin, history and music'.[22] For her, Alex, as the College was affectionately known, was a place where she was able to achieve her full potential. Interestingly she was the only one of the three Lynn daughters to attend Alex and train in a profession. Reverend Lynn does not seem to have been a supporter of female education, or his second daughter's desire to become a doctor. One of Medb Ruane's interviewees who spoke about the young Lynn said that 'if he'd had his way, he would have kept her at home'.[23] It is probable that it was the family's connection with Alex, (her mother was related to Archbishop Trench, a founding patron of the college), and her own determination to be a doctor, that got her to Alex.[24] When Lynn arrived in the college there was another pioneering Lady Principal in charge. This was Henrietta White, who like Jellicoe, was a vocal advocate for women's education and practical philanthropy. Under her guidance, Alex offered their 'girls' more than an excellent education; it also offered 'a context in which [their lives] could take shape'.[25] Students received lectures on women's rights from the veteran suffragist Anna Haslam, who often visited, and they also learned about 'local government reform, employment conditions for women, poverty, housing, Irish history and the Irish language', subjects which would be central to Lynn's public life in adulthood.[26] These ideas about an active life were very much part of new thinking on women's roles in society where 'philanthropic activity provided the middle-class woman with an enhanced public role in society and a number of women philanthropists entered the public world of politics through their charitable work'.[27] Lynn's mother had been engaged in charity, but this more active commitment to practical philanthropy would, for engaged students like Lynn, prove to be more political. Alex also provided her with an abiding interest in and knowledge of gardening, as White persuaded Frederick Moore, Head Gardener of the

---

20. Anne V. O'Connor and Susan M. Parkes, *Gladly Learn and Gladly Teach: A History of Alexandra College and School, Dublin, 1866–1966* (Dublin, 1984), p. 1.
21. Parkes, 'Anne Jellicoe' (DIB), pp 64–65.
22. Ruane, 'Kathleen Lynn', p. 65.
23. Ibid., p. 64, footnote 16, interview with May Cummins.
24. Ibid., pp 64–5.
25. Ibid., p. 65.
26. Ibid.
27. Maria Luddy, 'Women and politics in nineteenth-century Ireland', Maryanne Gialanella Valuilis and Mary O'Dowd (eds), *Women and Irish History* (Dublin, 1997), p. 98.

Botanic Gardens, to run courses in horticulture for her students. White also founded the hockey and cycling clubs in Alexandra, and Lynn remained a keen cyclist well into her older age. In 1897, after Lynn had graduated, White set up the Alexandra Guild to build a bond between past and present students, to encourage in them an understanding of 'useful work … and to interest them in, and inform them about, women's work'.[28] At the Guild's first meeting Dr Katharine Maguire, who would later co-found St Ultan's Hospital with Lynn, read a paper on 'The Social Conditions of the Dublin Poor'. In it she encouraged the members to improve the living experiences of the urban poor by 'buying and maintaining tenement houses in Dublin'.[29] The Guild began to address, in this practical way, the needs of the urban poor, and provide decent housing at affordable rents. According to Valiulis it was not simply a charity, it was a private venture with a sound financial basis which it hoped would 'inspire other private individuals to invest in the city's housing and alleviate the condition of the poor'.[30] Lynn would remain an enthusiastic member of the Guild all her adult life. That it influenced her social activism on housing is evident when she later adapted the guild model 'for inner city housing and community projects … generated by St Ultan's'.[31]

Alexandra College suited Lynn. She blossomed there, coming second in the Stern Scholarship, in 1892, and matriculating in the 1893 Royal University of Ireland (RUI) exams. Lynn had wanted to be a doctor from a young age, and, in 1894, aged 20, she began her medical studies, becoming part of the second generation of women to study medicine. Two decades earlier, a group of pioneering women had fought for the right to study and qualify in medicine, culminating in the Enabling Act of 1876. Dr Eliza Walker Dunbar was the first woman to register as a doctor in Ireland and Britain, when she received her Licentiate from the King and Queen's (now Royal) College of Physicians of Ireland in January 1877. Research by Laura Kelly has revealed that Ireland had a more permissive attitude in allowing women study medicine, and a policy of non-segregation of teaching by gender. As a result, Lynn had a choice of places to study, although neither at the Catholic University (now UCD) nor at Trinity College Dublin. This would have been her natural choice as it was her father's alma mater and the Protestant University, but Trinity did not admit women until 1904.[32] Instead she commenced her medical studies on 3 October 1893 at the Royal College of Science for Ireland.[33] She also studied at the Royal College of Surgeons in Ireland (RCSI), where she received the Barker Anatomical Prize in 1898.

28. Maryanne Gialanella Valiulis, 'Toward "the moral and material improvement of the working classes": The founding of the Alexandra College Guild Tenement Company, Dublin, 1898', *Journal of Urban History,* 23(3), 1997, p. 295.
29. Ibid., p. 296.
30. Ibid., p. 300.
31. Ruane, 'Kathleen Lynn', p. 65.
32. The Catholic University admitted the first women in 1898 and Trinity College in 1904. Laura Kelly, *Irish Women in Medicine, c.1880s–1920s: Origins, Education and Careers* (London, 2015), pp 44–5.
33. *Medical Students' Register* (London, 1896), p. 52. Throughout her medical career Lynn records her medical school as the Royal College of Science in the annual published *Medical Directory.* The Royal College of Science for Ireland was founded in 1867, specialising in higher education in physical and applied sciences, women were admitted from its foundation. It was absorbed into UCD in 1926.

Lynn seems to have had a flair for anatomy: in 1896, the Alexandra College magazine celebrated the 'brilliant success' of their former student who came first in her practical anatomy examinations, 'a distinction not hitherto achieved by a woman'.[34] Interestingly, anatomy, and especially dissection, was the most controversial area of medical education for women, due both to the sexualised nature of dissection, and Victorian ideas around female delicacy, but Lynn was not one to let such issues stand in her way.[35] She undertook her practical training in several Dublin hospitals, including the Richmond Lunatic Asylum and the Rotunda Lying-In Hospital, from which she received a Licentiate in Midwifery. Most of her time, however, was spent at the Adelaide Hospital, where she enrolled as a student in 1895. In 1898 she applied for the role of resident student in the hospital but, while the medical board recognised her ability, they were unable to appoint her due to a lack of any sleeping accommodation suitable for a female medical student.[36] She graduated in medicine from RUI, in 1899, receiving the Hudson Prize, awarded to the Adelaide student with the highest marks in the final examination.

Once qualified, Lynn began her life as a medical professional in a field dominated by men, albeit one in which women were beginning to make their presence felt. In the 1901 Census she described herself as a 'House Surgeon' living in Molesworth St and working at the Royal Victoria Eye and Ear Hospital. By 1903 she had moved to 9 Belgrave Rd, Rathmines, a house rented from the Plunkett family, and where she would live for the rest of her life. As noted by Ruane, Lynn was now moving in more nationalist, and later militant, circles; one of the Plunketts' sons, Joseph, would be a signatory to the Proclamation of 1916, executed after the Rising, while a daughter, Geraldine (later Dillon), later a member of Cumann na mBan, was part of Lynn's wider network of activist friends. She also knew Francis and Hanna Sheehy Skeffington, both suffrage activists and editors of the *Irish Citizen* newspaper, founded in 1912, to which she contributed. Francis was killed during the 1916 Rising, and Hanna would move to 7 Belgrave Rd, in 1918, becoming Lynn's neighbour. It was in 9 Belgrave Rd that Lynn established her successful GP practice: in the 1911 Census she is recorded as living there and described herself as a 'General practitioner MB Bch RUI FRCSI'.[37] She had passed the RCSI fellowship examination in 1909, only the tenth woman to do so since Dr Emily Winifred Dickson in 1893. She returned to the Royal Victoria Eye and Ear as Clinical Assistant, in 1911, but lost her post in 1916 as 'since the recent rebellion Dr Kathleen Lynn has not attended the Hospital. She has neither applied for leave, sent in her resignation nor offered any explanation for her absence'.[38] The trajectory towards her involvement in the 1916 Rising began early in her medical career when she became involved in various suffrage and representative medical bodies.

---

34. Quoted in Mary Cullen and Maria Luddy (eds), *Female Activists: Irish Women and Change 1900–1960* (Dublin, 2001), p. 66.

35. Kelly, *Irish Women in Medicine, c.1880s–1920s*, pp 94–5.

36. David Mitchell, *A 'Peculiar' Place: The Adelaide Hospital, Dublin: Its Times, Places and Personalities, 1839 to 1989* (Dublin, 1989), p. 258.

37. Census of Ireland, 1911, http://www.census.nationalarchives.ie/pages/1911/Dublin/Rathmines___Rathgar_East/Belgrave_Road/52501/, accessed 25/07/2023.

38. Meeting of the Council of the Eye and Ear Dublin 1916, quoted in Gearoid Crookes, *Dublin's Eye & Ear: The Making of a Monument* (Dublin, 1993), p. 105.

According to Kelly there were 42 female medical practitioners in Dublin in 1911, most of whom Lynn knew or worked with at some stage in her career.[39] In 1908, a number of these women came together to establish the Irish Association of Registered Medical Women, with Dr Katharine Maguire as its first President.[40] Lynn was involved from the beginning and, by 1911, had become Secretary of the Association, a post she would hold until at least 1915. As Kelly suggests the existence of the association shows 'a sense of community or network amongst these early women doctors in Dublin'.[41] The women involved in the association were engaged in suffrage activism, believing that professional women should have equality with men through the 'employment of medical women in connection with prisons, schools, public health'.[42]

These campaigns indicate that Lynn was, at this time, political in a way similar to many women of her class, religious background and educational attainment. She was interested in the recognition of women in professions and as citizens, but was as yet to make the intellectual jump to more radical politics. That, however, was not long in coming. There are hints that her politics were in the process of shifting from moderate to militant in her membership of the Irish branch (she served as secretary for a time) of the British Women's Social and Political Union (WSPU), the militant suffrage organisation set up by the Pankhursts in 1903. As unearthed by Ruane, she was named among the Suffrage fellowship in the WSPU records from 1908.[43] There were also female militant organisations in Ireland at that time, among them the militant, separatist and feminist organisation Inghínídhe na hÉireann (Daughters of Ireland) founded in 1900 by Maud Gonne McBride, and the militant suffrage group the Irish Women's Franchise League (IWFL), co-founded in 1908 by the Sheehy Skeffingtons. However, Lynn was more involved with the moderate, constitutional, non-militant Irish Women's Suffrage and Local Government Association (IWSLGA), which had been founded in 1876. It had achieved some notable successes, including securing, by the late 1890s, the local Government vote for women and the appointment of women as Poor Law Guardians. The parliamentary franchise for women remained its focus, but it was a limited and moderate lobbying campaign, drawing much of its membership from among the non-Catholic middle and upper class. Her religious background and social class fit with IWSLGA membership: by 1903 she was a member of its executive and would remain a member until 1916.[44] Among the IWSLGA membership were many women who would follow a similar political trajectory as Lynn, from constitutional to militant suffrage activism, including Hanna Sheehy Skeffington, several women doctors including Dr Katharine Maguire and Dr Ella Webb, as well as Louie Bennett and Helen Chenevix, later senior trade union leaders.

Of her own journey to radicalism, Lynn noted that she was converted to republicanism through suffrage activism: 'I saw that people got the wrong impression about suffrage

---

39. Laura Kelly, 'Irish medical women *c.*1880s–1920s: The origins, education and careers of early women medical graduates from Irish institutions', PhD Thesis, University of Galway, 2010, p. 183.
40. Ibid.
41. Ibid.
42. Ibid.
43. Ruane, 'Kathleen Lynn', p. 68.
44. Ó hÓgartaigh, *Kathleen Lynn,* p. 19.

that led me to examine the Irish question'.[45] Her developing friendships with the younger generation of more militant suffrage women, the influences of Alexandra College on her ideas about social change and helping those in need, and involvement in cultural nationalism and a developing sense of Irishness, certainly seem to have had an impact on her politics. As early as 1902, she was aware of the awful conditions of tenement living in Dublin: a newspaper report of 1902 records her attendance at a meeting of the Dublin Sanitary Association.[46] This association was set up, in 1872, to improve defective sanitary arrangements in homes and hospitals in Dublin; the 1902 meeting discussed campaigns to have separate wards for pulmonary consumption patients, the major problem of child neglect and infant mortality, and the need for urgent attention to sanitation in tenement dwellings. Ireland was, the attendees were told, 'fifty years behind in matters of public health compared to England'.[47] These concerns about infant mortality, unsanitary living conditions among the poor of Dublin, and proper hospital standards for treatment of infectious diseases would be issues which would be central to her work as a doctor.

It is also important to note Lynn's lifelong faith practice as a committed member of the Church of Ireland. Like many of her generation she felt a repulsion towards cultural Anglicisation in a secular sense. Her spirituality gave succour and support throughout her life, but she also sought ways to reconcile her Protestantism and her Irishness, a tension frequently alluded to in her diaries. Similarly to other women and men from non-Catholic backgrounds she demonstrated her Irishness through an Anglophobia expressed through cultural nationalism and separatism, using, consciously or unconsciously, 'Anglophobia and Gaelicisation [as] a way of demonstrating [her] nationalist credentials'.[48] Inghínidhe na hÉireann, for instance, expected its members to 'fight for the complete separation of Ireland from England' and to 'combat in every way English influences' on Irish language, culture and society.[49] Helena Molony, a key figure in the deepening of Lynn's radical politics, would take over leadership of the group when Gonne McBride returned to France, in 1905. Under Molony's stewardship, it became more radical 'emphasising, separatism, socialism and feminism more explicitly than before'.[50] Founded in 1908, with Molony as its editor, its newspaper *Bean na hÉireann* 'asked women to de-Anglicise even the smallest aspects of their lives in order to pursue meaningful political change'.[51] Among the contributors to the newspaper were many of the revolutionary generation with whom Lynn was already, or would soon be, politically involved; Molony, Gonne McBride, Sidney Gifford (John Brennan), Countess Markievicz, Maeve Cavanagh, Susan Mitchell, George Russell, Thomas MacDonagh, Patrick Pearse, Joseph Plunkett and the woman who would be central to her life, Madeleine ffrench-Mullen. As Oonagh Walsh has argued, the *Bean* articles, many written by Protestant contributors, were free of confessional rhetoric and

---

45. Ruane, 'Kathleen Lynn', p. 68.
46. *Irish Independent*, 21 February 1902, p. 5.
47. Ibid.
48. Roy Foster, *Vivid Faces: The Revolutionary Generation in Ireland 1890–1923* (London, 2014), p. 53.
49. Senia Pašeta, *Irish Nationalist Women, 1900–1918* (Cambridge, 2013), pp 39–40.
50. Ibid., p. 94.
51. John Burn Library, Boston College blog, Erin Sheehy, 'Bean na hÉireann (The Woman of Ireland)', https://johnjburnslibrary.wordpress.com/2022/04/04/bean-na-heireann-the-woman-of-ireland/, accessed 24/07/2023.

demonstrated 'the old Fenian virtue' of a secular republicanism.[52] Unlike some Protestant nationalist comrades, including Gonne McBride and Markievicz, Lynn remained a lifelong member of the Church of Ireland. Her growing Anglophobia and her developing socialism, however, combined with the influences of Molony and ffrench-Mullen, brought her to secular republicanism. This position would become increasingly evident in the 1920s and 1930s as she found herself living and running a secular hospital in an increasingly Catholic state.

It is at the end of the first decade of the twentieth century that Lynn comes into her political maturity. In tandem with her deepening commitment to advanced nationalism, her suffrage ideals became broader, more inclusive of campaigns for women workers, universal male suffrage and radical social change to eradicate poverty and deprivation. Many suffrage women were, like her, concerned with broader social issues such as child poverty, access to education, social deprivation, as well as the vote. By 1912, she was part of a campaign to have female suffrage included in the Third Home Rule Bill, attending mass meetings in Dublin. This campaign failed and the right to female suffrage was not included in the bill. On 13 June 1912, the first stone was thrown by militant Irish suffragettes at windows in Dublin Castle: the IWFL had begun its militant campaign. Among the militants arrested and imprisoned was Lynn's comrade, Hanna Sheehy Skeffington. Later, in July 1912, when the British Prime Minister Herbert Asquith came to Dublin, two WSPU suffragettes, Mary Leigh and Gladys Evans, followed him bringing a small hatchet which they flung at him, narrowly missing his head. Both were arrested, imprisoned in Mountjoy Jail and promptly went on hunger strike. The local suffragettes were not impressed with this WSPU intervention, 'unfortunately they did not leave heckling in Irish hands', but felt they had to show solidarity with Leigh and Evans.[53] Sheehy Skeffington and three others, still in Mountjoy, went on hunger strike. After five days, the Irish women were released, and the authorities began to force feed Evans and Leigh. Concern about the health and wellbeing of the women led to a letter, addressed to the Viceroy, from Kathleen Emerson, secretary of the IWFL, appearing in the *Evening Herald* on 13 August 1912. The signatories, including Dr Kathleen Lynn, Dr Katharine Maguire, and Dr Elizabeth Tennant, stated they wished to 'lay a memorial on behalf of Mrs Mary Leigh, Miss Gladys Baker and Miss Lizzie Baker'.[54] Leigh was released, on licence, on 20 September, and Evans on 3 October. As a result of the furore caused by the hunger strike, it was decided to imprison any suffragettes arrested in the future in Tullamore Jail in Co. Offaly, where they could be 'quarantined from a public which was potentially disruptive'.[55] By January 1913, with more windows smashed in Dublin Castle and more arrests, Irish suffragettes were sent to Tullamore Jail. At this stage Lynn had replaced Dr Elizabeth Tennant as the doctor to the suffragettes on their release, as 'Tennant's loyalties were found lacking'.[56] Lynn's loyalties were now with the militant suffragettes. In June 1913, she refused to allow the released women to

52. Pašeta, *Irish Nationalist Women*, p. 99.
53. Margaret Ward, *Hanna Sheehy Skeffington: Suffragette and Sinn Féiner: Her Memoirs and Political Writings* (Dublin, 2017), p. 76.
54. *Evening Hearld*, 8 August 1912, p. 3.
55. William Murphy, *Political Imprisonment and the Irish, 1912–1921* (Oxford, 2014), p. 22.
56. Ruane, 'Kathleen Lynn', p. 68.

be interviewed; she ordered that they be kept 'strictly quiet, to avoid all excitement, and see no one'. They were, she said, all suffering considerably from exhaustion because of five days without food, and in the case of Mrs Ryan, 'considerable weakness of heart'.[57] A few days later, on 26 June, she spoke at a public meeting in the Mansion House to protest the application of the Cat and Mouse Act to political prisoners in Ireland.[58] She was now operating among the more radical, militant, political women.

An entry in her diary, for 9 November 1944, mentions a lecture which Lynn attended, where a paper by Maud Gonne McBride on 'Inighni na hEirin' (Inghínídhe na hÉireann) was read by Rosamond Jacob.[59] Their work was 'trilling' particularly their 'Party of Victories, one in the Park' but she only 'vaguely remembered about of it, unionist then'.[60] Here we have Lynn retrospectively self-defining her politics in *c.*1900, soon after she qualified as a doctor although already involved in the cause of suffrage. Like Anna Haslam, and many of her compatriots in Alexandra College, she self-defined as a unionist, not an entirely unusual position for the educated daughter of a Protestant clergyman to have. In the intervening dozen years, she moved towards militancy in suffrage activism and towards cultural nationalism, but it is during 1913 that the final phase of her political development, moving towards socialist and militant republican ideologies, occurs. There are no diaries for this phase of her life but her witness statement to the Bureau of Military History (BMH) outlines, in her words, the 'casual way' she first got in touch with the 'national movement'.[61] Over the course of a number of months, in late 1949 and early 1950, Lynn had her 'Military Hist. interview' with Miss Kissane, which she noted 'only goes to 1921 so the Civil War doesn't come into it'.[62] The BMH interview lacks the immediacy of the diaries, coming as it does over three decades later, and is framed by what the interviewer was looking for, and by what the interviewee was willing to tell. Lynn noted that 'Miss Kissane is interested in little anecdotes'.[63] The Lynn of 1950 dwelt mostly on the Easter Rising, as she did in her reflections on the revolutionary years in her diaries. The period 1913–16, the BMH interview however gives some insight into how Lynn constructed the narrative of her political journey. These three years take up two pages, indicating that Lynn was recalling only broad outlines of her activities during these years. As mentioned, she credited Helena Molony with bringing her into the national movement, in about 1912. Molony herself also claimed that credit, indicating that this is a story accepted by both women and probably their wider circle.[64] Countess Markievicz also claimed she was the one who brought her 'kinswoman' into the National movement, having been drawn towards it

---

57. *Evening Hearld*, 20 June 1913, p. 1.
58. Ibid., 26 June 1913, p. 3. The 1913 Prisoners (Temporary Discharge for Ill-Health) Act, known as the Cat and Mouse Act, allowed for the early release of prisoners who were so weakened by hunger striking and force feeding that they were at risk of death. They could be recalled to prison once their health was recovered, where the process would begin again.
59. KLD, Tuesday 8 November 1944.
60. Ibid.
61. Lynn, BMH, WS 357, p. 1.
62. KLD, Tuesday 8 November 1949 and Saturday 4 March 1950.
63. KLD, Tuesday 8 November 1949.
64. 'Cathal O'Shannon and Helena Molony', Helena Molony's spoken recollection recorded 11 November 1964, RTÉ Sound Archives, Dublin, no. 172/68 in Ruane, 'Kathleen Lynn', p. 69, n. 34.

herself by Molony.[65] All of the above is likely to be true, and the influences of her comrades among the militant suffrage cohort brought Lynn to republicanism and another political ideology which was to frame her life: socialism.

In 1913, during the Dublin Lockout, Lynn, demonstrating sympathy with the striking workers, joined Markievicz, Molony and other activists in the soup kitchens in Liberty Hall, the headquarters of the trade unions. The push to unionise workers began in 1908 with the founding of the Irish Transport and General Workers' Union (ITGWU) by Jim Larkin, and its sister union, the Irish Women Workers' Union (IWWU), in 1911, which was headed by Delia Larkin. The backlash to unionisation from employers intensified after the founding, in 1911, of the Dublin Employers' Federation by William Martin Murphy. Tensions came to a head when Dublin tram workers, employed by Murphy and forbidden to join the union, went on strike on 26 August 1913. By 30 August a mass meeting of the striking workers was baton charged off the streets by the Dublin Metropolitan Police (DMP), with the death of one striking worker. As more and more workers were 'locked out', including many women workers from businesses such as Jacob's factory, with no strike pay, hunger and deprivation set in among the workers. In response to this, soup kitchens were organised at Liberty Hall, and it is here that Lynn began her lifelong involvement with the rights of women workers. It is also here that she met the man who would influence her thinking on socialism, James Connolly. As argued by Pašeta, at this time, the more radical Irish feminists were moving 'increasingly in a left ward direction'; the 1913 Lockout and Connolly were part of that move leftward for Lynn.[66] Connolly supported women's suffrage and 'believed an awareness of sexual inequality made people aware of other inequalities in society'.[67] As a response to the violent actions of the DMP and the employers, he founded a workers' militia, the Irish Citizen Army (ICA), to protect the striking workers. In line with his thinking on women's equality and unlike many militant organisations of the time, the ICA was committed to equality, leading to the involvement of many of the left-wing women, middle and working class. Connolly invited Lynn, who was now trusted by both suffrage and trade unions groups, to become its medical director. She was a woman he admired, telling his family that she was 'the most amazing of them all'.[68] Most remarkable to him was that she could, despite her upbringing and class background 'find her niche in the Citizen Army, be thoroughly at home and be so completely accepted by them'.[69]

According to her witness statement she began to train the ICA in First Aid, becoming a captain and its chief Medical Officer. She was now embedded in an organisation which was underpinned by socialist and egalitarian beliefs. Soon she was working with Cumann na mBan, the militant nationalist organisation founded for, and by, women in April 1914. It was through doing medical training with Cumann na mBan at its headquarters at 6 Harcourt St, that Lynn encountered 'Miss French-Mullen [*sic*] who became my closest friend'.[70] Soon after that meeting, the women moved in together at 9 Belgrave Rd, and

---

65. Ruane, 'Kathleen Lynn', p. 69.
66. Pašeta, *Irish Nationalist Women*, p. 123.
67. Ó hÓgartaigh, *Kathleen Lynn*, p. 21.
68. Ruane, 'Kathleen Lynn', p. 71.
69. Ibid.
70. Lynn, BMH, WS 357, pp 1–2.

remained living there together 'for 30 years – until her [ffrench-Mullen's] death'.[71] When they met in 1914, Lynn was 40 and ffrench-Mullen was 34; no records exist of either of them being involved in any prior relationships, with men or women. ffrench-Mullen's centrality to Lynn's life is critical, from 1914 until her death in 1944 they were rarely apart, personally, or professionally. ffrench-Mullen was born in 1880 to Laurence ffrench-Mullen, a Royal Navy surgeon, and his wife Margaret, née O'Callaghan. She had two brothers, one who died in infancy, and Douglas (*b.*1892), with whom she was very close. Mrs ffrench-Mullen and Douglas appear regularly in the diaries, with Lynn having a close relationship with both. As Madeleine's father was in the Royal Navy, she spent some of her childhood in Malta, but was back in Dundrum, Co. Dublin by the time he died in 1895. Unlike Lynn, her family were supporters of Home Rule, and her father was a Parnellite. As a young woman she had joined Inghínídhe na hÉireann and contributed to *Bean na hÉireann*, writing under the pseudonym 'Dectora'.[72] She spent time abroad between 1908 and 1913, in Leipzig in Germany, which meant that she did not encounter Lynn until Lynn's political journey to radical politics was almost complete. She was also involved in the soup kitchen during the 1913 Lockout, but it is in 1914 at the Cumann na mBan Hall that she met or, at least, made an impression on Lynn. While Lynn notes the meeting in her BMH statement, indicating its importance in her narrative of her revolutionary years, an interview with May Cummins, who knew them both, suggests a more instant, spontaneous connection. Cummins paints a picture of ffrench-Mullen 'as a robust young woman who fell off a chair and collapsed with laughter' at a First Aid meeting Lynn was conducting.[73] Lynn is said to have 'helped her up and the two became firm friends'.[74] Soon after that first meeting the two women were in all things, personal and public, 'a great team'.[75] Lynn now had a partner in her life and in her activism, and between 1914 and 1916 both were very involved in trade union activism, feminism, socialism and republicanism. Both women were active, as members of the ICA, in preparing for the 1916 Rising and, although Lynn said, 'I never drilled, I had no time for that sort of thing', like most of the senior women she knew the Rising 'was coming off altho' we did not know the exact date'.[76] Her trajectory from respectable medical professional, constitutional suffragist, and moderate unionist was complete: she was now a supporter of militant suffragette activism, a socialist and a revolutionary.

From now on, with the start of her diaries, we have Lynn's own words to understand her life, as a doctor, a socialist, a republican and a life partner to ffrench-Mullen. As Cynthia Huff has noted 'writers of manuscript diaries construct themselves and their texts through their use of space, extra-textual material, voice, ideology, and historical and family positioning, among other factors'.[77] The Lynn who began the diary in 1916 as a

---

71. Lynn, BMH, WS 357, pp 1–2.
72. Paŝeta, *Irish Nationalist Women*, p. 97.
73. Ruane, 'Kathleen Lynn', p. 69.
74. Ibid.
75. Ibid.
76. Ibid., p. 2.
77. Cynthia A. Huff, 'Reading as re-vision: Approaches to reading manuscript diaries', *Biography*, 23(3) (Summer 2000) p. 521.

42-year-old mature political woman, ends it in April 1955, when she was 81, and close to the conclusion of a busy, engaged, life. She had experienced joy and loss, the work of a professional woman, bitter political and professional disappointments, and setbacks, as well as personal happiness and sorrow. The voice in the diary is not passive: as she moves through the years, the impact all this has on Lynn is there to see. For the reader, there needs to be an awareness that diaries are not static and allow 'a continuous self-construction, a running report on identities both shifting and fixed'.[78] Following on from Paperno's thinking, the important thing to remember is that 'diaries are not "mere witnesses to their culture," but "active embodiments" of one of its organising principles: its temporality'.[79] In the way Lynn writes her diaries, the construct of the self, and her narrative of her life, and her engagements with politics, activism, friendships, faith and love, as she experienced each succeeding year, are plain to see. In her later years a self-reflexivity becomes more evident as she remembers back on periods of hope and activism, periods often succeeded by disappointment. Diaries are records of the writer's experience, emotions, feelings and are best read not as a linear history or telling of events, but as a process of the becoming or unfolding of a life: 'We should ask not what can be learned from the text of the diary, but what can be learned from the individual diarist's work of his/her life, in private, on a continuous basis within a calendar grid'.[80]

In following Lynn's life through her own words we have divided the selections from her diaries, from 1916 to 1955, into four sections. While certain themes of love, politics and activism continue through all four sections, different phases of her political life beak down into the following years.

Section 1: 1916–23 – Revolution
The Rising and its aftermath, the founding of St Ultan's Hospital, the War of Independence and the Civil War.

Section 2: 1924–32 – Post-Revolution
The early years of the Irish Free State, work as a TD (Teachta Dála) and local councillor, developing St Ultan's, the secular and religious forces of Free State conservatism, first Fianna Fáil Government (1932).

Section 3: 1933–44 – Political Afterlife
Fianna Fáil in Government, Maria Montessori to Ireland, hospital amalgamation, the 1937 Constitution and break with de Valera, death of Madeleine (1944).

Section 4: 1945–55 – Life without Madeleine
The 'Emergency' (WWII), BCG inoculation, Save the German Children, Noël Browne and the National BCG campaign.

Each section brings to life Lynn, self-constructing (consciously or unconsciously) an account of her life, both public and private. They give the reader an insight into her world, as it unfolded over four decades. In each section below the narrative of her life is told mainly though her own words.

---

78. Irina Paperno, 'What can be done with diaries?', *The Russian Review*, 63(4), (October, 2004), p. 566.
79. Ibid.
80. Ibid., p. 573.

1916–23 – Revolution

Three primary sources are central to understanding Lynn's participation in the 1916 Rising: her diaries, her BMH witness statement and a short diary kept by Madeleine ffrench-Mullen.[81] Lynn's diary gives a very succinct account of Easter Monday 1916. She begins with one word, 'Revolution', and then continues

> Emer and I in City Hall, Seghan [*sic*] Connolly shot quite early in day. Place taken in evg. All women taken to Ship St abt. 8.30. Mrs. Barrett, 2 Norgroves, B. Davis & I joined later on by B. Lynch, F. Shanaghan & B. Brady – we were locked up in a filthy store, given blankets thick with lice and fleas to cover us & some 'biscuits' to lie on, not enough to go round.[82]

The entry is almost breathless in its intensity, she began that Easter Monday morning as Dr Kathleen Lynn, GP and Clinical Assistant at the Royal Victoria Eye and Ear, Chief Medical Officer of the Irish Citizen Army (ICA), and because she was one of the only women who could drive, she was charged with taking First Aid equipment to City Hall. By evening she was a military prisoner and soon to be a well-known notorious rebel. Her witness statement elaborates on this entry: she and her ICA detachment were sent to Dublin Castle under the command of Seán Connolly. Lynn was late to arrive as she was delivering medical supplies. When she arrived in her car, the ICA detachment had failed to take the Castle and had instead taken over nearby City Hall, the railings of which she climbed over to join them. She described how Seán Connolly went out onto the roof and was hit in the head by a sniper's bullet, how she knew immediately that first aid was useless and how Jennie Shanahan 'whispered an Act of Contrition in his ear' as he died.[83] By evening, British soldiers had forced a way into City Hall, and, as the most senior officer still alive, Lynn offered the surrender to them. Everyone was arrested and 'taken to Ship St. about 8.30'.[84] Her Rising had lasted a day, but it would have a dramatic and long-lasting impact on the future trajectory of her life.

In Ship St she was very concerned about the unhygienic and dangerous conditions in which they were being held: the filth, lack of heating, lice filled bedding, and lack of proper food and sanitation.[85] Her position as a middle-class medical professional allowed her to speak as an equal with the Barrack's Medical Officer. He was, 'very nice and polite' and 'really kind'.[86] She recorded, however, the abuse received from other British officers, when she complained of the food and conditions she was told 'it was good enough for us, that lice, fleas and typhoid should content us'.[87] She had a hard time in Ship St, not sleeping and terribly bothered by the lice, 'the scratching was not so bad in the daytime but in the

---

81. Transcript of the Madeleine ffrench-Mullen diary, Brother Allen Collection, 201/File B. The Allen Collection is now in the Military Archives of Ireland.
82. KLD, Monday 24 April 1916. Seghan Connolly is Seán Connolly
83. KLD, 24 April 1916; Lynn, BMH, WS 357, p. 5.
84. KLD, 24 April 1916.
85. At the south-west corner of Dublin Castle, Ship St Barracks, built in 1750, were used as Officers quarters and not set up as a prison. In 1916 they were used to incarcerate female prisoners.
86. Lynn, BMH, WS 357, Part II, p.1; KLD, Wednesday 26 April 1916.
87. KLD, Tuesday 25 May 1916.

night-time it was perfectly awful. I always was very sensitive to that sort of thing'.[88] ffrench-Mullen's Rising had lasted longer at the RCSI outpost. Her short 1916 diary reflects her worry about Lynn, 'we had heard various stories that the Doctor was arrested, missing and the Countess and I feared we would not see her again'.[89] On 2 May, they were reunited in Kilmainham Jail; 'Met the Doctor going for water, had her to breakfast hip, hip'.[90] But there was a dark side as well, both record the executions of the 1916 leaders, most of whom they knew; it was, as Lynn later remembered, 'a very harrowing experience'.[91] All her life she regarded the men who were executed in 1916 as the ultimate patriots, as martyrs for a great and glorious cause, who 'went to [their] deaths with prayers on [their] lips'.[92]

After 10 days, Lynn was transferred to Mountjoy Jail, terribly unhappy that she was separated from ffrench-Mullen, writing that while Mountjoy was a more hygienic place, she would have given '£10,000 for Kilmainham and Madeleine'.[93] Soon after, her disapproving father and sister Nan visited; a 'very black Friday … so reproachful, they wouldn't listen to me & looked as if they would cast me off for ever'.[94] It would take several years for the relationship between father and daughter to fully recover. Entries in the diary stop on 17 May and do not resume until July 1916. During this period, she was released, weighing under eight stone, and still itching from the lice. Her family made representations that a friend take her under their charge as if she were a 'sort of a lunatic', which was 'a traditional way of classifying women's transgressive behaviour' as mad.[95] Lynn refused and was deported by the British authorities to Coltford near Bath in England. However she didn't remain long there and, by August, she was back in Dublin with ffrench-Mullen. She came back to a changed city and a changed country. She no longer had her job in the Royal Victoria Eye and Ear who refused to have her back, although she still had her GP practice. Many old friends did not accept her politics and new-found infamy, including her cousin Lizzie Smartt, who was very disapproving.[96] Lynn had betrayed her class and religious background; most were also aghast at the destruction wrought on Dublin during the Rising. Only her mother's unmarried sister, Florence Wynne, 'Aunt F', welcomed her into her home without judgement.[97]

Entries in the diaries are short and sporadic during the rest of 1916 and 1917. She is much more open about this time in her witness statement, indicating that she had, by the spring of 1917, become involved with Sinn Féin, the political wing of republicanism. In September, she witnessed the death of republican Thomas Ashe, mortally injured while being force-fed while on hunger strike in Mountjoy Jail. He died in the nearby Mater

---

88. Lynn, BMH, WS 357, Part II, p. 2.
89. ffrench Mullen diary, 201/File B, 1 May 1916, p. 4.
90. Ibid., p. 5.
91. Lynn, BMH, WS 357, Part II, p. 1.
92. KLD, 8 May 1916.
93. KLD, Wednesday 10 May 1918.
94. KLD, Friday 12 May 1916.
95. Ruane, 'Kathleen Lynn', p. 73.
96. KLD, Wednesday 17 May 1916.
97. Lynn's mother Catherine had died in 1915, Aunt F lived in Dún Laoghaire where Lynn visited and stayed with her regularly, spending most Christmases there.

Hospital with her 'finger on his pulse'.[98] While her republican credentials were solid, she had not forgotten her feminist ideals. A number of ICA women, and women from Cumann na mBan and Inghínídhe na hÉireann formed the League of Women Delegates, or Cumann na dTeachtaire, to ensure that women were represented on the executive of Sinn Féin, as it re-organised. Women had always been welcome as members of Sinn Féin, now they wished to be among its leaders. The secretary of the League, ffrench-Mullen, drafted, with Lynn, a resolution sent to the executive which insisted that 'men' should be understood 'to mean men and women and that should be in all speeches, leaflets etc'.[99] The League succeeded in getting four women appointed to the executive, including Lynn. She was, as Pašeta notes, at this stage 'trusted and respected and had a sturdy record of feminist activity'.[100] She had to go on the run in May 1918 when senior members of Sinn Féin were threatened with arrest. In her witness statement she gives a long description of her disguise, which she seems to have enjoyed: 'Miss Molony got a beautiful rig out for me'.[101] There was also serious work to be done, as the (so called Spanish) flu epidemic had come to Dublin. She was busy giving 'anti flu' injections, and she would immerse herself in caring for those with the flu, particularly members of republican families, members of the ICA and the poor of Dublin. She was arrested on 31 October but saved from deportation by representations from the Lord Mayor of Dublin, Lawrence O'Neill, because of her essential work in combating the flu. Her diaries reflect the desperate toll the flu took, 'hundreds lie awaiting burial in Glasnevin'.[102] She operated a deport for inoculations at 37 Charlemont St, a derelict building which, with the help of ICA women, was cleaned and 'made as presentable as possible'.[103] It was to be at No. 37 that Lynn was to spend the rest of her professional career as it was here, on Ascension Thursday 1919, that St Ultan's Hospital for Infants was opened with '£70 in the bank, and … two infants in the hospital'.[104]

Her involvement with Sinn Féin continued. As a Vice President, she attended regular meetings of the Standing Committee and the annual Ard Fheis (annual conference). Her diaries reflect a growing concern about the plight of political prisoners, and the intensification of British military and police raids, and reprisals on republican homes and on communities. Not only does she report on British violence in Ireland she also reports on their terrible actions in Amritsar, India where 'last April', 13 April 1919, a crowd of '1,000 fired on, 500 natives obliged to crawl on command of General'.[105] Lynn and ffrench-Mullen both ran, successfully, for seats on the Rathmines and Rathgar Urban District Council, as Sinn Féin candidates, in the January 1920 local elections. Their friend Rosamond Jacob, in her diary, records her brother Tom remarking that 'Rathmines won't know itself with Dr

---

98. KLD, Thursday 25 September 1916.
99. Pašeta, *Irish Nationalist Women*, p. 227.
100. Ibid., p. 228.
101. Lynn, BMH, WS 357, Part II, p. 9.
102. KLD, Tuesday 5 November 1918.
103. Lynn, BMH, WS 357, Part II, p. 11.
104. Ibid., pp 10–11. It was named after the seventh century St Ultan of Ardbraccan, bishop of Meath, who is reputed to have looked after the children of Meath during an outbreak of yellow plague.
105. KLD, Sunday 14 December 1919.

Lynn and Miss ffrench-Mullen ... helping to rule its destinies'.[106] She would prove to be an active and engaged councillor, elected onto the Public Health and Building Committees, 'being aware of the close connection between poor housing and ill health'.[107] As 1920 progressed she regularly recorded the growing violence, committed by the British military and police, during the War of Independence. The callousness of the raids, executions and murders disturbed her greatly. The killing of Tómas MacCurtain, Lord Mayor of Cork, in front of his wife and children, was 'cruelly brutal & callous', while a 'snap of the fingers would excite a massacre, God help us'.[108] In between reports of this violence she also detailed the developments in St Ultan's, the annual meeting was a great success on 22 May 1920, and on 15 July an outpatient room opened as well as the 'mortuary room, v. nice, a poor mite in it'.[109]

If Lynn had hopes of an early truce in 1921, she was very much mistaken. By February she had been appointed to the White Cross Committee and Saor an Leanbh (the Irish Save the Children) organisations which were to help alleviate the suffering of the most vulnerable during the war. Women and children were bearing the brunt of the raids and attacks by the military, including on her own home, and that of her neighbour Hanna Sheehy Skeffington, in June 1921. Her diaries continue reporting atrocities, as well as the excitement of the opening of the second Dáil in August 1921, where she says 'Dev' (Éamon de Valera) made a fine speech. By September, a truce had been declared and all the English papers seemed, she felt, to shrink from the idea of more fighting. By 6 November she had heard that 'our peace was signed & sealed & it was all right for us'.[110] On the same day she records a nice notice in the newspaper of the first two women to be called to the Bar and of four other Irish women, the first to break jail.[111] Lynn's initially positive reaction to the Treaty turned to anger when the text was released.

> 'Peace' terms but such a peace. Not what Connolly & Mallin & countless others died for. Please God the country won't agree to what Griffith, Barton, Gavin Duffy, Duggan and Mick Collins have put their names to, more shame to them, better war than such a peace.[112]

This was not what she had fought for, and she was happy that 'Dev' could not recommend 'acceptance of the peace terms'.[113] She was not the only republican woman to reject the Treaty, ffrench-Mullen did also, as did most members of Cumann na mBan. Her biases in recording the Treaty debates in January 1922 are evident, bemoaning that Arthur Griffith, who was the principle speaker in favour of the Treaty, was in Dev's place, that 'all our people

---

106. Ó hÓgartaigh, *Kathleen Lynn*, p. 53.
107. Ibid.
108. KLD, Monday 22 March 1920; Sunday 11 April 1920.
109. KLD, Thursday 15 July 1920.
110. KLD, Sunday 6 November 1921.
111. Ibid. On 1 November 1921, Frances Kyle and Averil Deverell, graduates of the Law School, Trinity College Dublin, became the first women called to the Bar in Ireland. The four women, members of Cumann na mBan, who escaped from Mountjoy Jail were Linda Kearns, Mae Burke, Eileen Keogh, and Eithne Coyle on 20 October 1921.
112. KLD, Wednesday 7 December 1922.
113. KLD, Friday 9 December 1921.

out of the Dáil' and that there was 'not a woman left in the Dáil now'. This was because all six female TDs were anti-treaty. It is obvious that 'F. Staters', i.e. those who supported the treaty and the establishment of the Irish Free State, who she felt behaved 'abominably to those who differ from them', now replaced the Black and Tans as the bête noire of her diaries.[114]

In March 1922, she wrote about the violence on the border with Northern Ireland, blaming the British who were, she felt, 'encouraging it to say they must interpose to prevent our exterminating each other'.[115] On Sunday 2 April she was delighted that the IRA, Cumann na mBan and Na Fianna rejected the Treaty and were all out for the Republic. This turned to disappointment when the Treaty was accepted by the majority of the population, in the June general election. She despaired that 'it feels as if the whole Republican structure was struggle and burnt up last Dec'.[116] Lynn could not accept the Free State, she could not betray the oath she had taken to the Republic in 1916. As Civil War escalated, she once more found herself embroiled in violence. Now it was a war of comrades, and the death of each of her republican comrades hurt deeply. She couched these deaths in terms of sacrifice, similar to those of the executed patriots of 1916. Cathal Brugha's death was 'heroic', he was 'calm and beautiful in death' a sacrifice 'which [will] do more to turn people back to the Republic'.[117] As the battle for Dublin was lost to the Free State, she travelled to Kilkenny where she saw military action as medical officer to the anti-treaty IRA, and was encouraged when the National Army 'lost many, killed & wounded & retreated' after a skirmish.[118] Her bitterness at those who supported the Treaty is evident when Michael Collins, chairman of the Free State Provisional Government and commander in chief of the National Army, was killed on 22 August 1922, writing that 'retribution has fallen swiftly on the murderers of poor Harry Boland'.[119] Most of her concern over the following year, however, was over the often violent mistreatment of anti-treaty women prisoners held in Kilmainham and Mountjoy Jails and later in the North Dublin Union; we must 'fight for the unfortunate prisoners' she wrote.[120] Many women she knew were in jail and on hunger strike, while she herself was almost one of them when her house was raided, in March 1923. She was taken to Oriel House searched and interrogated before being released home; 'M' she said 'had made a gt fuss'.[121] She was involved in the Women Prisoners' Defence League (WPDL) and worked with Kathleen O'Brennan and Charlotte Despard to deliver a statement from the WPDL on the conditions experienced by the women anti-treaty prisoners to the United States Congress. The Civil War finally ended in May 1923, although many of the imprisoned women were not released until December. Lynn remained very vocal about the mistreatment of the prisoners and eyewitness accounts of the often brutal violence the women endured are recorded in her papers. The final step in her political journey came in August 1923 when she stood in the general election as an

---

114. KLD, Monday 23 February 1922; *F. Staters* – Free Staters.
115. KLD, Tuesday 7 March 1922.
116. KLD, Sunday 18 June 1922.
117. KLD, Friday 7 July 1922.
118. KLD, Wednesday 2 August 1922.
119. KLD, Wednesday 23 August 1922.
120. KLD, Friday 10 November 1922.
121. KLD, Tuesday 13 March 1923. Oriel House, Westland Row, Dublin was the headquarters of the Criminal Investigation Department (CID).

abstentionist Sinn Féin candidate. Election day was fraught with 'armed police in and outside every polling sta. kept many away'. The next day, after her milkman told her she was elected, she prayed that 'God grant me grace to do right for my country'.[122] She was one of 44 Sinn Féin TD elected, and one of five women. However, like all Sinn Féin TDs, because of the oath of allegiance that all sitting TDs had to swear, she would not take her seat in the Dáil.

Lynn's diaries for this period are fascinating in her self-conscious construction of herself as part of a greater 'we'. She wrote often of the 'we' who faced the enemy, the British government and military during the War of Independence and the 'we', the true republicans, the die hards, who held out against the compromised and, in her eyes, illegal Free State. This 'we', the uncompromising, militant Republican, was a long way from her class, religious and social upbringing, but this 'we' was who she would remain for the rest of her life. The diaries also reveal a growing anti-imperialism and commitment to feminist and socialist activism. Other aspects of her character remained constant: her commitment to her medical work, through St Ultan's now, and as a local councillor. Her life with ffrench-Mullen is central to the diaries as they shared home and work, holidays and activism, friendships, and a love of the outdoors. Her network of friends, particularly those committed to the same ideals as herself, widened. Old comrades like Molony, Gonne McBride, Sheehy Skeffington and Clarke remained, but she now also worked with the MacSwiney sisters (Mary and Annie), Albina Broderick, Charlotte Despard, Kathleen O'Brennan and Caitlín Brugha. Her admiration for 'Dev', Éamon de Valera, grew. She was, however, also able to keep working with people, particularly women doctors in St Ultan's, who did not share her republican or her socialist principles. Ó hÓgartaigh argued that 'in political terms Lynn was a loser after the Treaty' and technically this was true.[123] She would never be at the centre of national political power, but she had other ways of carving an influential position for herself, through local politics, and her medical work. This would form a central part of the next phase of her life.

1924–32 – Post-Revolution

Politics remained a central concern for Lynn throughout the 1920s, although finding a role in a conservative state, which viewed the role of women through the constraining lens of respectability and domesticity, was a problem. She never deviated far from her republican principles, delighting, on 6 April 1924, in a huge procession to Glasnevin, held in honour of members of the Dublin Brigade of the IRA killed in the Civil War, reporting that republican Seán Lemass gave an oration which sounded the 'right heroic note'.[124] While the heroism of republicanism remained in her heart, the government of the Irish Free State could do no right, especially when they gloried 'in having executed good men, the best. It is awful.'[125] Although she had not taken her seat in the Dáil, she was a TD, a strong supporter of de Valera and remained active in Sinn Féin. She went with him on

---

122. KLD, Thursday 20 August 1923.
123. Ó hÓgartaigh, *Kathleen Lynn*, p. 47.
124. KLD, Sunday 6 April 1924.
125. KLD, Thursday 8 May 1924.

several speaking tours, and her friendship with fellow Sinn Féin TD Mary MacSwiney, and with Sinn Féiner Albina Broderick, deepened. Broderick, from a similar class and religious background, had opened a hospital outside Kenmare in Co. Kerry and was involved in the White Cross; they had much in common and would remain friends for the rest of Lynn's life.[126] Lynn was often on public platforms, including at Tuam, Co. Galway, when, on 29 October 1924, the 'boys executed' during the Civil War were returned to their families and communities for burial.[127] The treatment of republicans at public meetings was often noted, as on 2 February 1925, at a meeting 'every questioner was batoned, arms twisted, all the old D.M.P tactics'.[128] Her good friend Dora Maguire, a nurse at St Ultan's, continued to be a very active member of Cumann na mBan and was constantly in trouble, arrested for disrupting a film at the cinema when the Prince of Wales appeared on the screen. Lynn supported her throughout, accompanying her to court in August 1925 and visiting her in Mountjoy Jail in September. Interestingly Maguire gave her address as 9 Belgrave Rd, so she may have been lodging with Lynn and ffrench-Mullen at the time.

Her relationship with de Valera and many Sinn Féin republicans was, however, severely tested in 1926. On March 9, there was the 'momentous Ard Feis in Rotunda, about 600 delegates at it fr. 11:00am to 11:00pm', and a 'decision whether or not a principle not to enter F..S parliament to be taken at 11:00 tomorrow'.[129] For her, the next day was 'a terrible day', with

> long, long discussion & then diversion of F O'Flanagan's amend. passed by 5 votes, awful feeling of antagonism crept in at once & wasn't at all relieved by the losing of it as a motion by 2 votes. I can't say Dev showed up v. well, he seemed so personally affronted. We can't think this going into F.S. Parliament good, but the cause of Ireland goes on still D.G.[130]

This decision on whether to take their seats in the Dáil split Sinn Féin, although, as Ward argues, it was essentially a 'division over tactics rather than reflecting divergent political views'.[131] De Valera and his supporters left Sinn Féin and launched a new political party, Fianna Fáil, which intended to take its seats if elected. The split had an impact on some friendships, including that with Hanna Sheehy Skeffington. It would be almost a year before they reconciled; in early 1927 she recorded that 'saw Mrs Skeffington in evg. she is v. anxious we should be as friendly as before, personally, yes'.[132] Lynn's relationship with de Valera never quite recovered, and snipes at his politics and his leadership occur frequently over the following years. In the 1927 General Election, the first one contested by Fianna Fáil, she ran as a Sinn Féin candidate again and lost her seat. Her diary reflects her conviction that those who stood by the Republic were now a 'v. select' few.[133] She expected

126. Albina Broderick, or Gobnait Ní Bhruadair as she renamed herself, was the daughter of Viscount Midleton.
127. KLD, Wednesday 29 October 1924.
128. KLD, Monday 2 February 1925.
129. KLD, 9 March 1926.
130. KLD, 10 March 1926.
131. Margaret Ward, *Unmanageable Revolutionaries :Women and Irish Nationalism, 1880-1980* (Dublin, 2021), p. 334.
132. KLD, 9 February 1927.
133. KLD, Sunday 12 June 1927.

that 'F.F. will take the oath & go in'.[134] Two women candidates, Kathleen Clarke and Countess Markievicz, were among the 44 Fianna Fáil TDs elected. If she felt any animosity towards them, especially towards Madam (Markievicz), all of that faded when news came on 30 June that she was ill. Markievicz had been a constant in Lynn's life from around 1912, and now with the end approaching, Lynn was part of the inner circle who were with her in Sir Patrick Dun's Hospital. On 14 July, she wrote that Madam had 'a lovely day, enjoying everything. Count and Stasco with her'.[135] By evening she was unconscious and died 'peacefully at 12, God's time'.[136] Lynn wrote approvingly of Dev's oration at Madam's graveside in Glasnevin, but by 11 August she despaired, as all Fianna Fáil TDs 'signed oath to-day, how can they? Not a soul there, shows what a downward path does'.[137] Lynn would not run for national election again, but she would concentrate on her position as a senior member of Sinn Féin and continue her work as a local councillor for the next few years.

As her role in politics changed, St Ultan's increasingly occupied Lynn's energy and thoughts. It was a place where, as Ruane notes, she could deliver on her 'feminist, Christian and republican ideals'.[138] Her diaries record the comings and goings of doctors and nurses and show a female run space, with 'M ffM' in charge of staffing and administration.[139] Lynn was intent on introducing new and better standards and practices in medical care for the infants, and their mothers. She was part of an innovative team with Dr Ella Webb, who set up the Sunshine Home in Stillorgan to care for children with rickets and worked with Dr Katharine Maguire who worked in slum dispensaries.[140] By 1925, Dr Dorothy Stopford, later Stopford Price, had joined the team at St Ultan's and would play an instrumental part in their TB work. Lynn and her team were determined that their care was child-centred; they were inspired by visits to hospitals in the USA and Europe where they met leading paediatricians. They introduced new practices in social and infant medicine, including goats' milk, breast milk pumps, one of world's first Montessori wards, and plenty of fresh air and sunshine for the patients: 'bright sun all mg. babies out in it. D.G.'.[141] Lynn knew the children by name, she delighted in their recovery and was saddened by their deaths. Infant mortality remained stubbornly high for much of the 1920s and she mentioned, by name and with deep sadness, many of the infants who failed to recover. In October 1925 she lost 'poor little Edward, congen. stenosis bile ducts, dead too, bad, no x ray. Rare case'.[142] She believed in caring for the whole child and that 'a few hours of cuddling and comforting' would help improve a child's recovery.[143]

Politics was never far away and a comment on 5 December reveals who she held responsible for the troubles of many of her patients: 'Blythe says country is prospering, such

---

134. KLD, Tuesday 14 June 1927.
135. KLD, Thursday 14 July 1927. *Count and Stasco* – Count Casmir Markievicz, her husband and Stanislaus, her stepson.
136. Ibid.
137. KLD, Thursday 11 August 1927.
138. Ruane, 'Kathleen Lynn', p. 82.
139. M ffM – Madeleine ffrench Mullen.
140. Anne Mac Lellan, *Dorothy Stopford Price: Rebel Doctor* (Dublin, 2014), pp 117–18.
141. KLD, Wednesday 23 February 1927.
142. KLD, Monday 11 October 1925.
143. Ruane, 'Kathleen Lynn', p. 83.

an untruth when so many starve'.[144] Both she and ffrench-Mullen were concerned with the unhygienic living conditions of the families their infant patients came from. Through their positions on the local council Public Health and Housing Committee they pushed for investments in social housing. She spoke at council meetings about the interconnection between bad housing and illness and represented the Rathmines and Rathgar Urban District Council at the Royal Institute of Public Health in Geneva in 1929. Visits to hospital in Zurich and Basle in May gave her more ideas and by September 1929 she was in touch with a young architect, Michael Scott, about building a balcony onto her own house and developing more space in the hospital, hoping 'D.V. D.V. the money will come'.[145] Despite the constant worry of money, St Ultan's was growing; a new development happened when 'Sir T Myles came, wants us to take students & so become teaching hosp.', and the staff generally liked the idea.[146] Fundraising continued, wealthy friends and patrons sent what they could, donations came in from around the country and abroad, and monies were secured from the White and Red Crosses, but it was always in short supply. ffrench-Mullen was the chief fundraiser and had to be imaginative in her efforts, including organising annual festivals and events such as greyhound race nights, as well as holding hospital 'at homes' for visitors. The question of money became clearer with the beginning of the Irish Hospitals' Sweepstakes in 1930. The Sweepstakes fund was to subsidise the cost of running voluntary hospitals, and St Ultan's was among the six participating hospitals to benefit. While these monies were never enough to cover all costs, they certainly helped put the hospital on a better financial footing as it entered into its second decade. By 1930 it had 35 cots, an outpatient's department, where children up to age five were treated, and a laboratory; this was a long way from 1919 and two cots.

Helena Molony (Emer) remained a close friend, a comrade in many campaigns, and was also a cause for much concern over these years. Molony had remained, post revolution, a dedicated and radical political activist, republican and socialist. Like Lynn she was a local councillor in Rathmines and very involved in campaigns for social housing, and continued to pursue her republican and socialist activities.[147] She is mentioned in the diaries almost as much as ffrench-Mullen, certainly until the late 1930s, and it appears she was often living with the couple at Belgrave Rd. While Lynn supported Molony's work she was very concerned about her health; it is clear from the diaries that Molony was an alcoholic, given to binges, and Lynn was constantly trying to get her help with her addiction. On the morning of 9 January 1929, she found Molony 'pulseless, got priest, she rallied a bit. Had been on a terrible bend, poor thing. ... when will it all end'.[148] Luckily Molony recovered, and in between her binges, she continued her trade union and socialist work, going to Russia in 1929 as part of Dublin Trades Union Council delegation. Molony and Lynn's

---

144. KLD, Monday 5 December 1927. Ernest Blythe, Minister for Finance.
145. KLD, Tuesday 3 September 1929.
146. KLD, Friday 20 January 1928.
147. Nell Regan 'Helena Molony', Mary Cullen and Maria Luddy (eds), *Female Activists: Irish Women and Social Change, 1900–1960* (Dublin, 2001), pp 141–168.
148. KLD, Wednesday 9 January 1929.

socialist beliefs were similar. Lynn was involved in a 'hands off Russia' campaign and wrote, in 1930, that people could see the fear of and aggression towards Russia for what it was 'capitalism & war propaganda'.[149] When Molony returned from her visit to Russia she was instrumental in reviving the Irish Friends of Soviet Russia (IFOSR), Lynn and ffrench-Mullen attended the first meeting and joined the group. The issue of religious freedom under the Soviet system, which concerned those opposed to communism in Ireland, was dealt with by Molony who 'assured her audience that she had no trouble attending Mass' while there.[150] Lynn simply wrote that 'Russia practises Xtian society', demonstrating that her socialist beliefs did not conflict with her deeply held Christian faith.[151]

One major concern for Lynn was the rise of fascism in Europe, even when her love of Germany conflicted with hating what was happening there. Lynn mentioned the rise of Mussolini in 1924, saying he seemed 'v. high handed but perh. Sensible', but by November 1929, she saw Mussolini and his fascists as a threat to peace, 'Mussolini says too much talk of peace, terrible to say!'[152] She noted the rise of Hitler in Germany and the Fascist 'Blackshirts' under Oswald Mosley in Britain. It is obvious that, by 1932, she knew what was happening with the Jews in Germany, when she wrote about the 'great rejoicings' in Germany over Hitler's election victory but was despairing that he 'commanded clergy to throw out all Jews but D.V. some pastors won't have this unXtianity'.[153] In Ireland she drew a comparison between the British and European fascists and the Army Comrades Association (ACA), set up in 1932, in response to anxieties among those who supported the Free State and Cumann na nGaedheal, to the rise of Fianna Fáil; 'A.C.A. [who] call themselves 'National Guard', cheek of them. Eoin O'Duffy is President. Blue Shirts = kind of Fascisti'.[154] The 1932 election campaign had been bitter: clashes between republicans and the ACA were common, as Fianna Fáil were tarred as dangerous gunmen and communists, while a Cumann na nGaedheal TD Patrick Reynolds and a Garda detective were assassinated two days before the poll. Fianna Fáil won a narrow victory and formed a minority government with the Labour Party; for the first time since the foundation of the Free State, Cumann na nGaedheal were out of power. Lynn's complicated views on de Valera were suspended, temporarily, and it seems she had high hopes for a Fianna Fáil government. On 7 December she wrote 'Lemass says worst of our struggle over D. V. it is after such centuries of waiting'.[155] She was delighted when the republican prisoners, imprisoned by the Cumann na nGaedheal government, were released, and with 'Devs' plan to remove the oath. She fully participated in the 1932 Eucharistic Congress, and was invited to many of the State receptions, something which probably would not have happened had Cumann na nGaedheal still been in power.

---

149. KLD, Wednesday 19 February 1930.
150. Ibid.
151. KLD, Friday 4 April 1930.
152. KLD, Wednesday 14 January 1925; Wednesday 6 November 1929.
153. KLD, Monday 14 November 1932.
154. KLD, Friday 21 July 1933. Blueshirt was the nickname given to members of the ACA and National Guard, because of their uniform of a blue shirt.
155. KLD, Wednesday 7 December 1932. Seán Lemass, Fianna Fáil TD and Minister for Industry and Commerce.

The post-revolutionary decade, from 1924 to 1932, had been a mixed one for Lynn. St Ultan's was growing, and she was the dominant figure on the board, pushing through most of her agenda. Her national political career came to an end in 1927, but her involvement in national organisations, such as Sinn Féin, the White Cross, and the Friends of Soviet Russia, ensured that she was still a political player. On a personal level, her life with ffrench-Mullen was her bedrock and her emotional support system; most of the organisations she was in 'M ffM' was right beside her, as she was in the running of St Ultan's. In December 1926, she wrote 'we are living together nearly 11 years now D G'.[156] But life was not all about work and politics, both enjoyed their cottage in Glencormack in Co. Wicklow and visited as often as they could, always spending the month of August there. They would invite friends to join them, and many did over the years. They also enjoyed their pets, cats and dogs feature often in the diary entries, and both loved to work on their garden at Belgrave Rd. There were trips to Bath in England, a spa town where ffrench-Mullen could take the salts for her rheumatoid arthritis. There were visits to Europe also, which combined sightseeing and hospitals visits. They also made time for family, Lynn visited her sister Muriel in Warrenpoint regularly, and her 'Aunt F' in Dún Laoghaire. The couple were especially close to the ffrench-Mullen family, with regular breakfasts at the home of 'Mrs ff M' in nearby Moyne Rd, while Douglas ffrench-Mullen was a frequent guest in their home. Friends too were met with regularity or invited to tea, especially Mrs Sheehy Skeffington and Sighle Dowling, while Molony was practically a member of the household. Her Christianity remained at the centre of her life, she took solace in it when times were bleak, leaving much in the hands of God. As the second decade of the Free State began there was much to be thankful for, and much work to be done.

1933–44 – A Political Afterlife

January 1933 began with her usual busy tempo of work, politics, and friends. On New Year's Day she had to deal with Emer (Molony), who was drinking again, while the Dáil was dissolved at midnight the following day by 'Dev'. She felt that this was the right thing to do and that the people had to give the government a 'clear mandate to stop mouths of those who say country is divided'.[157] The result was that de Valera finally won an outright majority. She was happy to report on 29 January that the 'result of election = F.F. 77', and according to the newspapers 'the Irish have given clear mandate for independence & no talk of coercion at all'.[158] By 1933 Lynn's attitude to de Valera had softened somewhat, particularly since the divisiveness of 1926 and the Sinn Féin split over the oath. Now that he was in power, she hoped he would bring in more republican politics. Thinking that 'Dev.[was] all right' occured in tandem with a growing sense of disillusionment with Sinn Féin and the IRA. In October 1933 she and 'M ffM' went to a Sinn Féin meeting which degenerated into a squabble between 'SF and the I.R.A. members', it was she felt a 'waste of time to go'.[159] She now considered the IRA 'so self-centred that they would ruin Ireland

---

156. KLD, Wednesday 29 December 1926.
157. KLD, Tuesday 2 January 1933.
158. KLD, Sunday 29 January 1933.
159. KLD, Monday 23 October 1933.

to assert themselves'.[160] This disillusionment continued, and Lynn withdrew from active involvement in Sinn Féin, although ffrench-Mullen and Albina Broderick continued to attend meetings and Ard Fheiseanna. By 1936 she no longer had much belief in the new generation of IRA men and while her friend Mary MacSwiney lamented the imprisonment of young IRA leaders, Lynn felt that they were very different from the men of the previous generation.[161] In November 1933 she despaired that the IRA had 'fallen far fr. 1916 ideals, alas they are just freebooters now, on the make'.[162] The men of 1916 remained, always, her touchstone against whom she judged all republican men and women and their actions.

The continuing rise of fascism also remained a concern, in August 1933 she noted, happily, that 'Dev says Blueshirts + Fascisti & will not be tolerated'.[163] She wrote with obvious delight of a cancelled Blueshirt parade that month. They were, she wrote, the 'bluebottles buzzing around the carcass of C na nGael'.[164] As an astute political observer, she was not wrong in predicting the demise of Cumann na nGaedheal, by September 1933 the National Guard had merged with the National Centre Party and Cumann na nGaedheal to form a new political party, Fine Gael. She and Emer were of one mind in understanding why the Catholic Church seemed to be on the side of the Blueshirts. They believed the aim of the Blueshirts and the Church, directly inciting people through its anti-communist sermons, was to crush 'all non R.Cs out of the state', but 'we'll weather it like much else'.[165] Sections of the Catholic Church did portray the Blueshirts as 'saviours of Catholicism against the forces of communism', and with politics in early 1930s Ireland centred on the rise to power of de Valera, those who supported Fianna Fáil were often attacked; even Hanna Sheehy Skeffington was set upon by the ACA at a public meeting.[166]

Despite pulling back from active involvement she was still very engaged with politics, both as an observer and as a feminist. Her diary charts her growing disquiet at political violence in Europe, the civil war in Spain, the descent into war, and, at home, de Valera's treatment of republicans. Like many of the suffrage and republican women she was also very disappointed in Fianna Fáil's attacks on the rights of the women worker, as well as with the 1937 Constitution, on women's equal rights as citizens. She was aware of the policies against the Jewish community in her beloved Germany; 'Read terrible sufferings of Jews... on ret. here found Emer & Sighle & they feel there must be a protest from Xtians here'.[167] While she was initially ambivalent about Hitler, as Germany was in such a bad way both economically and politically, by the late 1930s she regarded him a dangerous warmonger. On the interference by Germany in the Spanish Civil War she wrote, 'Poor Bilbao taken at last & Franco congratulated by Hitler & Mussolini, Xtianity's gtst. enemies & the war is called Xtian', later agreeing with her friend Sighle Dowling that 'Hitler & Russia both out

---

160. KLD, Wednesday 6 September 1933.
161. KLD, Wednesday 6 May 1936.
162. KLD, 29 November 1933.
163. KLD, Monday 21 August 1933.
164. KLD, Wednesday 16 August 1933.
165. KLD, 4 April 1933.
166. Mike Cronin, 'The Blueshirt Movement, 1932–5: Ireland's fascists?', *Journal of Contemporary History*, 30(2) (April 1995), p. 324; KLD, Friday 31 April 1933.
167. KLD, Sunday 13 November 1938.

for world domination'.[168] The diary shows that she had knowledge of what was happening to Jews in Nazi-dominated parts of Europe. At a Sunday sermon in 1944, she heard of the 'horrors suffered by Jews in Nazi lands, Stuffed into trains & left for dead, packed into cells & steam turned on till dead etc'.[169] At home, she was friendly with members of the Jewish community and had agreed with Dr Bethel Solomons' suggestion that St Ultan's take in Jewish girls to train as nurses.[170] She expressed sympathy for the 'poor, poor Jews' many times, but she was also aggrieved that Erskine Childers TD, then of the Industrial Development Association, was acting 'scandalously to favour Jews'.[171] These complicated feelings of deploring the treatment of Jews by the Nazis, being personally friendly with members of the Irish Jewish community and also expressing antisemitic ideas on Jews as a group, and praying for their conversion, was not unusual in 1920 and 1930s Ireland. Her diaries indicate that her usual compassion for the suffering of prisoners, particularly given her knowledge of what was happening to Jews in Europe, was compromised by believing in these conspiracies around the idea of the international Jew.

This ambivalence is also evident in her entries about British policies and war. Her ardent republicanism and continuing Anglophobia are evident, with her constant delight that Britian was becoming a third-rate power. She was especially happy that so many colonies seemed to be following Ireland's example and demanding independence; she avidly followed the events in India, reporting on Gandhi's activism many times. At home, her activism was shaped by feminism once more, following the introduction, in 1935, of the Conditions of Employment Bill by Seán Lemass, Minister for Industry and Commerce. The most contentious part of the Bill was Section 16, 'Restrictions on the employment of female work', which gave the Minister the right to control the number of women working in any industry. Lynn, Molony, Sheehy Skeffington and many other feminists expressed concerns about the negative effect this would have on the rights of the women worker. By November 1936 she was happy to report that there was to be a 'new amalgamated womens' soc. to see we get our rights & truly, the men were quite willing we shld. share dangers of war but withhold fruits of it'.[172] This was a common complaint among republican women, that they had shared the risks with men during the revolutionary wars but had not benefitted in terms of equality in the Free State. By 1937, feminists were involved in a campaign against a draft of a new Constitution, published on 1 May. De Valera was 'much pained we shld. not think his constitution perfect for women when there is discrimination in many sections'.[173] By this stage her disenchantment with de Valera, suspended somewhat in 1933, was complete. She supported the Women Graduates' Association in opposing the Constitution and noted that 'we are all working hard for meeting of protest against new constitution and women'.[174] On 21 June they had a meeting in the Mansion House,

168. KLD, Monday 21 June 1937, Monday 2 October 1939. Xtianity means Christianity and Xtian means Christian.
169. KLD, Sunday 16 April 1944.
170. KLD, Saturday 6 May 1929.
171. KLD, Tuesday 16 March 1943; Friday 11 November 1938.
172. KLD, Friday 8 November 1935.
173. KLD, Tuesday 18 May 1937.
174. KLD, Thursday 17 June 1937.

where so many important demonstrations in Lynn's political life had occurred. It was another great occasion with many enthusiastic speeches by women, who were rightly fired up by this attack on their equal rights. While she was delighted that women were 'riz & rightly' against the Constitution, much to her disappointment, on the eve of the vote, Bridie O'Mullane of Old Cumann na mBan wrote a letter to the *Irish Press* expressing their support for the Constitution, now that amendments they had called for were included.[175] Old Cumann na mBan were particularly antagonised with a phase in Article 45.4.2 which referred to 'inadequate strength of women', noting that they engaged in 'heavy muscular toil conveying machine guns, heavy explosives' in the War of Independence.[176] De Valera removed this phrase and Old Cumann na mBan wrote the letter in support of the Constitution, accepting de Valera's word that the 'rights of women are not restricted'.[177] Lynn felt, however, that O'Mullane had been persuaded to write the letter as they, the Government, felt 'our opposition so much'.[178] Polling day was 1 July, for both a general election and a referendum on the Constitution. Lynn wrote 'No for Constitution & restore the Republic' on her polling card. Despite this opposition the Constitution was accepted nationally and, although disappointed, Lynn was happy that in her constituency in Dublin, it was rejected.

If politics in Ireland, Europe and globally occupied her attention and activism, her main focus was, as always, St Ultan's. In 1933, under the leadership of ffrench-Mullen, the St Ultan's Utility Society was set up to establish model tenement homes for Dublin's poorer citizens. These homes, inspired by the Alexandra Guild model, were planned to break what Lynn had always railed against, the connection between unhygienic, inadequate housing and illness in children. By December 1933, they had signed a contract and flats were to be built in Charlemont St. In November 1940, the first female Lord Mayor of Dublin and an old republican comrade, Kathleen Clarke, laid the foundation stone of these Charlemont St Flats.[179] Designed by architect Michael Scott the modernist flats were opened in October 1941. Everyone was 'delighted with the size of the rooms, the airy brightness, the individual balconies in wh. Mr. Scott has got geraniums etc. put'.[180] In St Ultan's, monies from the Sweepstakes helped with both expansion and new plans, the most ambitious of these being the amalgamation of St Ultan's with the Children's Hospital, Harcourt St to form a new National Children's Hospital. This was to be a larger and better resourced hospital capable of delivering a higher standard of care to infants and children. The suggestion had come from the Hospitals Commission, but Lynn and the St Ultan's Hospital Board, on which she was the dominant member, were enthusiastic. They began buying lands around St Ultan's, while a plan for the new hospital was designed by Michael Scott in partnership with Norman Douglas Good. Both ffrench-Mullen and Lynn were anxious that any new hospital be of the most up-to-date standard in medical design, and, with members from

---

175. Specifically, they wanted the phrase 'the inadequate strength of women' taken out of Article 45, which it was.
176. Maria Luddy, 'A "sinister and retrogressive" proposal: Irish women's opposition to the 1937 draft constitution', *Transactions of the Royal Historical Society*, Vol. 15 (2005), p. 190.
177. Ibid., p. 190.
178. KLD, Wednesday 30 June 1937.
179. KLD, Friday 1 November 1940.
180. KLD, Friday 12 October 1941.

Harcourt St Hospital Board, a committee was formed to carry the amalgamation forward. If, however, Lynn thought this proposal would be carried easily, the amalgamation was soon mired in a controversy which was 'orchestrated by McQuaid, articulated by Byrne', aided by Catholic secular allies such as Stafford Johnson, 'a leading light in the Knights of Columbanus', Dr Alice Barry, a Catholic member of the St Ultan's Board and Dr Marie Lea-Wilson in Harcourt St.[181]

The opposition of the Archbishop of Dublin, Edward Byrne and his ally and later successor, John Charles McQuaid (then President of Blackrock College), to the amalgamation did not come from nowhere. Neither St Ultan's nor Harcourt St was under Catholic management, and the Church wished all hospitals, especially those dealing with women and children, to be under Catholic control. This had both a moral and sectarian underpinning. Firstly from the moral point of view, issues of sex education, information on contraception and sterilisation, which might be offered in an amalgamated hospital were causes for concern. Secondly, from a sectarian point of view anxieties were growing about a perceived majority of Protestant doctors, trained mainly in Trinity College Dublin, working in both hospitals, as opposed to Catholic doctors, trained according to a Catholic medical ethos, at University College Dublin (UCD). There were also anxieties about the potential for proselytising among Catholic patients in a Protestant-run hospital. The work on amalgamation started well, but, by November 1935 Lynn was despondent. As Ruane points out, this fight was the first major battle of the Catholic ethics campaign, important in shaping the Catholic position on public policy, social work, hospital care, and medical research, a position centred on morality rather than health care.[182] Despite powerful opposition, the Amalgamation Committee and St Ultan's Board were determined to respond and refute all allegations. They succeeded in getting a deputation received by the Archbishop, with both Lynn and ffrench-Mullen in attendance, but he was terrible, 'domineering without reason' and accusing them of 'all the things we have never done & can easily say will never be done'.[183] In a response drafted by ffrench-Mullen, with the Boards input, they answered all accusations: sterilisation would never be an issue in patients under 16; they were never going to advocate for birth control or give instruction on sex matters; there would be no proselytising and Byrne was assured that half the staff were, and would continue to be, Catholic.[184] Despite these efforts to move the issue forward an impasse was reached and, in the end, amalgamation never happened. Occasionally, Lynn would return to this in her later years and regret that all their work on this had come to nothing. But she was never one to stay still and St Ultan's had already begun another scheme to help the poor in Dublin, through the work of Dr Dorothy Stopford Price, who in 1936 obtained a license to import and test the BCG vaccine. The fight against TB would be central to St Ultan's work into the 1940s.

The early 1940s were, for very personal reasons, hard years for Lynn. ffrench-Mullen never had good health. Again and again, Lynn records her not feeling well, her tiredness, her stiffness, her asthma and the worries she had about her, constantly advising that she take

---

181. Ó hÓgartaigh, *Kathleen Lynn*, p. 97.
182. Ruane, 'Kathleen Lynn', p. 85.
183. KLD, Friday 20 December 1935.
184. Ó hÓgartaigh, *Kathleen Lynn*, pp 102–3.

time off and stay in bed. In 1916, ffrench-Mullen had an operation on her thyroid, the after effects of which continued to impact her health. She also suffered from severe rheumatoid arthritis and often took holidays to English spa towns to take the waters for that condition. Like Lynn, however, she was a tireless worker for St Ultan's and for the Utility Society. Her work as administrator, fundraiser and organiser for St Ultan's had been invaluable and, in 1942, she was part of conversations with Dr Stopford Price and Michael Scott, about the 'new T. B. place, it may be started in 6 weeks'.[185] In late 1942 Lynn became worried about her sudden weight loss and insisted she go to their doctor who found nothing wrong, saying that the loss of weight was likely 'due to the old thyroid problem'.[186] Despite health issues, ffrench-Mullen continued her heavy workload into 1943 but, in August, her brother Douglas, to whom she was very attached, died suddenly. Her health declined rapidly after that and by April 1944 she was mostly bed-bound, having suffered several bad asthmatic attacks. On 11 May 1944, she went into a respite nursing home for a short time. Lynn rarely left her side and, over the coming weeks, she visited several times daily, always being there in the evening as ffrench-Mullen fell asleep. Unexpectedly, on 26 May 1944, just as Lynn went home after a visit, she died. Lynn rushed backed to say her final goodbye to her life partner, who looked 'lovely at rest, happy'. Two days later she

> got some wee flowers in garden & bunch of yellow roses & went & said good bye to the earthly M ffM & sat there a while in the stillness, the yellow roses make the coffin so sweet'.[187]

The funeral service was held in Whitefriars Church, and ffrench-Mullen was buried in the ffrench-Mullen family plot in Glasnevin cemetery. That the women were life partners was, consciously or unconsciously, acknowledged as such by many people, as is obvious in the diary entries. The crowds at the funeral 'all know me and not the family', and 'so many many mourn her and are kind to me', while 'Lily Reilly said they were relations, but she belonged to me'.[188] Lynn was treated, by all, as the bereaved widow. While she was appreciative of all the sympathies, her return from a brief visit, to her sister Muriel, is poignant to read even at a remove; 'the loneliness coming back, with no M ffM to greet me & say what barren wilderness it had been while I was away!'[189] ffrench-Mullen had left her money to Lynn who was determined to honour her memory and all her work, using it to improve St Ultan's in ways that they had planned together; Madeleine would never be forgotten as long as Kathleen lived.

1945–55 – Life without Madeleine

For the last decade of her life Lynn would live without her life partner, and she missed ffrench-Mullen terribly. In January 1945, on her birthday, which was always a special day for the two women, she wrote that while she was happy to have friends celebrate with her

---

185. KLD, Friday 27 February 1942.
186. KLD, Tuesday 24 November 1942.
187. KLD, Friday 26 May 1944; Sunday 28 May 1944.
188. KLD, Sunday 28 May 1944; Tuesday 30 May 1944; Wednesday 31 May 1944.
189. KLD, Monday 5 June 1944.

she did miss 'dear M ffM.'.[190] In St Ultan's she missed her guiding and calming influence, where 'she made all work for love'.[191] There were moments in her busy life, especially when alone, that she felt her absence most keenly, as on a Saturday in October 1947, when working late in the hospital; 'how I miss dear M ffM … Office closed, all gone by 1 o/c so diff. MffM always stayed & worked in peace Sat. aft. & was as late as usual for dinner'.[192] At other times of difficulty, she felt that the spirit of 'dear MffM' was helping in the way she had done in life. As the work on the proposed 'B.C.G Project for Ireland' progressed she wrote that all in St Ultan's felt ffrench-Mullen was helping them towards success.[193] Even in 1955, more than ten years after ffrench-Mullen's death, there was nothing more she liked to do than to meet old friends who remembered 'M ffM' and have a 'great pow wow over old times'.[194] Friends and family filled the gap left by Madeleine, as her brother John returned to Ireland, in 1948, and lived with her until his death in 1954, while there were regular visits to her sister Muriel who lived in Warrenpoint. Her close friend and fellow socialist and revolutionary, Sighle (Sheila, née Bowen), and her husband Frank Dowling had moved into No. 8 Belgrave Rd and were a real support to Lynn. May Cummins who had grown up nearby, and Frances Clarke, remained her friends. Lynn also developed close and loving relationships with the next generation of the Wynne family, many of whom were living in Dublin. She often visited Geoff and Stella Wynne and their children, and was invited to baptisms, confirmations, birthdays, and other celebrations within the family. Eric Craigen, his wife Margery (née Wynne), and their young daughter Marjorie were also now part of her extended family. Emer (Molony) was still active in politics. Although they met less often now, as Molony was living on the North Circular Road with her partner Dr Evelyn O'Brien, their meetings were always recorded with warmth. Albina Broderick continued to visit from Kerry, staying with Lynn when she attended Sinn Féin meetings. Lynn continued her regular visits to the cottage in Glencormack where she met with her Wicklow friends and neighbours. She also had her colleagues at St Ultan's and, as the 1940s went on, she had a new generation of women, and some men, to work with. Despite the absence of ffrench-Mullen, Lynn had a life filled with people who cared for her. As she aged, however, she lost more of her older friends and comrades, and after the funeral of Winifred Stack, wife of Austin Stack, in October 1950, she wrote that funerals now served more as 'reunions of ancient friends'.[195]

Her work in St Ultan's was, as always, her mainstay. In January 1945, she was delighted when Professor William Craig, a pioneer in community and preventive paediatrics, came to visit St Ultan's. At a lecture by him later that evening, at which she recorded that she was the only woman, she noted that 'they say Teac is unique'.[196] While the plans for the amalgamation with Harcourt St Hospital were over, she focused on expanding the bed capacity in St Ultan's, especially providing space for the care of infants with TB. Pulmonary

---

190. KLD, Sunday 28 January 1945.
191. KLD, Thursday 22 August 1946.
192. KLD, Saturday 11 October 1947.
193. KLD, Thursday 19 May 1949.
194. KLD, Saturday 12 March 1955.
195. KLD, Tuesday 5 October 1950.
196. KLD, Monday 8 January 1945.

TB was common in those in St Ultan's care, and mortality rates among under fives remained stubbornly high into the 1940s. Building on the pioneering work of Dr Dorothy Stopford Price with the BCG vaccine in the 1930s, St Ultan's was becoming a centre for TB treatment with ambitious plans for expansion.[197] The involvement of St Ultan's in the BCG project would again bring clashes with the Catholic Church and a complicated, sometimes fraught, relationship with Dr Noël Browne, the man credited with the eradication of TB in Ireland, sometimes to the determent of acknowledging the work of Dr Stopford Price in St Ultan's.[198] In 1942 Stopford Price set up an Anti-Tuberculosis League which included Catholic and Protestant medics. In his ongoing aim of complete Catholic control of medical care, Lynn's old nemesis John Charles McQuaid, now Archbishop of Dublin, objected to this and insisted that the Catholic-controlled Red Cross would take the lead on fighting TB. Undeterred, Stopford Price continued her BCG work at St Ultan's and, in April 1945, the new TB wing was formally opened. In May 1946, Lynn proudly reported that the *Irish Times* featured 'Dr Price's B.C.G. vaccination'. It was, she wrote, 'a great day for Teac Ultain & we are all so proud & pleased'.[199] There were occasional tensions between the women and moments when Lynn thought Stopford Price was moving too fast in her attempt to make St Ultan's a national centre for BCG inoculation. She was concerned that Stopford Price wanted to turn St Ultan's into an exclusively TB hospital, something Lynn could not countenance.[200] Most of the time, however, she was incredibly supportive of Stopford Price's work. On Monday 20 June 1949 the big day finally came when the first dedicated BCG unit in the country, designed by Michael Scott, was opened at St Ultan's. Dr Noël Browne, as Minister for Health, performed the opening ceremonies. Lynn was delighted that he spoke 'so well & nicely about Dr Price & her European fame. It was a day to be proud ...'.[201]

By July 1949, Browne had approved the location of the National BCG Committee at St Ultan's, with Stopford Price as its first Chair. Relations with Browne were not always so cordial. As a member of Clann na Poblachta, he had been elected as TD in 1948, and was part of the coalition government with Fine Gael. Lynn felt that he unfairly blamed the medical profession for the high death rates from TB, noting that they were not 'responsible for housing, feeding, resting the people'.[202] At a meeting with a deputation from the hospital in November 1950 he launched at 'us' because things were moving too slowly in TB work. Lynn believed it was better to move slowly but 'that's not Dr Browne'.[203] Neither did she appreciate his attacks on the medical association, and she was wary of his Mother and Child Scheme, proposed in 1950, to provide free medical care for all mothers and children. She was quite annoyed that those, meaning St Ultan's and herself, who 'started Baby treatment' had not been consulted about the scheme.[204] When the board of the hospital

---

197. KLD, Wednesday 8 March 1942.
198. See Mac Lellan, *Dorothy Stopford Price* (2014) for a correction to this impression.
199. KLD, Friday 31 May 1946.
200. KLD, Friday 18 July 1948.
201. KLD, Monday 20 June 1949.
202. KLD, Monday 8 November 1948.
203. KLD, Monday 13 November 1949.
204. KLD, Tuesday 9 May 1950.

met to deliberate on the scheme, the main consideration on which Lynn was focused, was a worry that under the scheme St Ultan's would no longer be an infant's hospital, it would become just like all other children's hospitals. She also feared they might have to accept 'Drs on Staff that we didn't chose ourselves'.[205] Lynn need not have worried as there were forces with more power than she or St Ultan's ranged against Browne and his scheme. Unsurprisingly, these included Archbishop McQuaid and the Catholic Church, but, more importantly, also included the Irish Medical Association. An impasse was reached between Browne and those who opposed his scheme, and with no compromise appearing from either side, Browne's resignation was requested and accepted by his party leader, Seán McBride, and his Mother and Child Scheme was not taken forward.

Lynn continued to comment on both politics and the war in Europe. Her complicated relationship with Britain meant that while she deplored the bombing, death, and destruction in English cities, she did not celebrate British victories once the Allies had invaded Europe. She was determinedly anti-Imperial and hoped that the war effort would see Britain decline as an Empire when, one by one, the colonies demanded their freedom. On 15 June 1947 she wrote 'India passed to Indians at 12 o/c y.day. Marvellous rejoicings Hindus & Mohamadans rejoice together D.G. Egypt will be next'.[206] Immediately after the war it became clear that in a defeated and destroyed Germany there was a refugee crisis of enormous proportions. She was horrified at the accounts from her friend and fellow paediatrician, Dr Bob Collis, who worked in the liberated Bergen-Belsen camp. She would not believe her beloved Germans 'could have tolerated such appalling conditions'.[207] By October 1945 she was concerned that the refugee organisations were helping all except Germans, and that 'poor Germans die of hunger'.[208] She was persuaded by her friend and St Ultan's colleague, Dr Kathleen Murphy, to join a new organisation, Save the German Children Society, of which she became a vice president. The organisation was controversial from the beginning, as the proposal to only bring Christian German children to Ireland, was seen as an 'unchristian and politically unwise move'. Several of its members also made anti-British and pro-German statements at its inaugural meeting.[209] Despite this, the scheme was popular and, by July 1946, German children began to arrive in Ireland to be placed with families. Lynn continued her involvement until the organisation wound up at the end of 1951.

In the early 1950s it becomes obvious that she was finding her large workload more and more onerous, both in St Ultan's and her private practice. Her diary is full of patient meetings, committee meetings, funerals of friends and comrades and reignited worry about Molony, who was drinking again. Her interest in politics was unabated, and she was happy to have her brother John in the house for company and discussions. In autumn 1953, she

---

205. KLD, Monday 7 May 1951.
206. KLD, Friday 15 June 1947.
207. KLD, Wednesday 13 June 1945.
208. KLD, Tuesday 16 October 1945.
209. Cathy Molohan, 'Humanitarian aid or politics?', *History Ireland*, Issue 3, 1997, https://www.historyireland.com/humanitarian-aid-or-politics/#:~:text=In%20October%201945%20a%20Dublin,wariness%20in%20the%20British%20authorities, accessed 23/07/2023

was avidly following the uprising in Kenya. She loved her breaks in Glencormack, feeling revitalised after 'plenty of sun & breeze & grateful heat. I was singing in my heart like the river for joy'.[210] Sadness came in January 1954 with the death of 'dear Dr Price', and on 4 March, on the eve of what would have been ffrench-Mullen's birthday, her brother John 'passed without a struggle. How thankful I am I was able to mind him to the last'.[211] More and more her thoughts turned to the past and there is a sense, in several diary entries, of her reflecting on her life. The British were using 'real Black & Tan treat' on the Mau Mau rebels in Kenya. She believed that the killing of the Mau Maus was as 'they attempted to help their bombed villages & it was not denied or affirmed, of course it is so & well we know fr. our treat. here'.[212] Sometimes she felt like a 'ghost from the past', and reflecting on all that had happened and all that she had been through she wondered if anything much had changed for women since they got the vote: 'I had thought' she wrote, that getting the vote 'would have transformed the world & it didn't. I thought the same wld. be when the British were gone, but that was a much greater disappointment'.[213] Lynn may have been disappointed with the position of women, and the fact that Ireland was not the Ireland of the Proclamation, and the Republic for which she had fought, but she had done a great service for her country. Her second last diary entry was on Sunday 24 April 1955, 39 years after the Rising and after she began the diaries. She attended a 'Commemoration Service. S. Mary's very nice, tho' not over many there. A beautiful day like 1916 was'.[214] The following day she made one final entry, a happy day in Glencormack where it had 'rained all day since we came & blew', but 'quiet now'.[215] She also used the phrase 'braineen annuas' – now that the storm is gone.[216] It is possible that she had some sort of attack or was feeling something amiss in her head (braineen) as 'anuas' can mean 'down' in Irish. Whatever the cause there are no more diary entries so we have no private insights into Lynn's final months. It is likely she spent some days in Glencormack and returned to Dublin. A few months before her death on 14 September 1955, she entered St Mary's Nursing Home in Ballsbridge where she spent her last days. She was buried, with full military honours, in Deansgrange Cemetery, in the Lynn family grave. An appreciation in the *Irish Times* said that Ireland had lost one of 'the most remarkable women' of the century.[217]

CONCLUSION

The diaries of Dr Kathleen Lynn allow us a window into the private life of a very public woman, revealing much of the complex interiority of her thoughts and emotions. While we know much of the historical events of Lynn's life, reading that life through her diaries reveals her emotions, her ups and downs, her joys, her traumas, her likes and dislikes.

---

210. KLD, Friday 18 April 1952.
211. KLD, Thursday 4 March 1954.
212. KLD, Wednesday 2 December 1953.
213. KLD, Thursday 24 April 1947; Thursday 15 March 1951.
214. KLD, Sunday 24 April 1955.
215. KLD, Monday 25 April 1955.
216. Ibid.
217. *Irish Times*, 16 September 1955, p. 5.

They offer a unique first-person perspective on the people, events, and ideas of her times, in a way other primary sources may hint at, but rarely reveal. To read in the diaries her motivations for her revolutionary activism, the foundation of St Ultan's Hospital, her work with her colleagues on the eradication of TB, and her continued feminist socialist and republican politics, gives us an understanding of the life and world of a radical woman operating in a patriarchal conservative society. Questions asked, prior to reading the diary, about what motivated the daughter of a Church of Ireland clergyman to become an Irish revolutionary, are answered, and through the diaries we see how Lynn enmeshed her deep-seated faith with an equally deeply held desire for freedom for women, workers and Ireland. She remained steadfast in her republicanism, her feminism, and her socialism to the end. The nuance and complication of her relationship with Britain, from whence came her ancestors, and with which many of her immediate family still felt connected, are reflected throughout the diary. Her Anglophobia, in terms of British political and military actions, and desire for the end of Empire was deep rooted, as was her friendship with both Anglo-Irish and English people. She could despair at the destruction of English cities in the war, while at the same time hoping the socio-political and economic cost of war would mean the end of the British Empire. She experienced a comradeship with all those who battled against Empire, regarding revolutionary men and women overseas as 'their Cumann na mBan or IRA'. She also noted a similarity between British colonial repressions elsewhere to those experienced by people in Ireland during the War of Independence. She could separate out British people from the idea of Imperial Britain, like one and wish for the end of the other.

In Ireland she, like many other radical revolutionary women, soon recognised a common enemy, a conservative state in alliance with a powerful Catholic Church. As a woman, as a diehard anti-treatyite, as a republican and as a Protestant, she was an outlier in a Catholic, patriarchal state. While Lynn was not anti-Catholic, how could she be when her life partner ffrench-Mullen and so many of her friends and comrades were Catholic, her diaries reveal her despair at the machinations and power of the institutional Church, its successful takeover of hospital care and its imposition of a Catholic ethos in considerations of medical care, especially care of women and children. Towards the end of her life, she wrote of her regret over the failed amalgamation, and feared that the church-supported and run Catholic Children's Hospital at Crumlin would swamp St Ultan's.[218] The diaries allow us a clearer understanding of how radical, revolutionary, women self-defined themselves, how they represented their actions and ideas, and how those identities did not remain static. When moving from a revolutionary to a post-revolutionary world, Lynn's diaries reveal how the events, ideas and people around her impacted and shaped her engagement with these worlds. They also demonstrate how her radical feminist, republican and socialist thinking, and her commitment to helping the poorest and most vulnerable, remained central to her work and her thinking. One of the most hidden areas of her life was her relationship with ffrench-Mullen. The diaries make visible the intimate connection between the women, their devotion to each other, their shared domestic and public life, and the

---

218. KLD, Wednesday 1 July 1953.

unspoken acknowledgement by others of the importance of that relationship. In providing these selected extracts we seek to represent Kathleen Lynn in all her complexities, an exterior or public life as radical revolutionary, feminist, socialist, and professional woman and an interior life as partner, sister, friend, comrade, and Christian. These interrelated and intersecting parts of her personality informed her life's work, her activism, and her relationships. She is a woman worth knowing through, and in, her own words.

PART 2: THE DIARIES OF KATHLEEN LYNN

SELECT ABBREVIATIONS AND EXPLANATIONS

A.C.A.	Army Comrades Association.
A.G.O.W.	All goes on well.
Ard C	Ard Chomhairle, the national governing body of Sinn Féin.
A.R.P.	Air Raid Precautions.
BMH	Bureau of Military History.
B.brack	Ballybrack, in south Co Dublin.
B & Ts	Black and Tans, nickname for temporary Constables recruited to assist the Royal Irish Constabulary (RIC) in 1920.
B.Rock	Blackrock, suburb of Dublin.
B.Stone	Broadstone, railway station in Dublin.
City Hall	Built between 1769 and 1779, the City Hall, Dame St, Dublin, originally the Royal Exchange, became one of the main sites of the 1916 Rising, garrisoned by the Irish Citizen Army.
C.I.D.	Criminal Investigation Department, short-lived plainclothed counter-insurgency police unit of the Irish Free State.
C na mB	Cumann na mBan.
C na nGael / C na nG	Cumann na nGaedheal, the main pro-treaty political party in the Irish Free State. It was in power between 1923 and 1932, and merged with other parties to form Fine Gael in 1933.
C.P.	National Centre Party which began as the National Farmers and Ratepayers League, was a short-lived political party in the Irish Free State.
Dail Eireann / Dail	Dáil Éireann. The lower house, and principal chamber, of the Irish Oireachtas or Parliament. The upper house is the Seanad Éireann or as it was most often called, the Senate.
D.cdra /D.Condra	Drumcondra, a suburb of Dublin.
Dean's Grange	Deansgrange Cemetery in Dublin.
D.G. / DG	*Deo gratias* (thanks be to God).

D.L. / D/L / Dun Laogh.	Dún Laoghaire, a coastal town on the outskirts of Dublin.
D.M.P.	Dublin Metropolitan Police.
D.V.	*Deo volente* (God willing).
Elin.	A hospital or convalescent home – unidentified.
F.F.	Fianna Fáil. Founded in 1926 under Éamon de Valera following a split from Sinn Féin following a decision by some members to take their seats in Dáil Éireann if elected.
F.O.S.R.	Friends of Soviet Russia.
F. G.	Fine Gael, political party founded in 1933 from a merger of Cumann na nGaedheal, the National Guard (Blueshirts), and the National Centre Party.
F.S.	Free State – the Irish Free State.
G. Men	Plainclothes divisional officers of the D.M.P.
G.P.O.	General Post Office, on O'Connell Street, Dublin.
G.S.R.	Great Southern Railways.
Harold's X / H.X.	Harold's Cross, a suburb of Dublin.
H.S.	House Surgeon.
I.C.A.	Irish Citizen Army.
I.M.A.	Irish Medical Association.
I.R.B.	Irish Republican Brotherhood.
I.T. / I. Times	Irish Times newspaper.
Kilmainham	Kilmainham Jail.
Lab.	Labour. Depending on the context can mean either the Irish Labour Party, founded in 1912 by James Connolly, James Larkin and William O'Brien, or the English Labour Party.
L.G.B.	Local Government Board.
M.O.	Medical Officer.
MtJoy / Mt.Joy	Mountjoy Jail.
N.D.U.	North Dublin Union Workhouse.
O.F.M.	Order of Friars Minors, the Franciscans.
O.P. / O.P.D.	Outpatients Department.
P.H.	Public Health.

Pts.	Patients.
RCPI	Royal College of Physicians of Ireland.
R.C.S.I.	Royal College of Surgeons in Ireland.
Red X.	Red Cross.
R.Drum	Rathdrum, a village in Co. Wicklow.
R.Mines	Rathmines, the suburb of Dublin where Lynn lived. Used in conjunction with a time at the start of an entry, this means Lynn attended a service at that time in the Holy Trinity Church in Rathmines.
S.B.'s	St Bartholomew's Church, Clyde Rd, Dublin.
S.cove	Sandycove, a coastal town on the outskirts of Dublin.
S. Fein/ S. F.	Sinn Féin. Political party founded in 1905 by Arthur Griffith, after 1916 it became the main republican party. It became the anti-treaty party from 1922.
St Ann's	St Ann's Church of Ireland, Dawson St.
St Enda's	St Enda's School, Rathfarmham.
Senate	Seanad Éireann. The Upper House of the Irish Oireachtas or Parliament. Members of this house are referred to as Senators.
T.D.	Teachta Dála, a member of Dáil Éireann, the lower house of the Oireachtas (the Irish Parliament).
Teac or Teach	St Ultan's Hospital for Infants.
T.W.F.L.	The Irish Women's Franchise League.
U.C.D.	University College Dublin.
W.I.L.P.F.	Women's International League of Peace and Freedom.
W.Point / W.P	Warrenpoint, town in Co. Down.
W.Row	Westland Row, train station in Dublin.
W.W.U.	Women Workers' Union.
Xtians / Xtianity	Christians / Christianity.

SELECT BIOGRAPHIES

Barry, Alice (1880–1955) – founding member of the Women's National Health Association and one of the founders of St Ultan's Hospital.

Bennett, Louise (1870–1956) – leading member of the Irish Women Workers' Union (IWWU).

Brodrick, Albinia (1861–1955) – Gobnait Ní Bhruadair, Irish republican and radical.

Brugha, Caitlín (1879–1959), *née Kingston* – Sinn Féin politician and TD, wife of Cathal Brugha. In the diaries she is referred to as 'Mrs C Brugha', 'Mrs Brugha'.

Byrne, Edward Joseph (1872–1940) – Archbishop of Dublin, 1921–40, opposed the amalgamation of St Ultan's with Harcourt St Children's Hospital.

Ceannt, Áine (1880–1954), *née Ní Bhraonáin* – Irish revolutionary and humanitarian leader, wife of Éamonn Ceannt.

Chenevix, Helen (1886–1963) – Suffragist and trade union activist, worked with Louie Bennet in the Irish Women Workers' Union (IWWU). In the diaries she is referred to as Miss Chenevix.

Childers, Erskine (1870–1922) – writer, politician, revolutionary, anti-treaty, executed in November 1922.

Clarke, Frances (*c.*1864–1949) – a neighbour of Lynn's on Belgrave Road, also from a Church of Ireland background.

Clarke, Kathleen (1878–1972), *née Daly* – founder member of Cumann na mBan, TD, Senator and first female mayor of Dublin. Wife of Tom Clarke. In the diaries she is referred to as 'Mrs Clarke', or 'Mrs Tom Clarke'.

Collins, Michael (1890–1922) – revolutionary, politician, pro-treaty, leader of the National Army, killed in an ambush in 1922. In the diaries he is referred to as 'Mick', 'M. Collins'.

Comerford, Máire (1893–1982) – writer, journalist, Cumann na mBan activist and anti-treaty.

Cosgrave, W. T. (1880–1965) – revolutionary, politician, Sinn Féin TD, pro-treaty, leader of Cumann na nGaedheal, President of the Executive of the Irish Free State.

Cowell, John (1912–2008) – physician and medical administrator, director of the National BCG Committee.

Despard, Charlotte (1844–1939), *née French* – suffragist, nationalist, socialist, and writer. In the diaries she is referred to as 'Mrs Despard'.

De Valera, Sinead (1875–1975), *née Flanagan* – teacher, folklorist, writer and wife of Éamon de Valera. In the diaries she is referred to as 'Mrs Dev'.

De Valera, Éamon (1882–1975) – revolutionary, politician, leader of Fianna Fáil, Taoiseach, and President of Ireland. In the diaries he is referred to as 'Dev'.

Dowling, Sheila 'Sighle' (c.1896–1957), *née Bowen* – Cumann na mBan, close friend of Lynn, lived next door with her husband Frank Dowling at No. 8 Belgrave Rd from the 1940s.

English, Adeline 'Ada' (1875–1944) – psychiatrist, republican and Sinn Féin TD.

ffrench-Mullen, Douglas (1892–1943) – member of the Irish Volunteers, participated in the 1916 Rising, brother of Madeleine ffrench-Mullen. In the diaries he is referred to as 'D' or 'Douglas'.

ffrench-Mullen, Madeleine (1880–1944) – Irish revolutionary, suffrage and labour activist, co-founder and administrator of St Ultan's Hospital. Lifelong partner of Kathleen Lynn. In the diaries she is referred to as 'Madeleine', 'M', 'M ffM'.

ffrench-Mullen, Margaret (1857–1929), *née O'Callaghan* – mother of Madeleine and Douglas ffrench-Mullen, (and two others) married St Laurence ffrench-Mullen, Fleet Surgeon, Royal Navy, in 1879, at Booterstown Church, Co. Dublin. In the diaries she is referred to as 'Mrs M ffM'.

Gilmartin, Matilda – appointed secretary to St Ultan's hospital in 1944 after the death of Madeleine ffrench-Mullen. In the diaries she is referred to as 'Miss Gilmartin', 'Miss G'martin', 'Miss G.M.'

Ginnell, Alice (1882–1967), *née King* – Cumann na mBan and Sinn Féin member, widow of Laurence Ginnell.

Gonne McBride, Maud (1866–1953) – Irish republican, suffragette, actress and muse of W. B. Yeats. Founder of Inghinidhe na hÉireann, widow of executed signatory Seán McBride, campaigner for the rights of republican prisoners and supporter of St Ultan's. In the diaries she is referred to as 'Maeve', 'Madam', 'Mrs McBride', 'Madam Gonne', 'Madam McB'.

Jacob, Rosamond (1888–1960) – writer and political activist. In the diaries she is referred to as 'Roisin', 'R. Jacob'.

Jane – Lynn's maid at her home 9 Belgrave Road, Rathmines.

Kennedy, Margaret 'Loo', (1892–1953) – Inghindhe na hÉireann, Cumann na mBan, anti-treaty, Fianna Fáil politician, Senator, 1943–8. In the diaries she is referred to as 'Commandant Kennedy'.

Kettle, Mary (1884–1976), *née Sheehy* – feminist, republican, local politician, sister of Hanna Sheehy Skeffington and widow of Lieutenant Tom Kettle, killed at the Somme in 1914. She was elected to Rathmines Urban District Council in 1920.

Lemass, Seán (1899–1971) – revolutionary, politician, Fianna Fáil TD, Minister for Industry and Commerce (1932), later leader of Fianna Fáil and Taoiseach.

Lloyd, Miss Ormsby – appointed Housekeeper at St Ultan's Hospital in 1934.

Lynn, Anne (1873–1931) – Kathleen Lynn's older sister. She lived in Cong with Reverend Lynn until his death. She never married and is buried in Deansgrange cemetery in the Lynn grave. In the diaries she is referred to as 'Nan' or 'N'.

Lynn, Muriel (*b.*1876) – Kathleen Lynn's younger sister. She lived in Cong, and later in Warrenpoint, Co. Antrim. In the diaries she is referred to as 'Muriel' and 'M'.

Lynn, John (1877–1954) – Kathleen Lynn's younger brother, he lived for many years in Australia, returning to live with Kathleen in Dublin a few years before he died. In the diaries he is referred to as 'John'.

Lynn, Robert (1844–1923) – Kathleen Lynn's father, married Catherine Marion Wynne. In the diaries he is referred to as 'Fardie' and 'F'.

Macardle, Dorothy (1889–1958) – republican, Cumann na mBan, writer, propagandist, anti-treaty republican.

MacSwiney, Annie (*d.*1954) – sister of Mary and Terence MacSwiney.

MacSwiney, Mary (1872–1942) – republican, Cumann na mBan, Sinn Féin TD, sister of Terence MacSwiney. In the diaries she is 'Miss MacSwiney' or 'Mary Mac'.

MacSwiney, Muriel (1892–1982), *née Murphy* – wife of the Lord Mayor of Cork, Terence MacSwiney, who died after 74 days on hunger strike in Brixton Prison.

McGrath, Joseph 'Joe' (1888–1966) – revolutionary, politician and businessman, Director of the Hospitals Trust, he ran the Irish Hospitals' Sweepstakes.

McQuaid, John Charles (1895–1973) – Archbishop of Dublin, 1940 to 1972. Opposed the Hospital amalgamation plan.

Maguire, Katharine (1863–1931) – doctor, one of the founders of St Ultan's Hospital.

Maguire, Dora (1889–1931) – nurse at St Ultan's and Cumann na mBan member, active in the organisation and in the Women's Prisoners Defence League in the 1920s. In the diaries she is referred to as 'Nurse' or 'the Nurse'.

Markievicz, Countess Constance (1868–1927), *née Gore-Booth* – Irish revolutionary, 1916 rebel, socialist, distant relation to Kathleen Lynn. In the diaries she is referred to as 'Madam', 'M', 'Markiev', 'the Countess', 'Madam M'.

Moloney, Helena (1883–1967) – Irish revolutionary, feminist, and labour activist. A member of Inghinidhe na hÉireann, she adopted the pseudonym 'Emer' for Inghinidhe work and was known by this name within her circle of republican women comrades. In the diaries she is always referred to as 'Emer'.

Montessori, Maria (1870–1952) – Italian physician and educator, developer of the Montessori educational method.

Mulcahy, Josephine 'Min' (1884–1977), *née Ryan* – member of Cumann na mBan and wife of Richard Mulcahy (1866–1971), IRA Chief of Staff in 1920.

O'Brien, Evelyn (1901–1981) – psychiatrist, partner of Helena Molony.

O'Casey, Seán (1880–1964) – political activist and playwright. In the diaries he is referred to as 'Sean O'Casey', 'O'Casey', 'O'C' and 'Casey'.

O'Donnell, Peadar (1893–1986) – revolutionary, teacher, socialist and writer.

O'Doherty, Rose – graduated NUI 1921, Honorary Visiting Physician to St Ultan's.

O'Duffy, Eoin (1890–1944) – revolutionary, soldier, policeman and politician, pro-treaty, first commissioner of the Gardaí, leader of the Blueshirts, first leader of Fine Gael.

O'Higgins, Kevin (1892–1927) – politician, Sinn Féin TD, pro-treaty, Cumann na nGaedhael, Minister for Home Affairs 1922–3, Minister for Justice 1923–7, assassinated in 1927.

O'Kelly, John J. 'Scellig' (1872–1957) – writer, journalist, Irish language activist, Sinn Féin TD, anti-treaty. In the diaries he is referred to as 'Scelig'.

Plunkett, Countess Mary Josephine (1858–1944) *née Cranny* – married to George Noble Plunkett, Papal Count, mother of Joseph Plunkett, revolutionary, poet and journalist, who was executed in 1916. In the diaries she is referred to as 'Countess P', 'Countess', 'Madam'.

Reddin, Teresa (1865–1949) – treasurer of Cumann na mBan, one of the founders of St Ultan's and first Hon. Treasurer of the hospital, St Ultan's.

Rhodes, Fanny M (c.1865–1934) – a neighbour of Lynn's in Rathmines. Normally called Miss Rhodes in the diaries.

Sheehy Skeffington, Hanna (1877–1946) – suffragette, political activist, teacher, journalist, writer. She lived on the same road, Belgrade Road, as Lynn and ffrench-Mullen. In the diaries she is referred to as 'Mrs. S. S', 'Mrs Skeffington', 'Mrs S Skeffington', 'Mrs S. Skeff'.

Stokes, Barbara (1922–2009) – paediatrician and disability campaigner, Stokes remained at St Ultan's until it closed in 1984 and was responsible for the transfer of the archives to RCPI. In the diaries she is referred to as 'Dr Stokes' or 'our Dr Stokes'.

Stopford Price, Dorothy (1890–1954) – paediatrician, medical officer to a Cork brigade of the IRA during the War of Independence, her medical career was spent mainly in St

Ultan's Hospital for Infants where she introduced BCG to St Ultan's in 1937. In the diaries she is referred to as 'Dr Stopford' and after she married as 'Dr Price'.

Tennant, Elizabeth – one of the founding physicians of St Ultan's Hospital.

Webb, Isabella 'Ella' (1877–1946), *née Ovenden* – active in the Women's National Health Association and was the first female to be appointed to the Adelaide medical staff. She worked at St Ultan's from its foundation.

Wyse Power, Jennie (1858–1941), *née O'Toole* – Sinn Féin politician, and founder member of Cumann na mBan. Voted for the Treaty, left Cumann na mBan and co-founded the women's pro-Treaty organisation, Cumann na Saoirse.

Wynne, Florence (1844–1941) – Kathleen Lynn's maternal aunt, lived in Dún Laoghaire. In the diaries she is referred to as 'Aunt F'.

Young, Ella (1867–1956) – poet, republican, mystic, Cumann na mBan, later lecturer in Irish myth and lore at University of California, Berkeley.

SECTION 1: 1916–23 REVOLUTION

The first section of Kathleen Lynn's diaries, beginning in 1916 as the Easter Rising breaks out and ending in 1923 as the Civil War draws to a close, reflects her deep involvement in this revolutionary period. Like Lynn, by 1916, the more radical middle-class suffrage campaigners had begun to lean left in their thinking, influenced by the thinking of James Connolly and other socialists, by their participation in the 1913 Lockout and membership of the Irish Citizen Army. After the Rising these women were determined to play their part in mainstream politics, campaigning for seats on the revitalised and reorganised Sinn Féin Executive and fighting as militants in the War of Independence. Lynn records the violence, raids, and reprisals of the War of Independence, particularly those aimed at militant republican women. Her entries on her disillusionment with the Treaty and the men who led Ireland into an Irish Free State reflect the intransigence of many of these republican women. The possibilities of radicalism which feminist and socialist women engaged with prior to 1916, which they saw reflected in the 1916 Proclamation, had been, according to their thinking, betrayed through the Anglo-Irish Treaty.

One of the central elements in Lynn's diaries is her work in St Ultan's Hospital for Sick Infants. The founding of the hospital in 1919 was inspired by a desire to 'make some effort to check the needless waste of infant life in Dublin'. Infant (under one year of age) mortality rates in Ireland at this time were 88 per 1000, slightly below the rates in Scotland, England and Wales. However, the rates in Dublin were much higher, at 141 per 1000, considerably more than in London (85 per 1000). The main causes of infant mortality in this period were diarrhoea and enteritis, bronchitis, pneumonia, convulsions, premature birth and a group of 'wasting diseases' often caused by malnutrition. 1919 also saw a spike in the number of deaths from influenza, as the pandemic hit. The hospital annual reports make it clear that they saw the high infant mortality rates in Dublin as directly linked to poverty and malnutrition. Issues intensified by the 'unsettled state' of Dublin during the War of Independence and Civil War.

Resources were a constant issue for the Hospital in this period. St Ultan's opened in 1919 with two cots and less than £100, in a building that was only just habitable. Thanks to constant fundraising by 1923 the hospital had expanded to 24 cots, money was also invested in the infrastructure with new windows, laundry (1920) and nurses' accommodation (1921). The hospital also kept goats to provide fresh milk for the infants, although they were a constant source of conflict with the matron. In 1923 the hospital opened a pathological laboratory, to address one of its key aims of 'research into disorders of nutrition of infants'. Despite limited resources 187 infants were admitted to the hospital during 1923, the death rate in the hospital had fallen from 55 per cent to 39 per cent. 901 additional outpatients registered during 1923, as well as medical treatment the outpatients' department offered nutritional advice and the masseuse attended twice weekly.

Lynn's diaries for this first period show a woman engaged in militancy, republicanism, politics, and medicine. They show a woman who kept a close eye on national and international events, who had strong opinions on the British, as well as showing her growing and deeply held anti-imperialism and Anglophobia. The diaries also show her movement away from moderate to radical ideologies, especially militant feminism, socialism, and republicanism. Privately the diaries tell us of a contented life with her partner Madeleine ffrench-Mullen, their shared domestic and work life, their holidays, their friends and their extended network of colleagues and comrades who supported their efforts in St Ultan's and on the Rathmines Urban District Council. They also reveal a woman with a deep commitment to her Christian faith. Lynn comes through the cauldron of revolution somewhat disheartened and disillusioned, but what is in evidence is a determination to continue working for St Ultan's, for the poor and for women.

1916

April

Monday 24

Easter Monday. Revolution. Emer and I in City Hall, Seghan Connolly shot quite early in day. Place taken in evg. All women taken to Ship St abt. 8.30. Mrs. Barrett, 2 Norgroves, B. Davis & I joined later on by B. Lynch, J. Shanaghan & B. Brady–we were locked up in a filthy store, given blankets thick with lice and fleas to cover us & some "biscuits" to lie on, not enough to go round.[1]

Tuesday 25

Ship St. barracks. Halpin brought in, utterly exhausted having been in chimney, without food, since evg. of 24th. We objected to lavatory accommodation & heard it was good enough for us, that lice, fleas & typhoid should content us. Another officer had the W.C. cleaned & was quite civil. Had good dinner, same as soldiers.[2]

Thursday 27

Heard Halpin died in hosp. this mg. Last night had our first night visitor, a drunken prostitute, fired in on us, it gave those who were asleep a great fright. She quieted down soon. Firing on & off all day – siege fare, bully beef & biscuits, Tea without milk. Many tales of headquarters being gassed, burnt out, etc. Very heavy firing all night, we thought place would come down any minute. Much perturbation in barracks sentries evidently every few yards, challenging passers to & fro.[3]

---

1. *Emer* – Helena Moloney (1883–1967). *Seghan Connolly* – Seán Connolly (1882–1916). *Mrs Barrett* – Kathleen Barrett, née Connolly, (*b.*1887), sister of Seán. *2 Norgroves* – sisters Annie (1899–1976), and Emily (1897–1977), Norgrove. *B. Davis* – Brigid Davis. *B. Lynch* – Elizabeth 'Bessie' Lynch (*b.*1895). *J. Shanaghan* – Jane Shanaghan. *B. Brady* – Brigid Brady (*b.*1896), all members of the Irish Citizen Army.
2. *Ship Street Barracks* – built around the 1750s and converted to Officer headquarters in the early nineteenth century. Although unsuitable it was used to incarcerate the female prisoners taken from City Hall for four or five days during the Rising. *Halpin* – William Halpin (1887–1951), Irish Citizen Army sniper, hid in a chimney in City Hall after the surrender until he was discovered and taken to Ship St Barracks.
3. *Heard Halpin died in hosp. this mg* – despite Lynn's fears William Halpin survived, living until 1951.

May

Monday 1

Taken to Kilmainham. Miss O'Farrell came in prisoner at dinner time, she had been round all our centres, under British escort advising surrender, as Connolly prisoner, most centres v. averse, doing well, why all gave in we can't understand, some trick behind that. She was promised safe convoy home & taken prisoner at Ship St. so much for British honour. In aft. about 50 men and we 12 women marched off via Thomas St. to Richmond barracks, great ovation as we marched along, only separation women hooted. In Castle Yard officer told soldier to prod Nurse Treston with bayonet for not at once falling into line saying he had seen her shoot 6 police & others all in barracks since Mon. Saw Fr. Columba at Richmond, who got Miss O'Farrell released. Men stayed in Richmond and we went Kilmainham, 3 in cells, one bed. B. Davis, J. Shanahan & I together. Gruel & dog biscuits for our supper. I can't sleep, fearful irrit. Nightly.[4]

Tuesday 2

Saw M.ffM early this mg. Greatest joy. Emer, she & I have cell together, such joy, cheerfully we do with one basin of water for washings, hog wash of cocoa & dog biscuits for b.fast. Madam Markiev. here in solitary. We had loan of her comb & soap. Day = b.fast 7.30, exercise some time in mg. for hour. When we are all together. about 70. I.C.A., C na mB etc. Saw many we knew & heard much news – M.O. here absolutely useless, looks like drug manic. Dinner 12.30, good soup – potatoes, dog biscuit, cheese nice change fr. eternal bully beef. Sleep after dinner. I searched & found body lice cause of my trouble. Supper 5.30 porridge dog biscuit. Bed when dark, no candles.[5]

---

4. *O'Farrell* – Elizabeth O'Farrell (1883–1957), Cumann na mBan, had spent Easter Week in the GPO. She was chosen by Pearse to take the surrender notice to the British, and subsequently took, under military escort, official notices of surrender to all the rebel outposts. *Connolly* – James Connolly (1868–1916), socialist, trade unionist and signatory of the 1916 Proclamation. *Nurse Treston* – Catherine Treston, née Ryan, Cumann na mBan, had been in the GPO. *Fr Columba* – Fr Columbus Murphy OFM (1881–1962), from the Capuchin Friary on Church St who ministered to the imprisoned rebels. *Men stayed in Richmond and we went Kilmainham* – the male prisoners remained in Richmond Barracks, Inchicore until either imprisoned in Kilmainham or Mountjoy Jails or deported to prison camps in Britian and the women were taken to Kilmainham Jail.
5. *M .ffM* – Madeleine ffrench-Mullen (1880–1944), also referred to as *M* in this section of the diaries. *Madam Markiev* – Countess Constance Markievicz, née Gore-Booth, (1868–1927), often also referred to as *Madame* or *M* in the diaries. *M.O.* – Medical Officer.

Monday 8

Heard 3 shots this mg, told later on Mallin, Ceannt & Colbert had been shot. That makes 7. What other country shoots its prisoners in cold blood! God bless them, they did not fear to die for Ireland. All had exercise this mg. Delighted to see Emer again. Heard Madame came back last night (was taken away y.day) and that she has a maid to attend her & tea & egg for b.fast. They say she has had life sentence. Aft. some appeared before 2nd tribunal but M & I were reserved for the General. Later saw Fr. Albert. He was with Malin, Heuston & Colbert this mg. They were wonderful in their consciousness of the Unseen & went to deaths with prayers on lips. He could have wished to be in their place. We were so sad after he left. We looked out on the hills and thought of psalms wh. have been such a comfort to us. When all in bed gt. reaket began – all unimportant people to go – hurry & scurry to get them out & in a very short time all were back again, it having just struck governor that young girls couldn't go alone thro' streets at that hour.[6]

Tuesday 9

The girls got off about 7.15, some came to say goodbye at our door, but soon the dragon, Barrett saw & stopped them. All gone now of our special set but Emer, Miss Gifford, Madeline & myself. There are 8 others, some recently taken – hear now Countess upstairs is Plunkett not Markieviz who is in Mtjoy. Heard Grace Gifford & Joe Plunkett were married in his cell on Sun. & that he was shot next mg. Little chap Cain came with Lavengero & kind message on Carletons but had cheek to advise me to give up my Rep. friends, told him I would follow my conscience. Heard very pitiful crying, it was Miss Gifford, her brother told her that 2 brothers in law were shot, Macdonagh & Plunkett. Kind matron let me go to her for a little. Just at bedtime we were scurried off in Black Maria to Mtjoy, travelled with Countess Plunkett. Went by bye streets for fear of a rescue.[7]

---

6. *Mallin, Ceannt & Colbert* – Michael Mallin (1874–1916), member of the ICA, Éamonn Ceannt (1881–1916), and Con Colbert (1888–1916), both members of the Irish Volunteers. All three were signatories to the Proclamation of Independence, 1916 and all three executed. *Fr Albert* – Fr Albert Bibby OFM (1877–1925), Capuchin priest. *Heuston* – Seán Heuston (1891–1916), Irish Volunteers, executed.
7. *Mtjoy* – Mountjoy Jail. *Miss Gifford* – Nellie Gifford (1880–1971). *Countess Plunkett* – Josephine Plunkett, née Cranny (1858–1944), mother of Joseph Plunkett (1887–1916), who was a leader in the Irish Volunteers, signatory to the Proclamation and executed after the Rising. He and Grace Gifford (1888–1955), sister of Nellie, married in Kilmainham a few hours before his execution. *Carletons* – a family of friends of Lynn's outside the Republican movement. *Macdonagh* – Thomas MacDonagh (1878–1916), Irish Volunteer leader, 1916 proclamation signatory, executed in Kilmainham, married to Muriel Gifford (1884–1917), the sister of Nellie and Grace Gifford.

Wednesday 10

Mtjoy clean & comfortable, but I'd give £10,000 for Kilmainham & Madeline. Matrons v. kind. Hot bath with M. & G. dinner soon after. Heard F. & L.S were here to see me. I am so sorry he came, it is hard to grieve one's Father, but I could not do otherwise. He didn't look too bad, I thought. N was there but didn't see her. Had to talk thro' gratings with passage between. Heard Carruthers was all right. Glad. Jane keeps house at No. 9. Good Jane. Exercise in aft. Allowed to talk, such a comfort. Good messages fr. Deutchland. N. Gifford looks better, Emer very well, M. not bad.[8]

Friday 12

A very black Friday. Fardie & Nan were here, oh, so reproachful, they wouldn't listen to me & looked as if they would cast me off for ever. How sorry I am for their sorrow! Erin needs very big sacrifices. I am glad they go home to-morrow. Why do they always misunderstand me? Had dear little sympathetic note fr. N. Whitley this mg & sweets & marmalade fr. [Courry]. Their message gave much joy. Heard that Sean McDermott, the lame boy & Connolly have been shot & that Asquith is here, that Dillon has upheld us in Parliament.[9]

November

Thursday 30

Madeline had goitre removed by Mr. Taylor. [I] gave anaesthetic. After op. met Canon Carleton, who saluted me![10]

---

8. *F* – Lynn's father Rev. Robert Lynn (1844–1923), also referred to as *Fardie* in the diaries. *L.S* – Lizzie Smartt, family friend and cousin of Lynn, from Mayo. *N* – Lynn's sister Anne Elizabeth Lynn (1873–1931), also called *Nan* in the diaries. *Carruthers* – possibly Christopher Carruthers, a 'Boy' in the ICA stationed at St Stephen's Green. *Jane* – Lynn's maid at her home 9 Belgrave Road, Rathmines, Dublin. In this entry *M* means Madame, Countess Markievicz.
9. *McDermott* – Seán MacDermott (1883–1916), *Connolly* – James Connolly (1868–1916), two of the seven executed 1916 leaders. *Asquith* – Herbert Asquith (1852–1928), British Prime Minister, April 1908 to December 1916. *Dillon* – John Dillon (1851–1927), MP, supporter of Irish Nationalism and Home Rule.
10. *Mr Taylor* – William Taylor (1871–1933), surgeon, President of RCSI and later Consulting Surgeon to St Ultan's Hospital, also referred to in diaries as Sir or Colonel Taylor. *Canon Carleton* – probably James George Carleton, Prebendary of Rathmichael in St Patrick's Cathedral.

1917

June

Thursday 21

Madam's homecoming, crowds greater than ever turned out for royalty.[11]

September

Tuesday 25

Thomas Ashe died in Mater while my finger on his pulse. Dev. came at night & he & Emer went to Bruagh.[12]

---

11. *Madam's homecoming* – the celebration on the release of Countess Markievicz from the Women's Prison in Aylesbury, a town to the north-west of London. She was discharged from Aylesbury on 17 June, returning to Dublin to a tumultuous welcome.

12. *Thomas Ashe* (1885–1917), a senior Irish Volunteer and military leader during 1916. Imprisoned post Rising and released in early 1917. He was rearrested and imprisoned in Mountjoy Jail in August 1917. He and others went on hunger strike demanding political prisoner status. He died after being force fed. *Dev* – Éamon de Valera (1882–1975). *Bruagh* – Cathal Brugha (1874–1922), Chief of Staff of the Irish Republican Army, later Minister for Defence and first president of Dáil Éireann.

1918

May

Friday 17

Madame M came to garden. We, M, Madame & I had lunch in garden. Evg. meeting of Standing Committee. Heard that whole Executive are to be arrested. I went home, went into Dr Dillon's, G men came while Dr D & I were at the door. He was taken. I walked out & off. Nearly all the others taken.[13]

September

Sunday 22

Inignie protest meeting for women prisoners. Mrs. S.S. M & Emer taken & released in 2 hrs. Poor M. Much mauled by police.[14]

October

Monday 28

3rd sitting Miss Williams. 90 Belfast prisoners 'Flu'. Saw & injected Fr. Sherwin. Saw Mr Curran who advises immediate coming out on account of epidemic.[15]

Thursday 31

Thurs. Arrested early, brought to Rathmines (F. Clarke came to R.mines P. Station) & Arbour Hill, deportation order cancelled, when guaranteed with Lord Mayor, 'no politics'. M & all worked well for me. Plenty pts. fr 5 p m.[16]

---

13. In this entry *Madame M* – Markievicz. *M* – Madeleine ffrench-Mullen. *Standing Committee* – National Executive of Sinn Féin. *G men* – plainclothes divisional office of the Dublin Metropolitan Police. *Dr D* – Thomas Dillon (1884–1971), Irish chemist and nationalist, husband of Geraldine Plunkett.

14. *Inignie* – Inghinidhe na hÉireann. *Mrs S. S.* – Hanna Sheehy Skeffington (1877–1946). *M* – Madeleine ffrench-Mullen.

15. *rd sitting Miss Williams* – Lynn was sitting for a portrait by Lily Williams (1874–1940), sister of her good friend Florence Williams, both of Rathmines. *90 Belfast prisoners* – These were republicans from all over Ireland arrested and incarcerated in Crumlin Road prison in Belfast.

16. *F Clarke* – Frances Clarke (*c.*1864–1949), a neighbour on Belgrave Road, also from a Church of Ireland background. *R.mines* – Rathmines the suburb of Dublin where Lynn lived.

November

Monday 11

They say Peace declared, at least it is armistice. Hohenzollerns gone, Republics all round. Much flagwagging here. At night officers on cars & motors attacked by rabble & beaten. Spoke to Foran re closing Factory. All goes well in Hosp.[17]

Monday 25

Maeve's return announced in papers, foolish. She will prob be taken. Election work proceeding well. Mrs. S. S. won't stand for Harbour Div. schade. Pts doing well.[18]

December

Saturday 14

A glorious sunburst sunrise & a lovely day, memorable for Ireland. We all hope. May our women's vote be used for good. Went to Aonach in evg. It was very nice & I saw many friends.[19]

Sunday 15

Great Public Funeral for Coleman, 1500 at least at it. I went fr. Westland Row to Rotunda with it. Much uneasiness felt re. ballot papers, left now in charge of enemy till 28th. Overwhelming S.F. majorities.[20]

Monday 30

Huge meeting in O'Connell St last night, Madam M only woman in, nothing further fr. Belfast jail, where machine guns are trained on Austin Stack, Freeman has done volte facie. M's birthday, she & Mrs here to dinner. We are to have Flag Day for no 37.[21]

---

17. *Hohenzollerns* – The House of Hohenzollern is the former royal German dynasty whose members were variously princes, electors, kings and emperors of Hohenzollern, Brandenburg, Prussia, and Germany. Kaiser Wilhelm II of Germany abdicated in 1918.

18. *Maeve* – Maud Gonne MacBride (1866–1953). *Pts* – patients. *Schade* – German for a pity or a shame, a word often used by Lynn when disappointed.

19. *Aonach* – Irish, an assembly or most often a festival or fundraiser.

20. *Coleman* – Richard Coleman (1890–1918), Captain in the Irish Volunteers, died of the flu while imprisoned in Usk Prison, Wales. His funeral was a propaganda coup for the Republican movement.

21. *Madam M* – Countess Markievicz, the only woman elected in the 1918 General Election. *Freeman* – the Freeman's Journal. *M* – Madeleine ffrench-Mullen. *Mrs* – her mother, Margaret ffrench-Mullen, née O'Callaghan.

1919

January

Tuesday 21

Dail Eireann. It was all it should be, simple, solemn, impressive – a great voice, God grant a continuance to the end! Went to S.B's a.m., then pts, then Dail. The evg entertainment was most successful, many press people present. D.G for this day, fine & bright all things. Much consternation when military seemed to be in possession of Mansion Ho, till they evacuated & we walked in.[22]

Wednesday 22

Almost all reference to Dail censored out of papers, murder of 2 police in Limerick arranged to synchronise with it. Limerick proclaimed same day. Another lovely day for 2nd meeting of Dail (private). Esther Hurford came to tea and wants to help in Teac Ultain.[23]

Tuesday 30

Cold miserable day, satisfactory meeting of C na dT re women on L.G.B. etc. J.J Welsh & others tried to meet Labour men in mg at Mansion Ho, only succeeded in summoning G men. Strike still rages in B.fast much to dismay of those who don't have to see Hibs .& Orange arm in arm.[24]

February

Tuesday 4

Great news. De Valera, Milroy & McGarry have escaped fr. Lincoln, hope they may be safe. I heard it first from Nunan in Jervis St. Saw Shelley there, who knew his father in old Parnellite days. Saw Foran, there may be great happenings soon. Bolshevism seems to be rapidly

---

22. *S. B.'s* – St Bartholomew's Church on Clyde Road. *D. G.* – *Deo Gratias* (thanks be to God).
23. Two Royal Irish Constabulary constables were killed in an IRA ambush in Soloheadbeg, Co. Tipperary. *Teac Ultain* – St Ultan's Hospital, often referred to by Lynn simply as Teac.
24. *C na dT* – Cumann na Teachtaire/League of Women Delegates. *L.G.B* – Local Government Board. *J J Walsh* – James Joseph Walsh (1880–1948), Irish Volunteer, later Postmaster General. *Hibs and Orange* – Nationalists and Unionists.

coming to the front on all sides. D.G. How puny are the efforts of the rich to resist the spirit of freedom.[25]

Wednesday 12

Mrs Clarke released, she must be very ill. Mrs P holds on well. A fearfully rushing day. 'Flu everywhere. There is hope of money for Hosp fr. Corporation. Saw O'Neill re repairs of 37. Mrs S Skeffington had good London meeting. Going to Glasgow for Self Determ. meeting there.[26]

Wednesday 19

Mrs Clarke & Miss Daly have 'Flu, it is spreading fearfully. Madam G came re. Mrs G. Patients all day, even Jane down. Madeline had satisfactory interviews re Baby. Hosp. Fearfully wet mg, cleared up afterwards. Went to Mrs Hungerford's. Elin. Full.[27]

Saturday 29

Mrs Clarke, a little, wee bit better, got thro' night & day fairly, she is so tired. Poor Mrs Daly came to her & Daly & Tom. Emmet has a cold. I was out fr 10 a.m. till 9 30 p.m. & did not get all done. Concert very badly attended, tho' I think tickets went well. Many military motor lorries in the Green. Mrs Skeffington says why?[28]

March

Saturday 15

Great day for Ireland, Madam's return, beautiful weather. We, Citizen army, met her at K.town in motors. Had tea there & returned for public entry into Dublin. Madam looks very well, Milroy & McGarry too. Madam went to Liberty Hall & we were photoed there, then she had meetings in New St & at St James' fountain. Great crowds.[29]

---

25. *De Valera, Milroy & McGarry* – Republicans Éamon de Valera (1882–1975), Seán Milroy (1877–1946), and Seán McGarry (1886–1958), all escaped from Lincoln Jail in England on 4 February 1919.
26. *Mrs Clarke* – Kathleen Clarke, née Daly, (1878–1972). *Mrs P* – Margaret Pearse, née Brady (1857–1932). *37* – 37 Charlemont Street, the location of St Ultan's Hospital. *Mrs S Skeffington* – Hanna Sheehy Skeffington.
27. *Elin.* – hospital/nursing home where patients from St Ultan's were transferred.
28. *Mrs Daly* – Catherine Daly, née O'Mara, mother of Kathleen Clarke. *Daly & Tom. Emmet* – Kathleen Clarke's three sons with Thomas Clarke who was executed in 1916.
29. *Madam* – Countess Markievicz, just released from Holloway Jail. *Liberty Hall* – headquarters of the trade union, the ITGWU, and the Irish Citizen Army

April

Wednesday 9

Mrs Clarke went home, nice day, very busy. Munroe Gov. Mtjoy suspended, must pay £2,000 fine, at least. Ella Young in garden, we had lunch there, 1st time this year. Madam went over Teach. The poor Byrne boy in Limerick Union Hosp was foully murdered by the police, on his attempted rescue, fr evidence at inquest to-day.[30]

May

Tuesday 6

Ard Chormarle at 10 o/c. Saw pts first. Not much business done but election of St. Comt. 4 women on now. Delegates went to Maynooth with Dev & Griffith. A most lovely day. Madam & Sylvia Pankhurst came to dinner after Ard C. Sylvia seems nice & quiet. Evg went with M to Moyne Road & planted gentian. Pearl's reception to-morrow.[31]

Thursday 8

Papers (Unionist) still very full of rage abt Limerick Delegates being here. Preposterous English Peace Terms announced. Heaps of people here in aft including Miss Douglas. Evg went to meeting of Inignie at Madam Gonne's, then to see Delegates return fr south. Countess Plunkett took M & me into Mrs McGarry's & we saw them & heard them speak well for Ireland. A memorable evg.[32]

Tuesday 20

V busy day with arrangements abt Teac, interviewed Mr Webb & Lord Mayor, latter to speak 'At Home'. Standing Comt meeting arranged many things especially B. Brennan's position. Rumour we are all to

---

30. *Munroe* – Charles Arthur Munro (1869–1952), Governor of Mountjoy Jail. *Ella Young* (1867–1956), Irish poet, republican and mythologist. *Byrne* – Robert Byrnes (1899–1919), Irish republican and trade unionist, shot dead on 6 April 1919 while trying to escape from hospital where he was under armed guard.
31. *Ard Chormarle* – Ard Chomhairle/National Executive, Sinn Féin. *St. Comt.* – Standing Committee of the Ard Chomhairle. *Griffith* – Arthur Griffith (1871–1922), Irish writer and politician, founder of Sinn Féin. *Sylvia Pankhurst* (1882–1960), English feminist and socialist campaigner who supported the cause of Irish freedom.
32. *Inignie* – Inghinidhe na hÉireann. *Madam Gonne* – Maud Gonne McBride (1866–1953). *Countess Plunkett* – Josephine Plunkett, née Cranny, (1858–1944). *Mrs McGarry* – Thomasina McGarry (d.1957), with of Seán McGarry.

be arrested once more. The American Delegates have requested safe conduct for our leaders for Peace Conference.[33]

Friday 23

The Teac At Home a great success, everyone seems pleased & we got some money. A most perfect day. Had meeting in the garden under laburnum. Mr Baillie spoke very nicely. Bakers' strike settled D.G. Lord Mayor had to be there & not with us. Things seem unsettled in Paris. They are very upset over leaving of 9 delegates.

Thursday 29

Ascension Day. A perfect day. Went R.mines 8 o/c. Breakfast in Teac, 2nd goat milked with 4 holding her. Saw Mrs Clarke, she is better. Aft Mrs C Brugha arr. in hurry, had 8 lb daughter in evg, both splendid D.G. We opened Teac with 2 babies. May the Lord bless our work. Eng papers full of "Dominion Home Rule" for Ireland. The play goes splendidly in Abbey.[34]

June

Monday 16

Meeting of women Drs to consult over Constitution. We all agree, I think. M went to Mtjoy & saw Mr Ginnell, he is fairly. No news of Madam Markievicz. Saw Mr O'Callaghan in evg (of Glasgow). Many rumours & certainties of arrests & searches. Ketterick looks well. Some rain to-day. We are all upset over baby Susanna's death.[35]

July

Thursday 10

We are anxious abt. babies, why have so many temp. up & undigested motions? Malachi very fragile. I went to Elin, but didn't stay long, went down to Teac & relieved M, she came back late & kept me for night.

---

33. *Mr Webb* – possibly James Henry Webb (1873–1955), of O'Callaghan and Webb architects. *Lord Mayor* – Lord Mayor of Dublin, Laurence O'Neill (1864–1943). *B. Brennan* – Robert 'Bob' Brennan (1881–1964), Irish nationalist writer and diplomat. *Standing Comt* – Sinn Féin Standing committee. *Peace Conference* – The Paris Peace Conference, 1919–1920.
34. *Mrs C Brugha* – Caitlín Brugha, née Kingston, (1879–1959), wife of Cathal Brugha.
35. *women Drs* – the group of women doctors who founded St Ultan's Hospital, Drs Lynn, Webb, Barry, Maguire, and Tenant. *Mr Ginnell* – Laurence Ginnell (1852–1923), Irish nationalist politician and lawyer.

Bed very small. I do feel very tired. Went in mg. to have Xray photo of jaw done by Dr Hayes.[36]

Tuesday 15

Preparation for Peace celebrations on Sat. God grant there may be no bloodshed. Babies all better to-day. Little Malachi's funeral to Dean's Grange this mg. He would have been 4 mos. to-morrow. Dr M very critical still of goat's milk & things in general. Her baby had bad turn this mg, she says depressed fontanelle doesn't matter. Antrum better. Supper Hurford's, nice.[37]

Thursday 31

Op. Col Taylor 9 a.m. Portobello saw Dr Crofton, Elin. 10.30, no chance for poor Molly Smith. Saw Dr O'Carrol 11.15 & handed over many pts. Saw Dr Maguire 12.30 in Teac & handed over babies did disp. Madeline & I came back to No 9, many there, not much peace, she looks well. Saw Dr Tennant 6 o/c & handed over more pts. Very tired evg. in bed abt. 11.[38]

August

Tuesday 5

Cycled into town. No pumps for motor tyres, schade. Brought fruit & flowers for Matron & M. All goes well in Teac D.G. Babies have grown since Fri. Saw Dr Keogh, he is pleased with my nose. Grand to see M again, looking well. Back late for dinner. After that saw a sick twin. A glorious sunset. Heard 1,200 rifles got in Dundalk. 50 mil. British securities transferred to U.S.A Bolshivick terror. Val much better.[39]

September

Friday 12

6 Harcourt St. raided, I saw them, armfuls of papers carried out, Griffith & others watched fr. windows, poor P. O'Keeffe & Blythe taken. Raids all over Ireland, demons. Little Jerry very low, poor child. Carmel

---

36. *M* – Madeleine ffrench-Mullen. *Dr Hayes* – probably Richard Atkinson Hayes (1850–1940).
37. *Dr M* – Dr Katharine Maguire (1863–1931).
38. *Dr Crofton* – William Mervyn Crofton. *Dr Tennant* – Dr Elizabeth Tennant.
39. *Dr Keogh* – Dr Peter John Keogh (1886–1944), ENT specialist.

& Liam to go, took photos of them before they left. Saw Fardie off by 1.30 train, well pleased with dentist. N better. Many raids in Dublin.[40]

Thursday 25

Nan & I went to Dean's Grange in mg. a lovely warm day. Very busy in aft. Heard all silver being called in. N says they would like me at home, only no one must know I am there. Strange. Teac does well. We are anxious abt. Mr Ginnell. M stayed in bed to rest aft y.day & Sunday. Question of prayer for Ireland's deliverance started.[41]

Sunday 28

R.mines 8 a.m. new baby Semus in Teac, a little better. Madeline, Matron, nurse McArdle & I went & collected at Croke Park, football Final. We got abt. £7. Lovely day. Evg. D.cdra Ch. lovely Southwark Psalm music. Tea Miss Hurley & Rhodes. Fine sunset. The thought came to me that we women must make the prayer for Ireland, saw Mrs. Clarke abt. it. Strike in England in full swing.[42]

October

Thursday 9

8 a.m. S. B's. Poor M had to start at 7 for Mrs D'Arcy's funeral. She brought Snowball the black cat back, poor homeless thing now. We got 2 new babies, [Mona] fr. Holles St. [ ] of poisoning such a mite, born 8 lb, now 4, 10 days old. I stayed in Teac till 1 a.m. Matron so tired, Esther moribund. At Standing Committee in evg. Good scheme of work & lectures for Clubs.[43]

Thursday 16

S.B's 8 a.m. Ard Feis held last night & all affairs settled. Large force of military & police hold Mansion Ho. M & I went down & after parley, she was allowed in to see Lord Mayor. A lovely day. Madam arrived fr. Cork at 6.30. Jane saw her. Only a few there. Many bad cases to-day. All well at Teac. Mrs Brennan told me fine stories of Y.F.W.

---

40. *Harcourt St* – Sinn Féin Central Offices and HQ of Cumann na mBan. *P.O'Keeffe & Blythe* – Patrick 'Paidin' O'Keeffe (*b.*1881), and Ernest Blythe (1889–1975), both members of Sinn Féin. *N* – Lynn's sister Anne 'Nan' Lynn.
41. *Dean's Grange* – Deansgrange cemetery, where Lynn's mother was buried.
42. *R.mines 8 a.m* – 8 o'clock service in the Holy Trinity Church, Rathmines. *D.cdra Ch.* – Drumcondra Church. *Miss Rhodes* – Fanny M. Rhodes (*c.*1865–1934), neighbour of Lynn's in Rathmines.
43. *Clubs* – Sinn Féin Clubs

Saturday 25

8 a.m. S. B's. Lovely day. M, Miss Ellis & I went to Old Connaught to Miss Whitty's & bought black goat, hope she'll be good. President rather better. Dr Crofton advised normal horse serum, wh. we gave at once, with benefit, I hope. Aft. Matron & I went to Lime Hill, all packing there. Evg. Pres. better. Went to Madam's reception, T.W.F.L met Mr & Mrs Brown of Australia there. Madeline's new costume arrived. Strange searchlights.[44]

November

Friday 7

Murky day, cold & damp. M went to Lady Shaw with Tipperary matron & interviewed architects in evg. Dr Hayes came to Teac & was amazed at improvement in it. M heard much of workings of C na mB, where Maeve is concerned. All motors to have permits. What shall I do? Mr Ginnell went to Arran. Mrs Weddall & other girls let out of Mountjoy after hunger strike. Petrograd lost to Allies.[45]

Wednesday 12

Rumours of other & larger raids. All Dail & S.F. Executive to go. Motor permits are a worry if we are all 'on the run' it doesn't matter. Dev does well in U.S.A. The strikes there quashed, but they fear only to break out with redoubled vigour. Nice day, all babies do well.

Tuesday 25

Op. Elin early, much protest against motor permits, many shops etc. won't have deliveries. M & I bought 2 birch trees to plant on Sat. Cold day. All well in Teac but '5/='. Everyone protesting against infamous new regulations re political prisoners. The new Teac book will be beautiful, the garden is getting quite nice. The tanks waited all night in Orwell Park for raid, didn't come off.[46]

---

44. *President* – one of the patients in St Ultan's Hospital, Lynn refers to patients throughout the diary normally by their first name or a pet name like 'President' or 'Matron'. *T.W.F.L.* – The Irish Women's Franchise League.
45. *C na mB* – Cumann na mBan. *Maeve* – Maud Gonne McBride. *Mrs Weddall* – Emily M. Weddall (1867–1952), member of Cumann na mBan. *Petrograd* – St Petersburg, Russia.
46. *new Teac book* – Leabhar Ultáin / The Book of Saint Ultan, a fundraising book published in 1920. It contained images and poems by Irish artists and writers.

December

Wednesday 3

Permit protests good. Dev does well in U.S.A. Fr O'Donnell claims compensation for unjust arrest etc. Went to L. Smartt's wedding. I was only one who thought of flowers. No taxis to be had, they had carriages. Wedding in Harold's X Ch. Fardie married them & Dean Reilly. Back to lunch in Leinster Rd. It was a nice comfortable kind of homely wedding. Evg. many pts.[47]

Sunday 14

8 a.m. R.mines. Busy day. Terrible revelations in paper re action of British in [Amritsar] last April, crowd of 1,000 fired on, 500 killed natives obliged to crawl at command of General. They call themselves Xtians. Lord Mayor is working to get Tom Kelly out. Our 1st Guild Office at 5, good many there. F Williams & another told good tales.[48]

Monday 22

Independent raided & machinery destroyed for felon setting. All carried out in most businesslike way. It was time to give them a lesson. I hear Savage is to have public funeral to-morrow, the jury sent condolences to relatives on this sad death. The President is better, D.G. & all others do fairly well. More rumours of great round up, preparing for 600 in Mtjoy.[49]

Wednesday 31

M stayed here last night. Busy mg. with pts. Good article in Telegraph re France & Ireland. Permits now necessary to enter or leave Park. Election work progresses well. M down at meeting in Harold's X & R.mines. Was going to see P. S. O'Hegarty's child as new year came in, back here after 12.30, moonlight, frosty night. What will 1920 bring?[50]

---

47. *Dev does well in U.S.A* – Éamon de Valera undertook a republican propaganda and fundraising tour of America between June 1919 and November 1920. *Fr O'Donnell* – Fr T. J. O'Donnell of the Australian Imperial Force and of Irish descent, arrested in Dublin for 'disloyalty towards the Sovereign'.
48. *Amritsar* – The Amritsar massacre took place on 13 April 1919 when a largely peaceful crowd protesting at the arrest of pro-independence activists were fired on by troops under Colonel Reginald Dyer. *Xtians* – Christians. *Tom Kelly* – Thomas Kelly (1868–1942), Sinn Féin politician and Alderman for Dublin City Council. *F Williams* – Florence Williams.
49. *Savage* – Martin Savage (1897–1919), Irish Volunteer, killed while attempting to assassinate Lord French, then Lord Lieutenant of Ireland, on 19 December 1919.
50. *Harold's X* – Harold's Cross, a suburb of Dublin. *P. S. O'Hegarty* – Patrick Sarsfield O'Hegarty (1879–1955), Irish revolutionary and writer.

1920

January

Monday 5

Much excitement, 2 police barracks attacked in Cork, in one police left by raiders in handcuffs, they might have been shot only we are so merciful. Evg. went to Dalkey. Pt. brought up to Portobello emergency op. Ald Flanagan gave £25 for handsel for Teac, bless him. Canvassing goes well. We gave in our nominations to-day for Urban Councils.[51]

Sunday 11

8 a.m. R.mines, busy day, meeting 12, dinner ffMullen, then to Harold's X., meeting, F Joseph spoke & Madeline, Citizen Army Pipers' band, torchlight procession to Ch. Ave., meeting there, then to Milltown & back to Ranelagh. Very stormy, wet day, home 6.30, had tea & got dry, M went to bed. I off to see people in Ch. Place, then Teac, poor Seumus low, then Schofields' party, lovely music, home 11.45. I do hope Thurs. will go well. Much lightening.[52]

Thursday 15

8 a.m. S. B's, the eventful polling day. Lovely mild, spring-like day. V busy, all of us going back & forward fetching people etc. Little Byrne (septic head) better D.G. In Teac Seumus still there, but very weak. Polling went on to last moment. Police wouldn't allow Dwyer, O'Connor & me into Town Hall to see ballot boxes sealed = illegal. We seem to have done well, so far as we can judge.[53]

Saturday 17

8 a.m. S.B's. Madeline elected & Sears topped poll in Harold's X. B. Brennan & Mr Mulcahy got in for Rathgar so there are 9 S.F. on council, D.G. fine for R.mines. Evg. Ceilidh for Teac in Gaelic League place, very nice but small. Mr Schofield sang. We got home at 5.15 &

---

51. *Ald Flanagan* – Alderman Michael Flanagan (1833–1931), Irish nationalist politician and long-time member of Dublin Corporation.
52. *Schofields* – Home of Joseph Schofield and family. He was a cello teacher at the Leinster School of Music.
53. January 1920 was polling day for the Local Elections. Sinn Féin had major successes across the country.

were dead tired. Deschanell defeated Clemenceau by large majority for President of French Republic.[54]

Friday 30

8 a.m. S.B's Great excitement over meeting of new Dublin Corporation & R.mines Council. We had lively time & made the old set see we were not to be trifled with before the end tho' we were outvoted every time, of course. Meeting lasted 2 ½ hours. In Dublin Ald. Tom chosen Lord Mayor, we'r so glad.[55]

February

Wednesday 4

First ordinary meeting of R.mines Council. We did well, got opponents to pass recommendation for Irish in schools. They are sorry they made set on Dwyer abt. bankruptcy. New babies in Teac. One seems v. bad. Influ. coming, it seems. I spoke a bit in meeting to-day. We had sholes of people here, lovely. Got help fr. America, so glad, good letter fr. Bob.

Wednesday 11

L. George's speech as tricky & false as usual, maravellous how Britain upholds rights of very small nations but ours. They hope to pass their precious Home Rule bill wh. no one wants, at once. Saw kids, dear little things & proposed playground. Goats' milk available again for Teac, D.G.[56]

Friday 20

Military patrols in city all night. 2 plain clothes police fired on some of our men in Grafton St. at 2 a.m., one on each side killed. When will this provocation cease? & people walk the streets unmolested. McGrath's house raided 4 hours & every man in O'Hara's arrested. Took President to Elin., child sick in O'Kelly's. Visited Mrs Clarke & saw Madge Daly there.

---

54. Madeleine ffrench-Mullen was elected for the Rathmines and Rathgar Urban District Council as was Kathleen Lynn, Min Mulcahy and Áine Ceannt for Sinn Féin. *9 S.F* – nine Sinn Féin local councillors elected in Rathmines
55. Although still in prison, Sinn Féin candidate, Alderman Thomas Kelly (1868–1942), was elected Lord Mayor of Dublin. However, due to ill-health, he was not inaugurated as mayor, so he never officially held the office.
56. *L. George* – David Lloyd George, British Prime Minister from December 1916 to October 1922.

Saturday 21

Martial Law proclaimed for Mon. No one to be out betw. 12 a.m. & 5 a.m. I hear it won't help them much. French to resign when country quieter [ ] to succeed. G.men retiring & resigning in large numbers, many police touts abt. Pres. still in Elin. No word fr. Cheeverstown. M went out 11.30, foolishly followed military patrol & got taken. I had a fearful fright when she didn't turn up I spent night in Donnybrook.[57]

Sunday 22

8 a.m. R.mines. In bed 2 hrs last night. Poor M charged with spying on Military, such rubbish, we all did [what] we could to help her, she is all right so far. It is dreadful to think of & all the anxiety about the country as well, God will help us, tho' times never seemed so dark. Already people have been shot in street for not answering challenge of plain clothes men.

Monday 23

8 a.m. S.B's. Went straight to M in Bridewell for fear she should be spirited away, she had slept well & was wonderfully cheerful, D.G. Mrs ffM came & very soon we were all in Police court. M's case came on in afternoon, charge obstructing military, Mr Lupton found no evidence of it & case dismissed, thank God, for it might have been serious. Poor B. Barton in Portland, hungerstriking. Mrs Mulcahy had bad experience.[58]

March

Wednesday 3

Council meeting 10 a.m., we made them uncomfortable over architect, lighting & salaries. Bob & [Sears] were not there. Castle mail held up in Dominick St. in broad daylight & mails for Castle taken, much perturbation & raids everywhere as result. F MacDonagh's raided again & children pulled out of bed. L.G.B. inspected Teac & were pleased. Poor baby came in in convulsions & died at once.[59]

---

57. *French* – Sir John French (1852–1925), Lord Lieutenant of Ireland. *G. men* – plainclothes policemen from the G Division of the Dublin Metropolitan Police
58. *Mrs Mulcahy* – Josephine 'Min' Mulcahy, née Ryan (1884–1977), member of Cumann na mBan and wife of Richard Mulcahy (1866–1971), IRA Chief of Staff in 1920. *B. Barton* – Robert Childers Barton (1881–1975), agriculturalist and Irish revolutionary.
59. *F MacDonagh* – Sister Francesca, born Mary MacDonagh, sister of Thomas MacDonagh and guardian of his children.

Tuesday 16

Council meeting 10a.m. re prospective strike, no wonder when men like Anderson on Council. Madeline stayed at Moync Rd. last night. L.G.B. is sending £405 for Teac, D.G. Dr. [Massy] came over it & was pleased. Madeline faint in aft. had to go to bed. Evg. practise S.Andrew's, went to Victory Concert, a great success, also Ceilidh. Home early to bed. Erskine Childers came abt. letter.[60]

Saturday 20

M the one with 'flu this time. Lord Mayor of Cork shot dead in his house by masked assassins, awful crime. Had very busy day, settled many things. Took M down to Glencormac in taxi in evg., she stood it well, but went straight to bed, poor child. All so kind there. Miss Gardiner & her German Governess are here.[61]

Monday 22

Back fr. Glencormac early. Cork Lord Mayor's murder, cruelly brutal & callous, all evidence points to police murder. Widow & 5 children & another expected, whole city in mourning. Mrs Pearse & Ceannt gone to funeral, they wanted M & me. Count P helped abt. Mr Berry. Saw Mr Ginnell, got pts. into Elin., full now. Teac does well. Coming home 10.45, saw crowds, heard soldiers were firing on people, bayonet charge at Portobello Bridge.[62]

Tuesday 23

8 a.m. S.B's. Ireland needs all our prayers, soldiers went wild last night, Man & woman shot dead Sth. Richmond St., many wounded around [ ] St. firing 60 rounds a minute, civilians helpless. Mrs Pearse & Ceannt back fr. Cork, a wonderful funeral & tale of honour & calm bravery. Irish republic recognised by U.S.A. Judge, D.G., we can thank God & hope there may not be too much more to endure. Soldiers confined to barracks to-night.

---

60. *Erskine Childers* (1870–1922), writer and politician.
61. *Cork Lord Mayor's* – Tomás MacCurtain (1884–1920), Sinn Féin politician and Lord Mayor of Cork was, on 20 March 1920, shot dead, in front of his wife and son, by masked men who were later found to be members of the Royal Irish Constabulary. *Glencormac* – Co. Wicklow, where Lynn and ffrench-Mullen had a holiday cottage.
62. *Mrs Ceannt* – Áine Ceannt, née Ní Bhraonáin, (1880–1954), Irish revolutionary and humanitarian leader, widow of Éamonn Ceannt.

Tuesday 30

8.a.m. R.mines. Mr Ginnell released unconditionally in aft. D.G. D.G. we heard it at 10 p.m. Council meeting in mg. for estimates for year. Went well. Hospitals got their £300. "Butcher" Macready has arrived here, so we suppose more frightfulness will begin, maybe not, who can tell? Baby Denny very ill with 'Flu. A nice Spring day. Machine gun practice all afternoon[63]

April

Sunday 11

8 a.m. R.mines. Restless night with Emer, she is better to-day. Such an anxious day on account of hungerstrikers in Mtjoy. Madam Gonne & I went there in evg. None of them actually in danger yet, Dr says. Soldiers there in full war array, [keeping] guns, tanks & armoured cars. A snap of the fingers would excite a massacre, God help us.[64]

Thursday 15

8 a.m. St. B's. Went to enquire for D. Humphries & Mrs asked me to see him, very weak he is but lies on happily & contededly in bed, a breath would blow him away. Spent night in Elin., a terrible round up last night, 200 taken on suspicion for shooting of Pleasants St. policeman. They say a 'young one' can identify man. Evg. news of gt. raid in R.mines. Captain White hungerstriking.[65]

Friday 30

Macready won't allow papers to publish any but his accounts of military doings! Good beginning. 15 prisoners released from Wormwood Scrubs collapsed. The President is in Elin. v. sick but holding his own. All well in Teac. We had field out pt. day. Baby Byrne (head abscesses) came to see us, fit & blooming D.G. Went late to see Mrs Clarke, she isn't bad D.G.

---

63. *'Butcher' Macready* – General Sir Cecil Frederick Nevil Macready (1862–1946), was appointed Commander-in-Chief of the Crown Forces in Ireland, by Prime Minister Lloyd George in early 1920.
64. *hungerstrikers in Mtjoy* – between 5 April and 14 April 1920 over 60 male republican prisoners undertook hunger strikes as a protest over their lack of political prisoner status.
65. *D. Humphries* – Richard 'Dick' Humphries (1896–1969), IRA hunger striker in Mountjoy. *Captain White* – Captain Jack White (1879–1946), republican, socialist and ICA leader.

May

Friday 14

Any number of police barracks & Income Tax Offices raided & destroyed all over the country, good work Madeline, very busy preparing for the Week. Miss Ball very ill, lumbar puncture in evg. I had letter fr. Waller Young inviting me to Harristown, strange after abt. 30 years silence. A most lovely day. Poor little President looks lovely in death.

Monday 17

Left 63 early, Miss Ball rather better but wandering still. Fierce riots in Derry, organised by British, Orange against R.C. Policeman & soldier shot. Madam got murder letter written on Dail paper. The wretches stole plenty fr. Harcourt St. Teac well. Went to Riversdale in mg. on car, Strachan driving, mare goes well. M v busy about "Week". Nothing doing now in Four Courts or Land Commission.

Saturday 22

Met Dr Chisholm at 6.30 a.m. At W.Row. Brought her to Mrs Mulcahy's, busy mg. poor Miss Ball bad. 1st Annual meeting of Teac a great success. We had 1st `at Home' afterwards & many old pts. there. All went well & the weather was lovely. Wonderful sunset. We got £26, all were pleased. French's nerves gone, he must rest, also Lawlor. Their end here is near & their master's.[66]

Saturday 29

The Teac is a year old to-day. Thank God for all He has so far done for us. Now we have 10 little ones, how many shall we have next year? 20 D.V. Col. Taylor removed my ganglion in heel at 9 a.m. M brought me to Aunt F & I stayed the day in bed. Very wet in evg., hope Celidhe wont be spoilt. Great fight in Kilmallock y.day. S.F. victory.[67]

---

66. *Dr Chisholm* – Catherine Chisholm (1878–1952), founder of Manchester Babies Hospital and one of the founders of modern neonatology.
67. *Aunt F* – Lynn's maternal aunt Florence Wynne (*b.*1844).

June

Monday 7

Polling day for P.L.G. elections, our people are pleased. McGrath, they say, was rescued fr. K. George's Hosp. last Thurs Hope it's true. Military patrol (surprise) & arms & cycles taken at Fermoy. V big guns coming in, they say England will fight with U.S.A. [ ] preparing. Looks rather like Prophesy coming true. Matron better.[68]

Tuesday 8

8 am. R.mines. Mr Crosby is having weekly celebrations on Tuesdays now. I hope people will come. Mrs Pearse got in with over 2,000 majority, Misses Doyle & D. O'Connor, too, & McCabe. Lovely day. It isn't true abt. McGrath, schade. The Pope has allowed pronouncement of his approval of our Republic. Meeting to censure [S.] Doyle for his action on Council.

Sunday 20

3 A.T Ch Rathcoole 10.30 saw C na mB in brake & snapped them. 1,000 pressing to Bodenstown, we went abt. 12, nice ride there. Gt crowds there. Madam passed us on road. S. O'Mirrile spoke. Grand to see I.R.A aeroplanes overhead all the time, lovely wreaths & cross. P barracks at Sallins = I.R.A. for day. Evg. went to Naas & found nice place with Mrs White just opposite v. nervous P Barrack.[69]

July

Saturday 10

Had microben fairly early, stayed quiet at cottage all day, much better than last time. M went in to Town to see her Aunt at Moyne Rd. & was not back till late. Got thro' barricades well. A terrible report in Freeman of speech to R.I.C. in Listowel by Chief Inspector telling them wholesale slaughter rule of day, the police at once resigned, decent men.[70]

---

68. *McGrath* – Patrick McGrath (1894–1940), Dublin IRA, wounded in an operation and treated under military guard at King George V Military Hospital. *K. George's Hosp* – was the King George V Military Hospital, it's now St Bricin's Military Hospital, Arbour Hill, Dublin.
69. An annual republican pilgrimage to the grave of Irishman United leader, Theobald Wolfe Tone (1763–98), at Bodenstown cemetery is held on the nearest Sunday to 20 June every year.
70. Divisional Police Commissioner for Munster, Lt.-Col. Gerald Bryce Ferguson Smyth reputedly said, in Listowel RIC Barracks, that the RIC should, in pursuit of their duty, shoot IRA suspects on sight. This led to the 'Listowel Mutiny' when several policemen resigned rather than follow Smyth's orders.

Thursday 15

Started off early to be in time for Teac Board Meeting. We decided unanimously to retire fr. Assoc. Hosp. Fete. Lunch with M. The new Outpt. Dept. open to-day. Mortuary room v. nice, a poor mite in it. Wonderful raid on G.P.O. by I.R.A. Castle mails again taken. Late aft. went over Clonskea Hosp., it is v. nice, fine garden & farm. Matron wonderful. Great re-organizing of Dublin Union.[71]

August

Tuesday 3

8 a.m. R.mines. R.C. Abp. of Hobart held up & insulted in S. The infamous bill for "Better Govt. for Ireland" passed in British Parliament. Mrs Bennett's Ruth brought up hurriedly fr. country & ovarian cyst removed by Col. Taylor this evg. He brought his son, a nice boy. M did good work at Comt. meeting. I got grazing for the goats. Now sentences of death etc. revoked long ago, can be executed.[72]

Tuesday 10

8 a.m. R.mines. Baby Murray looks very frail, poor scrap, hope she'll get on. Busy aft. Couldn't go to Hosp. Board (Conjoint) meeting. State of Belfast terrible, [?2/20] of R.Cs thrown out of work by other side. Boycott becomes more general, in consequence. M got nice picture of Abp. Mannix, beautiful face. He is very calm & dignified.[73]

Monday 23

Left Enniskerry 8.30, nice ride home. Meeting Clonskea 10 a.m. Met M there. Insp. Swanzy shot dead & 4 other R.I.C. former was bad lot in Cork. Cork's L. Mayor v.low, it is tragic & so many others. E. Ryan & M couldn't sleep for fear house here might be burgled by police, like

---

71. *G.P.O.* – General Post Office on O'Connell St, Dublin.
72. *C. Abp. of Hobart* – William Barry (1872–1929), Archbishop of Hobart, Tasmania. Born in Middleton, Co. Cork, he was on a visit to Ireland, when, on 3 August 1920, he was held up by the Crown Forces while visiting the South (Cork and Middleton). *"Better Govt. for Ireland"* – The Government of Ireland Act 1920 / the Fourth Home Rule Bill.
73. *Boycott* – In August 1920 Dáil Éireann imposed a boycott of goods from Belfast and a withdrawal of funds from Belfast-based banks. *Abp. Mannix* – Daniel Mannix (1864–1963), born in Charleville, he was Archbishop of Melbourne for 46 years and one of the most influential public figures in Australia.

Griffiths. Nice day. Did some begging for Teac, babies do well D.G. Our liberty comes fast. God grant too many valuable lives may not be lost.[74]

Friday 27

8 a.m. S.B's. Lord Mayor sinking, collapse feared, how cruel are Imperialists! All well in Teac, another lovely day. I.Times very satirical over Bolshevicks' reply to British vote, they may laugh the other side of mouth soon. Hundreds at Marlboro' St. Mass for L.Mayor. I went to Glencormac in aft. Lovely there. Biggar visited hosp.[75]

Tuesday 31

8 a.m. R.mines, it looks as if Mesopotamia & India were slipping from the grasp of the dying British Empire. L. Mayor of Cork still alive & triumphant, C naB marched thro' streets to pray in Whitefriar St. I asked for prayers in S. B's & S. Columba's, saw & had long chat with Williamses. Did good deal of Teac work & had busy aft. here. Enquiry at Clonskea Hosp. this mg. Letter from John & photo., he has changed.

September

Monday 6

8 a.m S. B's., nice day. L.Mayor still alive, 28th day. L. George coming home. 3 of my babies rather bad but a bit better to-night. Matron of Clonskea here to-day, many people came about many things. Got £1 from U.S.A in answer to Mrs Ginnell's appeal. We were not v. tired after all the long y.day. We all feel, somehow, more comforted abt. the L. Mayor to-day. Nice account in Herald of y.day in Navan.

Thursday 16

8 a.m. Xt. Ch. Still weary struggle in Cork & Brixton. It is cruel. Cullenswood & several other places in R.mines raided again, no one arrested, 7 hrs in Cullenswood. Housing Comt. 10 a.m. then Castle. Baby Murray has gained 1lb D. G. Hosp. Board Meeting, busy aft., went to dentist, much drilling, till pain relieved. The day has passed &

---

74. *Insp. Swanzy* – RIC District Inspector Oswald Ross Swanzy (1881–1920), presumed killer of Lord Mayor of Cork, Tomás MacCurtain, who was shot dead in Lisburn on 22 August 1920 by members of the Cork and Belfast IRA. *Cork's L. Mayor* – Successor to MacCurtain, Lord Mayor of Cork, Terence MacSwiney (1879–1920), on hunger strike in Brixton Prison.
75. *Biggar* – Edward Coey Bigger (1861–1942), physician and politician, medical inspector under the Local Government Board.

no gt. or wonderful pronouncement so far. Evg. Mrs Kettle spoke well at Ch. of Commerce.[76]

Monday 20

8 a.m. S. B's., in Cab. felt better all the same. Miss Ellis left this mg. so sorry not to see her, she looks well, I hear. The affair in Dublin mts. = party of young men, unarmed, out for walk, surrounded & taken off to S. Columba's college, then Bridewell, one shot dead. To-day fierce affray in King St., 6 dead, soldiers & civilians, more wounded, sergeant in Portobello, mad, shot 2 fellow soldiers, wounded more. All over fighting & shooting – Lord how long![77]

Thursday 23

No fresh horrors to-day, D.G. but plenty of details of Black & Tan shooting or rather bayonetting poor Lynch in Exchange Hotel in Parliament St. No sound heard by people in next rooms & they said he fired on them & was shot then himself, really was transfixed thro' chin with bayonet. L. Mayor same. God makes him live, whole world aghast at affairs here. All quiet this evg. 'Flu prevalent.[78]

Monday 27

8 a.m. S. B's, an eventful day. Poor Madam arrested & Seghan Gonne, who next? Saw Mrs Clarke, heard of raid of her house this mg. Trim now wrecked by Black & Tans because Police barracks taken day before. Had consultation re babies in Unions with Mrs Roberts. Some Black & Tans have resigned as result of Balbriggan. The other Hosp. in Charlement St. Xt. Ch. School is given over to them. Reappearance of M. O'Neill.[79]

76. *Mrs Kettle* – Mary Kettle, née Sheehy (1884–1976), feminist, republican, local politician, sister of Hanna Sheehy Skeffington and widow of Lieutenant Tom Kettle, killed at the Somme in 1914. She was elected to Rathmines Urban District Council in 1920.
77. *The affair in Dublin mts.* – Seán Doyle of Emmet Road Inchicore, member of the 4th Battalion, Dublin Brigade IRA, was shot by British Armed Forces at Kilmashogue, Co. Dublin. *To-day fierce affray in King St* – Sixteen members of the 1st Battalion, Dublin Brigade, IRA held up a party of British soldiers at the junction of North King St and Church St, Dublin. Three soldiers died and IRA member Kevin Barry was arrested.
78. *poor Lynch* – John Lynch, Sinn Féin county councillor from Limerick, shot dead by a group of 12 soldiers in his room at the Exchange Hotel in Parliament St, Dublin. *L. Mayor same* – Terence MacSwiney on his hunger strike in Brixton Prison.
79. *Madam* – Countess Markievicz. *Seaghan Gonne* – Seán McBride (1904–88), member of the IRA, son of Maud Gonne and John McBride. *Balbriggan* – Balbriggan, Co. Dublin was burnt by Crown Forces in a reprisal attack on 21 September 1920. *Major Smyth's funeral* – Major E. Smyth and Captain A. P. White were killed during a military raid in Drumcondra, Dublin on Tuesday, 12 October 1920.

October

Monday 4

8 a.m. S. B's., fine day after storm. Repudiations of all statements re Black & Tans & of Griffiths by Castle, won't carry far, I think. Black & Tans in Ranelagh y.day, firing, F. Williams & I arranged a day of prayer. It is observed that once the Irish in Brit. army realise `reprisals' they will cost British Govt. more than they bargained for. Saw Miss Ellis at F. Douglas', she is well. Teac does well. If only we had money.

Tuesday 5

8 a.m. R.mines. Last night, just when we were in bed, exhaustive raid by British troops & one D.M.P. man, officer painfully civil, nothing stolen, we were all kept up an hour. Mrs S. Skeffington raided too. Evg. Mrs Tom Clarke raided too last night, 30 lbs of grapes stolen. Two fine coups in country on police & military, arms etc. taken. Pouring day & night. M Stack & Mr Crosby will come on deputation to Abp. Tired to-day after all.[80]

Thursday 14

A day of horror. 7 men killed in explosion in New Ross, & 5 injured men shot at Phibsboro' by men in armoured car. 3 then shot by soldiers in Talbot St. as they were coming back fr. Major Smyth's funeral to Amiens St, we used to think permits bad! All well in Teac. Saw K. Gahan & her mother. At Elin. Rollo v. big & fat. Mrs Ceannt's ankle bad. D.G. she is not worse. She arrived at 1.55 last night.[81]

Sunday 17

20 A.T. 8 a.m. R.mines, pouring night, went to see poor Mrs O'Carroll whose husband was brutally murdered in Manor St., they were all at Mass, poor things. Dinner Fisher. Churchill's speech worse than L.George's scoffs at L. Mayor. Saw military lorry dash round corner & almost annihilate 2 trams. Aft. Gaelic office. Evg. S. Columba's. Poor old man shot in Capel St. this evg. Did Walls of Jericho & saw 4 loads of B& T leave Castle. Great distress. D.V. Prayer.[82]

---

80. *D.M.P.* – Dublin Metropolitan Police
81. *A day of horror* – Seán Tracey (Tipperary IRA) and two civilians were killed in a shoot-out in Talbot St, Dublin, as was a British intelligence office.
82. *went to see poor Mrs O'Carroll* – Peter O'Carroll was shot dead by British forces, after answering the door of his shop/home at 92 Manor St, Dublin. The British were looking for his sons who were members of the 1st Battalion, Dublin Brigade, IRA. *Churchill* – Winston Churchill (1874–1965), British politician. *4 loads of B& T* – Black and Tans. *D.V.* – *Deo Volente* (God Willing).

Thursday 21

In British Parliament Govt. resorted to barefaced lies to excuse & explain away Irish situation, foolish, for so many eyewitnesses of truth. Madam courtmartialled for speeches on arrest, 4 Independent reporters arrested. The despicable Brixton Dr says he will forcibly feed L. Mayor & has given nourishment while pt. unconscious. Evg went to R.C Truth Reception, saw M's relations & Apb. of Tuam.

Saturday 23

8 a.m. S.B's. lovely day, warm, went to see Madam Markievicz at 10 o/c, she looks well but nervy, v. excited abt. her trial, courtmartial. Saw pts. Madam Gonne nearly well. Terror in Athlone to-day, usual proceedings. Railway strike coming off, they say, no compromise this time, England will show she won't be ruled by Unions, she says! The Bps have refused Day of Prayer, how sad it is![83]

Monday 25

8 a.m. S. B's. At least the Brixton tragedy is over & the L.Mayor at peace. C.Brugha's raided by murder gang on Fri. night. Mrs kept 1 ½ hrs in lorry, they tried all means to make maid tell where he was, had bloodhound, broke into 17 houses in terrace, smashed much. Council Meeting passed payment for C.C., it is coming on. Nursing Board afterwards. There are 1,000 of spies all round now, outside C. Brugha's before raid. The moderates lose hope, we do not, D.G.[84]

Friday 29

8 a.m. S. B's. The great mourning day for Terence McSweeney. All arrangements carried out as if the body were there. Corpse literally placed under arrest at Holyhead with no relative, only Black & Tans, taken to Cork. M ffM, M & I went to Cathedral for the Mass at 11 o/c, place packed, Apb. Walsh there. D.G. there were no shootings in Dublin to-day. L. Mayoress still v. ill. Mrs Clarke ill, went to her. Babies do well D.G. Saw many friends to-day. Had a rushing day.[85]

---

83. *Madam Markievicz* – Countess Markievicz had been arrested on 26 September 1920 in Rathmines and her court martial was set for 2 December. Lynn, Maud Gonne MacBride and Hanna Sheehy Skeffington were permitted to attend.
84. *L. Mayor* – Terence MacSwiney, Lord Mayor of Cork, died on 25 October 1920 in Brixton Prison, after 74 days on hunger strike.
85. *M* – Countess Markievicz.

November

Monday 1

8 a.m. R.mines, just then the heroic Kevin Barry hanged in Mtjoy, a sad, dark, dreary day, but he died so nobly, how the tragedies follow one another. Still our spirit grows & strengthens in spite of all malignities. Six police & D. T [J] shot to-day, barracks taken & all in it & burnt. Teac Pound Day, did well. Much more one can't say. Now Republican flag at half mast from Nat. Univ. K.B. prayed for in R.mines.[86]

Wednesday 3

8 a.m. S.B's. S. Malachi's Day. M says he brought U.S.A. Presidential election for us. Harding, not Cox, England's man. Agnes Daly's hair cut off by Black & Tans & her [pal/imal] arch deliberately cut & she left to bleed to death in curfew hours only that Norah knew 1st Aid. M's cousin, Mrs Kieran gave £1 for Teac wh. does well. The Coughlan's house raided y.day & we never knew.[87]

Friday 19

A day of raids, all over everywhere, esp. R.mines. Mrs Conn Murphy's boy, Fergus, only male member of family in, Dr M & boy Conn, 16, wanted. Terrible pictures of boys in Leitrim, flogged, thrown into icy water, half hanged, thrown on lorries & shown to boys of next place for example for not informing. No more shooting in Cork to-day. Babies do well, D.G.[88]

Monday 21

8 a.m. R.mines, terrible day, 1st battle in Mount St. In all 12 Secret Service men shot dead & 4 wounded, Castle in a ferment. All trains & motors stopped at Jones Rd. football match B & T took gates, brought in armoured cars & machine guns, wrought havoc on 1500 people,

---

86. *Kevin Barry* (1902–20), medical student and IRA member, captured while taking part in a raid on British forces at King's Inn, Dublin on 20 September 1920, during a street fight between IRA men and Crown Forces, held in Mountjoy and hanged on 1 November 1920. *Teac Pound Day* – a fundraiser for St Ultan's hospital
87. *Agnes Daly* – Kathleen Clarke's sister, Limerick Cumann na mBan. The Daly house was raided many times as reprisal. Agnes Daly's hair was forcibly cropped during this raid and her hand badly cut.
88. *Mrs Conn Murphy* – Cornelius J. Murphy ('Conn') and his wife Annie (née Byrne), sons Fergus and Conn, all staunch republicans. *Terrible pictures of boys in Leitrim* – Bernard and Frank Ryan, Annaghacoolan, Co. Leitrim were subjected to half hanging and then forced to stand for an hour and a half in ice cold water while being beaten with whips by members of the Auxiliary Division of the RIC.

7 dead & numbers wounded. We called off Abbey Play. What will to-night be? It looks bad. 2 fires reported.[89]

December

Wednesday 1

8 a.m. S.B's. Union Jack gone. Council Meeting, they wouldn't have Kay's letter head, disgraceful jobbery the whole thing is. We had only Mrs Mulcahy, O'Connor, M & F of course were outvoted at once. Two poor boys shot in Ardee, one a schoolteacher. Evg. papers full of 'Truce of God', not taken up by anyone who could speak for Ireland. Many Labour troubles in England, ex-soldiers take over Town Hall in London. Labour representatives here no good.[90]

Thursday 2

Madam's courtmartial at Royal Barracks. We were all there at 10 & it didn't begin till 11.30. She looks fat & well, but naturally very agitated. M & I left when we saw her & I went to see people whose relations have been shot by military, to bring English Labour people to them. Evg. went to Shelbourne with Madam Gonne, saw Henderson, Adamson. Nevinson came back to supper with Madam. He looks so old now.[91]

Thursday 9

8 a.m. Xt.Ch. Glorious sunny day, not much news, some more arrested. Terrible find near Gort , 2 boys were missing, friends dreamt vividly they were in pond, went there & found them, mutilated beyond recognition, almost burned, quite charred in parts & then thrown in 3 feet water. Abp. Clune of Australia doing negotiations, please God

89. *terrible day* – Carried out by Michael Collins' 'Squad' of IRA men, the shootings took place in and around Dublin's south inner city and resulted in 14 deaths, including six intelligence agents and two members of the British Auxiliary Force. In reprisal soldiers attacked and fired on a match at Croke Park killing seven civilians and wounding 80.

90. *Labour representatives* – Members of a British Labour Commission came to Ireland to gather testimony on what was happening. Feminist and Labour activists gave testimony and guided then around the country. *Two poor boys shot in Ardee* – IRA men Patrick Tierney and John 'Seán' O'Carroll (who was a teacher) taken from their beds in Ardee, Co. Louth and executed by Crown Forces.

91. *saw Henderson, Adamson*– Henderson is most likely Frank Henderson (1886–1959), member of the IRA in Dublin, by 1921 he was OC of the 2nd Battalion, Dublin Brigade. Adamson is possibly George Adamson (1897–1992), IRA, Commandant in the Athlone Brigade. *Nevinson came back to supper with Madam* – Henry Wood 'H. W.' Nevinson (1856–1941), British writer and journalist who was friends with and was later married to British suffragette Evelyn Sharp (1869–1955), both of whom denounced the operations of the Black and Tans in Ireland during the War of Independence. Both were known to Lynn and Markievicz.

there will be Peace with Honour. Saw Miss Murray, dear child 7 mos. 12 lb healthy. B & Ts in road last night.[92]

Friday 17

8 a.m. S.B's, nice day, dolls' Sale went well in Teac. Little Mickie better, it is a miracle, sme others bad, one of Dr Webb's died last night. Poor Mrs Ceannt had horrible raid last night, they were drunk men & stole all before them including Xmas cakes & things of poor Eamon's. We saw prisoners taken in the road last night. They say Dev ill. Fr Albert & Fr Dominic taken. Fr Albert out again, bad raid there too.[93]

Friday 24

Letter by this mg.'s post to say I may go home for Xmas if I won't have demonstration (do they picture bands?) or see people who are not their visitors, I'll go joyfully but come back Mon. Left B.Stone at 1.45, crowds going. Train searched at Athlone by R.I.C. assisted by military. D.G. I wasn't arrested, home at 9.30. N & M met me in motor. They were twice stopped but had permit right. They look well, lovely to be home.[94]

Tuesday 28

8 a.m. R.mines. Innocents' Day. Many children's prayers. Most glorious sunrise glow, much to do when I hoped for lull. Poor little Eliza died in Teac, she had gone off fearfully while I was away. Epidemic of cerebral 'flu I fear. People hopeful on account of England's financial crisis. So many shot & killed during Xmas, it is fearful. Mrs MacSwiney gives evidence in Washington.[95]

---

92. *boys were missing*– Brothers Patrick and Harry Loughnane of Spanglish, Co. Galway, members of Sinn Féin and the local IRA were kidnapped, tortured, killed and mutilated by Black and Tans and Auxiliaries on 26 November 1920. Their bodies were found on 5 December 1920. The photographs of their mutilated bodies make headlines nationally and internationally.
93. *Dr Webb* – Dr Isabella 'Ella' Webb (1877–1946). *Fr Albert & Fr Dominic* – Capuchin Friars, Fr Albert Bibby OFM Cap. and Fr Dominic O'Connor OFM Cap. Both very supportive of and involved with republicans.
94. *N & M* – Anne 'Nan' and Muriel Lynn (1876–1968), Kathleen Lynn's sisters who were living at home in Mayo.
95. *Mrs MacSwiney* – Muriel MacSwiney, née Murphy (1892–1982), Irish republican and left-wing activist, widow of Terence MacSwiney.

1921

Saturday 15

Slept long again to-day. Poor Murphy will be hanged, I'm sure, tho' I.R.A. declare he had no part in ambush. Nice day, saw Baby Keating in his home, hope he'll do. My babies fairly, D.G. Hurried home to go out in aft. to Dean's Grange with F Clarke. Hot day, rather muggy. 3rd lecture at 1 o/c, scurry to get ready for it. M had children's jumble sale in Hosp. in aft.–beargarden. Evg. dinner with M, Maire [Forster] & Miss MacNaughton.[96]

Sunday 16

2 A.E. 8 a.m. R.mines. Nice day. Emer & I had supper & b.fast alone, she & I had good talk. Pts. in mg. all doing well. Saw M. in hosp. where she takes Matron's place for weekend. Dinner Nugent's, tea Douglas. Met Mrs P Snowden, very English, didn't much take to her. Police had exciting chase after soldier thieves & caught them. Eric Geddes has left U.S.A. in secret. Trouble financially in B.fast helped by Munster Leinster Bank

Saturday 21

8 a.m. S.B's lovely day, birds beautiful. A great ambush in Clare. D.G. 1 sargent & 4 police killed & much booty taken. Ambush also in D.cdra to-day, 3 cadets killed. Unemployment increases. Teac does well D.G. My babies were in garden to-day & all the better of it. Baby Fox better, Sir Wm saw her to-night. It was a rushing day with me. No news we wait for so far.[97]

Friday 28

8 a.m. S.B's. very mild. M grussed me as the clock struck last night. V. busy all round. I think Teac people fairly. Roger Sweetman has

---

96. *poor Murphy* – Captain Cornelius Murphy (1890–1921), 2 Cork Brigade IRA, arrested on 4 January 1921 and charged with the illegal possession of a revolver. He was the first member of the IRA to be executed under Martial Law for possession of firearms.

97. *A great ambush in Clare* – The Glenwood Ambush near Sixmilebridge, Co. Clare when the IRA ambushed an RIC patrol resulting in the deaths of six policemen. *Ambush also in D.cdra* – An IRA ambush on an RIC lorry at Drumcrondra Bridge, Dublin was foiled, six IRA men captured.

resigned. That's good. Mr C has turned up & trial goes on. They say 50 were released on Sat. night. Dan Carroll among them. M v. tired & resting this aft. Jane made beautiful cakes, one came fr. home too.[98]

February

Saturday 5

Plenty of daisies & all kinds of things this year, one flower on Forsythia, etc. They threaten further curfew restrictions here because of ambushes etc. Bombs & firing in direction of Fitzwilliam Sqr. this evg. Man, police shot in Gloucester St. this mg. Six girl teachers arrested for not giving names, in convent. Put a baby out with Mrs Behan. Mrs Fisher had 2nd S. Brigid's sale in Teac & did well. Everyone who should know things seems pleased.[99]

Saturday 12

Nice day. Saw Mrs Childers & had lunch there, she says White Cross will be quite good & a great undertaking. I am glad, for we had fears. M saw Mrs N Watson & heard abt. Sale. Aft. she, M ffM & I went to country dressmaker, splendid. Evg. Matron & I went to Joan of Arc. It was wonderful indeed. All goes well, in spite of Desmond Fitzgerald's arrest, he was foolish. Nurse Rankin went to Cork St. German measles. Poor Chris at the last. Others well.[100]

Tuesday 15

8 a.m. R.mines, nice day. Teeling & Simon Donnelly escaped fr. Kilmainham, how, a mystery, they say smart officer & heavy guard came for them. M & I asked to Madam Gonne's to meet U.S.A. Whitecross people. I went but they disappointed, saw some others there, they say Americans no good. I am put on Wht.X Comt. now. Poor little Maura v. collapsed for no reason to-day.[101]

---

98. *Grussed* – German, grüßen (to greet). *Roger Sweetman* (1874–1954), Sinn Féin politician and barrister.

99. *Six girl teachers arrested* – six trainee teachers at the Dominican Training College, Eccles St, Dublin were arrested in the course of a military raid there, when they refused to give their names. They were taken to the Bridewell but later released.

100. *Desmond Fitzgerald* (1888–1947), Irish revolutionary, poet and politician. *Mrs Childers* – Mary 'Molly' Childers, née Osgood (1875–1964), Irish writer and nationalist, wife of Erskine Childers. *White Cross* – The Irish White Cross established on 1 February 1921 as a mechanism for distributing funds raised by the American Committee for Relief in Ireland. *M* – Countess Markievicz. *Nurse Rankin went to Cork St* – as she had German measles, which was very contagious, Nurse Rankin had to convalesce in Cork St Fever Hospital.

101. *Teeling & Simon Donnelly* – IRA men Frank Teeling and Simon Donnelly escape from Kilmainham Jail, along with Ernie O'Malley. *M* – Madeleine ffrench-Mullen.

Monday 21

Called out early to find little 3 week Ultan Ganter dead, they don't know what happened him. V. full day. Mrs N Watson & I saw Mr Law early & talked things over with him, little Moira no worse, 2 new babies in, one cleft palate & hare lip, one pyloric stenosis. Terrible slaughter in Midleton & elsewhere. Would to God it would soon stop. Most 'Flu babies better. Aft. meeting Save the Children fund, more satisfactory. Lovely day & evg.

Thursday 24

8 a.m. Rmines, a wonderful day for Teac, Celtic cross 500 dollars came & Corporation gave £100, very generous of them, they had only just got in money. Rumours of Cabinet split over Irish administration. Greenwood going, they say. God grant the whole lot may soon be gone! More accounts of bad govt. Gen. Crozier's resignation because his judgment wasn't upheld abt. B & Ts robbing, made public at last. Rumour of more money for us.[102]

March

Saturday 5

Muriel's birthday, slept late. Papers full of ambushes etc., hear casualties are v. heavy for British, in Cork lately 500 went out 20 came back. Aft. had nice walk to S.mount, lovely mild day, tea F. Clarke, at it message fr. Mrs Martin came & I had to go to her to Dunlaoghaire. Phoned taxi, men all gone, very anxious but got one fr. A & B. Wild race to be in time for curfew 9 o/c. Nurse couldn't come. Mrs M has nice house. Slept till 2. Baby came 3.[103]

Monday 7

News of ambushes everywhere. Hear 2 escaped fr. Mtjoy y.day & 8 to-day, hope its true. Brig. Gen. Cumming shot dead in Cork & many others. Sligo gives trouble, we hear. Mayor & L. Mayor of Limerick murdered in their beds by B & Ts y.day. Great hopes all the same. Loads of dead soldiers constantly being shipped to England. I was

---

102. *Greenwood* – Sir Hamar Greenwood (1870–1948), last chief secretary for Ireland
103. *Muriel's birthday* – Lynn's sister Muriel. *hear casualties are v. heavy for British, in Cork lately* – Lynn is likely referring to the Clonbanin ambush of 5 May 1921 when an IRA ambush lead by Seán Moylan attacked a mixed convoy of British Army and RIC, leading to the deaths of five soldiers, although initially it was believed that upwards of 13 were killed.

held up & searched in taxi to-day & shot fired in Leeson St. as I was there.[104]

Monday 14

The six poor boys were hanged in Mtjoy this mg. in batches of 2 at 6, 7 & 8, wonderful scenes round it, about 10,000 praying C na B with banners, all were brave but v. sad. Churches thronged at every Mass. All work off till 11. I couldn't get in fr. D.Leary but by cycle. Many babies to be attended to, poor things. Doyle's 2 twins dead now, wife v ill. Bryan's wife ill too. Day v. wet, then sleety snow but the Dawn comes D.G. after the Dark.[105]

April

Tuesday 5

8 a.m. R.mines, very full day. Mrs Despard coming to live with Maeve. She gave £100 to-day for Teac where babies are fairly. Great indignation abt. poor Reynolds 'enquiry'. 1st it was to be public, then when the George V [Dr] got into a hole, they would let no one in. Coal strike proceeds gaily. Many mines destroyed. We have battles all over country. Got new goat.[106]

Sunday 17

A lovely mg. tried for 8 o/c at Kilbride but no Service, went to 11.30. it was v. cold in night but cottage v. nice. Mrs Heatley home. I saw her in evg. M & I washed hair & then went to Enniskerry side. Lovely sorrells & violets in Kilcroney Lane & wild geraniums. Primroses & violets everywhere. Poor Lily Cathcart took bad. The view fr. cottage is wonderful. We had a lovely day & were not tired. Thunder in aft.

---

104. *Brig. Gen. Cumming* – Brigadier-General Hanway Robert Cumming, commander of the Kerry Infantry Brigade of the British 6th Division, was killed at the Clonbanin ambush. *Mayor & L. Mayor of Limerick* – George Clancy, the Mayor of Limerick, and his immediate predecessor, Michael O'Callaghan were shot dead in their homes by Black and Tans on 7 March 1921.

105. *six poor boys were hanged in Mtjoy* – six republican prisoners, Bernard Ryan, Patrick Doyle, Thomas Bryan, Frank Flood, Thomas Whelan, and Patrick Moran were hanged in Mountjoy Jail. *10,000 praying C na B with banners* – crowds gathered outside Mountjoy Jail praying the rosary, led by Cumann na mBan.

106. *Mrs Despard* – Charlotte Despard, née French (1844–1939), suffragist, nationalist, socialist, and writer. Collected first-hand evidence of Black and Tan atrocities with Maud Gonne McBride. *Maeve* – Maud Gonne McBride.

Thursday 28

9.45 Council Meeting, O'Neill & Daly co-opted in place of B. Brennan & MacDonagh, well, M. & I were there to propose them for rest were late. Board Hosp. meeting, went well D.G. U.S.A Lady fr. Mr France came & saw all over Teac & promises much, hope she'll do it. Babies fairly. Mrs P. Lawrence gives thrilling tales of Ireland to match Lord Parmours. Horrid forged notice published abt. us fr. enemy source.[107]

May

Friday 13

Nomination day, all our people returned unopposed, a very fine warm day, saw nurse O'Carroll. We think she'll do as Sister. D.V. she'll be good. Terrible affair in Grafton St. last night, several killed & wounded. Eyewitness says B & Ts drop bombs fr. their lorries = reason of such a thing in crowded streets. Partition dead now, anyway. God grant Freedom soon.[108]

Saturday 21

Left early for Derry. Miss O'Connor, Emer & I had v. nice journey & arrived safely, put up in City Hotel, rested in aft, came by Portadown & saw orchards. Saw Dr O'Dougherty, went over fever hosp. with her, then drove out a bit, good horse. Evg. saw Dr Barrymore & several fine boys who came with him for meeting to-morrow. All preparations well forward. Derry = armed camp. Ulster specials in R.I.C. dress live at home & terrorise countryside with revolvers.[109]

Wednesday 25

Eventful day. Custom House burnt to ground = seat of L.G.B. & real seat of Govt. Nothing left of Income Tax etc. Just now many distant shots, say they'll burn L.H. & Mansion Ho. in revenge. Fearful intimidation in B.fast y.day, wholesale personation by Orangites & intimidation.

---

107. *Council Meeting* – Rathmines Urban District Council. *Mrs P. Lawrence* – Emmeline Pethick-Lawrence (1867–1954), British suffragette. Aided by Hanna Sheehy Skeffington, Meg Connery and others, she came to Ireland on a clandestine visit in 1921 to report on Black and Tan atrocities, particularly those against women. She included her Irish experience in her autobiography, *My Part in a Changing World* (London, 1938).
108. *Terrible affair in Grafton St* – An IRA attack on a lorry carrying Auxiliaries near Grafton St, Dublin, 14 civilians and one DMP man injured.
109. *Ulster specials* – The Ulster Special Constabulary was a quasi-military reserve special constable police force, set up in October 1920

Much trouble in Egypt wh. = pivot of Empire. D.G. got £5 from Mt. Mellary for Mrs A. Teac nicely.[110]

June

Saturday 4

Slept late, whole day racing, after to Elin. Miss Ryan better, then Teac. Pat has developed Chicken pox, sent to Cork St. was to have gone to Guild picnic at Williams' but Bride wrote fr. Bridewell for things & Mrs C had no one, so I went, found her at the Joy, got parcels into her. Mrs C. distracted, no news of where Claud is. We went to U.S.A. Tribune corresp. at Shelbourne, who will do all possible. D.V. they won't torture him.[111]

Tuesday 7

8 a.m. R.mines. We were raided by military about 3.30 a.m. They searched for people first, then went thro' papers, took a few, were over an hour there & went, no.10 raided too. Mrs O'Leary taken, Mrs S. Skeff. raided too, gt. excitement in road. Saw twin in S. Ult. v.thin & tiny, tried to get goat for him. Three poor men were executed this mg. Mt.joy. More reports of shooting hangmen. Lovely day.

Saturday 11

S. Barnabas 8 a.m. R.mines. To-day Smuts on arrival in England declares for free choice for all nations, U.S.A. our recognition in Senate. Sims (Admiral) recalled & reprimanded for pro British speech. We hear L.George is prepared to state offer in writing now, in advance. All well with Teac. Fete made abt.£200, a lovely day. Many preps. for departure. Hostel for war weary at Baldoyle.[112]

July

Saturday 2

8 a.m. S. B's. We all feel we must pray much in this critical time.

---

110. *Custom House burnt to ground = seat of L. G. B.* – British government's most important administrative buildings in Ireland, seat of the Local Government Board (LGB). *Much trouble in Egypt* – 23 May 1921, rioting broke out in Alexandria, Egypt, with dozens killed and hundreds injured.
111. *the Joy* – Mountjoy Jail
112. *Smuts* – Jan Smuts (1870–1950), South African military leader and politician, Prime Minister of South Africa from 1919 to June 1924. Puts pressure on PM George to publicly offer Dominion Status to Ireland. *Sims (Admiral)* – William Sowden Sims (1858–1936), admiral in the United States Navy.

Much rejoicing over B. Barton's homecoming. Went to Childers & saw 2 Englishwomen there, horrified with Limerick atrocities. Women have suffered much there.[113]

Saturday 9

8 a.m. S. B's, then straight to Kingsbridge for Limerick, hot journey. Aft. saw Mrs O'Callaghan etc. re Rest Homes. Mrs O'Toole nee Daly put me up, poor Dalys burnt out. Wakened often by lorries in night. Saw Laura & her eldest. Poor Mrs.O'C. is so sad. Queer old parson in Barrington St. knew little of hrs. of Service.[114]

Wednesday 27

Went in at 10 for P.H. Meeting. Dr Jackson ill, McKenzie in chair, Child Welfare after, we are to get Dr & nurse & rooms at once. At Teac matron very upset, another baby dying. M & I decided I'd stay in Hosp. & let matron go with M for a break & rest. Had a fairly busy, anxious day. Bereaved relative came abt. cot in memory of Dolores. F. Rhodes v. good to me.[115]

August

Monday 15

8 a.m. S. B's. We pray for guidance of Dail to-morrow. British peace terms perfectly unsatisfactory. We won't have them. Shelia & Larry very low, poor scraps. Matron back in good form. Sister such a comfort. Evg. dinner Cypress Grove, met Hungarian there, de Radnotfay, seems nice & simple. Got ticket for Dail for him. They are hard to get. Lovely day.

Tuesday 16

8 a.m. R.mines. Day of opening of 2nd Dail. Mrs ffM, Miss Duffy & I got in with much difficulty. C. Bruagha, M. Staines gave me a ticket each, only standing room. Very impressive ceremony, swearing in new members. Dev made fine speech, no compromise. Saw many old

---

113. *B. Barton* – Robert 'Bob' Barton (1881-1975) was released in early July 1921 to help with the truce negotiations.
114. *Dalys* – family of Kathleen Clarke. *Poor Mrs O'C* – Kathleen O'Callaghan, née Murphy (1885–1961), Sinn Féin member and widow of the murdered Lord Mayor of Limerick, Michael O'Callaghan.
115. *P.H.* – Public Health.

friends, it was a memorable day. John Parnell was there. Teac fairly but Larry v. low. Now arrangements for progress.[116]

Friday 26

Great Day. Public session of Dail. Dev's reply to L.George read by him at 12 precisely, profound silence for 2 mins. before, many prayers, he said the nation's mind fully made up, no power in earth or hell can change it. Revolt spreading in India, all Mysore involved. Serious for the Enemy. We took in 16th baby to-day for Mrs J Connolly, others doing v. fairly, D.G. Matron, S Nugent & E. Ryan at Dail. Now busy in Teac, nice day.[117]

Saturday 27

Full text of Dev's note & L.George's reply. Latter answers nothing & gives no ground for Eng. claim to hold us, clearly as always everything must be subordinate to England's interests. Revolt spreading in India, prob. it will go too. Eng. will be chastened then. Teac nicely. Miss Hay got to Jervis St. appendix. Miss Dockrell took me to Glencormac via. Old Connaught & Scalp. Lovely misty effects. Heather glorious.

September

Monday 5

Another lovely day, all Eng. papers seem to shrink fr. idea of more fighting. Some disagreement btw U.S.A & Japan. Eng. sending not only ships, but troops to Japan, I hear. V. nice reports of S. Ultan's Day in papers. D.G. all were so pleased. M. Collins made gt. speech in Armagh. Dail reply to L.George so wonderful in its simplicity. Babies fairly but Daisy. M & her mother got back safe. Madam & I at Mrs Ceannt's.

Wednesday 21

Up at 9, left Mullingar 11. Mrs Clarke, Pearse, Dr English & I, a very pleasant outing it was, all well on return, railway troubles seem imminent. Teac very fairly. Mrs Kieran came, M's cousin, with small

---

116. *2nd Dail* – The Second Dáil consisted of those elected in the 1921 election, including six women TDs, only members of Sinn Féin took their seats.
117. *Dev's reply to L.George* – this was a reply to the 'Proposals of the British Government for an Irish Settlement' which were published on 20 July 1921. Full Dominion status was offered to 26 counties, with Northern Ireland remaining within the United Kingdom.

child to Teac. V. busy aft. evg. new nurse helpful. The M.gar asylum very spacious & well-appointed Dr's rooms.[118]

October

Saturday 8

A day in bed, antigen had such reaction. I couldn't stir, v. bad headache, etc. Delegates left for London by mg. boat, about 22 in party. M. Collins didn't appear, wise. Griffith, Barton, Gavan Duffy & Duggan. They have taken 2 houses in Chelsea for 2 mos. Letter fr. Mrs Archer, they do well, D.G. Little Eileen still with us, temp.down to 100.[119]

Monday 31

8 a.m. S.B's. Saw all pts. possible. There was much to do. All excitement over escape of 4 girls fr. Mt.joy, Nurse Cairns, Miss Keogh, Coyne & Burke. There are still 5 in. Would God all were out & from camps too! Rode to D.L. to spend Halloweve with Aunt F. Turret & armoured car passed me in B.rock a reminder of last year. Aunt F & E there, had nice evg.[120]

November

Sunday 6

23 A.T. 8 a.m. R.mines, cold, bright day. Last day of novena to Irish saints in R.C. Ch. Heard our peace was signed & sealed & it was all right for us. Nice notice in paper of first 2 women to be called to Bar, Irish of course, & of other 4 Irishwomen the first to break jail. Dinner ffMullens, tea Rhodes. In Teac Kathleen shade better & Henry. Several released fr. Spike island D.G.[121]

---

118. *Mrs Clarke, Pearse, Dr English* – Kathleen Clarke TD, Margaret Pearse TD, and Dr Adaline 'Ada' English TD. *M.gar asylum* – St Loman's psychiatric hospital, Mullingar.
119. *M. Collins* – Michael 'Mick' Collins (1890–1922). *Gavan Duffy & Dungan* – George Gavan Duffy (1882–1951), and Eamonn Duggan (1878–1936), all members of the Irish negotiation team for the Anglo-Irish Treaty.
120. *Nurse Cairns, Miss Keogh, Coyne & Burke* – escape of imprisoned Cumann na mBan members Linda Kearns, Aileen Keogh, Eithne Coyle, and May Burke. *D.L.* – Dún Laoghaire, coastal town outside of Dublin, home of Lynn's maternal aunt, Florence Wynne.
121. *first 2 women to be called to Bar, Irish of course, & of other 4 Irishwomen the first to break jail* – On 1 November 1921, Frances Kyle and Averil Deverell, graduates of the Law School, Trinity College Dublin, became the first women called to the Bar in Ireland. *Spike island* – in 1921 Spike Island, in Cork Harbour, was the largest military prison holding republican prisoners.

Saturday 19

A nice day, went to Ballyboden & trees perfectly glorious, esp. beeches, veritable fairyland. Papers full of secret document got by us & pub. in Bulletin re raising Ulster "C" Specials to army strength to be used when & where necessary to slaughter us. Well plot exposed. Dev installed as chancellor of N.U.I. gt. enthusiasm. Guild Gift Sale, v. nicely, saw [ ] there. Teac nicely. Much rioting in India to welcome prince of Wales.

Wednesday 23

Mr Griffith gone to London D.G. 47 escaped fr. Kilkenny, who had just come fr. Spike, conference still hangs fire, were it were ended one way or other, too long drawn out. Awful scenes in B.fast again, Orange fanatics shot down 11 in streets. Sir J. Craig still ill. It was 56 were smothered in India. Miss Cruice has pictures of her place in Freeman to-day. Guns are taken fr. barracks in Windsor. Sir W. Taylor home.[122]

December

Wednesday 7

"Peace" terms but such a peace! Not what Connolly & Mallin & countless others died for. Please God the country won't agree to what Griffith, Barton, Gavan Duffy, Duggan & Mick Collins have put their names to, more shame to them, better war than such a peace. Council meeting from 10 to 4, we did good work, however. It is terrible how many who should know better seem quite pleased with terms.[123]

Friday 9

Dev makes pronouncement that he cannot recommend acceptance of peace terms. D.G. for that, life seems brighter again. Arbor Day in hosp. Went very well D.G & all were pleased. Evg. saw Dev, Griffith, Stack, M. Collins & Duggan. Mick very truculent to Dev. I never saw anyone so changed for worse. Hear he has nearly whole I.R.A. with him, even, so may my country stand by the Truth.[124]

---

122. *escaped fr. Kilkenny* – On 11 November 1921, 44 IRA prisoners escaped from Kilkenny Gaol. *Awful scenes in B.fast again* – major sectarian riots broke out in Belfast between 19–25 November 1921, leading to at least 32 deaths. *Sir J. Craig* – James Craig, 1st Viscount Craigavon (1871–1940), leading unionist politician and Prime Minister of Northern Ireland.
123. *Connolly & Mallin* – James Connolly and Michael Mallin, executed signatories of the 1916 proclamation and Irish Citizen Army leaders. *Griffith, Barton, Gavan Duffy, Duggan & Mick Collins* – Arthur Griffith, Robert Barton, George Gavan Duffy, Eamonn Duggan, Michael Collins, all negotiators, and signatories of the Ango-Irish treaty.
124. *Dev, Griffith, Stack, M. Collins & Duggan* – Éamon de Valera, Austin Stack, Michael Collins, Eamonn Duggan.

Monday 12

8 a.m. S. B's. Praying all day for the country's soul. Papers full of Mick, who shows more & more clearly as the creature of the British Govt. They have bribed the papers well to pretend all love the treaty. M much better, several new babies in Teac, all fairly there. Art O'Brien wrote good letter to Times saying no one could [ ] over terms. Sad that Mick & Griffith shld. be traitors now.

Monday 19

8 a.m. S.B's, at last public session of Dail. Griffith opened debate on treaty, very unimpressive speech, motion seconded by McKeon, poor dupe! The President made a most glorious speech, no one after it can doubt that treaty means slavery, worse than before because willing . The other side have no argument. Barton excluded himself bravely, one felt sorry for him. Press reports only G's side. Childers fine.[125]

Wednesday 21

8 a.m. R.mines, felt v. anxious in mg. Saw pts. & went to S. Ann's, then to Dail, load passed off D.G. Heard Duggan, horrid speech with reference to Dead wh. hurt living, then Ruttledge spoke clear & well. Hope all will be printed. Lunch with Madam & Carroll O'Carroll. Hear Miss McSwiney spoke for 1 ½ hrs. & wiped the floor with Cosgrave & all opponents. Windy again to-night.[126]

---

125. *McKeon* – Major General Seán MacKeon (1893–1973) IRA leader and pro-Treaty politician. *The President* – Éamon de Valera, President of Sinn Féin. *Barton excluded himself bravely* – Robert Barton (1881–1975), 1916 rebel, Sinn Féin TD, and Judge, he was one of the plenipotentiaries who negotiated the Anglo-Irish Treaty although he was a reluctant signatory. He later repudiated the Treaty and stood, successfully, as an anti-treaty Sinn Féin candidate in the 1922 election, a seat he lost in the 1923 election. *Childers fine* – Erskine Childers, anti-treaty, made a good speech against its acceptance.
126. *Miss McSwiney* – Mary MacSwiney (1872–1942), republican, Cumann na mBan, Sinn Féin TD, sister of Terence MacSwiney. *Cosgrave* – William Thomas Cosgrave (1880–1965), Irish politician.

1922

January

Saturday 7

Alas! that the Dail should to-day ratify the 'Treaty' by 7 votes! Still we do not feel very depressed over it, the right will triumph still & those who sold Ireland will rue it yet. What will happen now? God knows. D.G. Mrs ffM, Madeline, Miss Rhodes much better so that it was a day of thankfulness, despite the evening's news. God will over rule for good.[127]

Tuesday 10

8 a.m. R.mines. Alas! the day that sees Griffith in Dev's place & all our people out of the Dail, wh. is no Dail now only the instrument of England. Dick Mulcahy in Brugha's place & they behaved so insultingly. Not a woman left in the Dail now. However, Madam was in this mg. with cheering news. we are strong & will be stronger of missing the self seekers. Barton is with us, I am glad. God save Ireland.[128]

Friday 13

8 a.m. S.B's. Madam came at b.fast time, M., Emer, she & I all glad to meet, she gave Emer coat & went off with her. M much better, gt. news abt. resignation of French Cabinet & collapse of Washington Conference. Bad for Mother England. Had fairly big disp. Matron v. upset over loss of £9, we fear stolen. Evg. sent to Ch. Home & saw them all & babies & children, finished with compline. M up for 1 ½ hrs.

Thursday 19

8 a.m. Xt. Ch. Poor Baby Boland died at 3 a.m. they are terribly sad, sent much of their things to hosp. Papers full of M. Collins, no one else. D.M.Ps are to salute him now. `Republic' v. good if I had time to read it. Griffith was scandalous to Childers in Dail. Hospital Board

---

127. *ratify the 'Treaty' by 7 votes* – The Dáil approved the Treaty by 64 votes to 57.
128. *Griffith in Dev's place* – de Valera resigned, and Arthur Griffith was elected President of the Dáil in his place. *Dick Mulcahy* – Richard 'Dick' Mulcahy (1886–1971), appointed Minister for Defence.

meeting v. tiring. Miss Griffin criticising our action & she alone in dismissing unreliable nurses. Poor meeting. Much 'Flu still.[129]

Saturday 21

The Dail anniversary & now we have the Free State but D.V soon the time servers will play themselves out. A nice bright, blue skied day, busy all day, saw sad little motherless baby who is to come to us. Mother England is to help the Freestaters to frame constitution, just what one expected. Went to Clonskea, Matron there would like 'Flu cases. Card from M. The Pope dead of 'Flu.[130]

Monday 23

8 a.m. S. B's. A quiet night D.G. Rang up Emer in mg. & found she was all right too, long round in mg., found Madam Gonne had gone to Paris. F.Staters behaving abominably to those who differ from them. They have kicked out B. Brennan & F. Kelly will go next. English are so jubilant over Craig-Collins agreement that it shows how rotten it is. F.Rhodes off to Glencormac. A letter from M. She will soon be home D.V.[131]

February

Wednesday 1

8 a.m. S. Ann's, a glorious S. Brigid's sunrise & a lovely day, tho' v. muddy still. Council long, they hadn't all their own way there. Teac fairly well, poor matron has lost her sister in U.S.A. Rumours that B & Ts are not to be disbanded but sent north with soldiers, Free State army being so small, only abt. 50 could be got to take over Beggar's Bush, vacated y.day by B & Ts.[132]

---

129. *M. Collins* – Michael Collins. *Miss Griffin* – Miss L. J. Griffin chairman of the board of St Ultan's Hospital.

130. *The Pope* – Pope Benedict XV, born Giacomo Pablo Giovanni Battista della Chiesa (1854–1922).

131. *Craig-Collins agreement* – first agreement between Sir James Craig (as Prime Minister of Northern Ireland) and Michael Collins (on behalf of the Irish Free State) – on how the boundary commission will be set up, ending the Belfast boycott, and allowing Catholic workmen to safely return to work in Northern Ireland.

132. *Free State army being so small* – The first 40–50 Volunteers of the new National Army came from the Dublin Guard, an IRA unit that included members of Michael Collins's 'Squad'. *Beggar's Bush* – 46 members of the National Army marched to Dublin's Beggars Bush Barracks to take over from the departing British Garrison.

Monday 6

Left Glencormac early. F. Clarke met me in Ranelagh, home 9.35, great joy over C na mBs vote for Republic, 600 to 60, D.G. The Free State is in gt. difficulties, has no powers, we hear, for even Collins jibbed at Privy Council oath & so they are left between Heaven & Hell & are nothing. New Pope = Card. Ratt. There is Revolution in the Land. Teac fairly, much work done to-day.[133]

Friday 10

Nice day. M went for me to S. Enda's in mg., then we both went to Teac to special Board re estimates for cottage, had to leave for 1.20 train to Bray. F. Clarke at station, faithful person. Had warm welcome at Glencormac. Lovely quiet. Miss O'Brennan here in gt. form. Papers full of difficulties of Free State & disgraceful doings on border, much dissatisfaction over Griffith Collins regime. Bill passed for Treaty.[134]

Saturday 11

A very lazy day in bed feeling only tired, glorious sunshine in mg. made one ashamed not to be out. Moonlight to-night as wonderful. Read, wrote & talked all day. Soviet has seized railways in Cork, good move. Budget prospects don't please British. Bernard to make good Free Staters of Trinity boys. Hope all well in Dublin.[135]

Wednesday 22

8 a.m. S. B's. P.H Comt. 10, hurried fr. it to Ard Feis where we waited till 1 before Dev came. Interval filled by talking to Miss L O'Brennan & Mr O'Grady from U.S.A. There were songs & McDevitt gave Pearse's oration at O'D. Rossa's grave to point of giving England undying hate, then Dev came, they had reached fair agreement, if Griffith etc. kept to it. We had fine Republican meeting after D.G. We would have crushing majority if vote taken. [Disloyal] Eire.[136]

---

133. *C na mBs vote for Republic* – At its national meeting on 5 January 1922 in the Mansion House, Dublin, Cumann na mBan voted overwhelmingly to reject the Treaty. *New Pope = Card. Rath.* – Pope Pius X, born Ambrogio Damiano Achille Ratti (1857–1939).

134. *Cottage* – in 1922 St Ultan's received funding from the White Cross to convert 'the Cottage' for the use of the night nurses.

135. *Soviet has seized railways in Cork* – a number of short lived soviets, mainly in Munster, occurred during 1920–2 including one on the north Cork railways in early 1923. None lasted very long.

136. *Ard Feis* – Sinn Féin Ard Fheis, Mansion House, Dublin, the first to be held since the party split over the Anglo-Irish Treaty.

March

Tuesday 7

8 a.m. R.mines, nice day, cold. India troubling, Limerick taken by Republicans, we hear, what does it mean? J.J. fighting hard with Prov. Govt. Hear men who shot Max Green in Mick's pay, terrible L. George gone to Criclith in a huff, they are wanting him to resign. Teac v. fairly D.G. Padraig rather better. M much worried because Water Colour people unfairly won't let us have our concert in Engineer's Hall.[137]

Wednesday 22

S.Enda's mg. then rounds. Teac does nicely D.G. My babies have gained. Cottage looks very, very nice, nearly finished now. Cold day. Terrible fighting on border of N & S, seems as if the enemy were encouraging it to say they must interpose to prevent our exterminating each other & they armed the Specials. Belfast boycott may be renewed, they say. Fergus' mother objects to him wearing our clothes.[138]

Thursday 23

V. busy day, Board meeting to arrange abt. Miss Jones going to Berlin re Lab. & to arrange abt. furniture etc. for nurses quarters. Teac fairly D.G. I. Times has leader on ill effects of doles which is significant coupled with Wh. X closing up & rumours abt. it. Rory O'Connor gave fine interview to U.S.A. journalist. Army has rallied finally to Republic. Talked over women candidates for elections.[139]

Tuesday 28

8 a.m. R.mines. Evg. Club did well. I.R.A. convention has decided no elections till adult suffrage, v. good. B.fast boycott to be vigorously enforced. In Teac, cottage washed down & v. nice. Poor Mary & Kevin rather low, little Kathleen going like Dolores. A very cold day, the early rising, very hard to put up with.[140]

---

137. *Limerick taken by Republicans* – Parts of Limerick city was taken by anti-treaty IRA.
138. *the Specials* – The Ulster Special Constabulary (USC) was established in late 1920, in response to the increased outbreaks of violence related to the War of Independence. They were overwhelmingly recruited from the Protestant communities and were known as Specials or B Specials.
139. *Miss Jones going to Berlin re Lab* – Teresa Jones was a medical student, she graduated from NUI later in 1922, and was appointed bacteriologist to St Ultan's. A new Bacteriology Laboratory and Pathology Department was being built at St Ultan's Hospital. *Rory O'Connor* – (1883–1922), Irish republican who took the anti-treaty side.
140. *I.R.A. convention* – held on 26 March, despite being banned by the Dáil cabinet as the majority of the IRA membership were anti-treaty.

Friday 31

Council 10a.m. Sibthorpe v. offensive in remarks re corporation, turned v. cold & snowy sleet all aft. Disp. v. interesting. M & I went to say Goodbye to Madam, who is off to U.S.A. Evg. St. Comt. meeting, v. stormy. Dev sees nothing ahead but civil war, if things don't mend. Milroy, as usual, v. offensive. Mrs W.P. seems really sorry at disagreement.[141]

April

Sunday 2

Passion Sun. 8 a.m. R.mines. Rebecca there. A lovely day, memorable for great turn out of Dublin Brigade I.R.A. how many marched, thousands, I'm sure, with C na mB & Fianna Smithfield was packed with them, such a sea of heads. We saw 3 speakers but couldn't get within miles of them. Looks as if I.R.A. was not Free State anyhow. All took new Republic oath. Teac fairly[142]

Tuesday 11

8 a.m. R.mines, frosty mg. again. Emer told us last night of boy she saw hanging limp over edge of Free State lorry, she was sure they had just shot him & so it was, they said, trying to escape. B & Ts could do no worse. Who can tell what this will lead to! God grant us Peace & Unity. Poor Miss Jennings died at 87. She was a lovely character.

Sunday 23

Low Sun. 8 a.m. R.mines. Rebecca wasn't there. Rathfarnham baby better. M & I went to Church St. & walked with procession of 1916 Cuman to Parnell Sq. on their way to Glasnevin. It was fine, many Free Staters there. 1916 men, oh that they would come back to the land only! We had wreath for Sean Connolly which Jennie Shanaghan took. Then to Aunt F. She told much family history, v. interesting. Nice day.[143]

---

141. *Mrs W.P.* – Jennie Wyse Power (1858–1941), Sinn Féin politician, and founder member of Cumann na mBan. Voted for the Treaty, split with Cumann na mBan and co-founded the women's pro-Treaty organisation, Cumann na Saoirse.
142. *C na mB & Fianna* – Cumann na mBan and Na Fianna (republican boy scouts).
143. *wreath for Sean Connolly which Jennie Shanaghan took* – Seán Connolly was killed in City Hall in 1916. Jennie Shanaghan was there with Lynn by his side as he died.

Tuesday 25

8 a.m. R.mines, v. busy, many meetings etc. Labour Manifesto re setting up Workers' Republic a hoax. We wondered at Foran & Johnston coming out like that. F.S. General shot in Athlone = agent [provocitoure] again. They say that if F.S. get in it will really mean war & perhaps it were best to fight to a finish now, God direct us. Emer in bed. Masonic Hall taken for Belfast refugees. Teac nicely on whole.[144]

May

Tuesday 2

8 a.m. R.mines, Ballast Office & Kildare St. Club taken over by I.R.A. Many Branches of Bank of Ireland robbed, they say, of course, by us. Four Courts v. busy sandbagging etc. We learn every day new things abt. Jim O'Neill & others with him, now Free Staters. Childrens affair in Town Hall great success, animals great attraction. M v. tired, home 11. No doubt at all Cork murders = Agents Procateurs.[145]

Tuesday 16

8 a.m. R.mines. Conflicting reports of Peace Comt., one says agreement reached, wh. they insist on Dail sanctioning, another prob. true, that no agreement possible. The [weeshy] does well so far D.G. she got too hot for a little, others nicely. B.fast S.F. Executive calls on Dail to protect them. I.R.A. makes strong pronouncement re looting, etc. Garden in cottage finished now, looks well.[146]

Friday 26

The opening day of Aonach Ultain, a perfect day. Much to do, of course. L. Mayor ill & could not come to open it so I had to do it instead. Poor fireman took faint & had to go off in ambulance to Meath, heart. A

---

144. *Foran and Johnson* – Thomas Foran (1883–1951), Irish Labour Party politician and Thomas Johnson (1872–1963), Irish Labour Party Leader. *F.S. General shot in Athlone* – Brigadier General George Adamson (1897–1992), Commanding Office of the Athlone Brigade, National Army, was shot dead in Athlone on 24 April 1922 by suspected anti-treaty republicans. *Masonic Hall* – The Freemasons Hall, Molesworth St, Dublin was used to house Catholic refugees from the sectarian violence in Northern Ireland.
145. *Four Courts v. busy sandbagging* – anti-treaty republicans in the Four Courts were preparing to defend their positions. *Childrens affair in Town Hall* – fundraiser for St Ultan's held in Rathmines Town Hall, including enactments of fairy tales with real goats and lambs. *No doubt at all Cork murders* – this refers to the murders of 13 Protestants in Dunmanway / Bandon, West Cork in April 1922, likely carried out by elements of the anti-treaty IRA.
146. *[weeshy]* – small. *B.fast S.F. Executive* – sectarian violence in Belfast and Northern Ireland escalated during the late spring and summer of 1922.

fine crowd there for 1st evg. D.G. D.V. all will go well. No time to read papers, hope all goes well.[147]

June

Thursday 1

Another lovely day, v. busy. Hottentot rising in S. Africa seems fairly serious. Everyone angry at Churchill's commanding us to make all Dail members take oath to K. George. Emer brought Shaw Desmond to Aonach & I had talk with him for a time, he is rather 'Figgish' but nicer. 10.30 stormy St. Comt. Meeting – O'Keeffe as usual, taking too much on himself. Dev, Stack, Boland & I waited on steps of No. 6.[148]

Friday 16

The great polling day, M & I voted early. Free State Constitution in papers, every 2nd word = the King! real Freedom! They seem pleased with voting on whole & say Madam is safe, hope so. Busy day, we are all tired, including Matron. D.V. she will be less worried soon.[149]

Sunday 18

1 A.T. 8 a.m. R.mines, election results so far 20 Republic, 22 Anti, 2 Indep. Things don't seem hopeful I fear but one does not want to throw up sponge after all the suffering. D.V. a way out will be found, a straight way. It feels as if the whole Republican structure was struggle & burnt up last Dec. God will work it out we know. Aunt F at D.L. M & I went to Willbrook 1st. No rain yet, God send it.

Tuesday 20

8 a.m. R.mines, a wonderful day, Wolfe Tone's birthday = Commemoration Day. We all went to Bodenstown, quite a good turn out of die hards, Mellowes spoke well, glorious day, wonderful free blue sky & white clouds, all spoke of the ban, [ ]. Evg. Emer, Matron &

---

147. *Aonach Ultain* – fundraising festival for St Ultan's held in the grounds of St Mary's College, Rathmines.

148. *Shaw Desmond* (1877–1960), Irish novelist and dramatist. *St. Comt. Meeting* – Sinn Féin Standing Committee of which Lynn was a member. *O'Keeffe* – Patrick O'Keeffe or Pádraig Ó Caoimh (1881–1973), republican, Sinn Féin TD, pro-treaty, Governor of Mountjoy Jail during the Civil War, later Clerk of the Senate (Seanad Éireann). *Dev, Stack, Boland & I* – Éamon de Valera, Austin Stack, Harry Boland and Lynn.

149. *The great polling day* – 1922 Irish general election.

I went to concert in Inc. Law Soc. hall, it was fine, traditional singers, violin, dancing, a memorable day. Dwyer defeated in R.mines.[150]

Friday 23

8 a.m. S. B's, fixed up & did Dispensary. Said goodbye to all at Teac, home, packed. Tea Mrs ffM. Taxi to L.pool boat. Emer not well. Started 7 p.m. good crossing but fearful accommodation. Poor cattle. M & I on deck all night, Emer went below.

Tuesday 27

Had b.fast in Café Nortre Dame, canal to [Sleuys], Holland. Passed hist. Damme, ramparts now cornfields. Stadt Huisfine, esp. crypt, torture instruments, old tiles & carved stones, it was important place once, great old furniture. Exhibition embroideries, magnifying, gt. to see, colours vivid still. Saw archers shooting at sky target. Tram to Heyst, passed Knooke, gt. old Ch. Heyst fine sea front. Ch. has nice S. Anthony. By train to Bruges via Blankenberg, remains of German guns.

July

Monday 3

arrived in good time at D. Laoghaire, no difficulty at all, so much for rumours. Shared car with priest going Parliament St. all well in Teac. Matron doing Red X night duty. Shelling much worse than 1916, 18 pounder now, then 9, but casualties v. light D.G. on our side. Lying reports in all papers. We left McK Harvey's. F.S. shelled it all night & now report 150 prisoners & much stuff. F.S. hard pressed in country, sending for reinforcements.[151]

Wednesday 5

Council Meeting. Mr Ceannt in chair, all went well. Quiet day till evg. Papers say fight over. Dr English went home by B.stone train. Drs Ryan & Stopford to Wicklow. C. Brugha never left his post till he sent his 10 men out with white flags & then dashed out himself when they

---

150. *Wolfe Tone's birthday* – Theobald Wolfe Tone (1763–98), United Irishman and a leader of the 1798 rebellion, executed on 19 November 1798, buried in Bodenstown, Co. Kildare to which Lynn and fellow republicans made an annual pilgrimage on his birthday. *Mellows* – Liam Mellows (1892–1922), revolutionary, socialist, and anti-treaty republican, one of the leaders of the anti-treaty IRA garrison in the Four Courts.
151. *Shelling much worse than 1916* – fighting in Dublin between anti-treaty republicans and the National Army. The Battle for Dublin had begun on 22 June with the shelling of anti-treaty republicans entrenched in the Four Courts.

were safe, to fall wounded in Ham. Artery v. badly. C na mB not let across barriers now nor Red X. Much shooting in R.mines. We got to Teac safely. D.G. at 11.30.[152]

Friday 7

8 a.m. S. B's. Heard soon Cathal Brugha passed away early this mg. My God it is terrible. I can't believe it. What an heroic death! His death will turn more back to Ireland than anything else could. His body would not be taken into Pro-Cathedral. Hear our boys surrounded on all sides in mts. but they will manage D.V. Tried to get D to R.farnham Red X hosp & were told it were well if all in Rebel. hosps. were dead & many more.[153]

Saturday 8

S. B's. Pouring day, cold, slept downstairs in Cullenswood in clothes, expecting raid. Much fire all night but no shelling. Emer to [ ] arrange things in Cullenswood. Left M in charge there & went to Suffolk St. for Dr to relieve me. Went with message to Mrs C Brugha, found her calm and brave. Fr Albert came with me. Funeral to be all women, our men fight. Saw Cathal Brugha, guard of C na mB round him, calm & beautiful in death. F. Staters refuse to let us bury him in Republican Plot.[154]

Friday 19

No trains fr. New Ross to-day, motor to 1 mile fr. W.ford, walked fr. there alone, heard no crossing fr. new Ferry but D.G. got Ferry across, shelling v. brisk, got to Power's unhurt, then to Infantry Barracks, then to each post. Shells telling much on jail, Caval. & Infant. barracks, heard all posts evacuated, but boys went back. Dev sent message help coming but none came. Surprised & delighted to meet Dublin girl at

---

152. *Dr English* – Dr Ada English (1875–1944), doctor, psychiatrist, and anti-treaty Sinn Féin TD. *Drs Ryan & Stopford* – Dr James Ryan (1892–1970), physician and politician and Dr Dorothy Stopford-Price (1890–1954), physician, member of Cumann na mBan and later physician at St Ultan's Hospital. *C. Brugha* – Cathal Brugha leader of the anti-treatyites in O'Connell St, shot and mortally wounded, he died 7 July 1922 in the Mater Hospital, Dublin.

153. *Hear our boys surrounded on all sides in mts* – after the fall of Dublin to the National Army, anti-treaty forces retreated to the Wicklow mountains around Blessington where they are surrounded by pro-treaty forces in early July.

154. *Cullenswood* – Cullenswood House, Rathmines, home of Mrs Margaret Pearse. *Mrs C Brugha* – Caitlín Brugha (1879–1959), widow of Cathal Brugha and later Sinn Féin TD. *Fr Albert* – Fr Albert Bibby, Capuchin, friend of Cathal Brugha. *guard of C na mB* – Mrs Brugha insisted that only members of anti-treaty Cumann na mBan form a guard of honour for Cathal Brugha.

"Ford's" wh. is no H.Q. Wish more like her. Attended to wounded, saw to feeding. Host. v. bitter! Lively night.[155]

August

Wednesday 2

A long day with little food & no rest last night or to-day. We beat off enemy 3 times, heavy fighting along 25 mile front, Slievenamon in it, our men in fine positions. They shelled us with trench mortars & all kinds of machine guns & we had one sl. wound in leg only. They lost many, killed & wounded & retreated at last fr. [ ]. I sat on road with rear guard to be handy, they sniped us. Evg. ret. to Carrick

Saturday 5

B.fast in bed, nice day, saw poor boy in Union, he is v. bad. Left by 1.15 train for home, slow journey past Abbeyleix, poor Alice. Too late to send Radium back for boy. All well here, glad & thankful to be home again. D.G. Teac fine. Lab wall coming on, stone looks well. Heard other side complain of overwhelming odds, etc. Troops landed in Kerry. Dublin swarms with British. Rifle fire now. God grant all well down South.[156]

Saturday 12

8 a.m. S. B's, Griffith died suddenly 10 a.m. cereb. haem. got surprise, sad that he shld go a traitor, he will be an irreparable loss to F. State. M & I went to Navan 1.50 train, so nice & peaceful there, went to Loreto Convent, Sr. Columba away, pity, others rather stiff & F.S. saw Eamon. [ ] friends, he is well.[157]

Wednesday 16

Slept till 9.30. too bad. Our successes in Dundalk & Drogheda were v. fine, lots of stuff captured. Griffith's funeral to-day. A year ago he swore allegiance to Republic for 2nd time. Collins there, looking well=one tale, Collins beaten nearly to death=another. Teac filling, one of mine

---

155. *No trains fr. New Ross to-day* – Lynn went to the southeast area of Kilkenny and Waterford to act as a medical officer for the anti-treaty forces fighting there.

156. *Troops landed in Kerry.* – National Army troops travelled by sea to Fenit in Co. Kerry and landed there to retake the county from anti-treaty republicans.

157. *Griffith died suddenly* – Arthur Griffith (1871–1922), Sinn Féin founder and TD, pro-treaty and President of Dáil Éireann at the time, died suddenly on 12 August 1922, aged 51.

v. bad. Poor child, green diarrh. M has bad cold. New H. Surgeon appointed. She looks nice. Many pts.[158]

Wednesday 23

8 a.m. S. B's. I am so glad I went. F. Williams told me of Collins death in ambush near Bandon. She is v. sad & indeed retribution has fallen swiftly on the murderers of poor Harry Boland. D.G. Griffith & Collins were not treated so. Teac fairly on whole. It was fine all day. They say Collins' loss irreparable. He was beloved of a certain set. Pts. do well D.G.[159]

Thursday 24

8 a m R.mines. Collins brought by boat, they say, in dead of night to Dublin, Vincent's Hosp. to be embalmed. Funeral Mon. Reports say he was really shot in ambush last Sat. in Stillorgan, which is true? Official account of death evidently faked. Evg. says Thornton dead & Dalton, a very important man shot in ambush in Harcourt St. Letter fr. home says poor Hessie Ellwood & Mrs McKeon dead, a day of wreathing.[160]

Monday 28

Left Clun Ruad early, lovely ride in, whole town given over to poor Mick's funeral, it seems. They say procession was ill arranged & straggling. Nora Cunningham walked, 1st time she ever did such. Two of our Fianna boys & another unknown boy shot in cold blood on roadside by F.S. & they tried to make out we did it. Great rumours of F.S.ers running amok & wholesale raiding.[161]

---

158. *Our successes in Dundalk & Drogheda were v. fine* – Frank Aiken, Commandant 4th Northern Division and over 300 men capture Dundalk and its pro-treaty garrison and release over 300 anti-treaty prisoners.

159. *Collins death* – Collins, then commander-in-chief of the National Army was killed in an ambush at Béal na Bláth, Co. Cork on 22 August 1922. Harry Boland (1887–1922), Irish republican, anti-treaty, shot in Skerries in July 1922 by the members of the National Army.

160. *Thornton dead* – car carrying National Army Colonel Commandant Frank Thornton at Redmondstown, Co. Tipperary on 21 August 1922 , he was badly wounded not killed.

161. *Two of our Fianna boys* – on 26 August 1922 two Fianna Éireann officers, Seán Cole, (aged 19), Commandant of the 2nd Battalion, Dublin Brigade and Alfred Colley, (aged 21), Vice-Commandant of the Dublin Brigade, were arrested by intelligence members of the National Army at Newcomen Bridge on the North Strand and taken to Yellow Road, Whitehall where they were shot dead.

September

Wednesday 13

8 a.m. S. B's, went to Ch. Home after v. showery day & wet night. Mulcahy made lying statement in Prov. Parlia. We think it was poor Brugha's plan for attack overland before truce, wh. he, Mulcahy had lost, he was alluding to as if date was June 1922. J. J. has posters out of preposterously low food prices & rent, showing wages cut [mystified]. Poor Sean MacEvoy's father declares himself quite satisfied with shooting of his son! Can servility go farther![162]

Wednesday 20

8 a.m. S. B's. Little Kitty holds her own in Teac D.G. Mrs Fisher thinks branding Republicans a useful way of identifying them. Madam Gonne & Mrs Despard turned out of S Parliament for protesting against the treatment of prisoners. Saw Mrs Fullerton who was shot in knee by stray bullet. Greenmount spinning people came, place to be auctioned in Oct. "Uncle Jarlath" thinks Eng. won't fight. All our accounts good.

Friday 29

8 a.m. R.mines. Nice warm day, babies out on roof. F. Williams has weird tales of Unionist plots to overthro' Treaty, poor Treaty, nobody loves it. 63 raided & poor Fergus Murphy & Reynolds taken, D.V. no harm will come to them. Papers all say postal strike over but it is a lie, another . The Cuman na Saoirse is spotting for all its worth. Mrs C. Brugha had gt. ovation Glasgow.[163]

October

Tuesday 3

8 a.m. R.mines. All getting into order for secret military courts to try, condemn & shoot Republicans in the slightest pretext, but such four methods always have & always will fail D.G. Russia intervenes near Eastern question & has the audacity to say the British are blockading

---

162. *Poor Sean MacEvoy's father* – Seán McEvoy, a UCD medical student and anti-treaty republican, member of G Company of 4th Battalion, Dublin Brigade arrested by National Army soldiers in Bishop St, Dublin, and shot dead, reportedly while trying to escape.
163. *& poor Fergus Murphy* – arrested with Seán McEvoy and wounded in the head, taken to Wellington Barracks. *Cuman na Saoirse* – Cumann na Saoirse, pro-treaty women's group, provide intelligence on anti-treaty Cumann na mBan and IRA activists to the National Army.

Dardenelles against her! Teac well on whole, D.G. Miss Spring Rice came to Teac & was pleased, C. hates the torturing.[164]

Monday 9

Those poor boys were riddled with bullets on Naas Rd., one was still alive & saw priest. O my God, stop such horrors. Mundania Conference seems to progress. I went to Town for books & things for baby. All well in Teac & have gained. Matron back, D.G. They had terrible raid. Fine meeting y.day outside Mulcahy's. F.S. soldiers fired & stampeded some, nearly killing children in Chapel. They had cheek to ask me to write for book celebrating Irish Freedom published in Manchester. Significant. A dull day.[165]

Sunday 22

8 a.m. R.mines, glad to be there, Emer came aft. b.fast. Roisin went to collect Emily Hanratty for Gaelic Service, then to big meeting in O'Connell St. at 12.30. Madam MacBride spoke splendidly, then Mrs. Despard, then myself. Dinner Rhodes, then off to S. Mobhi's, Glasnevin where Gaelic Service was wonderful. D.G. good many there. Canon O'Connell revelled in it. Emer painted walls, they turned hose on the crowd.[166]

Monday 30

8 a.m. S. B's, cold E. wind. Proclamation that I.R.A. supports Republic in all ways D.G. We hear the Bps. were promised peace in 3 weeks, if only they would come out strong enough. Miss McSwiney wrote re. pt. Mrs Buckley says Cork city is putrid! is this so? Babies all better who were [douched]. Maura had [ischio] rectal abscess opened. Dev wants S. Fein kept on, just like him. Great explosion.[167]

---

164. *Miss Spring Rice* – Mary Ellen Spring Rice (1880–1924), nationalist, member of United Irishwomen and the Irish Countrywomen's Association. Took part in the Howth gun running in 1914.
165. *Those poor boys were riddled with bullets* – Na Fianna scouts Edwin Hughes (17), Brendan Holihan (17), and Joe Rogers (16), arrested while putting up Republican posters in Drumcondra, Dublin. They had been arrested by Charlie Dalton and Nicholas Tobin, two high-ranking Free State officers, interrogated at Wellington Barracks and not seen alive again. Their bullet riddled bodies were discovered in the Quarries, Naas Rd, the next day.
166. *Roisin* – Rosamond Jacob (1888–1960), Irish writer and political activist. *Emily Hanratty* – née Norgrove, Irish Citizen Army, was in City Hall with Lynn during the Rising. *St. Mobhi's* – Church of Ireland church in Glasnevin.
167. *Mrs Buckley* – Margaret Buckley née Goulding (1879–1962), Cork born member of Sinn Féin, anti-treatyite, later President of Sinn Féin.

November

Thursday 4

8 a.m. S. B's. glorious sunrise, like y.day, sunny day. The big explosion we heard at 12.30 last night can't be traced. Military police have no knowledge of it! Strange. An hour's fright in Mrs Humphries house, Aylesbury Road. Ernie O'Malley wounded in shoulder, the whole household arrested except maid. Miss O'Rahilly wounded in neck.[168]

Wednesday 8

8 a.m. S. B's, bright day, gt. attack on Wellington by 4 of our boys, 2 machine guns, 2 Peter the Painters, about 6 or 7 F.S. killed & 20 wounded, that is not S.F. but Scottish regt. wh. had just arrived, gt. excitement. Hear reprisals are to be on our prisoners there to-night. God forefend! Tried to see Miss MacSwiney, sent fr. pillar to post in vain, at last heard that only Gov. Gen. could give leave. Teac well on whole.[169]

Friday 10

8 a.m. S. B's, v. busy day, went to Maeve early, pts. till 1.30. Gen. Council of County Councils 2.30, there till 6.30, v. stormy, we had to break up meeting at last, they would give no satisfaction re prisoners. Emer splendid. Hunger strikers weak. D. Macardle taken, & they say, Madam. We must fight for the unfortunate prisoners. Teac nicely, tho' Paddy, my worst baby, is very bad. Concert splendid in Mansion Ho. Turkey giving serious trouble.[170]

Saturday 11

8 a.m. S. B's. Lovely sunshiny day, fair account in papers of C.C. meeting y.day. Madam MacBride's house in Stephen's Green raided & broken up, almost like Cullenswood. Appears to be reprisal for D. Macardle living there. O'Brennan & girls in Mtjoy. Miss MacS. v. weak

---

168. *Mrs Humphries*– Mary Ellen 'Nell' Humphries, née O'Rahilly (1871–1939), anti-treaty Cumann an mBan. *Miss O'Rahilly* – Anna 'Anno' O'Rahilly (1873–1958), Cumann na mBan, sister of Nell. *Ernie O'Malley* – Ernie O'Malley (1897–1957), revolutionary, writer, and anti-treaty republican.
169. *gt. attack on Wellington* – attack on the National Army garrison at Wellington Barracks, South Circular Rd, Dublin by anti-treaty republicans. 18 soldiers were wounded and two were killed. Two republicans were wounded. *Tried to see Miss MacSwiney* – Mary MacSwiney was in Mountjoy Jail at this time.
170. *Maeve* – Maud Gonne McBride. *D. Macardle* – Dorothy Macardle (1889–1958), republican, writer, propagandist, anti-treaty. *Madam* – Countess Markievicz.

now. L. Mayor avoided us & slipped off to P.marnock. No money to pay unemployed dole to-day. Mulcahy admits defeat.[171]

Thursday 16

Again, wasn't very well in night, queer, same date 1921. Teac nicely. Cosgrave has returned with orders to execute O'Malley & Childers & let Mary MacSwiney die. Went to Aunt F in evg. seeing Madam O'Rahilly on the way, she is better D.G. Mary MacS. very weak. Aunt F v. glad I came. I went early to bed & had grand sleep.

Friday 17

Left Aunt early. Annie MacSwiney sent for me, she was not starting for Mtjoy, where she is now fasting till she is let see her sister, they threw buckets of water on her & twisted her arms & were most insolent. We heard in aft. the terrible news that 4 poor lads were executed this mg. for having had revolvers, their mothers never heard of it till they saw papers. How humane England was in comparison? We always think worst has come.[172]

Monday 20

Left Waterford 6.45 a.m. without molestation D.G. Saw in papers how meeting in O'Connell St. fired on & 6 wounded, terrible, heard fr. Emer & M who read out letter thro' attack, how terrible it was, officer shooting to kill. Lily Bennett has since died & newsboy is dying, it is horrible. Landmine explosion killed 4 of ours, so sad. Miss A MacSwiney wonderful. Mr Childers reprieved one day longer D.G. Internat. Red X intervenes. Saw Mrs Childers, she has the real spirit of martyrdom.[173]

Thursday 23

8 a.m.Xt. Ch. nice day. Master of Rolls refused Habeas Corpus for Childers & others, they may kill them now, horrible. Inquest on Lily

171. *fair account in papers of C.C. meeting y.day* – meeting of the General Council of County Councils held in Dublin. A deputation of women including Lynn, Helena Molony, Fine Maud Gonne McBride and others raised the issue of the treatment of republican prisoners.
172. *Annie MacSwiney* (d.1954), sister of Mary and Terence MacSwiney.
173. *Lily Bennett* – A member of Cumann na mBan, while attending a rally held by the Women's Prisoners' Defence League in Dublin, she was mortally wounded when National Army troops opened fire on the crowd. *Landmine explosion killed 4 of ours* – IRA members Thomas Maguire, Paddy J. Egan, Bernard Curtis and Thomas Phelan were killed in a premature landmine explosion at the Naas Road, Inchicore, 20 November 1922.

Bennett, verdict= shot by person unknown tho' witnesses could prove officer did it & they admitted bullet = 45 Webley & his revolver = 45, so much for F.S. fairness. Party of drunken F.S. soldiers under Dolan fell on Miss A MacS, threw her out of her bed on road & broke all she had, only police prevented them killing her.[174]

December

Monday 18

8 a.m. S. B's. stormy. esp. evg. In Mtjoy boys in D. div. on hunger strike because 2 of them have been removed, where? no one knows. Several peace moves on, all from S.F. wh. looks well, our boys have taken Blessington, they do well. Teac fairly D.G. Had stormy ride to Silveracre Mill to see Baby Murray 4.30 at Sod of Turf. Women's Peace & Freedom League, it wasn't much. The report of Hague conference, our statement never read.[175]

Sunday 31

Sun. after Xmas, 8.a.m Xt. Ch. went back to bed after b.fast & made out report re. Geneva etc. Aunt E came to dinner & she was expected to-morrow. She looks badly. I went to Dalkey to meet M. Play even better than y.day. 2 C. Brughas with M & her mother. Mrs Skeffington's raided y.day & Roisin Jacob arrested, terrible! Reports everywhere of O'Malley's & Barton's executions in mg. Evg. with Aunt F.

---

174. *Inquest on Lily Bennett* – Evidence given to the inquest by Maud Gonne MacBride and Charlotte Despard of the Women's Prisoners' Defence League.
175. *Hague conference* – The Women's International League for Peace and Freedom 1922 conference was held at the Hague where Lucy Kingston and Rosamond Jacob represented Ireland.

1923

January

Friday 5

8 a.m. S. B's. Many pts. Allies no longer D.G. D. G. Madam MacBride, E. Taaffe, O'Toole & Brady taken. 6 Harcourt St. & £100. Prisoners' Dep. Fund & many typewriters. They are demons. They will try to oppose having Dr Murphy for new Councillor in McDonagh's 'place, they are so mean. M & I v. tired.[176]

Friday 19

8 a.m. S.B's, then off to Miss Duffy. V. busy mg. Have to go to Manchester to-morrow with Mrs O'Callaghan. New paper Eire but v. good. Did disp. & many pts. Left Dr Jones in charge. Borrowed attache case fr. Mrs C.B. Sorry to leave M so soon again. C. Ryan & nurse went to Glencormac for a week.[177]

Wednesday 31

8 a.m. S. B's. Glorious sunrise D.G. A senator = Bagwell, kidnapped. F.S. Govt. makes proclamation that if he is not returned in 48 hours, they'll take punitive measures against prisoners & suspects. What insolence! Teac fairly. Kitty nicely. M in fortress of jackells on audit business, out safely D.G. Novena women welcomed Roisin out. Mary & Sheila off H.strike, have got Polit. treat. R.mines housing looks well.[178]

February

Thursday 15

8 a.m. Xt. Ch. Hear Daily Mail etc. suppressed for reporting Cosgrave's request for 25 mil. loan. Passengers searched for it. Girls in Mtjoy off hungerstrike. Irish World gives good account of our work at the Teac.

---

176. *Madam MacBride, E. Taaffe, O'Toole & Brady* – Maud Gonne McBride, Effie (Aoife) Taaffe, Miss O'Toole and Frances Brady all anti-treaty republican women. *6 Harcourt St* – Headquarters of Sinn Féin. *Prisoners' Dep. Fund* – Irish Republican Prisoners Defendants Fund (IRPDF).

177. *New paper Eire* – *Éire/The Irish Nation*, anti-treaty propaganda newspaper.

178. *Bagwell* – John Philip Bagwell (1874–1946), Irish Free State Senator. *Novena women* – Cumann na mBan women and supporters who kept constant prayer vigils outside Mountjoy Jail in support of the imprisoned anti-treaty republicans. *Roisin* – Rosamond Jacob, arrested and imprisoned in Mountjoy Jail for anti-treaty activities. *Mary and Sheila* – Mary MacSwiney and Sheila Humphreys.

Poor Kitty, the mite, dead y.day. After all our struggle Harry's mother took him out, too lazy to come 3 hourly to him. Poor Ann raided because she knew me. Report 100 executions after 18th amnesty up.[179]

Friday 23

8 a .m. S. B's. Nice day. We all think Mrs Philimore is English Agent. She is deep. Big display & interesting. Young girls searched by C.I.D. men in Portobello, shameful. Saw Mrs Ceannt's house, indescribable wanton havoc. Went Saor an Lanab & Ch.Guild, both good. Saw people then & rushed as usual. Poor C. Donnelly taken & his boy, who was badly beaten. Reports of gt. captures but unconfirmed. Susie raided.[180]

March

Tuesday 13

8 a.m. R.mines. Went early to say goodbye to friend, then to Ch. Long round, Roebuck. found C.I.D. in possession on ret. & nurse just being taken away. I was brought to Oriel Ho. too, searched & all letters, etc. taken, told I might go, sorry to leave nurse, re-arrested at Merrion Sqr. back to Oriel Ho. Nurse, another & myself kept till after 8. Nurse & I released, D.G. M had made gt. fuss.[181]

Thursday 29

Holy Thurs. 8 a.m. R.mines Council at 10, then inspected Kimmage houses. Heard at dawn raid in my house & 7 & 10, determined to go back usu. time. Called at E. Ryan's. C.I.D. opened door there. I was a prisoner till 10 p.m. There were civil enough there. F. Joseph came like roaring lion. No. 9 in fearful state of filth, Jane frozen & starved. Stole all my food & Cong eggs & Miss Cooke's cake.[182]

---

179. *Irish World* –Irish American newspaper.
180. *C.I.D.* – Criminal Investigation Department, short lived counterinsurgency policing unit of the Irish Free State. *Saor an Lanab* – Saor an Leanbh – the Irish Save the Children Fund.
181. *Oriel Ho.* – on the corner of Westland row and Fenian Street in Dublin, it was the headquarters of the Criminal Investigation Department or C.I.D. *Nurse* – Dora Maguire, nurse at St Ultan's, anti-treaty member of Cumann na mBan.
182. *No. 9 in fearful state of filth* – No. 9 Belgrave Rd, Lynn's home. Jane was the housekeeper at the time.

April

Monday 2

Easter Mon. 8 a.m. S. B's to pray all might go well with M. who went by mail last night & all at home. A perfect day, like this time 7 yrs. Most successful meeting at G.P.O. D.G. Good speeches, Mrs Pearse in chair. Countess P., Emer, Mary Mac & I with Madam McB spoke. In Teac another time of deaths, 4 of mine in 2 days, Ultan one of them. Aft. Glencormac, lovely there. Prayed at Fassaroe Cross & said D.G. Fairyhouse bridge blown up.[183]

Thursday 5

Wire at b.fast. F. taken suddenly ill, come. Did all I could before 1.30 train, saw last night's pt. Matron splendid. Arrived in good time, found poor F. had stroke too, like last night's pt., only semi-conscious, tho' I felt certain there was smile of recognition of me D.G. Sleeping all the time. Poor N & M. Boys taken off by soldiers & found shot dead, terrible. They can't get into Mt. Fastness near Swinford for inquest. Carnarvon dead=Pharohs.[184]

Tuesday 10

The funeral day, last night N, M & I had our last farewell together to our dear one. All ready in good time, people came & brought lovely flowers as hearse at door. Bp. of Kilmore came, motored all the way, so afraid he wouldn't be in time. Mr McQuaide, Wixon, Doube & Archd. Treanor there. Bp. in time for last look on dear face so unutterably serene & happy D.G. Beautiful lights as we brought him westward. Grave lovely, moss lined & deep. Peace.

Friday 13

A lovely day & quiet. Wire of love & sympathy fr. dear Madeline in aft. Poor Aunt passed away y.day a.m. Sorry I can't be there. Saw many pts. Susan Kenny, Mrs H & Mary C came. Mary MacSwiney,

---

183. *Mrs Pearse in chair. Countess P., Emer, Mary Mac & I with Madam McB spoke* – Mrs Margaret Pearse as chair while Countess Plunkett, Helena Molony, Mary MacSwiney, Maud Gonne McBride and Lynn all spoke. *Fairyhouse bridge* – it was a railway bridge a few miles from Fairyhouse Bridge which was blown up with a landmine.
184. *F* – Lynn's father, Rev. Robert Lynn, died 8 March 1923, buried in Cong, Co. Mayo. *N & M* – Anne 'Nan' and Muriel Lynn, Kathleen's sisters. *Carnarvon dead=Pharohs* – George Herbert, 5th Earl of Carnarvon (1866–1923), financial backer of the expedition which found the tomb of Tutankhamun. It was believed those who disturbed the tomb were impacted by the curse of the Pharaohs.

Mrs O'Callaghan & Count Plunkett arrested on way to Liam Lynch's funeral. F.S. say we are completely down & out now – are we![185]

Friday 20

Busy with pts. big disp. Little Laytown Moira better D.G. Others well D.G. not worse of y.day's excitement. Heard Mrs Despard waiting outside Kilmainham till Madam Gonne was released, went there, she was gone, not in Roebuck either, back to jail with E. Young who spoke of daily fulfilment of prophecies D.G. Saw F Sherwin who says no immediate danger for Maeve D.G. Evg. M & I to bed 8.30 & slept.[186]

Tuesday 24

8 a.m. R.mines. 7th anniv. of Easter Week. Emer came in mg. F. Clarke off to Inch. 80 prisoners escaped fr. Curragh. Heard later 200 soldiers down with virulent V.D. there. No more news of H.Strikers. Saw Dr Conn Murphy, he looks v. frail & shaken. Much election work to do. Got v. ill new babies into Teac. Mr Ginnell's funeral to be in Delvin, nice.[187]

May

Saturday 12

8 a.m. S. B's, v. showery, sleet & hail. Madam McBride weak still, she has no muscle. Iseulte not much better. Emer going to meeting in Granard. Saw many pts. Teac v. fairly. Arranging abt. lab. maid. The poor things in N.D.U are in terrible way. Evg. went to Aunt F.[188]

June

Saturday 2

The 1st warm day & busy too. Moira Deegan released, D.G. poor things. M.Comerford re-arrested & badly beaten, on hungerstrike. That's a pity. Miss Cox drowned herself in Dodder, had cancer, at ways queer,

---

185. *Liam Lynch* (1892–1923), chief of staff of the Irish Republican Army, killed by Free State troops on 10 April 1923.
186. *E. Young* – Ella Young (1867–1956), poet, republican, and mystic. *Maeve* – Maud Gonne McBride.
187. *prisoners escaped fr. Curragh* – 70 anti-treaty prisoners escaped from the Curragh internment camp by tunnelling their way out.
188. *Iseulte* – Iseult Gonne (1894–1954), daughter of Maud Gonne. *The poor things in N.D.U* – North Dublin Union, women republican prisoners were moved from Kilmainham and Mountjoy Jails to the NDU, a closed workhouse repurposed for the prisoners.

terrible for relatives. Nurse had ether & piece of [ ] abretus removed & was v. excited & screaming, night now D.G. Heard our Landlord will let us have site. D.G. Matron gone to Lough Derg with Dr Barry. Up Republic.[189]

July

Tuesday 3

8 a.m. R.mines. Started to go to 11 o/c, in 1 hr. taxi was packed. All Bel Rd. looking on, esp. No. 5. Miss Clarke & Dr Stopford waited to see us off. Lovely safe drive down by N.town Mt. Kennedy, Ashford, Rathnew, Rathdrum. Big down hill after that. It is a lovely quiet valley, rushing river, high bare hills. Ford fordable D.G. All came safe. It was beautiful. House awful after staters, nearly all broken or stolen. Said Compline by river D.G.

August

Sunday 5

5 A.T. Went to 8 a.m. R.mines, had to come out so stuffy, recovered after a while. Went to Mr Moore re Kells meeting & then to Countess P to get her to go. B.fast in Teac. Matron & M went to H. Boland's Mass & Glasnevin. I tried 2nd Celeb. in Xt. Ch. & R.mines, missed both. Alb. Broderick came in aft. Tea 63, saw Dr Hennessy. Org. 3 meetings. M spoke twice, I three times, home 12 o/c.[190]

Saturday 18

8 a.m. S. B's, hurry for G.D. at 10 in good time. Nomination Rooms Marlboro' St. till near 2 fearing objections, all candidates accepted. Terrible to be in room with D. Fitzgerald. Talked to G. Duffy, Col.Moore etc. Saw poor boy in Mater fr. Gormanstown, bad haem. V. murderous raid on Suffolk. St. E. Donnelly arrested, attempt to do him in, say he

---

189. *Moira Deegan* – Máire Deegan, Cumann na mBan and anti-treaty. *M.Comerford* – Máire Comerford (1893–1982), Cumann na mBan and anti-treaty. *Dr Barry* – Dr Alice Barry (1880–1955), one of the founders of St Ultan's Hospital.
190. *Countess P* – Countess Plunkett. *Alb. Broderick* – Gobnait Ní Bhruadair, born Albinia Brodrick (1861–1955), Irish republican and radical.

is hurt. Evg. meeting. couldn't get to Council Meeting or P.H. Meeting. Accounts of in papers still.[191]

Monday 27

8 a.m. S.B's, the fateful day, ballot not secret, papers numbered, no warning given! Much firing at night wh. they pretend was attack by us. W. Redmond's procession in W.ford fired on & many hurt. All went well as regards voting but one doesn't expect fair play. I was up & down all day fr. place to place. Armed soldiers in & outside every polling sta. kept many away. Evg. Psalms fit in wonderfully.[192]

Thursday 30

8 a.m. Xt. Ch. Milkman at door told me I was elected. God grant me grace to do right for my country. Nice day with pts. We do well this evg. 25 Republicans elected D.G. Italy sends ultimatum to Greece because of assassinated Italians. May cause Europ. war. Teac v. fair, busy with preps. for Turas on Sunday.[193]

September

Wednesday 12

Cosgrave to have gt. welcome by papers on ret. Fri. next. Bands etc. Italy warlike again, won't submit to League, worrying Britain. She took wind out of Cosgrave's sails when he craved admission to League. [Liam] got to London, why? Saw Mrs Dev, she'll give concert souvenir. Mrs Ginnell at lunch. Grievances & good sense. Man escaped over Mtjoy wall, rode off on cycle. Mellowes house watched? Barney.[194]

---

191. The 1923 general election to elect the 4th Dáil held on Monday, 27 August. Kathleen Lynn was nominated as a candidate in the Dublin County constituency for the anti-treaty Sinn Féin. *G. Duffy, Col. Moore* – George Gavan Duffy (1882–1951), politician and judge and Maurice George Moore (1854–1939), Irish author, soldier, and politician. *Gormanstown* – Gormanstown Military Camp where male republican prisoners were held during the Civil War.
192. *W. Redmond's procession* – William Archer Redmond (1886–1932), son of Irish Parliamentary Party leader John Redmond, elected as an independent TD for Waterford in the general election.
193. Lynn was elected to the 4th Dáil but as an anti-treaty Sinn Féin TD who had committed to not participating in the Dáil if elected she did not take her seat. *Turas* – pilgrimage to church of St Ultan in Ardbraccan, Co. Meath.
194. *League* – League of Nations. *Mrs Dev* – Sinéad de Valera, née Ní Fhlannagáin (1878–1975), Irish author, wife of Éamon de Valera. *Mrs Ginnell* – Alice Ginnell, née King (1882–1967), Cumann na mBan and Sinn Féin member, widow of Laurence Ginnell.

Monday 17

Left Galway by 9.30 train, pouring wet, stormy day, good journey up. Saw Mrs Skeffington at Athlone & B.stone, little notice of meetings or victory concert, tho' all huge success. Limerick Bp. wouldn't let priests on our platform unless we guaranteed no further arming, disgraceful! Spain in hands of Militarists like Italy. Ruhr tortures like here. Hosing & batoning in "Joy", bad work. All well at No. 9, piles of letters.[195]

October

Friday 12

8 a.m. S.B's. Windy, esp. in night. K O'Higgins read paper in Mansion Ho. 300 Stewards there, few else. They threw Madam Gonne out when she rose to speak. Evg. did resolution. Heard of county murder gangs under Dist. Inspects. to do for any Republicans who go to law with "Staters" over land questions. Terrible.[196]

Tuesday 16

S. Gaul's Day. 8 a.m. R.mines, rush for Ard Feis at 11. It was fine. I was in chair at 1, then Mary Mac, her address fine, A.P's fine too. At 2.30 we walked to Marlboro' St. funeral immense. Went around Mtjoy, they fired on us, still peaceful day, he is at rest at last, poor Noel. Then another sitting A.F. till 10.30. Mary Mac, Fr Flanagan, Ruttledge & I are V.Ps, Daly & Stack Secs. Mrs Brugha & S O'Mara Treas. Nearly 500 in M.joy on H. Strike. All Ireland to do Walls of Jericho.[197]

Thursday 18

8 a.m. R.mines. Last night 11.30 1,000 marched fr. Mansion Ho. to Arbour Hill singing hymns & saying Rosary, v. impressive. We were held up by v. menacing troops, more & more of them at Arbour Hill threatened fire, armoured cars & lorries, we knelt in prayer, tense moments, then v. quietly we moved off to Mt.joy where sim. crowd was

---

195. *Limerick Bp* – David Keane, Bishop of Limerick. *Hosing & batoning in 'Joy'* – Mistreatment of anti-treaty prisoners in Mountjoy Jail.
196. *K O'Higgins* – Kevin O'Higgins (1892–1927), Minister for Justice. *Dist. Inspects* – District Inspectors, officers in the newly formed police force of the Irish Free State, An Gárda Síochána. *Staters* – supporters of the Irish Free State.
197. *Poor Noel* –Noel Lemass (*d.*1923), anti-treaty officer abducted in June and murdered in October 1923. *sitting A.F* – Sinn Féin Ard Féis. *Mary Mac, Fr Flanagan, Ruttledge & I are V.Ps, Daly & Stack Secs. Mrs Brugha & S O'Mara Treas* – Mary MacSwiney, P. J. Ruttledge, Fr Michael O'Flanagan, and Lynn were Vice Presidents of Sinn Féin, George Daly and Austin Stack, secretaries, Caitlín Brugha and Stephen O'Mara, treasurers.

praying. Stayed all night & encircled jail praying. Left at Angelus. Abt. 60 bandaged moved fr. Mtjoy to Tintown.[198]

Tuesday 30

8 a.m. R.mines. Nice day. Long Housing Comt. but did good work, D.G. Teac fair, but John Flynn bad, poor child. No trace of pen so far. I hope it is not gone finally. No news of Hunger Strikers. Our people inclined to use Larkin. I hope he won't use them. all ready for releases wh. D.V. will come v. soon. D.G. the men stand firm.

November

Wednesday 7

D.G. all girls released this evg. but 4 who weren't on H. Strike & 7 who wouldn't take a drink of water. Melina Phelan says splendid! No news of men yet. Adverse criticism of docking old age pensions in Council. Some boys so sad they had to come off H Strike. F.S. faked many documents, touts write them in prison & send out for capture. Teac just fairly.[199]

Thursday 22

8 a.m. R.mines. V. cold night, hard frost now, trees beautiful. Poor Madam taken over by Military & in N.D.U. S. Mitchell v. anxious abt. her, didn't mind other H. Strikers. Forms fixed for Newcastle, Mulcahy sways, day for the present & none are to be released, H. Strike or not. G.D. better D.G . Many girls at lunch time. Service at S. Ann's.[200]

December

Tuesday 4

8 a.m. R.mines. M, Emer & I had talk re Income tax, seems no way but to pay, they get even with you no matter how. Dr Jones gives trouble. Interviewed Dr Webb on her a/c., hope to arrange something. Went to S. Enda's & Roebuck. Long St. Comt. Meeting wh. did good work. Howth by last tram. Pt. holds her own. George H. better D.G.

198. *Arbour Hill* – Arbour Hill Prison, Dublin where some republican prisoners were being held. *Tintown* – Tin Town internment camp for republicans at the Curragh, Co. Kildare.
199. *all girls released* – most of the female anti-treaty republican prisoners remaining in the Dublin prisons were released. *Melina Phelan* – member of Ranelagh branch of Cumann na mBan.
200. *Poor Madam* – Countess Markievicz.

Saturday 8

Off fr. Howth by 9.45. Mrs L v. nicely. Nurse good. At No. 9 Emer says that Christabel is not Sylvia P. as I thought. C is a fraud, I know, but an able one. How can she write so! Aft. Miss Clarke & I went to Nativity play, it is better than ever. V. tired in evg. after a round. Dr Jones caves in.[201]

Monday 31

Wakened too early & then too late for Ch. sorry. V. busy all day with Nurses & many pts. Earthquakes in S. America too, they say. Severe avalanches in der Schive, many killed. Eng. in difficulties with no party strong enough to form a Govt. India & Afghanistan trouble her. Peter still there D.G. D.V. he'll come on. Madam M came late & was contentious. M v. late.

---

201. *Christabel* – Christabel Pankhurst (1880–1958), British suffragette. Christabel took a pro-imperial position during the War of Independence, unlike her sister Sylvia whom Lynn knew and admired and who was vocal in her support for Irish independence.

SECTION 2: 1924–32 POST-REVOLUTION

The Irish Free State was created from the ashes of the War of Independence and the short but vicious Civil War. While the Constitution of the Free State adopted in 1922 guaranteed equal citizenship and equal suffrage, the promised equality for which women militants had fought and expected was not forthcoming. The Free State was a highly conservative country in which the State, in partnership with the Catholic Church, had control over education and health care, and ensured that women's lives and bodies were subject to legislative, legal and moral controls. From 1923, a litany of legislative restrictions on women's rights, including restrictions on jury service, divorce, access to contraception, and employment especially of married women, were introduced. Representation of women in politics declined. Notwithstanding the election of five women TDs in 1923, only one took her seat. The other four, including Lynn, were Sinn Féin TDs who refused to take their seats because of the Oath of Allegiance. Instead, many political women found an outlet for their work in local government and in left-wing politics. These women were often involved in campaigns for better educational and healthcare policies, and, like Lynn, were against bad housing and unhygienic living conditions.

Infant mortality rates in Ireland remained steady in Ireland during this decade, at just over 70 per 1000, with a rate of over 90 per 1000 in urban areas. The causes of infant mortality also remained consistent, in 1932 the principal causes were congenital debility, diarrhoea and enteritis, premature birth, pneumonia, convulsions, congenital malformations and whooping cough, accounting for 82 per cent of all infant deaths. St Ultan's continued to expand, the number of in-patients treated increased by just over 70 per cent from 169 to 292 patients a year, the deathrate dropped from 44 per cent to 34 per cent. The outpatients department, which was seen by Lynn as central to the prevention of admissions by early treatment, grew by over 450 per cent in ten years, in 1932 10,766 cases were seen in the department. A new outpatient department, funded by the Irish White Cross, opened in 1927: it had previously been operating from 'a shed'. Lynn and ffrench-Mullen visited the USA in 1925 to raise funds and visit hospitals, they brought back new ideas including improved record keeping practices and the need for an electric breast pump, purchased in 1927. Other improvements included running water in the wards, a violet ray treatment lamp and vita-glass in the windows. All very much in keeping with Lynn's views on the importance of fresh-air, sunlight, and cleanliness. The pathology lab developed antigens for the treatment of whooping-cough and other disease outbreaks, and from 1931 they Schick tested all nurses for diphtheria, the hospital had six probationer nurses a year. In 1930 as funding from the Irish Hospitals' Sweepstakes became available the hospital purchased more land and started work on a new purpose-built wing.

For most radical, militant, anti-treaty women the years after 1923 were difficult. They did not feel welcome in the conservative, Catholic Irish Free State, which viewed women as second-class citizens whose rightful place was in the home. They were also very critical of the Free State Government's attitude to and marginalisation of anti-treaty republicans. The splits among the republican political groups, including Sinn Féin and Cumann na mBan, weakened the ability of republicans, and women, to influence policy. Even with Fianna Fáil in power, the backlash against the rights of women and women workers continued. Civil society women's groups brought the concerns of activists regarding the constant legislative subversion of their rights as citizens to the upper echelons of political power, but rarely had much impact. In this period Lynn left national politics when she lost her Dáil seat in the June 1927 General Election. She revived her hopes in de Valera somewhat when Fianna Fáil became the party of Government but would be soon disillusioned again. She remained very much involved in left-wing politics, joining the Friends of Soviet Russia with ffrench-Mullen and her long-time friends, Sighle Bowen and Helena Molony. She supported the rights of women workers through the Irish Women Workers' Union and wrote often of the need for a new women's movement. She worked as tirelessly as ever to develop St Ultan's with ffrench-Mullen, as always, by her side.

1924

January

Thursday 3

Nurse & Emer arrived quite early. V. cold, glad to be home. Seig. overjoyed to see E. M & I had lunch with Macs at Ritz. Madam & Emer there too. Bought warm coat, v.nice. V. wet. Trouble in Moscow, they say? true. Frontier trouble in India D.G. New F.S. postal orders marked (water) G.V.R !!![202]

Thursday 17

Madam in early v. exercised over Barton's position & rather justly. Many tales of trouble in F.S. army. The demobbed formed Union to take power themselves. V. wet. Hosp. Board went well. I fear babies neglected by me so much 'Flu. Bearded Mr Ruth in Merrion St. y.day. I fear no Gaelic Service on Sun.[203]

February

Friday 1

8 a.m. S. B's Brigid. A lovely sunshiny day with the bursting feeling of Spring. Robberies everywhere with little control. In Mullingar stormy scenes in Co. Council over reduction of wages. Free fight. Police & Military had "soothing" effect. Craig adamant over boundary. Nice practice in evg. for Sun. D.G. for the day.[204]

Sunday 17

Septuagesima. 8 a.m. Xt. Ch., beautiful sunrise over Sandycove Point, red gold sun, hard frost in night. Nice day, slept after b.fast. We had my goose for dinner & old port wh. Aunt F produced wh. I thought v. nasty. To Dublin for Gaelic Service at 5. We were in nave & rather

---

202. *Nurse* – Dora Maguire (1889–1931), nurse and Cumann na mBan member, active in the organisation and in the Women's Prisoners Defence League in the 1920s.

203. *The demobbed* – with the ending of the Civil War, Richard Mulcahy, Minister for Defence sought to reduce the size of the Free State army by 37,000 men. This was resisted by elements, including senior officers, within the National Army.

204. *Craig* – James Craig, 1st Viscount Craigavon (1871–1940), leading unionist, and first Prime Minister of Northern Ireland. *boundary* – The Boundary Commission, which was to determine the final geographical division between the two jurisdictions, did not meet until November 1924.

lost but it was wonderful all the same. 3 babies dead in Teac, my little Elizabeth. Back to D/L 8 o/c.

Tuesday 26

8 a.m. R.mines, hurried after for funeral at 10, it was nice little Service, the poor wee mite, a nice day & place so peaceful. F. Clarke came, we visited her grave & Cousin Robert's & Aunt Rebeccas, he is dead 30 yrs now. Runaway horse passed us in Ailesbury Rd. hope he hurt no one. Hear F.S. is setting up Testimonial for Dan Breen, strange. Miss Young came re Memorial book. A.G.O.W. D.G.[205]

April

Tuesday 1

8 a.m. R.mines. This was Easter Day last year, dear F's last Sun. in this world. Ah, the time flies but the world isn't the same. Letter fr. N & M, glad, I'll go down soon. Terrible revelations in papers re money gone in F.S. army, all so sordid & low. How they have fallen! Emer has report of Wireless Enquiry. Figgis comes out v.badly. Sad. Matron back, her brother much better.[206]

Sunday 6

Passion Sun. 8 am. R.mines. Procession for all murdered of Dub. Brigade v. fine, plackards, wreaths & flowers, all marched Glasnevin. Sean Lemass gave oration, right heroic note. Back to Larkin's meeting. C.I.D. T.D O'Driscoll tried to forge car thro', fired 5 shots, no one hurt D.G. Dinner Susie, Irish Service v. nice. Prayed in S. Lawrence O'Toole's Chapel. Supper Rhodes. Whist Drive for Book. Lect. E. Young.[207]

---

205. *Dan Breen* (1894–1969), anti-treaty republican, later a Fianna Fáil TD. *Miss Young* – Ella Young, secretary from 1922 of the Irish Republican Memorial Committee, which commissioned Art O'Murnaghan (1872-1954) to decorate a volume of names, *Leabhar na hAiséirigh*, which combined Irish mythology with the people, places and events from the Easter Rising and the War of Independence. *A.G.O.W.* – All goes on well.
206. *Wireless Enquiry* – established in December 1923 to decide on how to establish a public radio broadcasting service. Darrell Figgis (1882–1925) was co-opted onto the enquiry, a decision that led to a series of allegations of corruption, with Figgis as the focus.
207. *Sean Lemass* (1899–1971), anti-treaty republican, elected a TD in November 1924. Fianna Fáil Taoiseach 1959–66. *Larkin* – Jim Larkin (1874–1947), republican, socialist and trade union leader, recently returned to Ireland from the US.

Sunday 13

Palm Sun. 8 a.m. S. Pat.'s in snow, ride K.bridge, M nearly late for Fermoy. Larkin ran train to Roscrea just after Marlboro' snowballs after summer. Ann, Jane, Susie came. Surely 50,000 in Fermoy splendid march to cemetery. All passed Liam Lynch's grave & on to field where Sean T gave oration. After we left F.S. made trouble. Saw many old friends, one of Larkin's men hurt, sunset glorious, ball of gold.[208]

May

Wednesday 7

8 a.m. S. B's. Glad to be there. V. showery, cold day. Papers say all internees to be out soon, we'll fight for all prisoners. Stormy council Meeting over Child Welfare but we carried it D.G. When in Teac more trouble with Dr Jones, she is dreadful. V. busy evg. v. late, many pts.

Thursday 8

8 a.m. Xt. Ch. v. cold day. In interview Cosgrave glories in having executed good men, the best. It is awful. Some say F.S. will proclaim Republic for 26 counties but doubtful, tariffs work out badly for people. Aft. spoke at Harold's X Ch. Welfare, fine crowd. Man killed in Stephen's Green was friend of Henry's, run down by racing motor cycle on Sun.

Thursday 29

Ascension Day. 8 a.m. R.mines. Beautiful 5th anniversary of opening of Teac. All went well D.G. Gt & enthusiastic crowd, all enjoyed themselves. We got nearly £30. Gas strike settled we don't know how. No news fr. Limerick, but that contest closed & re-count, which on whole looks well for us. Evg. S.F. meetings, making badges hard.

June

Friday 6

M up early. Teac as usual. Matron's scalded foot better. Arranged for Miss Steadmond. Meeting Mansion Ho. re scrapping of Corporation. Irwine & Moran not allowed to talk. All others well received. Poor L.

---

208. *Sean T* – Seán T. O'Kelly (1882–1966), anti-treaty republican leader, later President of Ireland 1945–59.

Mayor v. ill. Sent for at 2 a.m. to see new born infant with external band interfering with respiration & [ ] action.[209]

Wednesday 18

Smuts thrown out at S. African election, good, D.V. same will happen here. Dr Jones definitely resigned to Med. Board made hurtful insinuations. We accepted resignation. Teac fairly D.G. Many pts. to see & much work. Poor Hanratty off [ ] I.R.P DF & v. rheumaticky still. We must try W.X. for him. Bodenstown next Sun.[210]

Thursday 19

V. busy, rush to R.farnham & Clonskea before Board. Dr Jones wrote terrible letter, poor thing, it is a pity of her. V satisfactory talk in evg. with Dr McDonald re new Child Welfare Centre in R.mines. Hope to get it going soon. M & I met B. Brennan then, he is v. hopeful D.V. soon we'll be free. Emer has v. disquieting news of Larkin starting strikes just to smash Transport Union.[211]

Sunday 22

11.A.T. 8 a.m. R.mines. Glorious day, started by 11.45 train for Bodenstown, an anxious time for we didn't know what F.S. might do, but D.G. we didn't clash, they were at 1.30, we at 3. We had fine turn out. I had to represent Govt. & lay cross on grave. Brian O'Higgins gave splendid oration, inspiring. Sent Nurse home in taxi. Keane on lorry with the people. We didn't clear expenses.[212]

July

Wednesday 2

Awake early, finer, up abt. 7 & had run in wet grass with M & Shuler, back to bed to get warm & then bath in river, v. cold but lovely. Showers all day & some bright sun. Unpacked & fixed up. House really wonderful after the year. We broke bed getting it upstairs fr.

209. *scrapping of Corporation* – There was a strained relationship between the Irish Free State and Dublin Corporation; Dublin Corporation was scrapped in 1924, under the Local Government (Temporary Provisions) Act, 1923 which gave the government the power to dissolve local authorities. It was restored in 1930.
210. *Hanratty* – John Hanratty (1892–1965), Irish Citizen Army.
211. *B. Brennan* – Robert 'Bob' Brennan (1881–1964), republican, journalist, writer, and diplomat, director of publicity for the anti-treaty republicans.
212. *Brian O'Higgins* (1882–1963) Sinn Féin politician and anti-treaty republican.

sittingroom, too bad. Lipton send double supply of most things, whole bag of flour. Shuler & Cairogue good.[213]

Friday 18

Up v. early for Mrs ffM going by 1st train 9 o/c. M went with her. Nurse & I went back to bed for 3 hrs & slept. V. windy day, some showers. M & Susie arr. abt. 2 old time. All much pleased with all that has happened. We bathed & planted ash seedlings for all & sundry, a lovely Arbor day. In evg. we & Farrells had fine bonfires for Dev. Hear same in Rathdrum. V. good.[214]

Wednesday 23

Dev's reception in Mansion Ho. on Mon. was surpassing, solid block fr. Green to Molesworth St. Maher fainted in Mansion Ho. Dev spoke outside too. Said Indep. must be maintained at all costs. Susie arr. safe & saw it D.G. We had a quiet day, good deal of rain, couldn't wash, river rose a bit. Word still fr. W.D.G. Eng. Lab. Govt. defeated twice in one night. We baked & sewed & [ ].

August

Thursday 14

Saw pts. & hurried up for 4.40 train. Matron & her party came with me to Kingsbridge. M joined us there, fine crowd. Dev got gt. send off, royal progress all way to Limerick. crowds at station, gt. enthusiasm. Limerick outpassed itself, such cheering, all party tea Hanrattys, 9 motors Ennis, lunar eclipse & rainbow, 2nd in week. Triumph entry Ennis. Nearly every house illuminated, gt. day.

Friday 15

Such a contrast fr. last yr., cheering thousands. Mary Mac & I shared room in Queen's. Attended Dev's Mass, 12, Cathedral, 2 the gt. meeting say fr. 30 to 40 thousand there. Ennis had her own decorations, gt. boughs in barrels, mottoes & pennants etc. Brian O'Higgins' speech marvellous. Dev fine too, crowd so thick that heavy shower never

---

213. *Shuler & Ciarogue* – Lynn and ffrench-Mullen's dog and cat.
214. *fine bonfires for Dev* – Éamon de Valera was unconditionally released from Arbour Hill Prison on 17 July.

damped ground. Tyrone, Derry, Fermanagh represented as well as South. Not a hitch. We left by 7 train for Dublin.[215]

Friday 22

Awake 5.45. M down fussing abt. tea for 7.30, dentist 9, Nan did v. well had 6 out. We put her to bed & she looks well. Kitten fine, back here, all well. F. Clarke took triplets in Teac. Hear F.S. has lost much over boundary affair. Big meeting in O'Connell St. on Tues. Hear raids expected on account of D. Macardles tragedies in Kerry.[216]

Wednesday 27

8 a.m. S.B's. Nice day. Heard a [ ] prisoners in huts that guards might go & vote at elections, v. probable. Poor man at Clarecastle shot on 15th quite admittedly by military for not halting, awful. Poor prem. dead & another. Matron v. good. Saved my money for me to pay bill of Dr Crofton's. Got fright abt. Madeline who never turned up till 1 a.m. I had been asleep, got up to look for her. Not at 63.[217]

Thursday 28

Didn't get up early after late night. M v. penitent, went off with some Americans to Miss Cranwill's & forgot time. Did good work, however. Saw Hanratty, he is bad, poor chap. Wet all day. Aft. Comt. at Clonskea. hosp. All well there. Terrible hurricane on sea. 24 1st class passengers hurt. Saw boy in evg. going to U.S.A. Schada . All arranged now D.G. for Gaelic Services on 4th & 7th. Teac fair but Joseph gone.[218]

September

Sunday 14

13 A.T. 8 a.m. R.mines. Went with E. Donnelly & others to Kilkenny at 10, glorious day & sun, lovely car. Arr. in 2 ½ hours. Excellent convention there. Good work done. E thinks another round up

---

215. *Mary Mac & I shared room in Queen's* – Mary MacSwiney and Lynn stayed in the Queens Hotel in Ennis, Co. Clare, joining de Valera on his speaking tour in Munster.

216. *D. Macardles tragedies in Kerry.* – Dorothy Macardle's book, *Tragedies of Kerry*, about the National Army violence in Kerry during the Civil War, published in 1924.

217. *Poor man at Clarecastle shot* – Michael Hartnett, from Tipperary town, was shot dead by the Free State military coming from de Valera's meeting in Ennis. *63* – 63 Moyne Rd, home of Madeleine's mother.

218. *Miss Cranwill* – most likely Maria 'Mia' Cranwill (1880–1972), design and metal artist.

coming, D.V. not. We all went to S. Canice's & saw it as well as twilight permitted. Arr. home 12.15. Part of way only tipped road in places. All well here. Matron's sister does well.[219]

Monday 15

8 a.m. S. B's. Nice day till aft. when rain, high wind. Nurse saw Dr Keogh, tonsils & adenoids to come out. Saw Fr Ronane in mg., he is puzzled he says. Dev never had larger meeting in Cork. Mary Mac jubilant. We, M & I have housing scheme on. Poor Ramsay Macdonald in trouble over motor. Madam escaped safe in motor crash, drunken driver drove into them.[220]

Sunday 28

15 A.T. 8 a.m. R.mines. Rebecca not there. By 10 a.m. train to Dunleer for convention. Meetings to be at B.fast, Newry, Armagh, Omagh, Derry. Speakers may all be arrested. Mrs S.S. went to B.fast. We went to Anagassen, nice little spot, wonderful panorama of Mourne mts. along bay. Nice day. We walked a lot. Convention fair. All went well at home. M better & Nurse, D.G.

October

Wednesday 3

8 a.m. S. B's, nice day, no rain D.G. Nurse came back in evg. Miss Conroy had nice letter fr. Cardinal Logue. Hear they are raiding actively & following people again, horrid. The Shannon Electric Scheme is v. sinister, to supply Liverpool & Manchester with cheap electricity when they have no coal. Eng. is a demon, so cute. Little lad does well in country.[221]

Monday 13

8 a.m. S. B's. Lovely warm, sunny day. 10 a.m. went with Housing Comt. to Kimmage to view defects, it was beautiful there, defects not

---

219. *E. Donnelly* – Eamon Donnelly (1877–1944), Director of Organisation, Sinn Féin, later a founder member of Fianna Fáil.
220. *Ramsey MacDonald* (1866–1937) – Labour Prime Minister of United Kingdom 1929–35.
221. *Cardinal Logue* – Michael Logue (1840–1924), Archbishop of Armagh and Primate of All Ireland. *Shannon Electric Scheme* – The Shannon hydroelectric Scheme was the first major industrial development by the Irish Free State in the 1920s to harness the power of the River Shannon and marked the beginning of the electrification of Ireland.

much, D.G. I. Times says Miss Hales heckled Dev in Cork y.day abt. her brother, poor thing. Busy Comt. meeting in evg. All F.S. v. mad we contest elections in Ulster. P.T. Daly wants us to join with his party, no thanks, thunderstorm in night.[222]

Monday 20

8 a.m. S. B's. Brought Mrs Clarkin back to Elin. Nice, quiet day, v. good reports fr. Ulster. Mary Mac got good reception & so did Mrs Skeffington. Long round in mg. Evg. met N & M at B.stone, sad their leaving home, they had much luggage, saw them off at W.Row, then St. Comt. Much discussed. Burial of restored bodies, so many abt. 80–what a sight! A country's mourning.[223]

Wednesday 29

8 a.m. S. B's, the gt. polling day. All will be well in Ireland. Left 1.25 for B.inrobe, good journey, I have to speak at Cross for Tuam boys executed, brought wreaths wh. sent to Oughterard, Donagh Patrick & Athlone, so all had their laurels. O'Donnell drove me to Cross. Maguires, surprised, told how all way fr. Athlone last night saluted executed boys. Mrs M satisfied now she has body. Tom M is fine.[224]

November

Friday 7

8 a.m. S.B's. Hear all prisoners in F.S. to be released because they're frightened. New British Govt. may smash their election campaign going hard. Hear I am to go to Mayo, not Cork. Mrs Ginnell in, much bothered over I.R.B. Many children have kind of 'Flu so many in Disp. to-day. M busy over opening of Child Welfare in Harold's X.[225]

---

222. *Miss Hales* – sister of pro-Treaty politician Seán Hales (1880–1922), who was assassinated by anti-treaty republicans on 7 December 1922. *P. T. Daly* – Patrick Thomas Daly (1870–1943), trade unionist and politician.

223. *Mary Mac got good reception & so did Mrs Skeffington* – The republican women were campaigning in the Northern Ireland 1924 General Election. *N and M* – Nan and Muriel, Lynn's sisters, leaving the family home in Cong. *Burial of restored bodies* – the bodies of 77 executed republican men were handed over to their families by the military for reburial in family or republican plots.

224. *the gt. polling day* – The 1924 United Kingdom general election in Northern Ireland was held on 29 October. *Tuam Boys* – these were six anti-treaty republicans executed in Tuam Military Barracks on 11 April 1923, they included John Maguire whose family Lynn references here.

225. *I.R.B* – Irish Republican Brotherhood, a secret oath-bound fraternal organisation dedicated to the establishment of an Irish Republic, founded in the nineteenth century.

Friday 14

8 a.m. S. B's. Wet night, finer day, all preps. for opening at Harold's X. Child Welfare extension, it went v. well, the room looks nice & all were v. pleased, queer the 2 Republicans, M & I, got all the "cudos". McCreedy's mem among public to-day, why? What good will they do England? Emer v. unsatisfactory, all well at Teac. Mrs Despard denies putting wreath on cenotaph.[226]

Wednesday 19

8 a.m. S. B's. A Thanksgiving Day. Sean Lemass in with 957 majority D.G. Cork & Mayo doing well, heard terrible news that poor Mrs Darrell Figgis committed suicide last night, shot herself in taxi, poor thing, she was so much better than he. Cardinal Logue dead! In Council this mg. they put in F.S. in place of Rep. wh. ws most unfair.[227]

December

Tuesday 9

8 a.m. R.mines, sunny mg. babies out so rosy, railways now definitely made English, terrible. Wrote to I. Times repudiating statement that I founded Teac. Chevasses in Town, saw them in evg. Nice photos of [ ] Sebgrania. Evg. Miss Young's lecture on old Gaelic Hymns, v. wonderful. We sang out best to illustrate. It shapes an epoch. Shots in R.mines 4 at 10 & one just now – 1.30 a.m.

Wednesday 10

8 am. S. B's, such a dark, foggy day. Ard Chomairle at 11, it did few things, but well, on whole, D.G. Discussed Language, Economic position & elected St. Comt. Miss Broderick came with me to Teac & discussed school feeding, she is a fine soul. Teac fairly D.G. Fran robbed in Belgrave Sqr. last night. Hear prisoners in robbery case "absconded" were doubtless F.S.[228]

---

226. *McCreedy's mem* – this may refer to the fact that Nevil Macready, Commander in Chief of the British Forces during the War of Independence, published his two-volume memoirs, *Annals of an Active Life*, in November 1924.

227. *Sean Lemass* – anti-treaty Sinn Féin candidate, Lemass was victorious in the South Dublin constituency. *Mrs Darrell Figgis* – Millie Figgis, née Tate, committed suicide on 18 November 1924.

228. *Ard Chomairle* – Sinn Féin National Committee of which Lynn was a member. *Miss Broderick* – Albina Broderick.

Monday 29

Left Aunt F's 9.30, she is determined now L must go whatever it was happened last night. D.G. for that anyhow. L may resist however. Hear Mrs Skeffington & O'Millane up for nom. for S. City, hope Mrs S will be chosen. All went well over Xmas. E. Donnelly not back & no organist. Comt. M was going to Olga, lost hat in storm. D.G. she didn't go. Sweeps of rain & storm. Terrible.[229]

---

229. *L* – Lucy, Aunt F's maid. *O'Millane* – M. J. O'Mullane, Independent Republican.

1925

January

Sunday 4

2 A. Xmas. 8 a.m. R.mines. M arrived immediately after, safe & sound D.G. After fearful crossings, esp. last Tues. she was sure boat couldn't survive waves. She is fine & has lots to tell. Was to be aft. Ch. prisoners' meeting here, but we went by Mrs Hodges (1.10) & people gone before we got out, too bad. Aft. Aunt F. L is bad. N & M v. anxious. Went to pt. in Bray, baby, back as soon as possible, reaction after prick.

Thursday 8

8 a.m. Xt. Ch. Such a nice warm day! bright sun. Char here did well. Saw Mrs Dev & had long chat over Xt. State. Mrs Bonfield wants more advice again, I said get another Dr. Aft. tea with Scotts for N & M. I brought Shuler, he was good. Aunt F off again fr. sending L home. Dr Stopford married this mg. Emer stayed, Isult came, [ ] Sierg not better.[230]

February

Monday 2

Left Aunt F early, nice sunshine, all well here. M saw to B.P. stove. Cosgrave's meeting y.day = C.I.D. & all the D.M.P. in Dublin & Republicans, every questioner was batoned, arms twisted, all the old D.M.P. tactics. K O'H's meeting = 200, mostly police. Hear "F.S" will have to call moratorium, can't get money in. Poor Norgrove, got 6 mos. hard & £20 fine for discovered dump. Nurse better D.G. McCanns raided.[231]

Thursday 5

V. busy mg. We tried to put down congoleum sqr. & broke a bit out of it. M so delighted with film "America" took F. Clarke & me there, it is wonderful, we understand the fight for freedom here. Fine to see

---

230. *Dr Stopford* – Dorothy Stopford (1890–1954), married George 'Liam' Price, from now on she is referred to as Dr Price in the diaries.
231. *K O'H's* – Kevin O'Higgins, Minister for Justice, Irish Free State. *Norgrove* – Alfred Norgrove, an underground bunker containing arms and ammunition found at his house on North Stand, Dublin.

Union Jack retiring. In Teac had to send Nurse to Cork St. & disinfect dormitory, took 2 nurses here. Saw Miss Lahiffe, she may suit for here.

Saturday 7

A lovely day till 5 or so, such sun! Hurried in mg. & caught 2.30 for Carrick. Mrs Skeff. & Buckley with me. A Mtjoy wardress in carriage & E. Blythe in next going to Dromod. P.P. met him. We drove fr. Carrick to Manorhamilton i.e Cluan O'Rorke. N. Hoyne seemed well but abt. 11 had big haem. fr. lung, terrible shock. I stayed with her all night, D.G. she rallied. Dr Dolan v. good. He had accident same day. Hotel people most kind.[232]

Saturday 28

8 a.m. S. B's. Long busy day. Tea with F. Clarke, Mrs Fisher there. Mrs Skeff. M & I went with many more by 6.30 to Kilkenny. Miss O'Daly v. worried because she alone went to Carlow, our literature fine. G.D. better. Duffy in charge. Kenny does his best. V. grand hotel. Our room looks out over Castle grounds. Town like Bruges, such quaint old buildings etc. We'd like to stay weeks & explore.[233]

March

Tuesday 3

Sean Lemass, S. McBride, G.D. & Art O'Connor in train, said I was wanted in Ballina, so I came back fr. Athlone. Saw Cummins there. A.G.O.W. Papers full of unedifying F.S speeches. Arr. Ballina after 7, a glorious sunshiny day. Croagh Patrick looked like an enchanted mountain in the evg. sun with wonderful lights on it. Later Nephin all white, looked beautiful too & there was a glimpse of the home mts. Many military left Athlone, fully armed for Sligo & Ballina. Tommies unoffensive, officers thugs. Will there be foul work on Wed.? All hopeful in Ballina & glad to see me. Had a walk up past the Church felt so much F & M were with me in the lovely moonlight with sounds of rushing water. Had lovely quiet time in S. Mary's Athlone, nice Ch. Quaint 17th cent. monuments.[234]

---

232. *Mrs Skeff. & Buckley with me* – Hanna Sheehy Skeffington and Margaret Buckley. *N. Hoyne* – Nellie Murray (née Hoyne), anti-treaty Cumann na mBan, hospitalised after being on hunger strike during the Civil War.
233. *Miss O'Daly* – Agnes O'Daly, anti-treaty Cumann na mBan, from Limerick, sister of Kathleen Clarke.
234. *Art O'Connor* (1888–1950), politician, lawyer, and judge.

Tuesday 31

8 a.m. R.mines. Nice day. Dr Goulding says Child Welfare not wanted in R.mines, death rates low! The horror of a mind like his! Nurse Jackson left, poor thing. Teac nicely. Chrissie Doyle came there & wanted M's & my signatures in her book! Prep. for pig fight in Council to-morrow.[235]

April

Thursday 2

8 a.m. Xt.Ch. Cold, nice day. Special Teac Board re. O.P Dept. painting etc. N Hoyne v. well. Papers say we may get 2 in in North, fine! Aft. lect. on Mothercraft in H.X. V. well attended D.G. Miss Tyndall not v. well. Evg. our P.H. meeting. V. good. M. at special Mansion Ho. meeting re. Income Tax. Hear Dr Barry going to U.S.A. for F.S. under Rockfeller Scheme.

Wednesday 29

Council & v. long & worrying P. Health at 10 o/c. Mason terrible over pigs. Fine cold day. Mrs Dev won't meet Americans. She is dreadful. It is such a pity. They have got v. nice new house in own grounds. Teac nicely. Eng. budget takes off more than F.S. & gives widows pensions & to all over 65, good.[236]

May

Saturday 9

Disturbed night, fainted, so glad M with me. Have been eating too much & doing too little. Got all done in good time. M & I went to Amiens St. Met Aunt F, nice journey to Rostrevor. Met Mansfield girl going to Mourne College. Nan met us at W.point. Aunt F. delighted. Poor Jane away, sister dead. All looks v. nice, all well.

Friday 22

Warmer, sl. rain, Emer v bad, long talk with Miss Bennett. D.V. something will come of it. Miss Tyndall still there & conscious. Gt.

235. *Dr Goulding* – Henry Benson Goulding (*d.*1931). *Chrissie Doyle* – Crissie Doyle published her book, *Women in Ancient and Modern Ireland*, in 1917. Doyle was a former member of Inghinidhe na hÉireann.
236. *long & worrying P. Health* – Public Health Committee of Rathmines and Rathgar Urban District Council, Lynn and ffrench-Mullen proposed that pig keeping within Rathmines be regulated and piggeries cleaned out more often.

preps. for our annual meeting – Wolf Tone. D.V. some spirit will come in to things.[237]

Sunday 24

5 A.E. 8 a.m. R.mines. Nice sunny day. Emer wonderful, consents to have treat. & seems as if there was hope of her faith D.G, it is wonderful. God grant fulfilment of all. O'Hegartys gave £5.5 for Teac D.G. Dinner Nugents. Sylvie has a "flame" at last D.G. Evg. S. Columba's, went to Roebuck, a day of Thanksgiving.

June

Sunday 21

2 A.T. 8 a.m. R.mines. Gt. rumours of trouble to be at Bodenstown. M, Susie & Nurse stayed at home for election work. I went. Wonderful crowds, glorious day. Long, long procession. Dev headed it. Dev came soon after. 3 small Fianna boys sounded last post. Oration in big field for crowds. Saw heaps I knew. F.S. in official force, no gen. public. Returned, election work till 11.30. D.G. all was peaceful.

Thursday 25

M. v. tired after all, she is so good after disappointment. How foolish the H.X people were, to put Maddock before her! Now she is off raffling toy kitchen for Teac wh.goes well. D.G. I got off by 6.30 train for Corris. Cousin F. v. kind. Had long talk with L who is really better, I think, & Corris is restful & peaceful D.G. Cousin F says she will visit us in Glenmalure.[238]

Tuesday 30

8 a.m. R.mines. Council Meeting 10 re. Committees of course. Unionist & C. na nG. voted Maddock Chair. & Healy Vice. Comts. went all right, fair enough. M & I went to Shelbourne & saw Abp.'s niece, Miss Mannix, nice girl. M gave letter re. prayer into his hand. Saw Dev there. Evg. went Mrs C. B's but no Australians came, they are v. tall & portly. Conference in London. Tim Craig& Co.[ ].[239]

---

237. *Emer v bad* – concerned over Helena Molony's drinking, a recurring theme in the diaries. *Miss Bennett* – Louie Bennett (1870–1956), leading member of the Irish Women Workers' Union (IWWU).
238. *Maddock before her* – Sir Simon Maddock, Chairman of Rathmines Urban District Council.
239. *Comts. went all right* – Lynn was elected to the Housing and Building and Public Health Committees, while she and ffrench-Mullen were on the Child Welfare Committee.

July

Wednesday 22

Warm overcast day. M & I washed & bathed. Poor Shuler v. sick & sorry for himself in mg. but was quite lively & hunted plenty when F.C. & I climbed to amphitheatre. It was misty & splendid, 3 distinct tiers of Lug visible. Shuler lay in stream to cool at Grahams. A fisherman came early. Glorious golden sunset fading v. fast.

Sunday 26

7 A.T. Only Mattins & sermon. At Ballinaclash, Mr Hammond there as usual. Susie, Sylvie & I up abt. 6 new time, an hour too soon as we discovered, they went to 8.30 Mass (old time). I had rest, b.fast & started for 11.30 (N.T.). Nice to be in Ch. again. Hard ride home, V. tired. M here D.G. Dinner went all right for the 7, such a squash. Then D.G. men left. We showed girls stone cottage, rested then. V. heavy thunder, rain. Night absolutely deluge. High wind.[240]

August

Tuesday 4

Much better this mg. Quite anxious to be up before M would let me. We were expecting Madam & car fr. early. Argentine Consul & backup came fishing. Nice, v. calm day. Had all packed & N started for train before they arr. D MacArdle, Rosine Jacob & Madam, they were pleased with place, lovely drive home, found house spotless & all well D.G. Did good deal of unpacking & settling.[241]

Thursday 27

An eventful day. Housing sub Comt. went well. Special Teac Board approves of our U.S.A. plans. Teac babies hold their own, outside ones fine D.G. French getting gt. beating fr. Druses in Holy Land. Sent for 2-3 places at once. Went to S.cove to see Muriel's Miss Griffin, not bad. Got Council Group. Excellent. Mary has tidied it away. Nurse arrested again. Pr. of Wales as before. She'll get a month now.[242]

---

240. *(N.T.).* – New Time. The Summer Time Act, 1925 provided a default summer time period, when Irish summer time would be one hour in advance of West-European time.

241. *D MacArdle, Rosine Jacob & Madam* – Dorothy Macardle, Rosamond Jacob and Countess Markievicz all came to visit the holiday cottage in Glencormac.

242. *Sandycove* – a coastal town on the outskirts of Dublin. *Nurse arrested* – Dora Maguire, nurse at St Ultan's and anti-treaty member of Cumann na mBan, who caused a disturbance in a cinema when the Prince of Wales appeared on the screen.

Friday 28

8 a.m. S. B's. Lovely day, b.fast in garden. Emer & M went to hear Nurse's case. She wouldn't choose to be heard in Police Court & is sent for Circuit court wh. sits end of Oct. or Nov. She'll be on remand in Mt.joy till then. All v. sorry for her. I saw Mr [ ]Cubsen, magistrate re. her, v. nice, Many babies bad. Guild Practice for S. Ultan. Slum photos quite good.

September

Monday 7

M & I both v. sleepy in mg. Both went to see Nurse in Mt.joy & found Maeve Phelan had taken our visit & so we had all toil for nothing. M went about T. Ashe concert to [ ] at St. Comt. I asked abt. Dr Mannix & his Unity talk. We wanted Dr Mannix for T.A. concert & he would not give definite reply.[243]

Wednesday 9

Papers full of Drs Meeting y.day. No mention of De Burca, no mention of Dr Mannix. Teac nicely on whole. Saw Margt.'s solr. Mr Kerr, seems nice, says she got almost full amt., v. strange she is positive it was only £17.10. Saw over Leinster Soap Works, v. interesting, hope all will go well with it. Talked with S.Bowen & some more C na mB. Nurse is to have hot water bottle, D.G. Cold day.[244]

Tuesday 15

8 a.m. R.mines. Saw Nurse with S. Humphries at 10 o/c. long & satisfactory talk. Child Welf. 11, long & complicated, saw Mrs Kettle after 2. U.S.A. ladies expected at Teac, only one came. Aft. Hosp. Board, Healy such a stupid man. Evg. heard Mrs Joe MacDonagh to marry [ ] Murphy at 6 a.m. to-morrow. Heard poor Mr Kelly in Clonmel Asylum, what happened him! V. hard day, such difficult things to do.[245]

---

243. *Maeve Phelan* – Cumann na mBan member.
244. *De Burca* – Seamus De Búrca (1893–1967), Minister for Local Government and Public Health. *S. Bowen* – Sheila (Sighle) Bowen, later Dowling (*c*.1896–1957), trade unionist, feminist, member of Cumann na mBan.
245. *S. Humphries* – Sighle Humphreys, senior anti-treaty Cumann na mBan activist. *Mrs Joe MacDonagh* – Margaret 'May' (née O'Toole) widow of Joe MacDonagh, Sinn Féin TD, anti-treatyite and director of the Belfast Boycott, died in 1922 of burst appendix. She married Finton Murphy in September 1925.

Friday 25

> Early to Miss Dill Smyth. Nellie Gifford that was came after b.fast &
> her nice little girl. Disp.big. We all think advt. in papers for workmen
> for Shannon Scheme terrible. Conditions like barracks, v. evil. Emer &
> her Society are putting in counterblast D.G. tomorrow. Evg. letter fr.
> Mrs Kelly, Pittsfield, not at all encouraging.[246]

October

Saturday 3

> Only awake at 8. Sorry. V. nice day. Dublin Opinion fine on Shannon
> Scheme. Hundreds have left Hibernian Insurance because English
> now. D.G. Got many presents, chickens, widgeon, damson & plum
> jam, so kind. Long talk with Mrs Marlowe in evg. Emer & I gardened in
> Peace in aft. bulb planting. Saw Mrs O'Byrne re Nellie.

Monday 19

> We both slept well. M still unable to be up, happy in bed. Had nice sea
> water bath, it got rough at mid-day & is still. Everyone most kind &
> attentive. Wind fr. S., sea doesn't look so v. rough but boat tosses a
> lot & creaks. We are well off in airy deck cabin, terribly tuffy in lower
> ones. P. Farrer hasn't appeared yet. Young ones enjoy sliding about.
> Read [ ].[247]

November

Sunday 1

> 21 A.T. 8 a.m. Usu. Ch. Saw O'Brien & Solan 10.30, rush to Babies
> Hosp. v. nice, splendidly equipped, Labs. etc. Good Enceph. case
> treated with Serum. Lovely day. Black babies such darlings. Drs all
> v. kind & helpful. Dinner Kerley's 1.30. Mrts v. nice, 2 young married
> daughters & their husbands, jolly family party. Mrs K took us Riverside
> drive & round Central Park. sunset glorious, ball of fire in soft haze
> thro' trees. Saw a few original wooden houses of N.Y. one v. nice with

---

246. *Nellie Gifford* – Helen Ruth ('Nellie') Donnelly née Gifford (1880–1971), suffragette, republican and trade union activist, curated the first exhibitions about the revolutionary period in the National Museum of Ireland. Married Joseph Donnelly in 1918 in America, they separated, and she returned to Ireland with their daughter Maeve in 1921.
247. *boat tosses a lot & creaks* – Lynn and ffrench-Mullen sailed to the USA on a fundraising drive for St Ultan's and to view children's hospitals and child welfare provisions. They were particularly interested in hearing about new therapies and seeing new equipment.

verandah. Evg. went to Central Club, Mary Mac didn't come. Both v. tired, early to bed.[248]

Thursday 5

7.30 Usu. Ch. called "Little Ch. round corner" famed for kind of Gretna Green marriages. Nice day. Went to consultation at Babies Hosp. Saw some good cases. Lead poisoning, Syph. one just like Teac to have breast milk. Then Miss Leckie, then rush for photographer at 3 o/c. I never saw such lamps before, taken in Irish dress, then to Dr Kerley who has written such nice letters for us, then rush back in shuttle, in busiest time, never saw such a squash, swallowed supper, our party at Leckies, did well, Molonys, O'Brien, Solan Godfrey, Herbert, Moynihan. Bed 12 o/c.[249]

Friday 13

7.30 Usu. Ch. Early to Bellvue, Miss Ryan showed us over it, a wonderful place, over 2,000 there. Many remember Miss Brennan & her influence still works. About 12 babies born p. day there, charming Chinese Sister over them. Old ferry boat for T.B. children. Psychopathic Dept. for sick prisoners. Fine Kindergarten. Saw wonderful plastic face result. Dr Lavers motored us later. Lunch Mrs de Lisser. Nice evg. Keoghs Edgewater.[250]

Thursday 19

8.30 S. P's. Went 1st to Dr Emerson, he gave much literature re his [ ] fad, Perfect Health, says Drs only treat disease. Washington Ave. fine. Met M at Children's Hosp. Dr Smith showed us round & was v. nice. Saw Dr Stone also. Saw babies in Incubator room who did well. Lunch Wom. City Club. Mr. Hollowell showed Health Unit, v.perfect. Evg. dinner to Graham Brooks Hotel Vendome. Mr Pearmain talked abt. M. Childers, her uncle.

Wednesday 25

Packed in mg. & checked out. Went to Mrs Callender. M got carried on at 126th St. thought we should never meet again! She thought she was

---

248. *Babies Hosp* – the Babies Hospital was New York's first dedicated Children's Hospital, founded in 1887 by Drs Sarah and Julia McNutt, it is now the Morgan Stanley Children's Hospital.
249. *Little Ch. round corner* – Church of the Transfiguration, Manhattan.
250. *Bellvue* – Bellevue Hospital, the oldest public hospital in the United States. *Miss Brennan* – Agnes S. Brennan (*b.*1859), was director of the nurses training school in the hospital from 1888 to 1902, her father was Irish.

right, I knew I was. Just as I was despairing kind lady told me she saw her. I rushed & found her D.G. Had rushed lunch with Mrs C. Back in snow to Mrs Villard, saw over Catharine Blackwell's hosp, glad to see it. Evg. King's Park, Mr Brown & Anna met us. Mrs McCarthy v. nice.[251]

December

Friday 11

7.30 Usu. Ch. A gt. Peace came to me there & I know I may leave M safe in his hands & D.V. I'll be back soon to her. Was long in mg. getting ticket transferred, then got typewriter M had chosen y.day, then Mr Walsh, J.C. abt. office, saw likely place & beautiful Firenz tea rooms. Got few Xmas things. M so brave, dear child. Dr McGuinness came with $50 Xmas box Teac. Nellie soon off D.G.[252]

251. *Catharine Blackwell's hosp* – Lynn means Elizabeth Blackwell (1821–1910), the first women to gain a medical degree in the United States. She founded the New York Infirmary for Indigent Women and Children in 1857, now the New York-Presbyterian Lower Manhattan Hospital.
252. *I know I may leave M safe* – Lynn returned to Ireland before ffrench-Mullen who remained to continue fundraising.

1926

January

Thursday 7

8.a.m Xt.Ch. coldish day, gt. havoc of floods. Fair a/c of R.mines meeting in Times. Pea soup fog in N.York. I knew it would come fr. Eng. soft coal. Spoke at Child Welf. Section "Better Ireland" Conference in aft. Dinner Mrs ffM, nice, so lonely without Madeline. I miss her every turn.

Wednesday 13

8 a.m. S. B's, had pts. to go to & then Ard C. where came in on debate re Ard Feis to decide for or against new policy of oath removal & going into F.S. Parliament. Long talk with M Comerford, she is agst. it & Mary Mac & Alb. Broderick & E. Donnelly & I am sure many more. Late in evg. when I had almost done all pts. Eamon D. was upset overall.[253]

February

Thursday 11

8 a.m. Xt. Ch. A glorious sunny day. Matron & I interviewed Gordon Campbell re Wh. X funds, he was v. sympathetic. Lunch with L. Wellwood, discussed Lane etc. Nurse & I rushed for "Abbey" at 6.30, got in all right with many more. We showed what we thought of the Plough & the Stars, it is a horrible travesty on Easter Week, how can they write lies abt. dead? Letter fr. Fr Fitzgerald. He is not R.C. D. G.[254]

Friday 12

8 a.m. S. B's, nice sun again. Most unfair a/c of last night in I. Times,

253. *Ard C* – Ard Chomhairle, the National governing body of Sinn Féin. This Sinn Féin Ard Fheis was where de Valera proposed that elected members be allowed to take their seats in the Dáil if and when the oath of allegiance was removed. This was opposed by many of the republican women including 'M Comerford' (Máire Comerford), Mary Mac (Mary MacSwiney), Alb. Broderick (Albina Broderick / Gobnait Ní Bhruadair).

254. *Gordon Campbell* – Charles Gordon Campbell (1885–1963), Irish banker and civil servant. *Nurse & I* – Dora Maguire and Lynn. *the Plough & the Stars* – A riot erupted at the Abbey Theatre during the fourth performance of Seán O'Casey's play, *The Plough and the Stars*, on 11 February 1926. In attendance were some of the widows and participants of 1916 who protested at what they saw as a grotesque distortion of the events of the Rising, insulting to those who had died for Ireland.

Indep. better. They say the publicity will make Casey, as in old days "Playboy" made Synge, but that marked epoc in Nationality D.V. so will this! Big Disp. Mr Bell wanted me to see after old Miss Donovan but they got another Dr. Evg. P. Health, Mrs Kettle Chairman again D.G. Madeline is proposed by [ ] Dan Curran for council D.G. Talked with Mrs. Kettle.[255]

Friday 19

8 a.m. S. B's, a dripping wet day, walls, floors all wringing. O'Casey has said horrid things abt. Mrs Skeff. we hear. Got £3.3 for my fund so far D.G. Matron in good form, Teac babics nicely, but Michael. Nurse's shop nearly ready. D.G. Davy Crookes in Town.

March

Monday 1

8 a.m. S. B's. Nice day, lonely b.fast. Fine letters fr. M & money, D.G. £265, it is fine. My fund nearly £50 now D.G. Mrs ffM fell & cut her head last night, none the worse, D.G. she couldn't dine here after all or go to then debate. Miss Dufy, Nurse & I did, it was packed. Mrs S. S spoke fine & Mrs McCarville & Madam McBride, O'Casey & the rest v. halting. O'C has a filthy mind.[256]

Tuesday 9

8 a.m. R.mines, cold wind & some sl. snow shower. The momentous Ard Feis in Rotunda, about 600 delegates at it fr. 11 a.m. to 11p.m. with sl. intervals, decision whether or not a principle not to enter F.S. Parliament to be taken at 11 to-morrow. On whole good spirit, anxious for Peace but Scellig's recriminations & Mrs Clarke's vile. Dev v. fair D.G. It will be for the best, whatever D.G.[257]

Thursday 18

8 a.m Xt. Ch. Cold mg. clearing to lovely day. Burst up at Geneva nearly certain, may mean war again & Eng. difficulty. Med. & Gen.

---

255. *Mrs Kettle* – Lynn and Kettle served on the Public Health Committee of the Rathmines and Rathgar Urban District Council.
256. *Mrs S. S spoke fine & Mrs McCarville & Madam McBride* – Hanna Sheehy Skeffington, Eileen McCarvill (née McGrane), Cumann na mBan, and Maud Gonne McBride.
257. *Scellig* – John J. O'Kelly (1872–1957), writer, journalist, Irish-language activist, anti-treatyite, Sinn Féin TD. He was a leading opponent of de Valera's policy of flexibility on the oath and entering the Dáil.

Teac Board. Cable fr. M. another, dollars coming D.G. She is anxious abt. her mother, but I told her all. Women of both sides met & agreed to allow no recriminations. To-day the Devites are determined to enter the F.S. Parliament & in 1925?[258]

Sunday 28

Palm Sun. 8 a.m. R.mines. Saw abt. violets. T.D's meeting 11 o/c. We were defeated on quest. of principle & 2nd Dail but won decisively on policy. Dev, I grieve to say took it badly & wouldn't resign till another vote taken wh. confirmed 1st D.G. & left us Die Hards in possession. It is best so may there be no bitterness! D.G. the uncompromised Republic stands.[259]

April

Thursday 1

8 a.m. R.mines, nice mild day. Gt. cable fr. M sending $2,000, doesn't want to come home, it seems till all money raked in. No satisfactory explanation yet abt. Malahide tragedy. It is dreadful. Teac nicely on whole, v. full. Wrote much to M. John in N. York, D.G. They are starting new organization at once, I hear.[260]

Wednesday 7

8 a.m. S. B's. Glorious mg., raining later. Busy mg. Violet Gibson, Lord Ashbourne's sister, fired on Mussolini & wounded his nose. Strange, India reported quiet but 35 dead & 500 prisoners, not v. like an intercommunal row. Emer says both Republican parties will crumble & glorious new one arise. Matron's head v. bad. I wish M was home to help her.[261]

Monday 19

8 a.m. S. B's, v. busy, many pts. They're going to have Indust. Exhib.

---

258. *1925* – Lynn makes an error on the date here; it should be 1927 when the next general election was due.
259. *Die Hards* – a common term for uncompromising republicans. De Valera was defeated at the Ard Fheis and resigned, left and formed a new party, Fianna Fáil, which would follow his aims of flexibility on the oath and enter the Dáil.
260. *Malahide tragedy* – the murder of six people in La Mancha, a large house near Malahide. Henry McCabe was convicted on the murders and hanged in December 1926.
261. *Violet Gibson* (1876–1956), attempted to assassinate Benito Mussolini on 7 April 1926 in Rome.

to encourage Irish Trade, will it? Eng. Sec!! Good leader on ethics of oath taking i.e mental reservations. Statesman critises Dev. v. justly. Poor baby we worked so hard for Sat. night dead, too bad. Matron caused consternation saying returning Wed. I say mustn't. Good talk Stacks re Boyne Valley. Cold showers.

Wednesday 28

8 a.m. S. B's, a curiously dull, dark mg. Early I felt v. anxious, would Madeline get off all right? Later felt all well & D.G. before 7 p.m. had cable saying she had started & John was starting to-morrow. D.G. D.G. we are all rejoiced. More bloodshed in Calcutta, it is serious there. W.W.U. has grave case & D.V. they'll win out. Long talk Mrs Brugha. Nurse had more things stolen fr. shop.[262]

May

Tuesday 4

8 a.m. R.mines. Wireless fr. M 7.30. Gen. Strike on, no trains etc. how will M get home? Sent her a wireless asking a landing at Cove. Saw Miss O'Connor re same & Matron & I interviewed U.S.A manager. He remembered me in N. York! I. Times tells prophesy fr. Glencolumbkill when last Golden Eagle dead (Irish), it died last week "men will come fr. under the earth & stop ships going on sea & people on roads". Fullfilled to letter D.G.

Friday 14

Up at 10, heard children before, missed 11 train Cove thro' Mr King telling me of poor girl who tried to get away, a lovely mg. Saw many arum lillies & lupins & primroses blooming in open. To Cove 2.30. Old woman lamenting emigrants true. To Rob Roy, saw old Kilty, Visited Cathedral, old churchyard. Tender10 p.m, Reached Republic at last & found M well. Delighted with 4 leaved shamrock. Crowds came off, back in bed 2.30 a.m.

Saturday 22

Slept late after all, so sorry. Pts. till 12.30 then Ard Chomar. settled up fairly, T.D's at 5, Ard C has Resolution calling on all "Go iners" to resign wh. came apurth. gt. effect in conjunct. with their printed objects wh.

---

262. *W.W.U.* – Irish Women Workers' Union.

= now pure Republicanism- sweep country, scrap F.S. constitution & set up own Govt. A lovely day. God grant we get straight ans. fr. Dev.[263]

Sunday 23

Whitsunday. 8 a.m. R.mines, then to T.Ds meeting. Dev talked & gave no satisfaction, sad he is so unreliable. Meetings went on all day. In end we appointed Art O'C Dev's successor & refused coalition, they wouldn't have our terms. A lovely day. Thinking much of John & praying for him.[264]

Wednesday 26

8 a.m. S. B's, M had b.fast in Teac. I had Gaelic lesson & heaps to see to, wrote to Anna & John, how I think of them! Late in Teac. At last we got Dr Solomons to speak to-morrow. Papers have it, Dev. wants to go into F.S. & K O'Higgins will welcome them! What a change! did some work abt. Internat. Womens' recept. Must prepare for to-morrow. Warm to-day.[265]

June

Monday 21

Felt Aunt F & Eliza all well. rushed to No. 9, then to meet M at 23, satisfactory talk, then pts. galore & many bad, in Teac saw H.S. & Sister fr. Children's Harcourt St. Saw Miss O'Daly re advt. Poblacht. V. busy aft. & evg. S. Bowen came v. late & ret. after 12, had good talk with her. New Anti-imperial Assoc. formed. Won't forget dabbling in canal with bare feet y.day & all the restfulness.[266]

July

Thursday 1

Awake late after late night, had long round, R.farnham etc. Saw

263. *Ard C has Resolution calling on all 'Go iners' to resign* – Sinn Féin Ard Chomhairle called on all members who would take their seats if elected, 'go-inners', and take the oath of allegiance to resign.
264. *In end we appointed Art O'C Dev's successor* – Éamon de Valera resigned as President of Sinn Féin over the issue and Art O'Connor was appointed his successor as President. *John* – John Willoughby Lynn (1877–1954), Kathleen's brother.
265. *Dr Solomons* – Bethel Solomons (1885–1965), Master of the Rotunda Hospital, Dublin. *Internat. Women* – the Fifth Congress of the Women's International League for Peace and Freedom, was held in Dublin 8 to 15 July 1926.
266. *Poblacht* – an anti-treaty republican newspaper *An Phoblacht* was launched in 1925. *S. Bowen* – Sighle Bowen.

Margt. of 16 wonderfully well. Poor Evelyn Farrell died in aft. I am so sorry. Miss Gore Booth's death in paper, we are all so sorry for poor Madam & she looks so sad. Hear Internat. Women are pleased with our efficiency! Good. We had good meeting in evg. for our excursion. How we wish we were in Glenmalure.[267]

Tuesday 13

8 a.m. R.mines, hurried to Congress, Irish minority report by Rose Jacob quite good, D.G. another glorious day. D.V. to-morrow will be as fine & nice. They had to pay 2/- to go to Tim's Garden party, horrid! We're thro' with much difficulty with preps. for to-morrow. D.G. hope all will go well. There have been fearful explosions of munitions in U.S.A. by lightening, hand of God.[268]

August

Sunday 22

12 A.T. 8 a.m. R.mines, sunshine, wind, showers, hurried to Teac. Mrs McSwiney & daughter came, saw everything. D.V. they won't forget us. Heard gt. jealousy over our poor £2,000 White X money & we want so much more! The babies are truly terrible now, never saw so many bad together. I think Census shows all young men gone, towns grow, country desolate.[269]

September

Tuesday 7

8 a.m. R.mines. There were 48 out of 150 dead this mg. in Drumcollogher & by evg. it is 52, terrible. Saw D & Art after much discussion at last I said I'd go to-morrow early to bear our sympathy to the survivors. Poor Art isn't well. They are starting educating D.G. & progressing. It was a most rushing day & now D.V. I'm off to Drumcollogher to-morrow. M's cold better.[270]

---

267. *Miss Gore Booth* – Eva Gore Booth (1870–1926), suffragette, writer, poet, mystic, radical activist, sister of Countess Markievicz, and partner of Esther Roper.

268. *Congress* – Congress of the Women's International League for Peace and Freedom. *Tim's Garden party* – Timothy Healy (1855–1931), Governor General of the Irish Free State, his official residence was the Viceregal Lodge (now Áras an Uachtaráin).

269. *Mrs McSwiney & daughter* – Muriel MacSwiney, widow of Terence MacSwiney, Lord Mayor of Cork and their daughter Máire. *White X* – The Irish White Cross.

270. *48 out of 150 dead this mg. in Drumcollogher* – In Dromcollogher, Co. Limerick, a fire swept through the local cinema. Disaster on night of 5 September 1926, 48 people lost their lives. *Saw D & Art after much discussion at last I said I'd go to-morrow* – Lynn agreed with Art O'Connor to go to Dromcollogher to express the sympathies of Sinn Féin to the local people.

Wednesday 8

A heart rending day, arr. Newcastle West, got motor to Drumcollogher, driver much shocked, has been up & down all time since Sun. Saw huge grave being filled with black debris fr. ruins. In evg. it was green mound with flowers. Went to all I could & tried to comfort. All mourn in village. [McAuleys] have grandchildren safe. Jerry O'Brien, paralysed, lost wife & daughter. Mr O'Brien's only daughter & so on but they are wonderfully resigned D.G. for it.

Tuesday 14

8 a.m. R.mines. Bath Comt. 10. Came back after it, letter fr. John, he is in Manchester & hopes to be here end of week. D.G. D.G. He had good voyage & likes boat. Wrote at once to him & M. Drumcollogher inquest blames operator & lessee & lets civic guard off, it is so unjust. All are preparing for election. D.V. we'll let it alone. M had good time in Dunleer D.G.[271]

Thursday 16

8 a.m. Xt. Ch. A v. warm day, like heatwave. F.S. asked for seat on L. of Nations Council. Eng. pretends surprise. What window dressing is it? Emer is reported as saying to Commissioners she was trained nurse, 18 mos workless, really was N. Maguire, unwise for her. Heard Dr Lee of Chicago in C. of Surg. on dangers of preg. & lab., v. farfetched. Teac Board all right. Many pts. so many more since Nurse left. A.G.O.W. D.G.[272]

October

Friday 15

8 a.m. S. B's. Cold day, wrote in mg. large disp. Teac full again after 2 days of fever. V. excellent meeting in evg. in College Green right across fr. Bank to other side. Fr O'Flanagan, Scellig & E. Donnelly spoke, all listened well. All goes badly with England. In at Holles St. meeting. Quite late Mrs S.S. came with an evicted family of 3 wh. I had to house for night. D.V. they'll get place to-morrow. Baby a dear.[273]

---

271. *letter fr. John* – her brother John, who lived in Australia, was coming home to visit.
272. *L. of Nations Council* – League of Nations. *C. of Surg* – Royal College of Surgeons in Ireland.
273. *excellent meeting in evg* – Sinn Féin public meeting where Fr Michael O'Flanagan, John Joseph O'Kelly (Scellig) and Eamon Donnelly spoke.

Wednesday 27

8 a.m. S. B's. P.H 10. M v. busy re. 1st S. Ultan's Concert of Season. It went well. Miss E. Rhodes wants dinners for poor in R.mines. Council approve, can't help. Turf can be got, no coal. People so poor now can't buy turf. Madam M distributed on her own. Sister in Teac may leave for a Baby Club. We'll miss her. Matron rather perturbed. Eng. goes worse & worse & F.S. with her. Poor Margt. ill, went to her.

November

Wednesday 17

8 a.m. S. B's. Mrs Hurford came in mg. V. glad to see her, all went well there. Hurried to Teac but Sir Wm. gone. Matron to have op. week after next. They are rushing bill "Public Safety" thro' F.S. Parliament to deal with raiders etc. Evidently v. alarmed at any opposition. Met 1.5 train Amiens St., John never came. Rang up Belfast, Balsam expected early to-morrow. Muriel wired that he & I should go to her. Teac v. fairly D.G.[274]

December

Thursday 16

8 a.m. Xt. Ch., nicer day but cold. Kevin O'H made gt. speech in F.S. & said we were negligible & beneath contempt. Housing Comt. went well, McKenzie quite good. Teac Board also went well D.G. D.V. all our schemes for help will do well. Babies nicely D.G. No further news of George Gilmore, it is fearful. V. good meeting in Abbey St. Scellig spoke well. Sighle makes plans.[275]

Tuesday 21

8 a.m. R.mines, how thankful M & I are to be at home together. Ch. Welf. 11 went well, v. busy trying to fix Xmas things & all. A day with mg. sun. Report George Gilmore in Hosp. Hope it's true. Many presents for Teac, such lovely Pittsfield things & fr. here too. D.G. Aunt Julia sent £5 good soul, for my poor things. There is such distress. Madam brought some wood for them.

---

274. '*Public Safety*'–The Public Safety (Emergency Powers) Bill was introduced to the Dáil on 16 November 1926.
275. *George Gilmore* (1898–1985) anti-treaty republican and socialist, imprisoned several times in the 1920s. *Sighle* – Sheila 'Sighle' Dowling, née Bowen, (*c.*1896–1957), close friend of Lynns, lived next door with her husband Frank Dowling at No. 8 Belgrave Rd from the 1940s.

Thursday 30

8 a.m. Xt. Ch. Lovely last quarter moon. Madeline's birthday, D.G. she isn't in U.S.A. We buried poor old Rep. soldier fr. S. D.U. D.G the funeral was all right, though Madam & the Nurse insisted he was R.C. & had him in Chapel tho' registered not R.C. He was fine fighter. China will have none of Britain's proposals D.G. George Gilmore not on h. strike & fairly comfortable. The girls all right. A nice busy day.

1927

January

Saturday 1

It was a nice fresh New Year's Day. Some lovely sun. Now people can see in the dark by invisible rays, more of God's forthshowing of the next stage. Nurse Maguire has got 14 days for chalking walls, she wished for it. V. busy with epidemic, rushed to Aunt F, for dinner & back. Emer bad, 1st time since last Xmas. D.G. M working hard for Teac. Terrible way Germans = masters, Irish = serfs on Shannon works.[276]

Friday 14

Up 4.45 to meet John, boat not in till 5.45. No one stirring when I got to Pier. He came safe & well D.G. We had tea & all slept till 9.45. I left him to sleep & went in & did Disp. was well finished when he came. Dr Hill had op. case wh. she managed well, D.G. Aft. we bought tablecloths etc. good Irish designs. Evg. Emer, M ffM & I dined here & went to Jack & Beanstalk, quite good. Dr Lynch came too.[277]

Tuesday 18

8 a.m. R.mines, V. cold & frosty, cleared in midday, froze again in night. Hear Fianna Fail does badly in country & Dev will be much disappointed at elections. Comyn has left him & is an Indep. Rep. & will go in oath or no oath. V. busy day, so many here. Ch. Welf. went well D.G. Miss Butler improves. Teac v. fair D.G.[278]

February

Wednesday 9

8 a.m. S. B's, gt. rush for P.H. at 10. Mrs Kettle elected Chairman again D.G. It got v. cold abt. 12.30, like snow but none came. Teac better

---

276. *Shannon works* – The Shannon hydroelectric power station at Ardnacrusha was built by the German firm Siemens-Schuckert. Over 1,000 German workers, including 150 technicians worked on the Scheme. There were some tensions between the German and Irish workers.
277. *Dr Hill* – Dr Kathleen Enda Hill, qualified Trinity 1923.
278. *Dev will be much disappointed at elections. Comyn has left him & is an Indep.* – This is more hope than fact for elections were anticipated in June 1927, although the polls did not show Fianna Fáil doing well; Michael Comyn (1871-1952), a co-founder of Fianna Fáil did not in fact become an independent republican as a Senator.

D.G. I. Times leader plainly says F.S. must accept all Engs. risks, war etc. she has no separate entity, we all knew it. Another leader v. libellous abt. Corporation, but good re. bridges! Mrs Skeffington in in evg. she is v. anxious we should be as friendly as before, personally, yes.[279]

Tuesday 15

8 a.m. R.mines, mild sunny day, much 'Flu going, all Drs v. busy. Ch. Welf fr. 11 to1 went well. Negotiations with China broken off D.G. Letter fr. Muriel, she is v. glad abt. Nan. Mrs S. Skeffington wants to start new Women's movement to embrace all politics & be just feminist. Fog so dense this evg. I could scarce find my way. D.G. cleared later to lovely night. Emer came in with M ffM.

Friday 18

Slept late, v, tired with 'Flu pts. Nice sunshine. Nationalists go well forward in China, D.G. God help them. Eng. evidently prepares for war, has conciliated railway men & started sugar factories. Good letters re. women jurors. F.S. too crooked to let them serve. Unfortunate people in S.D.U. absolutely starving & herded together in small room as if in jail, no sanitary accommodation, door locked.[280]

March

Thursday 3

So tired, slept late, fine mg. v. busy all day, one to another constantly. Cosgrave worrying now abt. Lane Collection, we passed resolution demanding their return in Council y.day. McGuinness v. clearly shows if Dev means anything, he means revolution. F.S. & Britain wont calmly stand back & let him take over Govt. Not likely. China does well, anti[ ] army melted away.[281]

---

279. *she is v. anxious we should be as friendly as before* – Unlike Lynn, Hanna Sheehy Skeffington left Sinn Féin and joined Fianna Fáil, sitting on its Executive. The women agreed despite these opposing political views that they would remain friends on a personal level.

280. *Women jurors* – Under the 1927 Juries Act introduced by Minister for Justice Kevin O'Higgins women were automatically exempt, but not legally prohibited from serving on juries. In effect women had to opt into the potential jurors list which most did not do. Lynn and many feminists opposed the Act on equality grounds.

281. *The Lane Collection* – Sir Hugh Lane (1875–1915) was an Irish art dealer and philanthropist who died in the sinking of the Lusitania in 1915. An unsigned codicil in his will left his collection to a modern art gallery in Dublin but it was not honoured. A parliamentary commission in 1926 admitted that Lane's desire was clearly to leave the paintings to Dublin but the National Gallery in London which holds some of his paintings refused to honour this. However, it does share many of the paintings on a rota with the Hugh Lane Gallery in Dublin.

Monday 7

8 a.m. s. B's, it was a v. busy day, racing whole time. Mrs Connery says Kevin O'H was most insolent to deput. of women who went to him re. women jurors, she went to Glenavy who at least was civil. Teac got good deal of money D.G. it was a good day. Marconi scandal revives, maybe more disclosures re. F.S. entanglement with it. John safe in Avonmouth D.G. Billas lovely in window boxes.[282]

April

Saturday 2

8 a.m. S. B's nearly as wet as Thurs. Called to 2 urgent cases, one when back fr. Ch, the other on coming home fr. that, no time for bath etc. Indep. has published our vote re. no pact with F. Fail. They have list of F.F. candidates, evidently, & make guesses at our candidates fr. those not in it. A very weeshy prem. came, admitted. Miss Rhodes cheered over dinners.

Tuesday 12

8 a.m. R.mines, such a busy day. Still reports of Nationalist reverses in China, are they true? Gt. excitement = Kevin O'Higgins announcement that he was coming to meeting to-night. He heard what we think of him. M ffM spoke so nicely fr. body of hall. Mrs Kettle splendid, v. witty. Desmond Fitzgerald actually said "It didn't cost much, anyhow, to execute Childers" Has he no heart? Poor man.[283]

May

Saturday 7

Slept again, lovely sunshiny day. India & China do well, also Lab. In Eng. v. noisy in Commons over preposterous bill. Hurried & met Aunt F & we went to Sketching Club pictures wh. weren't bad. Gladys W. & Efa had pictures. Aunt F. enjoyed it & wasn't v. tired. Evg. M ffM & I

---

282. *Mrs Connery* – Meg Connery (1881–1956), suffragette, member of the Irishwomen's Franchise League. *Glenavy* – James Campbell, 1st Baron Glenavy (1851–1931), Independent Senator in the Free State Senate, chaired the Judicial Committee appointed to advise the Executive Council of the Irish Free State on the creation of a new courts system for the Irish Free State. *Marconi Scandal* – The Marconi Scandal 1912–3 revealed corruption in British politics.
283. *Desmond Fitzgerald* (1888–1947) – revolutionary, writer, pro-treaty, Cumann na nGaedheal, Minister for External Affairs.

went to Madam Gonne's show wh. was right good education tableaux & slides & songs. Then to Aunt F. A busy, full, nice day.[284]

Saturday 14

Susie found us in bed after up 2.45 a.m. last night, hurried off with her at 12, it rained good deal, walked & went astray, finally right for Bohernabreena & waterworks, cleared, lovely, heard cuckoo v. satisfactorily. Walked all up to far end Glenasmole, marsh, marigolds fine, then up Featherbed to Glencree Road, home by Lemass Cross. Tea Hell Fire Club, a long, glorious walk home, 9, tired & happy, stiff.

Thursday 26

Ascension Day. 8 a.m. R.mines, v nice day. We worked well & I never saw Annual Meeting go off with so little trouble. All went so smoothly & well D.G. We missed Matron v. much. Dr Cassidy was not approved of. Mrs Skeff. brought Mr Howard fr. Nebraska. M & I went to D.L & she off to London to Conference. I saw Aunt F. Evg. Emer & Sighle came, lovely time. A.G.O.W. politically D.G.[285]

June

Friday 3

Late again after late night. All working hard to get out election letters. 100,000 to be done, we were there, M & I till nearly 2 a.m. I went to 40 at 8, then to meetings in Chapelizod & Lucan. Mr Griffin, Emer & I, G. Plunkett drove us. Lovely sunset, we had nice time & Emer spoke v. well. Griffin was at exam till an hr. before meeting. A.G.O.W. D.G.

Friday 10

The weary Count, Sean MacBride, came for us at 8.30. We were down before 9 o/c. V. large Poll. At 1 a.m. announced to be 71,000 out of possible 101,000 – Kevin is leading well & Cooper & Belton, the rest are nowhere. I fear no chance for the Republicans. Russians

---

284. *India & China do well, also Lab. In Eng. V. noisy in Commons over preposterous bill* – Lynn was happy that Nationalist campaigns in India and China. The preposterous bill was the Trades and Disputes Bill which Labour opposed and which was a Conservative response to the General Strike of 1926 and sought to restrict certain actions by trade unions including 'sympathy strikes' and other forms of industrial action and reduce the levy paid by the unions to the Labour Party.
285. *Emer & Sighle* – Helena Molony and Sheila Dowling (née Bowen) were good friends and collaborators in left wing politics during this period.

have executed 20 spies & informers proved to have given Sir Hodgson information. Good.[286]

Sunday 12

Trinity sun. 8 a.m. R.mines. Sean came near 11 & went to B.rock, count went on, many eliminations, mine after Rooney, in end Good, Johnson, McEntee & B. O'Connor got in. Brian O'Higgins, Mary Mac, Art O'Connor, C. Murphy defeated. We are surely v. select now. F.F. & F.S about equal & F.S. seems v. unhappy over it. We know all will be for the best D.G.[287]

Tuesday 14

8 a.m. R.mines, glorious sunny day, cold in shade. Evg. sees C na Gael & F.F. almost quits, 41 to 44, everyone says what will be next move. Many say F.F. will take oath & go in. The expected little Erskine Childers not arr. yet, but all well. Gt. reception in N. York for Lindeberg. No Union Jacks flown D.G. All seems well with Soviets, D.G. We arrange for consolation Party Sun. 26th. Lovely moon.[288]

Thursday 30

Hurried fr. Aunt F who is fine. Dev is having Referendum wh. will keep people thinking they're doing something. It rained & rained whole time. Madam Markievicz has appendix. Emer came abt. her. I got Sir W T. & he agreed & I got her into Dun's D.G. D.V. she'll be all right. Saw pts. all day & packed & now at nearly 2 a.m. we're nearly done. Mrs Dow is to go to-morrow. D.V. & D.G. All well.[289]

July

Friday 8

A most lovely day D.G. We enjoyed every moment of it. Postman brought wire saying poor Madam was v. bad & had 2nd op. I fear there is little

---

286. *Weary count* – the June 1927 Irish general election was held on Thursday, 9 June. Lynn stood again as a Sinn Féin abstentionist TD. *Sir Hodgson* – Sir Robert Hodgson (1874–1956), British diplomat and consul.

287. *B.Rock* – Blackrock, a suburb of Dublin. *many eliminations* – Lynn lost her seat in this election. *Rooney* – John Rooney, Irish Farmers' Party. *Good, Johnson, McEntee & B O'Connor* – John Good (*d.*1942), Thomas Johnson (1872–1963), Seán MacEntee (1889–1984), and Batt O'Connor (1870–1935), all won seats in County Dublin in the 5th Dáil election.

288. *C na Gael & F.F.* – Cumann na nGaedheal and Fianna Fáil. *Many say F.F. will take oath & go in* – take the Oath of Allegiance and take their seats in the Dáil.

289. *I got her into Dun's* – Sir Patrick Dun's Hospital, Dublin.

hope in that case. I think she was just tired of life, poor dear Madam. We went, M to hotel, I to Kellystown, both to Macnamara & Byrnes where Grannie dead. A.G.O.W. in world, we think, Eng. not better.

Saturday 9

Lovely day, b.fast out, then Mrs Skeffington & Erskine Childers came. Madam's progress not good. Went with them to see & if nec. abandon Hastings Conference. Madam v. v. bad, op to relieve obstruct. not working, vomiting, complete paral. of gut. Had I.C.C. Pittuit. Sir W says she'll die in night. Terrible restlessness. Miss Roper staying night. Maeve Markievcz seems fine, honest girl. Mary arr. for. funeral already! Five of us staying night in place.[290]

Thursday 14

8 a.m. Xt. Cth. Straight to Dun's. Sir W delighted with her progress as was Sir J Craig, say she'll recover. She had lovely day, enjoyed everything. Count & Stasco with her. She was well at 7, at 8 in gt. pain, collapsed unconscious, died v. v. peacefully at 12, God's time. The Count Stasco, Mrs Skeff. M O'Byrne, Emer, Mrs & May Coughlan, Dr Cavanagh & I were with her. Dev came later. We each got one of the roses she loved so. D.G. for her, she had a happy entry into [safe].[291]

Saturday 16

Early at Rotunda, helping, for Lying-in-State, phone to say John at No. 9 D.G. Went to him & told him all, he came with me to funeral Mass at 10, sad & quiet. Gore Booths there. Coffin carried whole way to Rotunda, crowds. John walked too. Peace. Arr. in shadow, light only on her face, wh. is so peaceful & serene, turned straight to one side, flowers everywhere there. Someone left 8 eggs in bag on coffin, promised prob. J & I stayed there a while with Emer, then to Aunt F.

Sunday 17

4 A.T. 8.30 Xt. Ch. glorious day. J & I went to funeral. Just in time. I was put betw. Art O'Connor & Dev! Whole route thronged. Parnell St. Capel St. Parliament st. Dame St. George's St. York St. Green,

---

290. *Miss Roper* – Esther Roper (1868–1938), partner of Markievicz's sister, Eva Gore Booth. *Maeve Markievicz* (1901–62) – daughter of Countess Markievicz.
291. *Sir J Craig* – Sir James Craig (1861–1933), politician and physician to Sir Patrick Dun's Hospital. *Count & Stasco* – Count Casimir Joseph Dunin Markievicz (1874–1932), husband of Countess Markievicz and Stanislaus (1896–1971), Casimir's son by his first marriage.

Grafton, O'Connell & so to Glasnevin. 6 lorries of flowers took 3 hrs to cover route. Art O'Connor, Dev & such carried coffin in cemetery. Don't know length of procession, [6] bands. Dev spoke nicely. M ffM & her mother had accident, unhurt, all got back safe.

August

Thursday 11

Not v. well in mg. In bed til 12.30 D.G. better then & worked all day. Big lines in I. Times whole F. Fail party going into F.S. Parliament to-morrow. All signed oath to-day, how can they? Not a soul there, shows what downward path does. Hear whole F.S. Govt. will resign to-morrow & have another gen. election. Anyhow we're contesting C. Dublin & I have to attend!

Friday 12

On anniv. of Griffith's death, Dev & Co enter F.S. Parliament, no one took any notice, thing fell as flat as the Treaty. Just means so many more fallen fr. high estate. Tom to go up for County & C Murphy for City. We'll make a good fight D.V. success lies with God. It was nice day, lovely moon now. Used Abt's. breast pump for 1st time.[292]

Monday 22

We slept late, v. heavy showers. Gt. excitement. Independent says maj. of our 5 T.Ds favour going in. I immediately repudiated it & A. Stack sent to all rest, telling them to do same. Evg. papers full of my letter. V. busy all day, we had splendid meeting in Town Hall in evg. It was packed, Mary Mac spoke well & Emer surpassed herself D.G. she chaired. Mary Mac much pleased.[293]

September

Monday 5

8 a.m. S. B's, v. nice Autumn Day. Hear Mrs Wyse Power becoming v. dissatisfied with F.S. Letter fr. U.S.A. says American Republicans sit

---

292. *Abt's breast pump* – Dr Abt's electric breast pump was the first modern electric breast pump, developed in 1921. Lynn had seen it on her visit to America.
293. *A. Stack* – Austin Stack (1879–1929), anti-treaty Sinn Féin TD. *Evg. papers full of my letter* – Lynn's letter includes her vow that 'under no circumstances will I enter an Imperial provincial Parliament, oath-bound to a foreign king', *Evening Herald*, Monday 22 August 1927.

back disgusted & refuse to work more. Matron off for holiday. Dr Ball leaves, Dr O'Brien comes in.[294]

Friday 30

8 a.m. S. B's, Emer early, then special Council to protest agst. Greyhound racing course Harold's X. Floods again in evg. N.Z. Premier here, why? Many in Disp. rush whole time. Didn't say cycle came back safe on 28th. D.G. Rush for train to Armagh. Muriel met me. All well in Lime Park. Ready for drive to Dublin to-morrow. Blustery day. Jane Doyle not operated on yet.

October

Wednesday 12

8 a.m. S. B's, foggy & dull. Council re Coursing Track, it can't be prevented, talked with unemployed, poor men. Long P.H. Comt. Papers full of Cosgrave in tall hat & all the rest of the West British. Saw abt. several v. poor babies, oh the horror of the starving mothers & babies. Evg. went to Dominick St. & Roebuck. Mrs Despard thinks she won't last. Poor Madam thinks F.F. will save Sean.[295]

November

Monday 28

8 a.m S. B's. The gt. day that Teac O.P. dept. was begun, they are hard at fixing the temp shed. D.V. all will go well. Much prep. for to-morrow's meeting. D.V. it will be good. Emer gave me choice of 2 of Madam's pictures, nice to have them. Many pts. Work in garden goes on. Preps. for Xmas tree abt. 1,000 to be invited. S.F & C na mB offices raided y.day. Rumours of wars.[296]

December

Monday 5

8 a.m. S. B's, stormy & droughty all day. V. busy till after 11 p.m. Blythe says country is prospering, such an untruth when so many starve. I am so anxious that something should be done to feed them &

---

294. *Dr Ball, Dr O'Brien* – probably Dr Florien Isabel Ball, graduated Trinity 1922, and Dr Eveleen Josephine O'Brien, graduated UCD 1924.
295. *Madam* – Maud Gonne McBride. *Sean* – Seán McBride (1904–88), who was to be executed.
296. *Teac O.P. dept* – St Ultan's Outpatients Department.

everyone says they're hopeless, what am I to do? A.G.O.W. with Utility Soc. V. stormy this evg. Smith says our electric wiring isn't safe, must get it rewired.[297]

Sunday 11

3 in Advent, 8.30 Xt. Ch. Left 11 o/c for Ard Feis, mg. long, good but wearisome. Set of lectures by Scellig on all subjects, Hist. [ ] & Economics fr 11.30 to 2.30. almost lunch, back motions. I left 5.45, went to Aunt F. back 10.30. All hard at it still. Fr O'Flanagan left before Mary Mac had her say abt. his conduct, Army ticket defeated D.G. Scellig Pres., Mary Mac & Dr Madden V.Ps. D.G. I wasn't elected. We left them at 3.30 a.m.[298]

Monday 19

8 a.m. S. B's, colder than ever & such an icy wind & the poor make no sound & they must be frozen. V busy with pts. all day, tried to do Xmas thing. Taxi failed me & I had to walk. Told F. Rhodes she must stay in bed & keep warm. Cosgrave going to U.S.A. J McNeill has option of retiring after 2 yrs on £10,000 pension & the poor! No brick-laying to-day, everything freezing. Gladys Wynne came, v. nice. A.G.O.W. D.G.[299]

297. *Blythe* – Ernest Blythe (1889–1975), Minister for Finance.
298. *Ard Feis* – Sinn Féin Ard Fheis, 1927. *Dr Madden* – John Madden (*c.*1896–1954), physicians and Sinn Féin member.
299. *J McNeill* – James McNeill (1869–1938), politician and diplomat, second Governor-General of the Irish Free State.

1928

January

Tuesday 3

8 a.m. R.mines, now floods make havoc after all the cold & snow & loss of life fr. that. Gt. rush to be in time for dinner at Miss O'Donnell's. Mary & Annie Mac, M ffM & Miss Rynn there. We started with grapefruit & had turkey & gt. spread, pretty decorations, lanterns etc. Hear Liam & Dev together in Ennis with Dr. Fogarty. Evg. at Esther Pearson's to meet Miss Hurford. Esther nice lady, v. big & magnificent house. Small one homelike.[300]

Thursday 5

Up late after late night, v. busy all day. Hear gt. floods in Glenmalure, road washed away in places, after thaw. Liam's farewell dinner, it is horrible with such starvation around. Teac got money D.G. Evg. Mary Mac lectured on influence of women, good discussion then, fine crowd. V. wet & blowing hurricane, hard to get home. Mrs S.S. & Mrs C O'Brien & Sighle to supper. Nice.[301]

Tuesday 24

Just when going to Ch. called off, busy with pts. etc. Warder Grace shot near Mtjoy, he had cruelly tortured poor George Gilmore lately, nearly broke his wrists & danced on his wounded leg & chest. Poor G. pulped. Gen. raids on this a/c, 2 taken next door. G Gilmore's 2 brothers taken. All will make nice reading for U.S.A. V. cold winds, busy day. Many to see. Teac nicely D.G.

Monday 30

8 a.m S. B's, v. frosty & cold coming back. Council 10. Old Metcalf prop. Mrs Kettle for Chairman & we all agreed, that is fine, she is first woman in such a post, rest went well. Stop Press. Earl Haig dead. 2nd late in evg. = Cosgrave's train to Ottawa wrecked but his coach safe.

---

300. *Dr Fogarty* – Michael Fogarty (1859–1955), Archbishop of Killaloe, 1904 and 1955.
301. *Mrs C O'Brien & Sighle* – Kathleen Cruise O'Brien, née Sheehy (1886–1938), suffragist, Irish language advocate and teacher and Sheila Dowling.

M ffM at poor Tim Coughlan's funeral, immense, he was done in fr. behind, only Harry Boland more mashed up. Murder on 28th.[302]

February

Wednesday 15

P.H. 10 they wanted to make me Chairman but I refused, too gt. a responsibility, they waited for me! Was ever such a change! Mrs Kettle says we are the last Council, it wld. be a pity. Med Board went well. The Drs like the idea of teaching D.G. Many pts. aft. & not done till 8. Then had to take D.T. case to Nursing Home, such a job! Nice sun. Evg. wet. Cosgrave looks older after U.S.A.[303]

Tuesday 28

8 a.m. R.mines, a glorious sunny day, rushed thro' special Child Welf. Meeting, Convent visit etc. to meet Muriel at 1.30 & I sunned myself ½ hr. Mrs J.F. Kelly sent money for Teac D.G. M left by 3 train, pleased. I had fearful rush all aft. Didn't finish aft. people till 9 p.m. & then had outside visits. M ffM at Ceilidh wh. went well. She arr. here 2 a.m. Rain has come, schade.

March

Thursday 1

8 a.m. Xt. Ch. rather wet mg. then lovely sun all day D.G. Busy as usual. Saw Isulte, her boy Sean & his family & Madam McBride & Mrs Despard, latter with temp. insists on going to London to help local elections at 84. She's a terror! Evg. C na mB lect. by Miss Bennett re disarmanent, v. interesting, shows how things tend & futility of war. D.V. Reign of Peace comes soon. Matron normal, better.

Thursday 8

Stayed on to recover tooth pulling. Pain nearly gone, D.G. I feel better it's gone. Long a/c of Harling Enquiry, v. evident, they say, that he's guilty. They arrested 2 boys in Court to-day who were to give adverse

---

302. *Earl Haig* – Douglas Haig, 1st Earl Haig (1861–1928), British Army Officer. *Tim Coughlan* – Timothy Coughlan (1906–28), anti-treaty republican, participated in the assassination of Kevin O'Higgins on 10 July 1927. Coughlan was killed in controversial circumstances six months later, on 28 January 1928. The IRA claimed that he was ambushed and extrajudicially executed.
303. *Chairman* – chairman of the Public Health Committee of the Rathmines and Rathgar Urban District Council.

evidence, just like them! E. wind day. I tried to do things. M ffM in bed all day trying to rest. In Teac all babies coughing their heads off, we must close.[304]

Thursday 29

8 a.m. Xt. Ch. Cold & wet. Council 10. Mrs Johnson v. rude to Mrs Kettle, nasty to hear. Poor canary bad with asthma, gave him [Fod.] in his water. Ann never came, sick headache. Mary stayed in for my dinner & then Mary Jordan came. Evg. the gt. Sweep drawing. Miss H thinks she'll have £300 for us. D.G. for that & Violet Days are £120 D.G. Called to pt. at 1 a.m. Neuresthenia.[305]

April

Monday 2

8 a.m. R.mines, nice sunny mg. v. busy. Blythe shows huge surplus & N. Govt. What does all this overplus of money mean, when country goes down, down? Hear Dev promised in N. York to do nothing revolutionary & the Bankers granted Cosgrave loan. Strange that F.Fs. were sick during prisoners' debates so F.S. had majority of 3, are they too a convenient opposition? We got money.

Saturday 14

Late again, Joint Hosp. Board 10.30. Mr Nolan = Chairman, then Mary Mac, she is v. well. No. 27 raided 3 times this week. Florry McCarthy taken with any amt. of papers in her case, addresses & all. She is ill, poor girl. Heart bad. Remanded for a week. Bremen safe in N.foundland D.G. Nan rather better D.G. Evg. whist Drive Mrs Brugha's, good. Then Aunt F.[306]

---

304. *Harling Enquiry* – named after Seán Harling, who served in the secretariat of the First Dáil and was the main suspect in the death of Timothy Coughlan.

305. *Mrs Johnson v. rude to Mrs Kettle* – Maire Johnson (née Tregay), suffragist, trade unionist and wife of Labour Party leader, Thomas Johnson, Mary Kettle (née Sheehy) feminist and local politician, widow of Irish Parliamentary Party MP Thomas Kettle and sister of Hanna Sheehy Skeffington. Mrs Kettle sat with Lynn on the Rathmines Urban District Council and was a supporter of St Ultan's. Mrs Johnson was also a member of the Rathmines Urban District Council where this incidence of rudeness possibly occurred.

306. *Florrie McCarthy* – Florence McCarthy, republican activist, involved in the Cumann na mBan 'Ghost' campaign which sought to interfere with jurors in republican trials. *Bremen safe in N.foundland* – German Junkers W 33 aircraft that made the first successful transatlantic flight from east to west on 12 and 13 April 1928.

May

Monday 7

8 a.m. S. B's, another most lovely day tho' wind a bit cold. No word at all in I. Times about y.day's meeting & police rushes. Went with Sir Wm. to Kilmacud, he was impressed by Convent. All will go well D.V. Mrs Hungerford better D.G. Saw Emer & sort of got things smoothed over more or less unwittingly betw. them D.G. E. seems much better. Saw embroidery school in W.W.U. office.[307]

Thursday 17

Ascension Day. 8 a.m. R.mines, good showers to-day but cold wind still. Sighle & Emer were here to-night too. We had prelim. meeting of Madam's Memorial, hope it will cover cost of our new wing D.V. it would be a fitting memorial. A.G.O.W. Many pts. etc. Mary's Teddy not well, he is a v. fragile creature. Tried to realise the glory of the Ascension.

Thursday 31

8 a.m. Xt. Ch. A day to be thankful for D.G. all went so well for Teac, the board delighted at proposal that new wing shld be Madam's Memorial. Dull mg. then lovely sun. Annual Meeting went v. well & all were so pleased. We got £32.15. It was splendid all thro'. Poor Uncle Jarlath v. low, he doesn't want to get well. Jack gone back. Mrs ffM, M & I went out & stayed late. D.G. D.G. for all he sends.[308]

June

Wednesday 6

8 a.m. S. B's. Poor M so sad. Uncle Jarlath's funeral 10 o/c. I went to Council, v. unsatisfactory letter fr. Elect. Supply Board, won't let us get transformer, won't be responsible for breakdown!! Baths to go ahead. D.G. Teac well. Dr Casey taking Dr O'Brien's place as H.S. Poor Dr Hill in such a state abt. her father, it is dreadful! A lovely day,

---

307. *No word at all in I. Times about y.day's meeting & police rushes* – this refers to a refusal by the police to allow a meeting under the auspices of the Women Prisoners' Defence League outside Mountjoy Jail. The police baton charged the women to disperse them.
308. *Uncle Jarlath* – Lt Colonel Jarlath ffrench-Mullen (1856–1928), served in the Bengal medical service and was a member of the Gaelic League, uncle of Madeleine.

evg. esp. Girls on hungerstrike in Mtjoy for political treat. not right I think.[309]

Tuesday 12

8 a.m. R.mines, cold, fine in mg. then poured. Spent mg. with Edie Goorwick in Bray & saw one attack, poor child, they are all so worried abt. her. Mrs McDermott has been released uncond. fr. Mtjoy on 10th after H. Strike. Vomiting continuously, was sent to Mercer's, v. bad & annointed this mg. better when I saw her in evg. & wants to live. D.V. she will. Teac looks fearful without plaster.

Monday 18

Got specimens in mg. Much to do all day a rush, D.G. it went well on whole. Teac progresses fairly, cold & v. wet most of day, did some things for Glenmalure. Woman has flown Atlantic to-day for U.S.A. of course, came fr. N.F. Land, landed in S.Wales. Gardens look well in spite of all. Bodenstown y.day showed F. State patronising F.F. & F.F in turn patronising, what was the I.R.A. & C na mB. S. Fein alone true now.[310]

July

Saturday 7

A most glorious day. M came out & lay in sun all day. We tidied house, lay in sun, cooked for to-morrow. Susie & Sylvie came late laden with coal, wood, potatoes, milk, duck & heaps more. We made 3 journeys to ford for them, they had tea & went home happy. We gave some of the new potatoes to Byrne boy & Prince. Bliodana caught a fine rabbit. Lovely day.

August

Friday 3

M up early to go to 8 o/c Mass, 1st Fri. She wasn't back till 11, God's time. I was so hungry had porridge, it was v. hot a while then long

---

309. *Dr Casey* – probably Dr Hanora Casey, graduated NUI 1925. *Girls on hungerstrike in Mtjoy for political treat* – In June 1928, five republican women prisoners in Mountjoy Jail, Sighle McInerny, Eva Jackson, Sighle Humphries, Mrs MacDermott, and Florence 'Florrie' McCarthy went on hunger strike demanding political status.
310. *Woman has flown Atlantic* –Amelia Earhart's solo flight across the Atlantic.

overcast & thundry, then bright. We washed, wrote, did many little things. D MacArdle & F O'Moore went up Glen bathing, etc. & another party of girls. Britain spends 3 mil. on interdominion cable, talk of war betw. Poland & Lithuania.[311]

Friday 17

Determined to do all possible of remainder of Congress. At Child Welf. 9.30 to 2 or so, v. good papers, chiefly antenatal work. Gave Prof. McIlroy & Dr Chisholm their S. Ultan books, they were v. pleased. Lunch Shelbourne with Prof. McIlroy, Dr Barry, Gregory etc. they were nice & freundlich. Saw Eoin Byrne & talked to H.S. re him. D.G. he seems better. Took M ffM home, a washed out rag after y. day. Home after dinner. Matron stopped my preps. for to-morrow.[312]

September

Saturday 8

We gardened all mg. v. satisfactorily D.G. & got good work done but much still to do, v. much, then pts., waited impatiently for taxi, talked to poor "Count" Flinter, he is down & out. Mrs Larkin is starving. Sent eggs & oatmaal. What will the end be! M ffM & I went to Malahide to see house for Muriel, it wouldn't do at all. Nice day. St. Comt. meeting on. S.F. won't be dictated to by I.R.A.

Tuesday 11

8 a.m. R.mines, rather dark mg. M ffM back late fr. Whitefriar St. She packed for Clonmel delegate to Municipal Councils Conference. alas, no gardening! V. busy with pts. Saw Miss Oulton who gave me a ghost story she has written, v. interesting. Dr Collis came & had long interview with M in Teac. D. V. our big Hosp. scheme will materialise. They say France & Germany are sparring & Peace Pact only signed.[313]

Tuesday 18

8 a.m. R.mines. Child Welf. 10. Glorious day. Trouble in Child Welf. with Miss Butler, she is very rude. We came back & gardened a little,

---

311. *Britain spends 3 mil. on interdominion cable* – The Imperial Wireless Chain was to connect Britian with all the countries in her Dominion, the final link of which, between Australia and Canada, opened in June 1928.
312. *Prof McIlroy* – Dame Anne Louise McIlroy (1877–1968), Professor of Obstetrics and Gynaecology, London University. *Freundlich* – friendly.
313. *Dr Collis* – Robert 'Bob' Collis (1900–75), paediatrician and author, later doctor to Christy Brown.

it is very alluring. Then pts. & rush till evg. F. Williams brought bulbs. Went over plans for greater Teac of Future D.V. & signed paper re. it for Dr Collis for U.S.A. Matron came back fr. I. of Man, v. sunburnt & well. She is off again for more holiday.

October

Tuesday 16

8 a.m. R.mines, v. mild, muggy day. Child Welf. 10 o/c, went well but Miss Butler won't apologise for her rudeness. New York went wild with enthusiasm over wonder Zeppplin feat, it flew slowly up Broadway before landing. Was a moment in garden, all well there. V. busy all day. Saw F. Rhodes, she trod on her kitten by accident & killed it & was desolate, poor Fanny.

November

Friday 2

All Souls. 8 a.m. S. B's, arr. just when Aunt Emily's name was being read out, such a cold, wet day, it poured most of time & I got drowned going to pts. & St. Comt. in evg. Mary Mac is terribly under thumb of Peadar O'Donnell unfortunately. Teac v. fair. Matron pleased Miss MacHale sent such lovely blankets for Maher. Germany is surprised over Zepplin's wonderful feat. B. McQuaid troubled.[314]

Wednesday 14

10 a.m. P.H At last they are going to retire McKeogh, it is time. The Gas Co. says it had no idea of putting down new pipes till we had finished roads: they tear them up again gaily. Wrecked liner tales v. terrible, mothers & children in raft for hours, now disappeared, more than 100 lost, 200 saved. M ffM & I went to see R.mines utility houses, they are v. nice. Wire fr. Dr Graham, Belfast. I have to fetch Mary Nesbitt to-morrow.

Friday 30

S. Andrew 8 a.m. R.mines, rush for dentist, then going back to Teac heard M ffM had hurt herself, fall fr. cycle, rushed back, took her to Meath, Mr Stokes, X Ray showed fracture surg. neck of [ ]hilmerus, poor child, she was v. good, took her home here, to-night she had

---

314. *Peadar O'Donnell* (1893–1986), republican, socialist and writer.

pain, morphia, sleeping now. King George seems v. seriously ill, they prepare for worst. A v. busy day with M & all. Warm, muggy.[315]

December

Wednesday 5

Lovely sunny day for hours D.G. M doing v. nicely D.G. Rush for Council wh. went well. We're having another shot at the school meals. Med Board went fairly. Dr D Douglas to be asked to apply for post of Path. & bacteriologist. Hear how poor Henry Dixon was killed by motor car y.day at Gardiner Row. He was always a good Republican. They say King G. rather better.[316]

Saturday 15

Much to do. Got M ready for Teac. Mr Stokes came at 9, quite pleased with her D.G. Did pts. & rushed thro' them & to Teac as soon as possible. All went fine there. We had most successful At Home, all admired New Wing wh. looked lovely with soft lights & shining floors & beautiful colours. Miss Esmond says it is only up to date place in Town. To Aunt F abt. 8.30.

Wednesday 26

Up late. I came back here & found M ffM here D.G. We opened my presents happily together, I hate doing it alone. Susie came & was nice & got Sylvie to take Mary & me down quick to Aunt F for dinner. Got lovely box dried fruits fr. N. Hoyne & fine blotter fr. Scotts. Brigid & Jane great chums & all a happy party in N. Smiths. Muriel & I went to see Nan again in aft. Jane & B went to pictures & enjoyed themselves much.

---

315. *Mr Stokes* – Henry Stokes (1879–1967), surgeon.
316. *Dr D Douglas* – Dr Dorothy Herbert Douglas, graduated RCSI 1922. *Henry Dixon* (1859–1928), law clerk, cultural nationalist, founder member of Sinn Féin, interned after the Rising and during the Civil War.

1929

January

Tuesday 1

8.30 Xt. Ch. may the New Year see us, could it be, Free! God grant it if we are ready for it. How one longs to lose the heavy burdens & let the oppressed go free. Anyhow, China is free now & India does seem, if she holds out, to be making for it too. A lovely, mild, gentle day, tho' wind cold & frost. Teac got £210 to-day. D.G. D.G. babies nicely. Saw M Kenny in mg. had lovely walk there. Ret. here to busy aft. & evg. All well D.G.

Wednesday 9

Slept thro' alarm, v. dark. Susie long here at b.fast. Went to Frankfurt Ho. Found Emer pulseless, got priest, she rallied a bit. Has been on terrible bend, poor thing. Went to her late at night. She is still v. feeble, but better. What will be the end of it all? Another railway smash in England. Jugo Slavia seems to be gone to extreme of extreme Mussolini system. How do people stand it?

Monday 14

V. busy day. Racing the whole time. V. cold day but dry. Teac does well. New Wing & breast pump such comforts. Miss Purser came with subs. for Madam's Memorial from the Leslies of Glasslough & was charmed with place. Emer better D.G. Queen Mary's cold better. Miss Nancy Parnell a real Englishwoman, sees no difference betw. the 2 countries. How different fr. Charles Stuart?[317]

Monday 21

8 a.m. S. B's, resigned to what God wills, if we are arrested, we are arrested. Interviewed people in mg. M & I rushed for Dail meeting at 11. No excitement there. Stayed till 12. Mary Mac expounding her constitution wh. worries over trifles too much. It seems England now won't give F.S. face value of [ ] returning to her but only their bullion value, wh. is little. What a typically mean trick to play on poverty.

---

317. *Miss Purser* – Sarah Purser (1848–1943), artist. *Miss Nancy Parnell* – great niece of Charles Stewart Parnell (1846–91), British Liberal politician and trade unionist.

Saturday 26

Off by 6.40 to Muriel. Met Dr & Mrs Jim Ryan at Amiens St. her mother died suddenly in Belfast. I tried to comfort her on journey & she told much of wheat growing & grinding. V. frosty, Caledon quite Alpine. M & I had lovely drive to Augher thro' Aughnacloy, it was beautiful in sun. Then dinner & garden wh. was v. frosty. She hopes for a house soon. All well in Afghanistan.[318]

February

Sunday 17

1 in Lent. 11.30 Kilbride, beautiful walk in sunny snow. Mrs Heatley & Jackie there. Hurried back to dinner. Mrs Skeff, Rose Jacob, Miss Dowling & the Burns to dinner. V. happy party. Then I left, walked to Bray, bus to Dean's Grange, then to see M Kenny then Aunt F, she is v. well D.G. Rather footsore at end. Snow gone. Plenty still in Glencormac. Home all well D.G.[319]

Wednesday 20

8 a.m. S. B's, a race all day with pts. & P.H. 10 & Med Board 12.30. Dr Webb is coming back to us D.G. We, Emer, Mrs Johnson & I inspected Wash Houses on Hollyfields. Poor little Frances Moore buried to-day. The Derey Cookes came in evg. V. disappointed that Hon. Guinness gave so little to Teac, but he may do more. English Govt. nearly defeated on grant to Irish loyalists wh. is good. Windy to-night.[320]

March

Thursday 7

Up early to show Mary how to clean stove, it did well after, nice sunny day, did some house things & then pts. Matron off for a rest. Many raids & arrests, v. bad one in Cullenswood & 27 Dawson St. where

---

318. *Dr and Mrs Jim Ryan* – James Ryan (1892–1970), physician, anti-treaty republican and Fianna Fáil politician, and his wife Máirín née Cregan (1891–1975), writer, Cumann na mBan member and anti-treatyite. Her mother Ellen died suddenly in Belfast on 25 January. *M* – in this entry *M* is Lynn's sister Muriel, who lived near Newry.

319. *Mrs Skeff, Rose Jacob, Miss Dowling & the Burns to dinner* – Hanna Sheehy Skeffington, Rosamond Jacob, Sighle Dowling, née Bowen, and Cissie, née Cahalan, (1876–1948), and her husband John Burns. Cissie Cahalan was a trade unionist, IWFL member and president of the Irish Drapers' Assistants Association 1922–4. After her husband's death in 1936 she lodged with Kathleen Cruise O'Brien, later with Hanna Sheehy Skeffington and worked part time in St Ultan's.

320. *grant to Irish loyalists* – Southern Irish Loyalist Relief Fund.

Mark Byrne sat 6 hrs. while scouts outside warned his prey off. Electrical trades mad abt. Shannon Scheme. See in paper of a baby 14 ozs at birth, fed on whey & brandy!! who now at 5 mos. weighs 5 lbs.

Friday 15

Up & cleaned stove, got breakfast. V. foggy early. Day went well. Disp. large enough. Dr Price rang re haemoliticcoli, she patronised Dr Crofton's lab. again D.G. Election results = Higgins in by only 200, a gt. comedown for F.S. Nice sun in aft. Hear more people swearing by brown bread D.G. Miss Geoghan v. well all day D.G. Evg. saw Miss Carey in Dun's. The place is full of dear Madam.[321]

April

Friday 5

V. tired again but M went for 1st Friday. Dr Finnegan, our new H.S. in bed with cold so I had whole disp. alone. Special Rates Council10, went well D.G. We are not raising rates tho' County charges more. Felt v. cold in aft. & tired, to bed with temp. 100, went down before 12, only tiredness. Hope to go to Glencormac to-morrow. Dr Steen fr. Gt. Ormond St. in Teac. Pleased.[322]

Wednesday 17

Late as usual, too tired, M up, v busy with sleepy sickness man & all, another case of v. acute Flu. Hear they won't let any into France etc. unless freshly vaccin. since v. virulent smallpox landed in Marseilles. Baby Day off to-morrow. D.V. Teac goes well. P.H. 10, & Med. Board. F. Clarke v. excited over going to Jim's on Sat. Quite hot to-day, soft wind at last, rain soon D.V.

Tuesday 30

8 a.m. R.mines, fine day, cold wind. M & I went & bought dress, nice but v. dear we think. Gt. forest fires in France near battle fields, bombs go off at intervals wh. were buried in wood. F.S. has raided houses of Austin Stack's funeral Committee, so cruel. Many of Dev's crowd

---

321. *Higgins in by only 200* – Dublin north by-election, Cumann na nGaedheal candidate Thomas O'Higgins, younger brother of Kevin O'Higgins won a narrow victory over Fianna Fáil's Oscar Traynor.
322. *Dr Finnegan* – probably Dr Mollie Finnegan, graduated Trinity 1928. *Dr Steen* – Robert Steen (1902–81), Irish paediatrician working at Great Ormond Street Children's Hospital, he would return to Ireland in 1932 and work with Dr Stopford Price on BCG inoculation.

at Austin's funeral & even J.J. Walsh was there. Many, many cried. Flowers lovely.[323]

May

Sunday 12

S.A. 8.30. Xt. Ch. a quiet day with Aunt F. Saw poor O'Grady at Lourdes Ho. Lovely day. M ffM says big & v. fine Connolly demonstration. Wonderful lot of Unions represented. 5 bands. Madam MacBride arrested when leaving her house for something she said last Sun. in O'Connell St. Hear they [ ]felon set her in F.S. Parliament.[324]

Monday 13

8 a.m. S. B's. Showery, windy, sunny day. Got thro' last things & packed. M ffM helped. Just before I left M heard of her cousin's Ernest's sudden tragic death & his wife & 2 little ones have still a week's journey to get to him! Poor, poor M, she feels it so. I hate leaving her. She saw me off. We met Madam MacBride on way to L.pool boat. Sibthorp travelling. Couldn't find my suitcase for quite a while. Mrs Dr Cunningham fr. Vincent's in my cabin. Fairly rough.

Wednesday 15

Zurich 10, not 9-8. Lovely in early mg. thro' fields, heights, woods, blossoms, Freiiheit. B.fast Basle. V. glad to get it. Gothard v. near Bahnhof, nice, washed, dressed, went to opening, caused sensation thro' being only woman in robes. They took my photo specially. Aft. saw Children's & Orthopedic Hosps. latter excellent. Even recept. Dolder lovely, high up, by funicular. Flowers & nice things, too many Union Jacks.[325]

June

Saturday 1

Up late, nice soft rain on & off & now steady. M ffM approves of my Congress report D.G. Didn't get out till near 1 o/c & then busy, went

---

323. *F.S. has raided houses of Austin Stack's funeral Committee* – a committee of republicans was set up to organise the funeral of anti-treatyite Austin Stack, their homes were raided during the funeral.
324. *Madam MacBride arrested when leaving her house* – she was arrested for giving a seditious speech at Cathedral St, Dublin, on May 5.
325. *Dolder* – near Zurich, Switzerland. Lynn was in Switzerland for an international Public Health Congress.

to Dalkey & saw McConglin baby, not too bad. D.G. Asked to go & see Mrs Mcredy, she was nice & gave flowers. Eng. elections show big Socialist maj. so Liberal & Conserv. must join to defeat them. King George bad again. Supper F. Rhodes.

Wednesday 5

Uncle Jarlath's anniv. M went to Mass I had early call & got pt. to hosp. Council 10, long & interesting. Mrs Kettle, v. rightly, objects to being put out of proper place in R.C. emancip. procession because she's a woman. We all agreed. Emer got resolut. re hut rescinded. I gave report of P.H. Congress & they all sampled Pomol. Dr Keogh did my nose after wh. is much better. Evg.v.good meeting at Count Plunkett's Idealism & Life.[326]

Sunday 16

3 A.T. 8.30 Xt. Ch. Nice mg. After b.fast wrote to Muriel & came to Dublin before 1 o/c Met Miss Towers, Mrs Langan, M ffM & we all started for Bodenstown with Maher, such a happy day, met little Hyland boy cycling, took him up. Large crowd, 3 bands, fine turn out D.G. & heartening it was D.G. for reviving spirit. Madam McBride & her women there, Mrs Mallin & many more. 8 of us had tea together. Evensong 7. Gardened till 10.[327]

July

Wednesday 10

8 a.m. S. B's & then packing & rushing to be off to the Glen. M had to go to Teac, we were all ready before she came back. Nice uneventful journey down, came by Clash & avoided hill, road was better too. Got across ford well. I waited a moment to see pt. at Hotel. The cottage was so nice & spruced up, we never saw it so. Linoleum on Shuler's room & curtains! We just got beds ready & went to bed. River v. low, dear place.

Saturday 20

A lovely day, light & shade, had sun bath, then Susie, Sighle & I went

---

326. *P.H. Congress* – Lynn gave a report on the Public Health Congress in Zurich to the Rathmines Urban District Council Public Health Committee. *Count Plunkett* – George Noble Plunkett (1851–1938), nationalist politician, museum director and biographer.
327. *Mrs Mallin* – Agnes Mallin, née Hickey, widow of Michael Mallin, executed in 1916.

to climb up just in line with house, Lugduff, we nearly got up, v. stiff climb & felt we had enough, Susie had headache, had gt. clamber down, poor S. retired to bed & was sick, rest had nice lunch, read, then Miss Price & J. Shanaghan came & were v. delighted. J.S. never here before. M gave pot of tea to people up Glen who gave 4/- for Teac. D.G. Fish jumping in river.[328]

August

Thursday 1

A much stormier night but all fr. West River. D.G. not bad. Slept little. Early up, worked hard, Dan came & Maher abt. 11.00, all ready abt. 3, showers, found dear Mrs ffM passed to rest at 3. M came soon & was wonderful, D. rather excited. They took cast off her hand, D. wanted it, she looked v. sweet & peaceful. We'll keep D. here for present.[329]

Saturday 3

The day of funeral. I persuaded M to stay in bed till b.fast. Gt. rush to get all ready. F. Rhodes came & minded house & Matron came too. Mass Beechwood 10, then funeral, so many there & all truly sorry. M & D were v. good. I went with K. Healy, Mrs Kirwan, Matron, Miss D. M broke down a bit at grave. Back to Teac. Then she & D. went to Pearl & Winnies. I saw Muriel, she v. sympathetic. M & D not back till 10, played out, both.

Friday 30

8 a.m. S. B's. We were tired & we had such a day. I had 4 hrs. steady work in disp. Many bad babies there. Gt. preps. for Sun. D.V. all will go well. Zeppline has gone right round the world fr. Lake Hurst in N. Jersey to Deutchland, Russia, Japan & back in abt. 21 days with no mishaps. Wonderful. Evg. M & I went to Messiah. Rhodes to supper. Met v. interesting Austrian Baroness, now poor.[330]

---

328. *Miss Price & J. Shanaghan* – Kathleen N. Price, trade union activist, Irish Nurses' Union, and Jennie Shanahan (1897–1936), member of the Irish Citizen Army who fought with Lynn at the City Hall outpost.

329. *D* – Douglas ffrench-Mullen (*d.*1943), brother of Madeleine, also referred to as Douglas in the diaries.

330. *Zeppline* – refers to the Round-the-World flight of the LZ-127 Graf Zeppelin which began 7 August 1929.

September

Tuesday 3

8 a.m. R.mines. Lovely sun. I had kind of sun bath in window. Saw Mr Scott re balcon. he will get it in hands now. D.V. He settled up Teac things too, is architect for v. fine house in Bognor! Papers full of Snowden & Ben Tillet & all retrograde workers. Emer better, D.G. Mrs Hurley, Boston, in Teac, gave £5. D.V. D.V. the money will come. Wrote many letters. Evg. quite warm.[331]

October

Wednesday 16

8 a.m. S.B's, it was v. stormy in night & mg. Lovely day. Poor Mrs Boyce of Upr. R.mines killed by runaway horse y.day, she was out with her 4 little children, tragic. Emer is going, as delegate, to Russia for Trades Council, D.G. Connie Bennett's mother dead, long sick. Teac Med. Board went well. Invited out to Paediatric 8 o/c. Sent for to see wee baby, v. ill, Pneum. brought it to Teac.[332]

Tuesday 29

8 a.m. R.mines, v. busy, saw Matron early, looking fine & in gt. form D.G.D.G. Nice sun awhile, some survivors of aeroplane found in Mediterranean. More soldiers evicted fr. Portobello come for rooms fr. us. Poor things. M ffM & I went at 7.30 to see Emer & delegation start for Russia. D.G. she was fine. Miss Price went too. Much singing of Red Flag etc. D.V. they will do well.[333]

November

Friday 8

It was a lovely day. Quin came & he & M gardened & did lots. I had to go to Disp. wh. lasted fr. 12 to 4, going hard. Aunt F. better D.G. Miss

---

331. *Mr Scott* – Michael Scott (1905–89), architect. Scott designed several of the buildings at St Ultan's Hospital, and a balcony for Lynn's Rathmines house. *Snowden & Ben Tillet*– Philip Snowden (1864–1937), UK Chancellor of the Exchequer and Ben Tillet (1860–1943), British socialist, trade union leader and politician.

332. *Emer … to Russia for Trades Council* – Molony, as a member of its executive, visited Russia in 1929 as part of the Dublin Trades Council delegation.

333. *More soldiers evicted fr. Portobello come for rooms fr. us* – a shortage of housing for married solders in Portobello Barracks; Rathmines District Council were inquiring about lands in Kimmage for social housing for soldiers.

MacHale stood op.v.well D.G. saw her in evg. Then to Wom. League Peace & Freedom, move on to oust Mrs Desp. & Madam McBride thwarted by 2 votes. L. Bennett reprimanded them for shaking hands with a prisoner. Only Kidson now [survives] or in crash. V. big explosion 11.10 Ballsbridge area.

Monday 25

8 a.m. S. B's in v. deep gratitude for not being in Clonskea! Saw dentist early who agreed tooth must come out. Terrible thing in paper, Civic Guard shot poacher dead near Fermoy, I think, Judge warned jury, Guard unlawfully armed & anyhow, shouldn't have fired, said murder or manslaughter & jury acquitted Civic Guard!!! shows terrorism of countryside. Evg. got tooth out after 3rd pull, such relief, pressure gone. Thankful to bed.

December

Monday 16

8 a.m. S. B's, frosty bright day. Steps froze when Mary washed them. Money for goose club coming in v. well. Saw Miss Murray, no news of Sighle yet. Brought doll that M dressed to W.W.U. for Emer. Much admired it. relief to have Dr Hill home D.G. I am to see Pearl in consultation someday, M v. glad. Evg. M & I went to help with parcels for Child Welf. show, many helpers, work soon done, D.G. & to bed, v. tired.

1930

January

Thursday 2

8 a.m. Xt. Ch. Such a nice fresh, sunny day. All India Conference at Lahore ended & well ended it seems, reading betw. lines. the I. Times leader was almost blasphemous saying Eng. would be India's murderer if she loosed her stranglehold, that she is her brother's keeper, such hypocrisy! Egypt declares for complete independence too. All well in Teac. Went to tea McCurdy. Poor M. beth but wasn't hurt.

Saturday 4

Mrs Kettle called me up 6 o/c, her maid had had a baby, gt. fuss. Dr Hill there 1st. D.G. mother & baby all right. I took her to Rotunda in ambulance. Back 8 o/c. M ffM & I sorted her poor Mother's things till after 2 o/c & cleared out much. Mary's brother & friend here all day on way back to London. Aft. tea Clarke & evg. Rhodes. Brought gramophone both places. Called to Teac prem. bad. Canon Strong came & baptised her, poor lamb. V. stormy now.

Tuesday 7

8 a.m. R.mines. Lovely sunny mg., then rain as usual, not much in papers only Mrs S. Skeffington & Roisin Jacob were speaking at Rotary Club of visit to Prague & Internat. Women & Peace. My poor little god daughter Ellen, died this mg. She had such an unearthly sweet smile. She accomplished in a few days what takes others a long life, dear little soul, only waited to be baptized & went.[334]

Saturday 11

8 a.m. S. B's. V. cold, returning agst. wind. Mrs Kettle came & I explained all abt. her maid. She & baby leave Rotunda to-day & baby comes to Teac. Bought Nan birthday things & she liked them, she looks well. Saw Laisariona in bus & had gt. talk re Russia. V. cold & snow & sleet all day, freezing hard. Aunt F. had wire, Ida has cold & only up this Wed. Aunt F. fine.[335]

---

334. *visit to Prague & Internat. Women & Peace* – Sixth Congress of the Women's International League for Peace and Freedom, Prague, August 1929.

335. *Laisariona* – Elizabeth Somers (1881–1934), republican and writer, Cumann na mBan member, known by her pen name Lasarfhiona Ní Shamhraidin.

Tuesday 28

8 a.m R.mines, dull day but v. nice birthday, got nice things, snow drops fr. Flo & so on. F. Wellwood gave S. Teresa's bookmark. M & I went to Steven's to see new T.B. ward, but it is not open air, such a pity. We saw girls on balcony, picture of health, better than men downstairs. Evg. Mrs Ginnell came, v. well & in good form & I went to Jimmy O'Dea pantomime, splendid.[336]

February

Thursday 6

8 a.m. Xt. Ch. Up 7.30 & all ready for Mrs Hungerford's anesthetic at 9, all went well, v frosty & then lovely sun. Plants came for rock garden & they put in one gratis, v. nice. The missing postman, they say, was accidentally killed by civic guard when all were drinking at Xmas & body hidden in bog. Sad to see such things can happen. M in bed to rest. Teac well. Saw Aunt F. in evg. Terribly cold. East wind.[337]

Wednesday 19

A lovely sunny day & cold frost now. Miss Wilkinson, good Labour woman, has had the courage, it would take a good woman to do it to denounce all this religious!! fervour against Russia for what it is, capitalism & war propaganda. Gate Theatre opened y.day. I am sure Mr Scott is v. proud. Mr MacDonald says Muriel shouldn't buy site, right. Gramophone fine.[338]

Thursday 20

Was late because of cold, nice sun, put baby Noel in it & he breathed better, he is wonderful to be alive with such bronchitis. On all sides we hear of Eng. preparing for war with Russia, how terrible that this supposed war for Christ shld. be against the only country, wh. as a nation, practises his teaching towards all. Sighle & Emer came & we joined the Friends of Soviet Russia. D.V. they will hold firm & keep their place.[339]

---

336. *Jimmy O'Dea* (1899–1965), actor and comedian.
337. *The missing postman* – Larry Griffin, local postman, disappeared from the village of Stradbally, Co. Waterford on Christmas Day 1929.
338. *Ellen Wilkinson* (1891–1947) was a British Labour Party politician. *Gate Theatre* – Michael Scott, Lynn's favorite architect and friend, converted the Rotunda supper-room and ballroom into the Gate theatre.
339. *Friends of Soviet Russia* –Helena Molony, on her return, helped set up the Friends of Soviet Russia. Sheila Dowling became an active member of the group.

March

Friday 7

8 a.m. S. B's, rushed to Emer & May. V. busy all day. Poor Postman's body (Waterford) found buried on blanket in a field & all those arrested for his murder released. What does it mean if not that police did it themselves? Gt. rush to get to John Brennan's lecture in evg., it was fine & Gerard Croft's songs beautiful. Nuns send her 40 girls to lecture on history round Dublin.[340]

Thursday 13

8 a.m. Xt. Ch. Some heavy hail storms & much darkness before. All on tiptoe watching Ghandi in his march for Freedom. He is wonderful at his age 60, so old for India. Debate in Senate on Russia & persecutions. They hadn't it all their own way for Joe Connolly (who was good in 1923) said what of Belfast pogroms & so on wh. was so true. Britain always has ulterior motives when [highbrow].

Wednesday 19

8 a.m. S. B's, snow quite deep, could hardly manage cycle but did it D.G. Lock on Ch. gate frozen, had to enter by side. Sun was glorious & melted snow where it shon, hard frost now. Y.day & to-day in court cases agst. C.I.D. successful & damages awarded £75 & £80, judge old British type, so much better than rotten F.S. Evg. protest meeting in Town Hall agst. Gtr. Dublin bill, quite good. It is a rotten bill.[341]

April

Friday 4

8 a.m. S. B's, such a N.E. wind all day, like snow. The poor almonds & chestnuts are perished. Gt. rush to Dun's at 10. Brigid all right there for her tiny op. Teddy holding her hard. A baby & pram stolen fr. outside Woolworth's, terrible excitement. Hope baby will be found. M ffM & I went to opening meeting of Friends of Soviet Russia. Emer spoke splendidly. Russia practises Xtian society.[342]

---

340. *John Brennan* – pseudonym used by Sydney Madge Czira, nèe Gifford (1889–1974), journalist, broadcaster, and republican.

341. *Gtr. Dublin bill* – Local Government (Dublin) Bill, 1929, proposed to alter the administration of the city and county, including abolishing the urban districts of Pembroke, Rathmines and Rathgar (on which Lynn was a councillor) and their inclusion within the city limits.

342. *Friends of Soviet Russia* – many of Lynn's feminist and trade union comrades were members of this organisation including Helena Moloney, Hanna Sheehy Skeffington, Charlotte Despard, Maud Gonne McBride, Nora Connolly O'Brien, and Rosamond Jacob.

Thursday 17

8 a.m. R.mines, just dragged ourselves out of bed. M ffM had b.fast in Teac. I was late for both Building & Baths Comts. Teac Board went well, then we rushed for tickets etc. Got all done well D.G. India seems to be getting on fine. I hope they will hold out. Glorious sun but cold, cold winds. All preps. getting done D.G. for Brussells. Tired now.

Monday 22

Slept v. fairly, sea glasslike. Nice coffee etc. Antwerp. Arr. Brussells on time. Pension Thevenet v. clean & nice. Slept till lunch. Aft. Bois chestnuts, lovely in Avenue Louise. Ian v. brave. Wonderful equest. statue at gate of Bois, two wrestlers, one with benign face, has hand at other's throat. Kerbstones locked with iron bands or jointed. Too sleepy to write more.

May

Friday 2

Persuaded M not to go to early Mass tho' 1st Fri. Shopped near Ste. Gedulde, got Little Flower for Pearl, imitat. wood. I got Jeanne d'Arc for M. Rushed dinner, met Dr Delacourt Derscheid, Pres. Women's Sect., v. intelligent, worth seeing after our long search. Promised interchange of ideas. Got our last Glaces, packed, left on good terms. Saw Exposition building Antwerp fr. train. Sailed at once, sorry to leave.

Tuesday 20

8 a.m. R.mines, a nice day. England v. fierce over India. She feels her hold slipping. A v. busy day, Child Welf. 10.30, went well. Poor Brennan girl died this mg. so sad. I saw garden in aft. Went to Saor an Leanb. It went well, I think. Matron says Nurse O'Toole unreasonable abt. trifles, hope she'll settle again. Mr Scott rang re. M's water supply. Sacklaoala spoke v. well on Sun. I hear. M much better D.G.

Thursday 22

8 a.m. Xt. Ch. F.Clarke v. full of the news of her brother's death. D.G. he didn't die in the street. Coldish day. Mrs Naru arrested now & Mr Patel carries on in India, tactics just like here, they won't let prisoners be visited etc. Longed to garden, wrote in mg. & saw Scott. Teac does

well, wards being repainted & so on. Brigid gramophone to Aunt F. I thought v. orig. Houses newly built in Salthill, Galway.[343]

Saturday 31

It was a v. nice day, saw dear N who is well, we admired the goldfish a v. little while. Aft. M ffM & I went to Sunshine Home & enjoyed it, they are hoping to build more. Children looked well. I am hoping for new treat. for Mary B. D.V. it'll do some good. Miss Blandford & many more so glad to be at Stillorgan. Early to bed.[344]

June

Tuesday 10

8 a.m. R.mines. Dull coldish day, some rain. Hear Strickland now of Malta was Commandant of the Black & Tans here, note it well! Now one understands much. Indians complain like us, of how British violate all principles of civilized warfare. M ffM & I went to S. Columkill's & remembered much & poor M.B.Pearse. D.G. she got on well y.day. Hear we are to be wiped out in Oct. as a Council![345]

Friday 13

A lovely day & v. busy, breakfast in garden, sun quite hot. Bombay waited whole day, squatting on maidan with police all round, at last at midnight they left & 25,000 held meeting & sang patriotic songs, their C. na mB women in orange sashes. Australia wont have Eng. Gov. Gen. right. The garden is v. enticing with roses & pinks & gold fish etc. Jane came to stay till arranged for.

Monday 23

Such a cold day after all the lovely sun. M ffM & I went to Glasnevin & saw her Mother's grave, v. nice. The Republican plot looks v. neglected alas! We then ordered things for the Glen. & shopped & rushed round. Such showers, hail at times. They say Indian situation well in

---

343. *Mrs Naru* – Kamala Nehru (1899–1936), Indian independence activist, wife of Jawaharlal Nehru. *Mr Patel* – Vallabhbhai Jhaverbhai Patel (1875–1950), Indian nationalist and barrister.
344. *Sunshine House* – Children's Sunshine Home, Stillorgan had been founded by Dr Ella Webb in 1925 as a convalescent home for children, it is now the Laura Lynn Children's Hospice.
345. *Strickland now of Malta* – Gerald Strickland (1861–1940), Maltese and British politician. A Major General Sir Edward Peter Strickland was commander of the Sixth Division of the British Forces in Cork in 1920, they are not the same man. *M. B. Pearse* – Mary Bridget Pearse (1884–1947), writer, musician and teacher, and sister of Patrick Pearse.

hand, the vipers, they would crush if they could! but India is a tough proposition. Madam's Comt. went well.

July

Friday 11

A wettish cold mg. cleared abt. 5, fairly, only had 20 mins. atmosph. bath. Mrs Pearse & M Brigid arr. abt. 5 & were on whole, I think, pleased with Glen. tho' thinking it v. backward & horrible to get at. M. B. brought Lohengrin wh. is v. fine. We had pleasant time & they left abt. 10 F. Clarke & I went to ford, they thought walk & bridge & all v. hard going.[346]

August

Friday 15

8 a.m. S. B's. Slept last night on balcon. & it was lovely. No rain till 7.30 when I beat hasty retreat. V. busy day. Dr Hill off for 14 days. Miss O'Connor Boston & Dr Colles came & was nice. Gt. rush to meet Aunt F. at Amiens St at 5.15, now we feel holidays really over. Blie's 2nd back paw sore, took him to Lambert's & he fixed him, he says paw's v. well. Nice day & sun. Evg. 3 hrs with M.B. Pearse.

September

Wednesday 10

Mary came up 7.30. Jane bad all night. We took her off & baby girl born about 1 o/c, both well D.G. P.H. 10, fairly long, much to do then & many to see. The aft. & evg. were v. hectic. Mrs W Power has accomplished that the stones of City Wall will be preserved D.G. & it can be re-erected later D.V. Indians stone police. Poor old Willy Wally dead at 95, a nice Autumn day. All tired to-night.

Saturday 20

We stayed in & tried to clear up things fr. 63, got a good lot done. Fascisti & Communists = powers in Germany now. Fascists all for war, alas. India says they won't accept antireligious part of Bolchevism tho' they are keen on all the rest, wh. is v. good, I think. It was an even wetter day than usual, [ ] at night.

---

346. *Mrs Pearse & M Brigid* – Mrs Margaret Pearse (1857–1932), nationalist, and mother of Patrick and William Pearse, anti-treaty Sinn Féin TD, and her daughter Mary Brigid.

Monday 22

Off by 7.20 with Jane & baby to Tuam. M ffM went straight to Sligo Municipal Congress. J & I to Tuam, met Fr Benedict, v. enthus. Gaelic. Saw Children's Home. V. nice. D.V. Jane will be happy there. Nice lunch, missed train, raced it in car to Claremorris, such bumping, shaved it, got in as it moved D.G. Lovely aft. saw many raths etc. Went to Sligo Railway Hotel wh. is beautiful. Mrs Kettle & all there. Bed early.[347]

October

Thursday 2

Slept late on balcon, lovely night D.G. We were busy to-day. Mrs Kettle in all right & Ald. Tom D.G. Myles Keogh high up too. I did some prep. for lecture to Nurses in aft. It started rain early & ended in downpour. Nurses came at 3, about 50 in all, all v. keen to see all we had to show & were v. attentive to lect. Went to Aunt. F. after 7, B's temp. still up, but better.

Friday 17

8 a.m. S. B's, lovely night on balcon. & till evg. rain, rain 'Rifles for China' was gun running on large scale, by Northerners! How loyal! Teac nicely on whole. I thought much of poor Teddy. He turned up in evg. Couldn't bring himself to go to sea if Mary only saw her handiwork now! Evg. v. good. Meeting of International Women Mrs Skeff. Mrs Desp. spoke on Russia. It is a gt. land.

November

Friday 14

Breakfast early & then many visits before Teac. Dr Foley in great excitement going off for a post in the Lincoln. D.V. she'll get it. Terrible disaster in Lyons Whole hill fell on the town & demolished many houses. How could they have left people in such a perilous place? Hear now we are to get £1,400 fr. Sweep. Got roses & things for Aghaloo. Went to W.I.L.P.F. meeting.[348]

---

347. *Jane & baby to Tuam* – Jane was Lynn's maid and had a child outside of marriage. Lynn took her and the baby to the Bon Secours Mother and Baby Home in Tuam, Co. Galway. Decades later this Home would be at the centre of the controversy about its very high infant mortality rates and burial of infants in underground chambers.
348. *Dr Foley* – Dr Bridget Maude Foley, graduated NUI 1925. *W.I.L.P.F.* – Women's International League of Peace and Freedom.

Sunday 30

8.30 Xt.Ch. Advent Sun. Slept as usu. & after dinner went back to Ard feis wh. was crowded & v. keen, they did some foolish things, like forbidding F.S. to buy a flag, if a permit had been got fr. F.S. & forbidding us to have any dealings with those who had taken F.S. oath. When coming away Florrie McCarthy & Joe Clarke attacked by G. men & papers & books snatched fr. them.

December

Monday 8

M ffM went to Mass early. I had only just b.fast ready when she got back. V rushing day. This day in 1922 we were in Geneva. Kathleen O'Brennan & I in rain. Attempts to prevent more S.F. murders & how little we could & with the dreadfully British Red X there! New H.S. in Teac. I had only a rush in & out M cold all day. In India they shot Chief of Prisons dead, no [ ]understanding.[349]

Monday 15

Had nice night out, v. busy all day. Revolt in Spain said to be quelled by shooting officers & imprisoning 1,000 men! Strange piece in paper re. change in methods of Govt. in England: is it Soviet or what? Jane came & arranged to stay here & do late evg. & early mgs. till Xmas. Poor little Ciarogue cat sick. M went to the Bystander, excellent prison play. Not home till 11 o/c.[350]

Monday 29

8 a.m. S. B's. Cold N.W. wind. A rushing day. Poor M ffM was v. tired & sorry for being so long ill, this is a hard time on her, her father's anniversary & all. Dr Price gone to London, now Miss Price v. well now. D.G. F.S. govt. says it will cut off all hosp. grants because of sweep money, the essence of meaness! but what can one expect! We had gt. dinner, M's turkey, Susie, Sylvie & Douglas.[351]

---

349. *Kathleen O'Brennan* (1876–1948), nationalist, journalist, anti-treatyite, and campaigner for Irish independence.
350. *the Bystander* – a play about convicts in an English prison by Robert Brennan (1881–1964).
351. *Miss Price* – Kathleen Price.

1931

January

Wednesday 14

Late up, nice day tho' cold M ffM up nearly all day & v. busy, arranging, much re new building, lighting, ventilation etc. Hear Teac milk has formatin in it so sorry for Coard. Pt. told me her child must be demonstrating since she was 11- menstruating! Building strike goes on & F.S. has cheek to say it will make slums worse as if slum dwellers could afford to live elsewhere.

Friday 23

Lovely sun early then showers & cold N.W. wind. V. gusty. Teac v. busy Emer says W.W.U. has bailiffs on Govt. over decision of High Comt. re mental nurses fees writ out for £4,500. Mulcahy says he'll bring in bill to overthrow H. Court decision, if he does, whole edifice of F.S. collapses. In dark little lad prevented my plung into large puddle with a point to it & oh Miss! Mind child.

February

Thursday 12

8 a.m. Xt. Ch. cold mg. some frost. Rang Mrs Kettle & she was quite nice re Child Welf. It is all cut & dried now & we must make what we can of it. D.G. Mrs K is not [ ]frossle. Such a busy day, flying whole time. Molly H. nicely D.G. Teac fairly, building goes well. M ffM sent bits whin fr. Jersey. It is to-day the Pope is broadcasting. Jane, Mrs Despard, Dr Timoney is to go to F.O.S.R to-morrow. Emer approves of Stasco.[352]

March

Thursday 5

Up late, alas! v. cold winds. Teac lean tos being wrecked, how quickly it is done! Alas for the grass. Casement's Life is a horrid libel on us & all Easter Week. Denis Gwynn should be ashamed to be so anti Irish,

---

352. *F.O.S.R* – Friends of Soviet Russia.

no wonder England praises his book. Sighle came in mg. I gave much advice. Mrs Kettle at night & we talked Child Welf. fine now.[353]

Friday 20

8 a.m. S. B's. Mild day, v. busy. Posters say King George proposes to visit Ireland, D.V. such an indignity will not occur. Matron seems better D.G. Has McGilligan's rush visit Buckingham Palace any significance? Nice & Springlike. M ffM to have teeth out to-morrow. D.V. it will do much good. She walks better with crutch.[354]

Friday 27

8 a.m S. B's, lovely early sun & on balcon. Tim Healy dead & funeral private & no flowers. So passes the man who sold Ireland time & time again. Compare Madam's funeral! Hear England can't pay Northern subsidy longer & we are to be a federal state & Card. Logue is arranging it & is to be Papal Legate at Eucharistic Congress. Perhaps! Lovely Spring day.[355]

April

Wednesday 15

Great news! Spain has proclaimed a Republic & King Alfonso has abdicated. D.G. for a bloodless revolution. God grant ours may be the same. Med. Board went well. Matron delighted at idea of Hospitals' Congress in Vienna. At 5 there was meeting in R.C.S.I re Brit. Med. Assoc. meeting here in 1933. It was good. I seconded resolution & am on Executive.[356]

May

Tuesday 5

8 a.m R.mines, not so sunny. Went for tickets for Vienna, to Douglas & Jas. Dwyer hoping he'll get into Guinness. Teac v. fairly. V. busy

---

353. *Denis Gwynn* (1893–1971), journalist and historian, published his book *Traitor or Patriot; The Life and Death of Roger Casement* in 1931. It constructed Casement as flawed if patriotic, while Gwynn dodged the issue of the black diaries which reveal Casements' homosexuality.

354. *McGilligan's rush visit Buckingham Palace* – Patrick McGilligan (1889–1979), Minister for External Affairs.

355. 31st International Eucharistic Congress was held in Dublin 22 to 26 June 1932.

356. King of Spain, Alfonso XIII (1886–1941), abdicated on 14 April 1931. *Brit. Medical Assoc.* – British Medical Association, their annual meeting was held in Dublin in 1933.

aft. Evg. great long Cuman meeting, business to expel Emer, Cuman felt incompetent to do so & referred to St. Comt. We got parchment to Signora Ceannt & Emer, M ffM & I signed it. We felt it may be an historic night.[357]

Thursday 21

A busy day & anxious but D.G. we got thro' well. Teac Board 11.30, signed deed poll for new sweep. Dr De B Daly told us we must look to our laurels, perh. we compare favourably with mixed Boards. Talked to Dr Moorehead re clinical teaching, he isn't hopeful. Quite cold, E. wind all day, now mild, soft rain. We wish we were ready & off, for we, all 3, need freedom fr. care.[358]

Tuesday 26

8 a.m. R.mines, a v. nice day & bright sun in aft. M & I went to Child Welf. 11.30 wh. went not badly D.G. then we did much shopping & successful. M got hats, coat & smart dresses. The Teac in a hurry & back here to many. Evg. special Cuman meeting. Mrs Buckley came but not Emer. They can throw us out if they will.[359]

July

Thursday 16

8 a.m Xt. Ch. F. Clarke surprised & glad to see me. Fine in mg. & indeed all day, 1 heavy shower. Made out our balance sheet for Vienna etc. We had long & important Board Meeting. D.V. we made right decisions. New roof to old house = £300. Saw to many things, shopped, got thermosin case for Mrs Byrne. Good letter fr. John D.G. F.C. & F.W. saw me off, arr. in Glen safe. F.R. v. well D.G.

August

Tuesday 4

8 a.m. R,mines, thankful for all mercies. So glad Dr Maguire has entered into her rest. I Times notice v. bald & not a word of the self sacrificing life & I had impressed it on them! Ordered wreaths fr. Med.

---

357. *Cuman meeting* – Cumann na mBan meeting.
358. *Dr De B Daly* – Dr Charles Calthrope de Burgh Daly (*d.*1847). *Dr Moorehead* – Dr Thomas Gillman Moorhead (1878–1960), Professor of Medicine at Trinity College and President of the Royal College of Physicians of Ireland.
359. *Special Cuman meeting* –Cumann na mBan meeting.

Board & staff & Gen.Board. Brought Sighle to Dr O'Dougherty, she is all normal D.G. Visited & shopped. Teac quite nice D.G. & all goes well there. A lovely day for Horse Show. Many pts. already, man came in evg. said he was Dr McIlhinny, asked for money. Was he a fraud?[360]

Wednesday 12

Busy mg. Saw dear old Oultons, Miss Emma a darling, so grieved for Dr Maguire. Mr Scott in his new offices in S. Frederick St. & I had long interview re Laundry block & I think he has done it well tho' Matron's room must be curtailed, says there is springy grasslike stuff for flat roof wh. we must have. D.V. solarium will be v. good, I hope. A letter fr. M ffM, D.G. D.G. she will probably be home before end of month. It is splendid. Nurse does well, poor thing, her family are a burden to her.

Tuesday 18

8 a.m. R.mines. No news all day of M ffM. We wonder if she will come to-morrow. I do hope she will be wise & go to Glencormac. Child Welf. 10.30 went well. R.mines will keep its end up. Then to pts. & shopping. The North is behaving v. ill & attacking convents etc., curfew may be proclaimed, they say. Teac, all is ready in new wing & babies will be in D.V. to-morrow. Such glorious unaccustomed sun! Evg. F. Rhodes. Mr R. there, Tristan & Isolde [ ]

Monday 24

Up 6.30. Met M ffM & Mrs Bennett at W.Row, both so well D.G. M can walk quite easily with crutch D.G. She rested all day & Douglas & Miss Duffy came to dinner, rather surprised she was going to Glencormac. Stop Press. British Cabinet resigned Coalition formed to retrench, terrible to cut off the unemployed. Hear B. Specials being called & armed, feared renewed pogram in North. D.V. it won't be. Britain fights by all foul means as usual. Lovely day.[361]

September

Monday 7

8 a.m. S. B's to pray Teac Post Graduate course may go well. Three turned up for it & I had them an hour at disp. I think they liked it, it made Teac v. busy. M ffM went round Teac, to Mr Glynn & home, had

---

360. *Dr Maguire* – Dr Katharine Maguire (1863–1931).
361. *W.Row* – Westland Row, train station in Dublin.

Douglas to dinner & wasn't 'dead'. She sleeps well here, D.G.D.G. she is so well. More news of floods in Anglesey Rd. Water within 3 in. of kitchen ceiling. D.G. no lives lost.

Thursday 17

8 a.m. Xt. Ch. it was a lovely Mother's Birthday D.G. M ffM & Olga came & we had Mr Benson & Mrs Tom Clarke at Board Meeting. Mrs Reddin was away & we couldn't set key of seal to seal our Sweeps deeds poll. We have decided on building the Laundry on side garden so that D.V. it will fit in with large plan. I went about range & saw Liffey one wh. would do. Teac fairly. Irish Press has interview with Signorita Kent. Revolt in Navy seems serious? Revolution.[362]

October

Monday 5

8 a.m. S. B's, lovely warm day. M & I went shopping first & then to Teac, all v. fairly there & Matron back, looking v. well. M able to do so much more D.G. The dishwasher is on its way at last! Senators ' houses visited & they warned not to vote for safety bill, good. Rioting continues in England & U.S.A. says she is nearly finished D.G. Old Sir Thos. Lipton died on 2nd, same day as Bp. of Tuam. Emer came in evg. worried by meansesses.[363]

Friday 9

Wet to-day. V. busy, big disp. not back till 5. Y.day papers said Hindenburg setting up dictatorship in Germany leaving people no vestige of freedom. All Councils here almost speak out against Police Bill & are promptly going to be suppressed. M ffM goes on well D.G. She & I washed hair after dinner & isn't too tired. D.G. Saw swallows up to 27.9.31. All gone now I think.

Monday 12

8 a.m.S. B's, a nice day, rain in aft. The provisions of the Safety Bill are terrible, worse than the worst British bill ever was. Saor Eire, C na mB, Fianna, I.R.A. all proclaimed. all trials to be in secret & papers to

---

362. *Mrs Reddin* – Teresa Reddin (1865–1949), treasurer of Cumann na mBan, one of the founders of St Ultan's and first Hon. Treasurer of the hospital. *Senorita Victoria Kent* – Spanish woman who abolished flogging and introduced sweeping reforms in the prisons of Spain.
363. *Sir Thomas Lipton* (1848–1931), founder of Lipton tea.

be fined if they dare to. Nurse & I put on carpets in mg. then pts. then B. McQuaide to lunch at Teac. She was v. pleased. Mary E. won't have an op. Fanny Lynch here, her eyes are bad. M ffM in bed.[364]

Wednesday 14

Got specimens of M ffM early, fairly long day. Matron didn't mention last night at all. I gave orders, windows must be open at night. Cosgrave got his bill thro' by majority of only 18, he is losing his following. Emer says British Communists riddled with Scotland Yard men have got control of Saor Eire & I.R.A. be it so we'll conquer yet! Douglas came for his birthday dinner & cake, v. nice. Was at Dean's Grange & brought things to S. Patrick's.[365]

Wednesday 28

Still not quite N. in mg. lovely day, sunbath. Fianna Fail's Ard Feis seems good, as if Dev was getting a bit of back bone at last. Perhaps they may accomplish something. Quite nice & warm.

Saturday 31

Unveiling of Madam's tablet in aft. A mixed grill, many not seen together since 1921 but all poor Madam's friends. Mrs Wyse Power spoke so feelingly of her with tears in her voice. I had to thank for Teac. Alfie, L.Mayor O'Neill, Count & C.ess O'Byrne, Mrs Pearse & many more. All pleased with Teac. Then to Aunt F. Hallow Eve with "The Souls of the Righteous" in my ears. Poor Landlord buried to-day.[366]

November

Sunday 1

8.30 St. Ch. D.G. for day. Went to Dean's Grange & planted metal box with snowdrops on grave. So quiet, mild, fresh & beautiful. Faded birches. Evensong. Nice hymns, no Sermon. Canon had no

---

364. *Saor Eire*– Saor Éire was a political organisation established in September 1931 by communist-leaning members of the IRA. *Safety Bill* – The Public Safety Act 1931, which empowered the Executive Council to declare a state of emergency during which most provisions of the constitution could be suspended, and extra security measures taken.
365. *Cosgrave got his bill thro'* – The Public Safety Act. *Scotland Yard men have got control of Saor Eire & I.R.A* – Molony believed that British police spies were among the membership of Saor Éire and the IRA.
366. *A mixed grill* – many of those who attended the unveiling had split over various political issues since 1921, but all had been friends with Markievicz so came together to honour her.

voice. Madam McBride delighted with her huge meeting. 30,000 sang Soldiers' Song, fine & Felons of our Land & 1916 Proclamation sold like hot cakes as Phoblacht. Stop Press D.G. The spirit revives.[367]

Wednesday 11

8 a.m S. B's, got lilies & wore one & it was the only one I saw till I got back to Teac. Lovely bogus proclamation wh. was so realistic. I thought it genuine until I considered no one could be so fulsome over Empire. Many fine meetings. Fr Sweetman spoke well. Baton charges. F.S. men arrested & released. Emer, John & Madam all well to fore. M ffM went to Firhouse 8.30 & came back so tired. Pearl not well, alas![368]

Wednesday 25

S. Catherine, 8 a.m. S. B's. Mr Simpson mentioned S. John of X & S. Catherine of Sienna. I think M ffM had glorious cardinal cyclamen, always remembered. Emer much better. Cosgrave speaks of our love for England & gives it as reason why clause shld. pass, denying F.S. power to alter its constitution. Clause thrown out by 50 to 350, I think. Made up parcels of dear Nan's things & sent them off. Not busy day but got much done,

December

Thursday 3

V. stormy night & indeed day. More military trials. Lord Mayor of Cork to try to depose City Manager. Special Teac Board went well. He passed all Laundry things. M ffM went for Pearl & brought her to S. P's & D.G. she went willingly. We prayed all will go well. Many pts & out v. late. Stormy now.

Thursday 10

Only waked at 8.30 but thanked all the same for Gilmores. F.S. majority was only 1 y.day Would have been = only 1 F.F. was out . Alfie Byrne has retired fr. Senate. Why? Ann had wild tale of how Sean T accused him of taking Sweep money, sounds queer. Gt. epidemic of

---

367. *her huge meeting* – Maud Gonne McBride, Helena Molony, Charlotte Despard and others spoke at a People's Rights Association meeting held on Dublin's O'Connell Street.
368. *Fr Sweetman* – John Francis Sweetman (1872–1953), Benedictine monk, pro Sinn Féin, under an ecclesiastical ban for 14 years, 1925–39, because of his support of Sinn Féin.

Scarlet, Cork St. & Clonskea full. I had 4 cases to-day, all N.side got new Valor Perfect stove, hope it will do well, cost 17/6.[369]

Friday 18

V. busy but all went well D.G. Mrs Wyse Power seems more & more to be returning to us D.G. Nice letter fr Miss Herbert saying now the fight must continue till Liberty won. Sheila & Mrs Skeffington here in evg. Republican file suppressed now, they say. because George Gilmore's photo in it.[370]

---

369. *Alfie Byrne* – Alfred 'Alfie' Byrne (1882–1956), nationalist politician, Irish Party MP, Independent TD, Senator, Lord Mayor of Dublin.
370. *Mrs Wyse Power seems more & more to be returning to us* – Jennie Wyse Power, formerly a senior member of Cumann na mBan and Sinn Féin split with both over the Treaty which she supported. Now a Free State Senator, for her like many, the anti-women policies of the Free State government were proving a unifying platform for those who had split the Treaty.

1932

January

Tuesday 12

8 a.m. R.mines. Hear Frank Gallagher arrested for publishing treason in Irish Press & many more charges. People in Wynn's Hotel v. panicky over Fr. Sweetman's lecture, made him promise to say nothing political. It was crowded & I saw many old friends. His talk on how Communism's the highest Xtianity was excellent. Sighle & Frank came back with me to Pembroke Rd. Couldn't make pt. hear.[371]

Friday 22

Such a day. Sighle came early & we arranged for Mrs C to stay with Emer, then told Publican to send her no more drink. Met Mrs Gilmore & we interviewed Mr Wigham & he was v. nice & kind D.G. Then she came to Teac & saw all & Miss Rhodes liked her. V. big disp till 3.30. M ffM's cousins paid 1st visit to Teac & were delighted. We had fire drill, went well. More & more pts. to finish after 11.

Thursday 28

8 a.m. Xt. Ch. M ffM grussed me at midnight, 58th birthday & it was nice, got several things, big cake, record, basin & jug, grapes & so on. M ffM & I shopped. Saw about N. Hoyne's fruit. Mr Waldron kind. Emer v. depressed, God help her. She slept but unrefreshed. I never saw her so low. We had nice little dinner & she came in. Sister at murder trial of that poor Ticknock child. It was once in Teac.

February

Tuesday 16

8 a.m. R.mines. Most glorious day of brilliant sunshine. No excuse for not voting. Most people say F.F. will come well in D.V. D.V. We do hope & pray for the best for Ireland. They say even if C na G is beaten it will try to form dictatorship. Hear police, arm, civil servants all anti Govt. Shooting of Leitrim candidate will hold up that elect. Times says statutory Dail meeting might therefore be put off.[372]

---

371. *Frank Gallagher* (1893–1962), journalist and Irish volunteer. Gallagher was prosecuted for seditious libel under the Constitution (Amendment No. 17) Act 1931. *Sighle & Frank* – Sheila Dowling and her husband Frank Dowling.
372. The 1932 general election was held on Tuesday, 16 February.

Friday 19

Latest results F.F. 58, C na G 41. Lab. 11 Farm 5. that is wonderful, if only now F.F. will stand firm but ugly rumours of an agreement, could they descend so low! Sweep tops 2 mil.[373]

Monday 22

8 a.m. S. B's. A rushing day, Teac goes well D.G. & Mr Scott is seeing abt. the new cots. Elections still cause surmises. F.F. indignantly repudiates idea of Nat. Govt. & says C na G only now first mentions it & we heard it weeks ago fr. F.F. source. another dry day & all fairly well.

March

Wednesday 2

Felt a bit rested this mg. D.G. Wind not quite so biting. All packed. M ffM gave Mrs W. Power Stasco's book to review, hope it will be a worthy memorial of dear Madam. Sligo & Leitrim election day. D.V. all will go well there. Alfie Byrne is twister, got elected as Cosgraveite & now sides with Dev!! War Comt. in East, gt Powers could stop it. Davy & Mrs Cookes, Frank & Mrs Costello came. Such a fat, well fed quartet unlike starved Dubliners.[374]

Thursday 10

1st act of new Ministers was to order off all restrictions of prisoners in Arbour Hill D.G. D.G. Their relations visited them & at 4 they were released, all of them. Met by strings of cars. Wild enthusiasm. All went to An Stad in N. Frederick St. I saw Gilmores, Sean O'Farrell, Punch O'Rian & many more. Gt. gathering of clans, like old times. Used to have 2 small towels only on 6.30 a.m. till night for 10 weeks, often only bread & water & they lived triumphantly thro'.[375]

Friday 11

M ffM much better, rushed across to An Stad & saw the prisoners again, they look starved & weak after all. Terrible to think of them

---

373. *Sweeps* – Irish Hospitals' Sweepstakes, a lottery established in 1930 by the Irish Free State to finance hospitals.
374. *Stasco's book to review* – Stanislaus Dunin Markievicz (1896-1971) was the stepson of Countess Markievicz, his unpublished biography of his stepmother is held at the National Library of Ireland.
375. *order off all restrictions of prisoners in Arbour Hill* – On 10 March 1932, the new Fianna Fáil government released 23 political prisoners from Arbour Hill and other prisons.

naked but for towels all Dec. & up to now & mostly on bread & water & alone. They had excursion to Glendalough & Ceilidh in evg. I fear too much excitement for them. In Teac burnt baby dead, alas! John came abt. 11 p.m & is well, says M v. nervy & shld. smoke.[376]

Wednesday 23

8 a.m. R.mines. Much stir over Dev's proposal to remove oath caused gravest consternation in British H. of Commons & whole place humming with reporters trying to get opinions. British Cabinet meeting to-day. Will they try to repudiate Statute of W.minister? Nice Spring day. Babies out D.G. Emer came late, she & John & Fineen are off to-morrow. Nice sketch for Madden's bust.[377]

April

Thursday 7

We are both v. tired & have idea of going to Jersey for 12 days next week D.V. it would be lovely & would save M ffM. I hope Dev. & Co have sent note & say they won't go to London to confer, quite right. Mussolini was first to break off talks & return to Italy first to flout Britain, may we do same! Went to bed after dinner & sent Douglas home. We were too tired for words. Cold, wind & hail.

Tuesday 12

8 a.m. R.mines, a nice day, rush to pts. & Child Welf. M ffM saw Board of Works re Madam's statue in Green, they don't think they'll object. It now appears Cosgrave & Co. made secret arrangement to pay British Land annuities, not even telling their own Cabinet! Much British scandal! but perhaps they bluff as often before, D.V. we'll keep firm & straight.[378]

Friday 29

Bathed early, M's leg bad. I shopped, she rested on sand, got hair cut. I rushed to meet Mrs & Miss Reckett, lovely bus drive to Perrifer (?) &

---

376. *M* – here refers to her sister Muriel who had bad health.

377. *Dev's proposal to remove oath* – de Valera intended to keep his election promise to remove the Oath of Allegiance which all TDs had to take on entering the Dáil. The Constitution (Removal of Oath) Act 1933 provided for its removal.

378. *British Land annuities* – Under Article 5 of the 1921 Anglo-Irish Treaty, annuities were included as part of what the Irish Free State would pay to service the United Kingdom public debt. While the Boundary Agreement of December 1925 released the Government from these obligations, payment of annuities continued and, in March 1926, the Cumann na nGaedheal government agreed officially that the Irish state would continue to do so.

walk to Grosney. V. fine, saw Plermont to N. Got v. near precipices, lovely sun, remains of v. large castle on Grosney bigger than Orgeuil. entrance arch whole, remains of several towers at intervals. Home, packed, said good bye. Eng. papers give a/c of how Batt O'Connor behaved like lunatic in Dail. Irresponsible.[379]

May

Saturday 7

John & I went to Mr Scott in mg., he says roof needs much, wood rotten, we are to beard Couness next week over it. French President's assassinated by White Russian, insane Dr. poor man, he was old & feeble. Aft. J & I went to Spring Show & saw beautiful jumping in warm sunshine, reminded me of Hollymount so long ago. Exhibits nice too. Bought Foxford blankets.[380]

Thursday 12

Connolly & McDermott's anniversary & day of budget, it must be good for I. Times is so mad over it & so self contradictory. All possible British goods are on tarrif & large amts. goes to relieve unemployment. Income Tax 5/- in £, it will be hard on those who pay but will relieve distress. Gt. United Missionary meeting in Mansion H. Bishop Linton [ ]of Kilmore spoke well & liberally.[381]

Wednesday 18

The I. Times perfectly furious over tarrifs & gives report of C na nGael meeting where Cosgrave told lies galore & was terribly unfair about Dev. John fixed the range & perhaps it will work now. M ffM went to lectures of Hosps. Exhibition & W. Taylor was splendid on Nurses, how they shld. have good hours, games etc. Sighle & Frank came. Moon fine.[382]

---

379. *Grosney* – Grosnez castle on the island of Jersey. *Batt O'Connor* – Bartholomew 'Batt' O'Connor (1870–1935), revolutionary, pro-treaty, Cumann na nGaedheal (and later Fine Gael) politician.

380. Paul Doumer (1857–1932) President of France was assassinated on 7 May by Russian émigré Paul Gorguloff (1895–1932). *Spring Show* – Royal Dublin Society Spring Show.

381. *Connolly & McDermott's anniversary* – anniversary of the executions of 1916 leaders and Proclamation signatories James Connolly and Seán Mac Diarmada (Seán McDermot) on 12 May 1916 in Kilmainham Jail.

382. *Tariffs* – The Tarriff Commission was reviewing tariffs and the de Valera Government sought to impose its own tariffs on imports from Britain.

Tuesday 31

8 a.m. R.mines. Gt. rush to dentist & back & to Child Welf. wh. my letter fr. City Manager was a bombshell. God will arrange things I feel sure. If only we could have a proper scheme! M ffM had Hospts. Comt. at 6 wh. question of levy on Sweep's money, got more towards solution. John fixed in new bath wh. is gt. improvement. He is clever. Evg. gave Nurses lecture to 13.

June

Saturday 18

I forgot to mention Mary B reception in Mansion Ho. last night. M ffM & I went. Peter Murray, Los Angeles there & so many more. G. Gilmore & Mary Mac spoke. Saw so many. To-day Murray came to Teac & saw all round. He is quite nice. Here we slaved & had all done, beds made & all with Aunt F. by 10.30 a lovely warm day. I. Times thinks we'll be free, no fight.[383]

Tuesday 21

8 a.m. R.mines. Another glorious day. Saw Annie Carroll & talked to her, she is v. much on wrong lines. D.V. she will improve. The garden party at Blackrock was gt. success, we hear, John & I started for reception at Castle for Legate. Dev. did it well. There were millions & all so well arranged, no crushing, & all went well, saw state rooms & many fr. Garry Houlihan to City Manager, Fr O'Shea arrived.[384]

Sunday 26

5 A.T. 8 a.m. R.mines, rushed back & fed all & got them started for Park. Day dull, overcast. D.G. for that. Crowds & crowds came fr. all over place. Dr Hill drove us, J & me, to Aunt F's, & we had rest. D.G. Heard wireless fr. Park, not v. edifying. Rosary over & over 3 hrs = each sodality passing high altar. John Brennan heard well & McCormack sang beautifully. J has enough of visitors, didn't turn up till abt 1 a.m.[385]

383. *Mary B reception* – Cumann na mBan reception in the Mansion House for Irish American visitors to the Eucharistic Congress. *Peter Murray, Los Angeles* – member of the American Association for the Recognition of the Irish Republic (AARIR).
384. The 31st International Eucharistic Congress, held in Dublin 22–26 June 1932. The representative of Pope Pius XI was the Papal Legate, Cardinal Lorenzo Lauri.
385. *McCormack* – John McCormack (1884–1945), Irish tenor, sang at the Eucharistic Congress.

July

Friday 1

Slept thro' alarm, up 8.15, rush for dentist 9, no time for b.fast. Nice mg. Mr MacNamara sheltered 4 in Congress, like ourselves. Dev. rang, he will unveil Madam's statue at 1 o/c on Sun, so we must just be ready. Papers gave nice pictures of y.day's show & harpist much pleased. Showery. Teac fairly. Dr O'Leary new H.S. nice, but new. We asked Nurse Martin to stay on & that's for July. Nurse off to Lough Derg. I must pack alone.[386]

August

Friday 12

All enemies out against Dev., new kind of Taoists start purporting to be aiding distressed I.R.A. pre Truce with that enlisting volunteers to be ready to crush communities or the like, if nec!! I. Times v. poisonous also. V. busy day in Teac. Frau Grabish came to lunch, she is a dear. Evg. S.F. meeting, such rot as the St. Comt. talks! They are antideluvian. Heard some about Paed. Conference.[387]

Friday 26

Slept late, had b.fast, dressed & was at consultation at 10 fr 9.10. Teac disp. record = 63, bad enough babies still. Govt. going to set up enquiry re profiteering, rents included, shld be good, I think. All goes on in Teac busily. Glass & screen going up on roof & sink being fixed. We admitted practically dying baby fr. Rotunda. The toxic ones have done well D.G. Many such a comfort & so happy here.

Monday 29

8 a.m. S, B's. Papers full of Dr O'Callaghan & Tisdell's return fr. Olympic Games & their welcome. O'Duffy says Olympiad will be here in 1940. Gt. news, M ffM is wonderfully well & Dr Weir hopes for gt. things this time. Nan Lawless case hopeful too. All busy in Teac, many babies & v. sick & works coming on glass screen being put up. Mr Scott says he'll come on Sun.[388]

---

386. The memorial to Countess Markievicz was unveiled by de Valera in St Stephens Green on 3 July 1932.

387. *Evg. S.F. meeting, such rot as the St. Comt. Talks* – Lynn becoming disillusioned with Sinn Féin and its Standing Committee.

388. *Dr O'Callaghan and Tisdell* – Dr Patrick 'Pat' O'Callaghan (1906–91) won the gold medal in the hammer throwing and Robert 'Bob' Tisdall (1907–2004) won the gold medal in the 400-meter hurdles at the 1932 Summer Olympic games.

September

Friday 2

8 a.m. S. B's, soft,v. wet, damp, warm. Alfie Byrne re-elected 3rd time Mayor, he got 20, Mrs T.Clarke 10. V. busy Disp. not over till 3.30. Then Conaty sent form re exemption on tax on Dance said I was to sign all & of course that was wrong, had to get new form, fill in my part & send back to him. Cotton strike v. embarrassing to England. Saw Jellett Sullivan, they were all round home places, Corrib, Cong, B.robe, Maam etc.

Monday 26

8 a.m. S. B's, v. busy all day. Hear Dev made good speech at Geneva, he is wonderful. John came abt. 3, saw Sir Wm. who said foot must be opened wh. was done in Dun's at 4.20. Saw Mr Macnamara, too, who said J's teeth must come out soon. We ret. here & J much relieved, went to bed & I had millions & on till v. late. Emer came, v. well D.G & talked to John. V.v. cold to-day.

October

Monday 10

8 a.m. S. B's, nice mg. sun, then soft day. Army comrades fired on F.F. meeting, a C na nGael one, on same time, free fights A.C.A. tried to break up F.F. Hear v. probably a 26 county Republic shortly (therefore) all money being transferred to 6 counties or Britain, for £ would only be 15/-. Good news if true. Ard Feis wasn't bad, some signs of common sense at last. Went to Draw & saw drum ship & ports. It was v. fine. Saw Duggan & Lord Powerscourt.[389]

Wednesday 12

8 a.m. S. B's. Rioting more severe, people shot dead, barricades, trenches, armoured cars in streets, fires & darkness. Terrible joy ride in Dr Lane's car they nearly killed a woman & quite killed a man, police have warned all Drs to look out for them. Med. Board went well, rain in aft. The provisions of the Safety bill are terrible, worst than the worst British bill ever was.

---

389. *A.C.A.* – Army Comrades Association, a quasi-fascist, paramilitary organisation founded in 1932 by former army officers, nicknamed the Blueshirts because of the colour of the uniform shirt they wore. They were a response to the victory of Fianna Fáil in the 1932 election, leading to street battle between supporters of Fianna Fáil and Cumann na nGaedheal.

Thursday 20

8 a.m. Xt. Ch. sun early, much rain at night, so lovely to have M ffM back & she is so well & walked quite a lot in Spa & she did well to-day. All so pleased to see her in Teac. Board went well D.G. Papers of course, say Dev. is fine, or a nothing. In England many admire him much because he works for his people. Gold found in Cork, maybe in quantity = 2nd place in Ireland lately.

November

Tuesday 1

8 a.m. R.mines, nice sun later. Fianna Fail has nearly doubled Cumain & these have trebled members D.G.. Their Ard Feis on 8th demands removal of Senate & C.I.D. Press quotes Daily Mail showing agricultural depression worse in Britain than here. M ffM says knee better & she was at Mass D.G. Evg. went to Grangegorman, v. nice but all new hymns but one. Mr Hamilton there. Mr Bell preached v. otherworldly.[390]

Friday 4

8 a.m. S. B's, so nice to have Mr Waring there. Nice day. I. Times seems to rage & storm & misrepresent but Dr Ryan showed plainly farmers are only one 1/- behind last year's prices per cwt. in Liverpool, much better for them to have home markets as they soon will, D.V. Comt. of References seems to take much on itself & blame us for not admitting baby when we had no cot. Sighle came, long chat. A.G.O.W. but Shanaghan gave Emer whiskey.[391]

Monday 21

8 a.m. S. B's, v. cold N. Wind but nice & dry. Dean Swanzy killed by motor in London remember H. Smartt speak of him re Newry. Dev has momentous task in Geneva & he is universally respected there, unbiased. Mrs W. Power anxious but glad. Papers report Prince of Wales in B.fast addressing Orangemen fr. wall after beating their drums "I like a good time, you like a good time" quite maudlin. Alas for dignity. They are taught how to play to gallery.[392]

---

390. *demands removal of Senate & C.I.D.* – refers to plans to abolish the Senate (the upper house of the Irish Parliament) and the Criminal Investigation Department of the police.
391. *Dr Ryan* – Dr James Ryan (1892-1970), Fianna Fáil Minister for Agriculture. *Shanaghan* – Jennie Shanahan, friend and comrade of Helena Molony since their Irish Citizen Army days.
392. *Dean Swanzy* – Henry Biddall Swanzy (1873–1932), Dean of Dromore. *Mrs W. Power* – Jennie Wyse Power.

December

Friday 2

Never waked till 10. V. wild & wet & again to-night, better in day. V. busy day. Dr O'Leary at her exam. & I never knew. Dr Mulcahy came & helped D.G. Many bad pts. Wire in evg. fr. Stasco saying the poor Count passed peacefully away this am. Stasco is so gentle & longs for sympathy. Mrs Skeffington & Sighle here till 12. The Phoblacht is scandalous about Emer comparing her to W. Martin Murphy.[393]

Sunday 4

2 in A. 9 a.m. Gaelic S. Patrick's. D.G. to be there once more. Gt. news, Mr McCann wants Matins every Sun. in S. Auden's, Gaelic of course, it will be great. I.R.A. burnt film in Dundalk. Armistice in London. They are brave now there's no Safety Act, alas! how they've fallen. Playing England's game all the time. Aunt F. D.G. Cold but nice. Wrote to Stasco. Sighle knitting under M's directions.

Wednesday 7

8 a.m. S. B's, such cold wind. Our statement at Geneva, tho' Joe Connolly re. Jap. manufactured "Free" state in Manchuria splendid. Ireland doesn't stand for Imperial aggression. Nice sun but now v. cold wind, colder than snow. Girl came re Montessori training in Teac, M ffM asked her. Lemass says worst of our struggle over d.V. it is so after such centuries of waiting.[394]

Monday 26

Up late, J. came to No. 9 & found all well. Another lovely day, not quite like y.day tho' all v. well here. We saw round & I went to Teac. all well there D.G. & we hurried back to Auntie. M ffM not so well on S. Stephen's day for years. Saw Capt. White's grandson, a fine child. Aft. we went to L Wynnes, nice there, saw Foxrock Wynnes, then we saw Miss Hogg, v. feeble. nice, v. gracious.

---

393. *Dr O'Leary* – probably Dr Mary M. O'Leary, graduated NUI 1915. *Dr Mulcahy* – Dr Aileen Mary Mulcahy, graduated RCSI 1925 *Stasco* – Stanislaus Markievicz, stepson of Countess Markievicz. *W. Martin Murphy* (1845–1919), Irish businessman who led opposition to unions led by Larkin, culminating in the 1913 Lock-out.
394. *Joe Connolly* – Joseph Connolly (1885–1961), revolutionary, anti-treaty, Sinn Féin organiser, joined Fianna Fáil, Minister for Posts and Telegraphs in 1932. With de Valera at the inaugural meeting of the League of Nations assembly at Geneva (September 1932) and represented him at the working sessions of the assembly.

12.5.16. This is a very black Friday, Vardies &c were here, oh so reproachful, they wouldn't listen to me & looked as if they would cast me off for ever. How sorry I am for their sorrow, Eirin needs very big sacrifices. I am glad they go home tomorrow - why do they always misunderstand me?. This m[orning] had a dear little sympathetic note fr...well Whitley, with some sweets & mar malade &c coming their message gave much joy. Heard that Shown Macbe... the little boy &connolly have been shot, that as...orth is here, that Dillon has up- held us in Parliament.

17.5.16 There hasn't been much to note, nothing happens here, but everyone is kind & we have many gifts of fruit, flowers etc from kind friends. Saw & Maguire yesterday & S.C. both very disapproving L.S. to day the same.

KL/2/1 (6)

Original diary entries made by Kathleen Lynn on 12 and 17 May 1916 while in Mountjoy. KL/2/1(6) Courtesy of the Royal College of Physicians of Ireland.

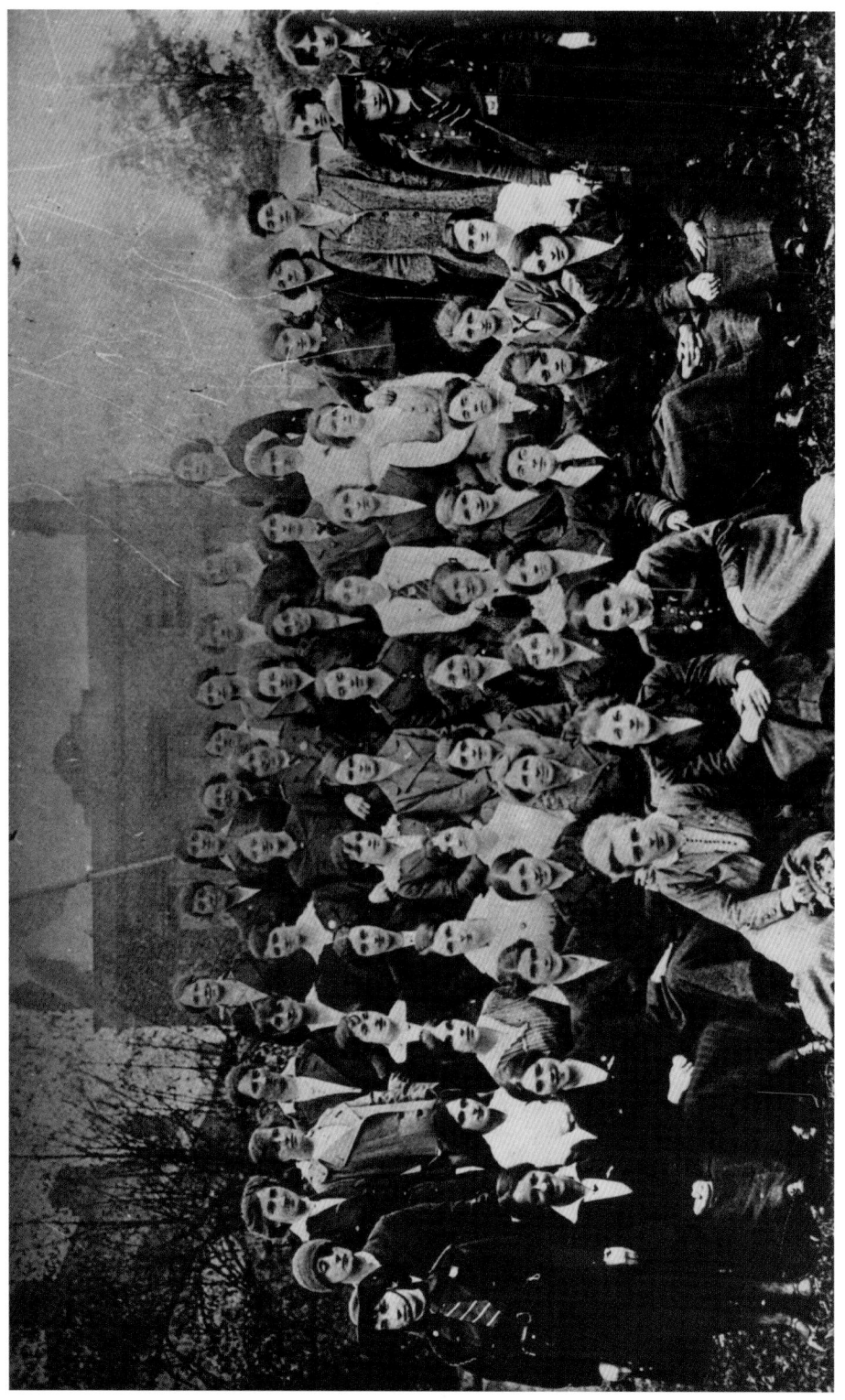

Women who participated in the 1916 Rising, in the Garden of Ely O'Carroll's house in Peter's Place Dublin, summer 1916. Madeleine ffrench-Mullen and Kathleen Lynn in front row, left and right respectively. KMGLM.18PC-1B53-02 Courtesy of Kilmainham Gaol Museum/OPW.

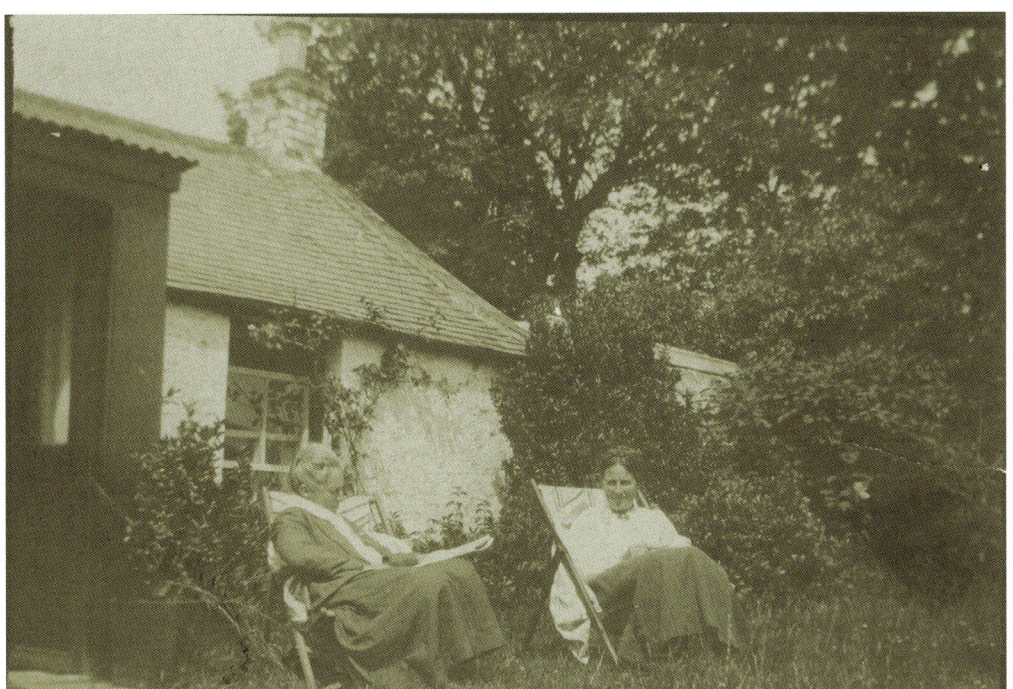

Kathleen Lynn and Madeleine ffrench-Mullen in the garden of the William's Cottage, Glencormack, Co. Wicklow, *c*.1917. The Kathleen Lynn collection within the Brother Allen Collection, IE/AL/KL/5/4. Courtesy of the Military Archives, Ireland.

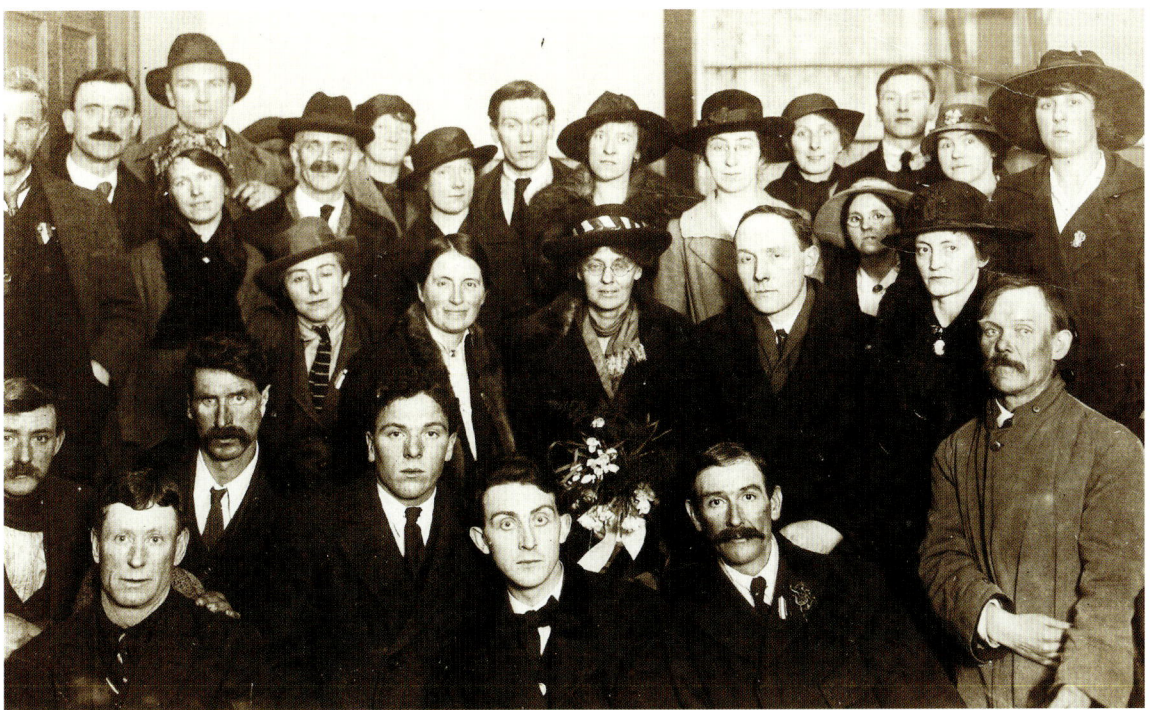

Photograph taken in Liberty Hall the night Countess Markievicz was released from prison, 15 March 1919. Second row (women seated from left) Madeleine ffrench-Mullen, Kathleen Lynn, Countess Markievicz. National Photographic Archive, NPA POLF202. Courtesy of the National Library of Ireland.

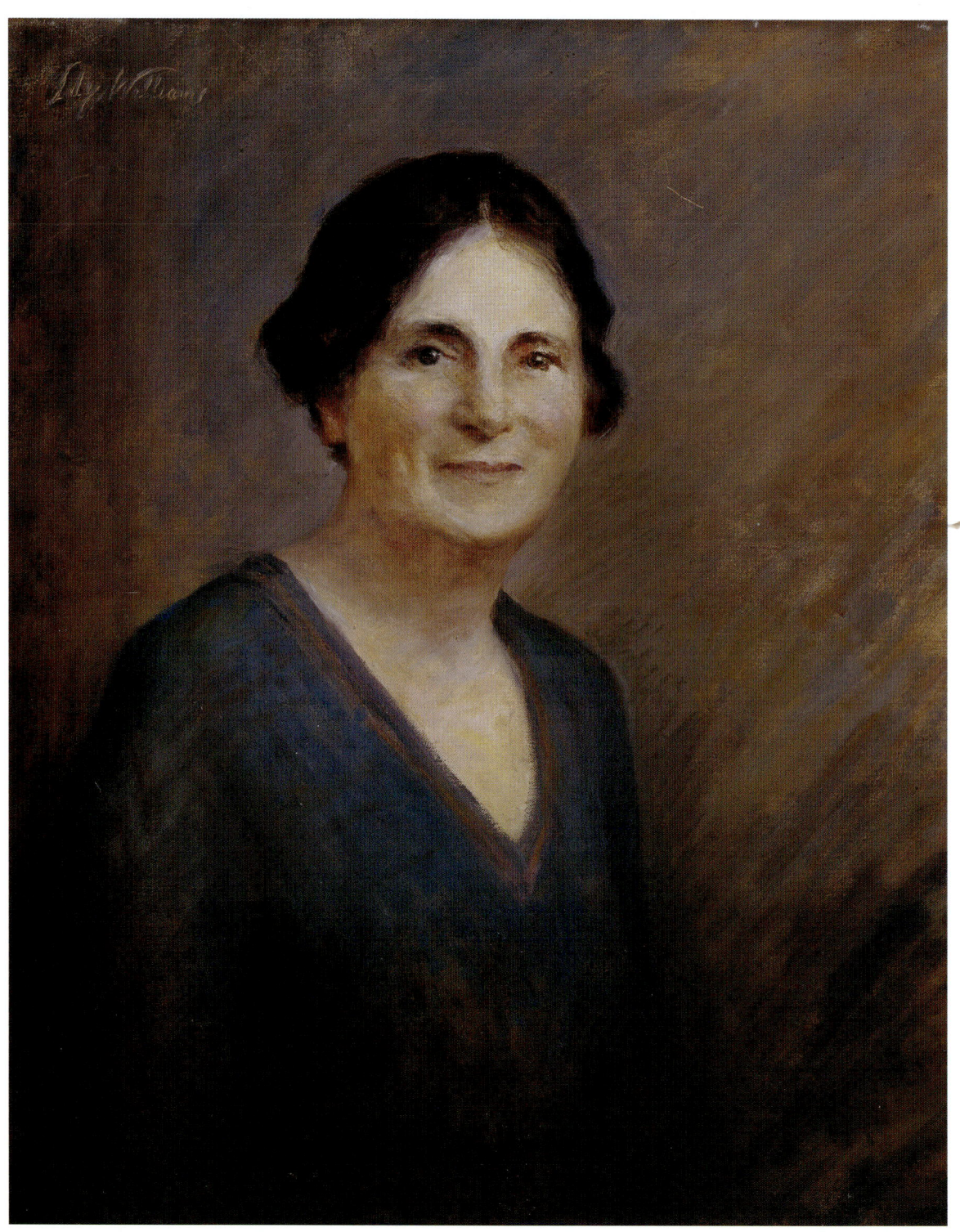

Portrait of Dr Kathleen Lynn by Lily Williams, 1919. SU/9/4 Courtesy of the Royal College of Physicians of Ireland.

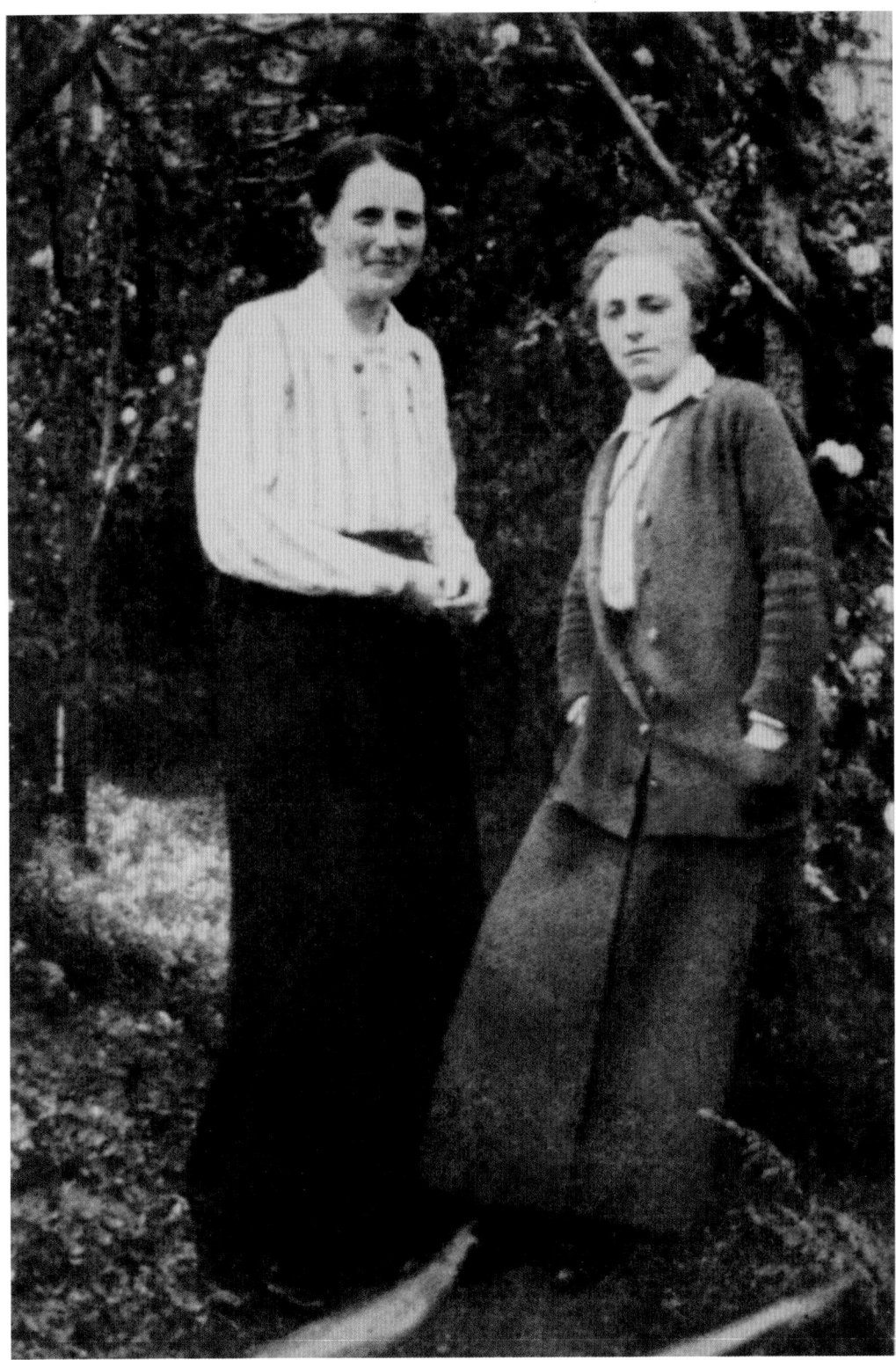

Kathleen Lynn and Madeleine ffrench-Mullen, *c*.1919. SU/1/1 Courtesy of the Royal College of Physicians of Ireland.

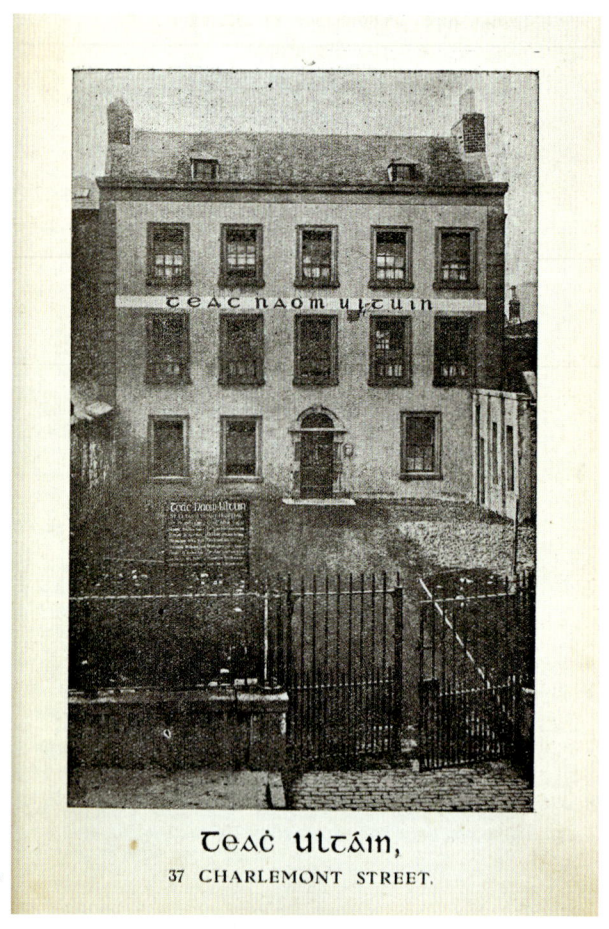

TeAC ULTÁIN,
37 CHARLEMONT STREET.

St Ultan's Hospital, *c*.1920. SU/1/1 Courtesy of the Royal College of Physicians of Ireland.

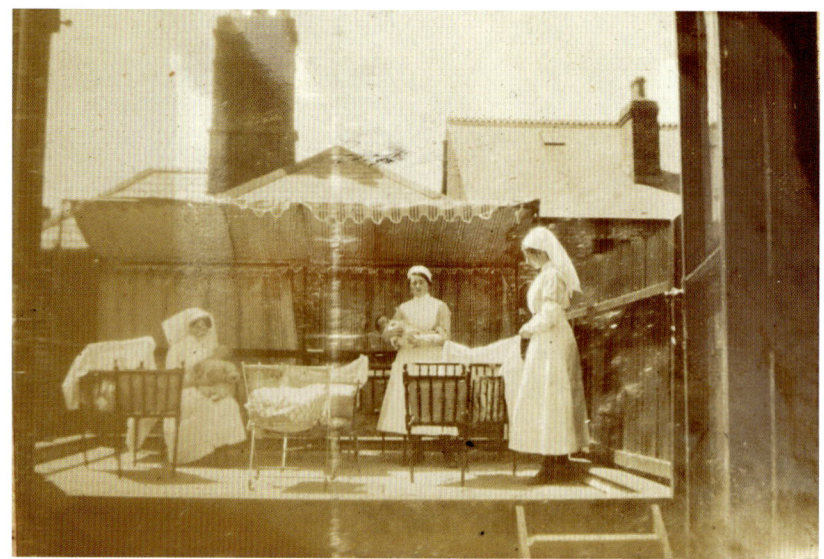

'Sunshine ward', St Ultan's Hospital, *c*.1920. SU/8/3/1 Courtesy of the Royal College of Physicians of Ireland.

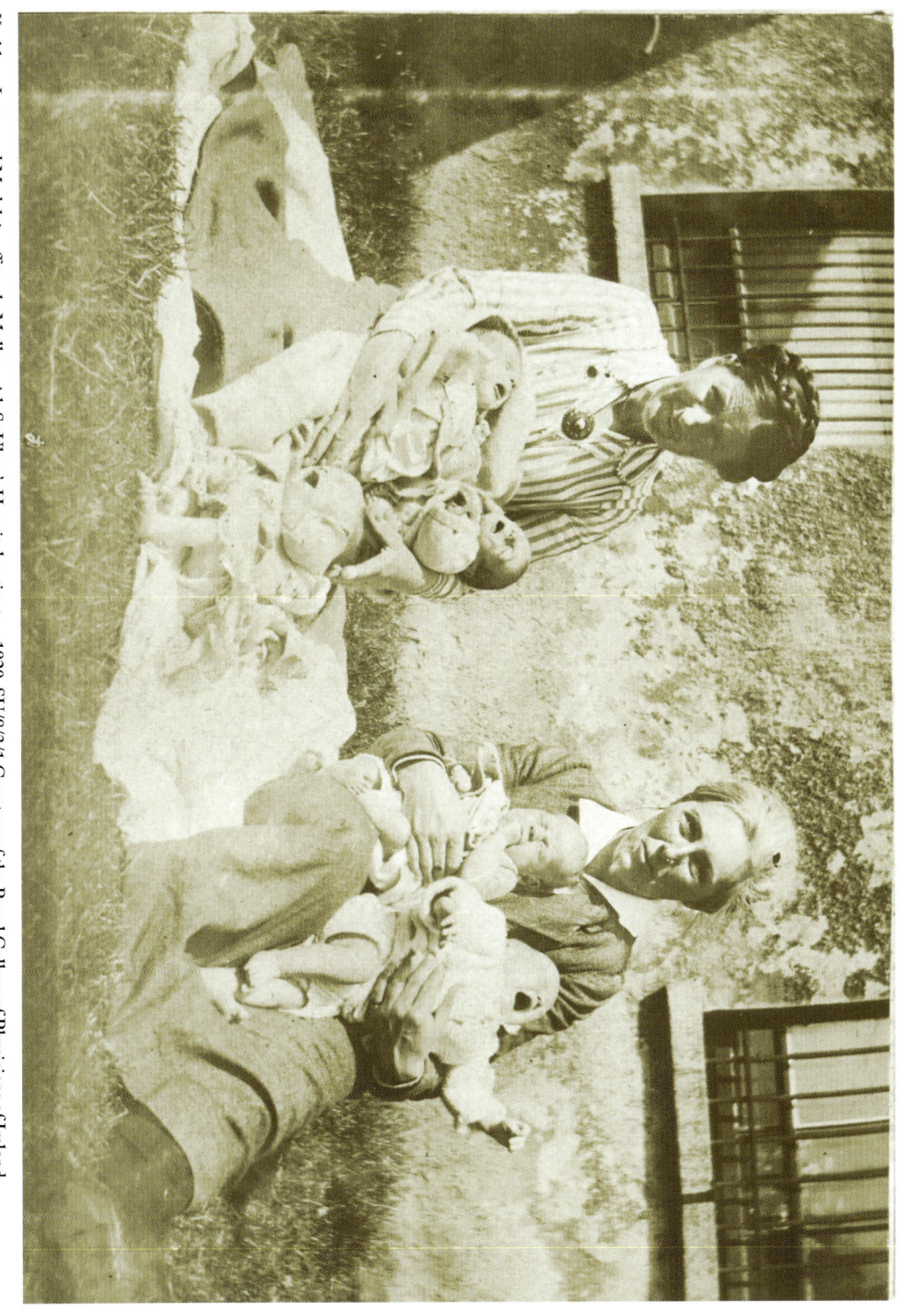

Kathleen Lynn and Madeleine ffrench-Mullen with St Ultan's Hospital patients, *c*.1920. SU/8/3/1 Courtesy of the Royal College of Physicians of Ireland.

April

given blankets thick with lice & fleas to cover us down
Emer, Mrs Barrett, 2 nonproyers, B Davies &I joined later on by

1916. Easter Monday. Revolution — Emer & Sim City Hall, Eoghan Con

1917.

1918.

1919. can't agree about Sinn Fein — Will there be war aga

1920. A quiet busy day with me. American goes on us
Mayee Kavanagh in evg. she is so kind. Her pla
quiet nice parlor. don't & patients my — we a no

1921. 4. A.E. 8 a.m. R mines beautiful warm day. Poor Fray
hall, to get, he was alive & Barry Boland. I never knew more agree

1922. 8 a.m. S.B's a very hard day for me, had to go miles on cycle, no ti
work to do. got ? ill poor native in the place. We been hall to w

1923. 8 a.m. R mines to ? — Jimmy ? Easter ree'n. Emer came in w
good lad. good journey. all fair in reac & no 8. g. out

1924. Anniversary day, snow all gone, pours of rain, we

1925.

1926. 8 a.m. S.G ? endeavoured 10 yrs ago, it was such a lovely
D.G. for it. emily dangerous red hangover here, she is well
in the Gaelic. M. Scarlett wants me to tea. Spent evg. qu

1927. 8.30. If. Ch. ref. to show very quiet day with plenty. Slept
much work, but all goes well o.g. But Muriel 1 K. ealio 8

1928. 8.30. R mines wedding at 8, palms etc, nice day, went
shower, but to shore Richard at 11. 8.40 a.m. went

1929. 8 a.m. S.B's M went to mass too in honour of the day
come to galway and we. got Laqcam saw outside of anim
proletariate. five mins to. picturesque, got hangups particulars

1930. 9. Ch. of Resurrect. V. high Priest let us say confession over in
their methods here, not dignity enough. Dr Ellis reports w

1931. hoped for Celebration, but was too dead tired to get up. 9
nice service, they have the long east window, d. altered, magical gr
ann fort dear little spot. lovely drive, saw white & red camelias. snapped

1932. 4. Δ E 8 a.m. S. Helier's parish Ch. rather 'high'. after breakfast promenaded wit
In evg. they rang nurse Byrne called off. S. v. alarmed of
interest as Europeans are united, show disasterous it will be for

1933. 8 a.m. S.B's l. day of memories. nice soft rain in plenty &
Eleanor's death, nowhere amidst radiant ? board father paced
the Church. Child Welf. went well. o.g. got P. c of Ashford castle m

1934. 8 a.m. R mines. Poor v. Clarke so safe for Jim & so like her to be a
a bent agre got in by protest. death false. Had the Engl co
first used electricity. A night of, water cut off no one t

1935. V. tired in my. a v. busy day. Plaza burnt to ground,

1936.
Red white & blue not apparent. Emer & ? were b
& nurse B. meeting ? ? anti-imperialist & ? ?

1937. 8 a.m. S. B's lovely warm sun all day, got into our

24 April 1916 to 1937 of Kathleen Lynn's diary. KL/1/1 Courtesy of the Royal College of Physicians of Ireland.

24th

ocuts "to ligan, not enough to go round
nch, & Shenaghan & B. Brady. We were locked up in a filthy store,
not quite early in day. Place then in coq. all woman taken to whip at abt 8.30.

people were busy going about for past hour (12.45 a.m.)
all British usurpations in ferment. America & Italy
wish improved.
own trodden ... & ... every day went to ly in mage to
... scheme & lot of signatures old ... relief ... &c.
... necessary and now everyone thinks, 3 inner regents! ...
be hanged in my for having worked how unequal we are &c!
... station too. all day we had memory of this non. ...
... crowd. we couldn't ... out, no room. Mass ... Dr. ... ...
... cold showers all day, evg. most enormous meeting at ...
... Delvin ... v.nice v. frail & shaken. much election ...
... ... murphy he looks ...
... off to ... 80 prisoners escaped fr Curragh. Not a letter
... by 10.30. tired warm welcome. did I see ... so a
... thing ready for Dublin, only I went to train, so wet. Driver
... ... heard more than ever before, v. good ... next night. I went aunt &
... youth & age, both clever. evg. Hardwicke Hall, official anniv ...
... golden 10.30. joint Hosp Board, ... Walsh chairman, I Vice-ditto,
... shode in ... wh. is nicely b. & ... R. ... Rebecca so steady & good
... gaelic service 5.15. v. nice, Easter lessons wonderful
... then Harrison & saw her & fat 3, back to
... club picture v. good, then ... she phoned she had arranged it
met, she may take holiday, later ...
... lecture to hospice child self at 3.30.
... ... this ... just 5 mos. before. there was so good
... those who are gone, help with us still. Poor
... ... those who are gone, help with us still, ... said ...
... gap tower, both with wonderful ...
... narrow streets in old town v. sleep. saw well fed
... marvellous succes ... new ... no sign
... a little better & saw Russell re gommoch in & ... girl
... right up to ... effective. S. Catharine's harbour coat ...
... met Wendy ... likely, they know some by masses. evg. ...
... bank manager, rather nice, had lovely ... both. aft ...
... to fill gap. Celebrations went well & day ... spoke out for ...
have her in debt ... paid her! strange logic! saw ... & Sally & ...
... in it. & times hopes U.S.A. will see how closely her
... came in cage we had great ... she told of victor
... with sympathies so ... at that hour & ... attached
... only civil marriage
... ... Mass suffered. heard ... died of
... too late. no ... Mass suffered. ... England did it for ..., but perh.
very malicious, that England did it for ..., but perh.

... coronation ... there is little here
... busy with us ... things, couldn't go to

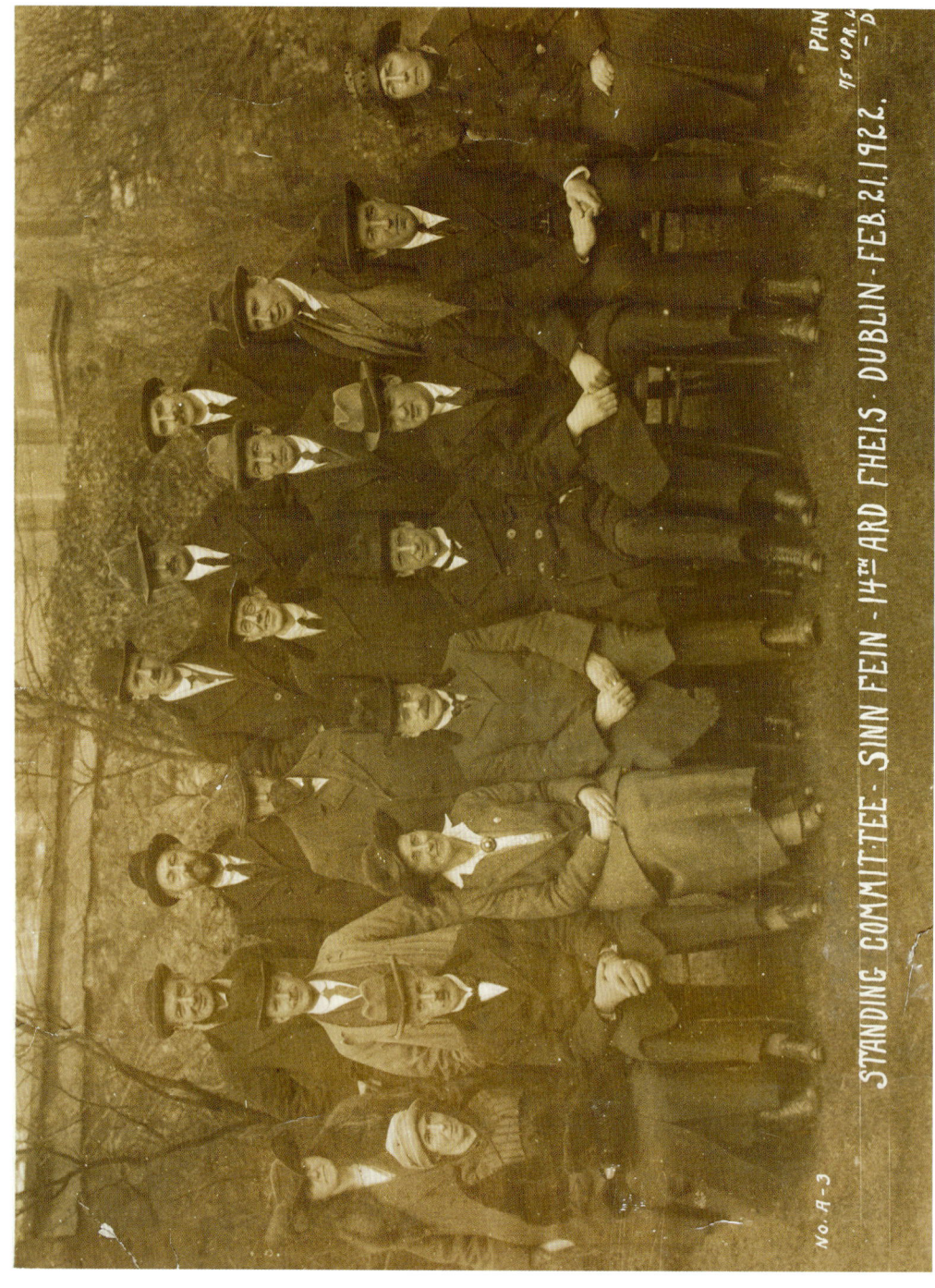

Sinn Féin Standing Committee,14th Ard Fheis Dublin, 21 February 1922. Kathleen Lynn is seated front row, third from left. The other women members included are Jennie Wyse Power (second row, left), Kathleen Clarke (seated front row, left), Hanna Sheehy Skeffington (seated front row, right). National Photographic Archive. NPA KOS. Courtesy of the National Library of Ireland.

To the Electors of Co. Dublin

VOTE

VOTE

No. 1

No. 1

Dr. Kathleen Lynn

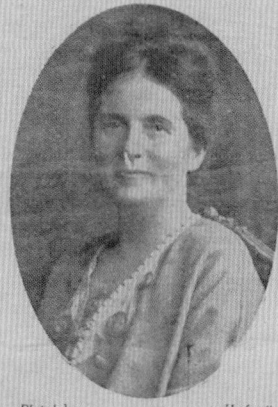

Photo by]   [Lafayette

Dr. Kathleen Lynn

At the last Election you entrusted me with the representation of the County Dublin. I came before you then as a follower of Wolfe Tone and James Connolly, believing with them that *complete separation from the British Empire* is the only way of achieving an honourable and permanent peace for Ireland.

I am a Republican because I desire, in the words of the Proclamation of Easter Week, "equal rights and equal opportunities for all our citizens," and I hold that under a Republican form of Government this can best be accomplished. I hold that "equal rights and equal opportunities" should be no idle phrase; that it should mean the abolition of privilege of every kind—privilege of birth, position, or possessions—not earned by personal service to the community. I hold that a payment of £40,000 per annum, on the one hand (the amount paid to the British King's representative) and a wage of 32/- a week (the standard set by Free State for workers on Shannon Scheme) is not a division of wealth that should exist in a Christian community.

I believe that we, ourselves, could mould a Republican form of Government to suit the special needs of Ireland. We need not slavishly model it on other Republics, under some of which the people have a less endurable existence than under the most tyrannical of Monarchies.

I hold that a Republican form of Government can be more cheaply maintained than any other; that extravagant display on useless institutions such as a standing Army, ornamental figureheads, etc., is unseemly in a country temporarily impoverished by its fight for freedom.

I am opposed to a standing Army as being a pernicious influence in any country, as well as being highly expensive.

I believe that the Revenue of Ireland could be administered in such a way as to ensure a proper standard of living to all its able-bodied citizens. I believe it should be used to provide an adequate pension to its aged and disabled citizens. Recognising that the child is the Nation's most precious possession, proper provision should be made to enable the mother to bring up her fatherless family.

With judicious fostering of our industries, by tariffs and prohibitions, and by the fostering of a steady home market for our agricultural produce, we would speedily gain our economic balance.

We have in this country mineral and other natural resources which will never be fully developed as long as we are governed in the interests of another country. Therefore, the aim of all true patriots must be that of Wolfe Tone—" to break the connection with England, the never-failing source of all our political evils."

That I will be constant to this aim and ceaseless in my efforts to secure it, my fidelity to the Republican cause in the past, and my refusal to compromise in the present, must be my guarantee.

KATHLEEN LYNN, F.R.C.S.I.

Published by Liam Gilmore, 23 Suffolk Street, Election Agent for the Candidate, and Printed by the Fodhla Printing Co. Ltd., Rutland Place, Cavendish Row, Dublin.

Dr Kathleen Lynn's election handbill, 1927. KL/2/15 (1) Courtesy of the Royal College of Physicians of Ireland.

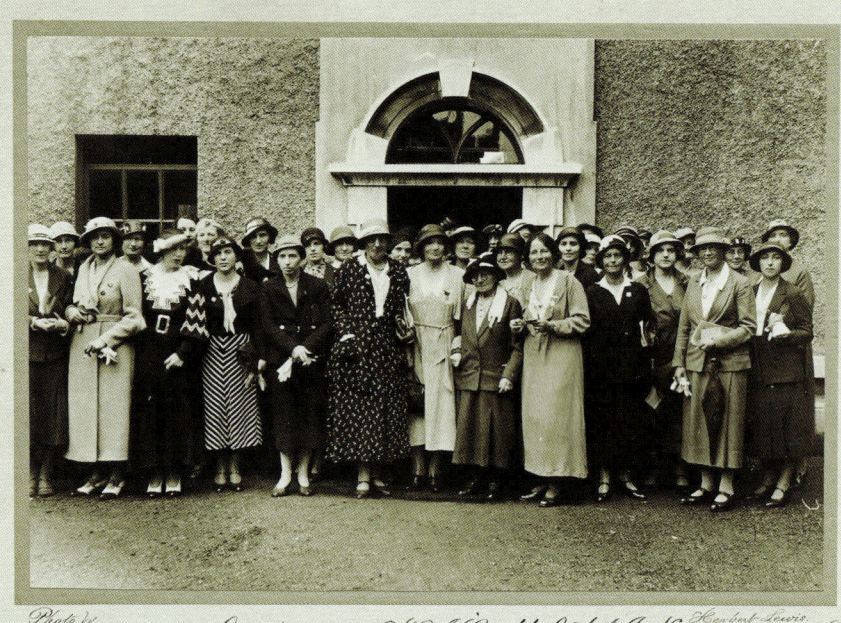

Luncheon at Teac Ultáin for the visit of the British Medical Association to Dublin, 1933. SU/8/3/5
Courtesy of the Royal College of Physicians of Ireland.

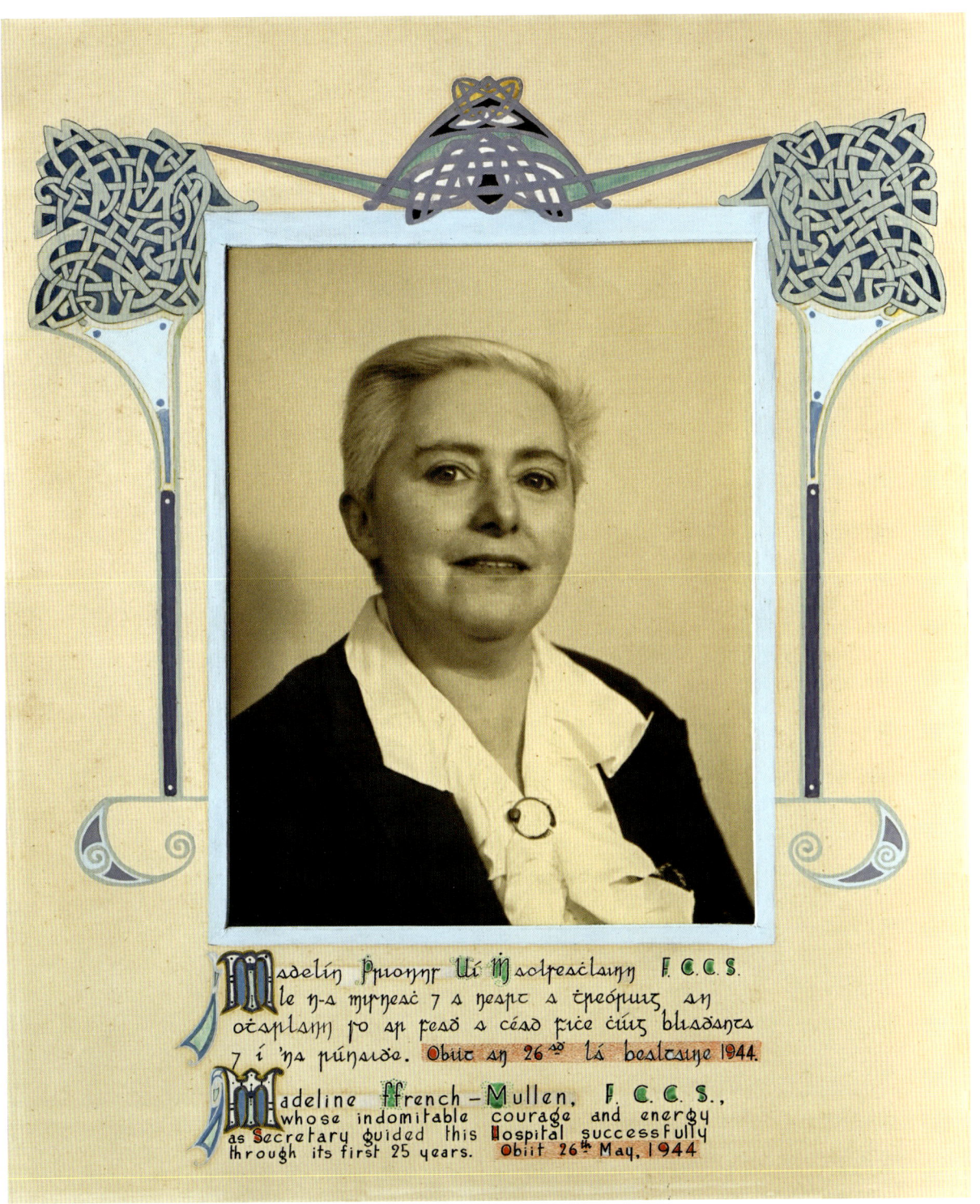

Madelín Fhuonn Uí Maolpeaclaunn F.C.C.S. le n-a mípnead 7 a neape a tpeópuic, an oéaplainn po ap peað a céað pice cúig bliaðanta 7 í 'na púnaíðe. Obuit an 26ªª lá bealcaine 1944.

Madeline ffrench-Mullen, F.C.C.S., whose indomitable courage and energy as Secretary guided this Hospital successfully through its first 25 years. Obiit 26ᵗʰ May, 1944

Madeleine ffrench-Mullen. SU/8/3/7 Courtesy of the Royal College of Physicians of Ireland.

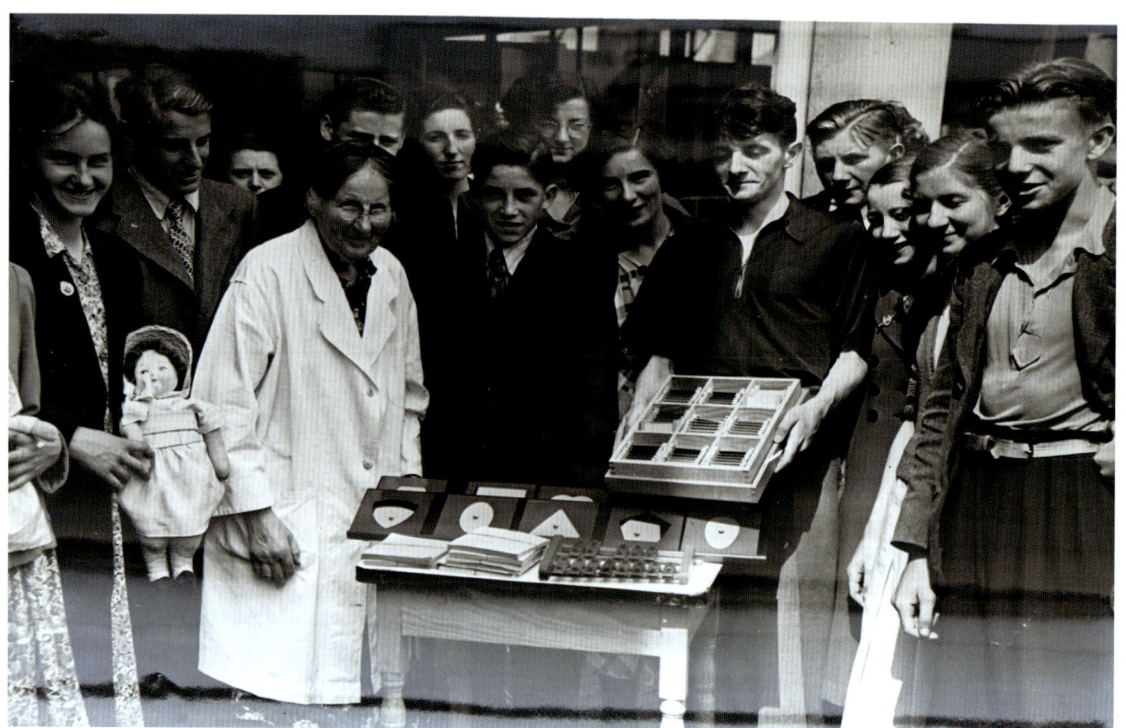

Junior Red Cross donation of Montessori equipment to Kathleen Lynn at St Ultan's Hospital, 1950. SU/8/3/12 Courtesy of the Royal College of Physicians of Ireland.

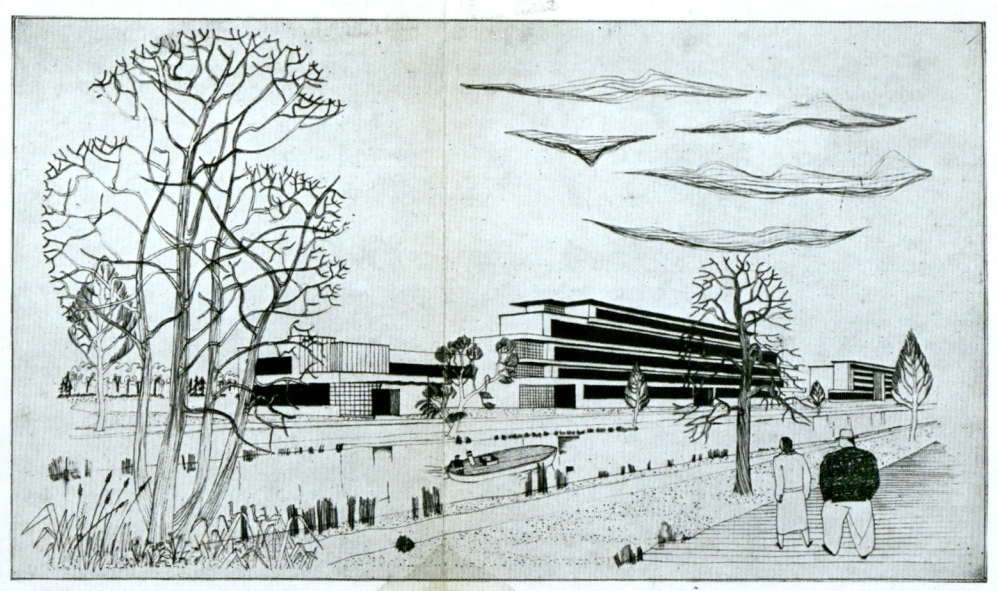

Still waiting !

THE DREAM HOSPITAL

THE NEW TEACH ULTAIN FACING
SOUTH ACROSS THE GRAND CANAL

GOD AND ST. ULTAN LEND YOUR AID: TO CARRY OUT THE PLANS WE'VE MADE !

The Dream Hospital flyer, c.1945. SU/7/3 Courtesy of the Royal College of Physicians of Ireland.

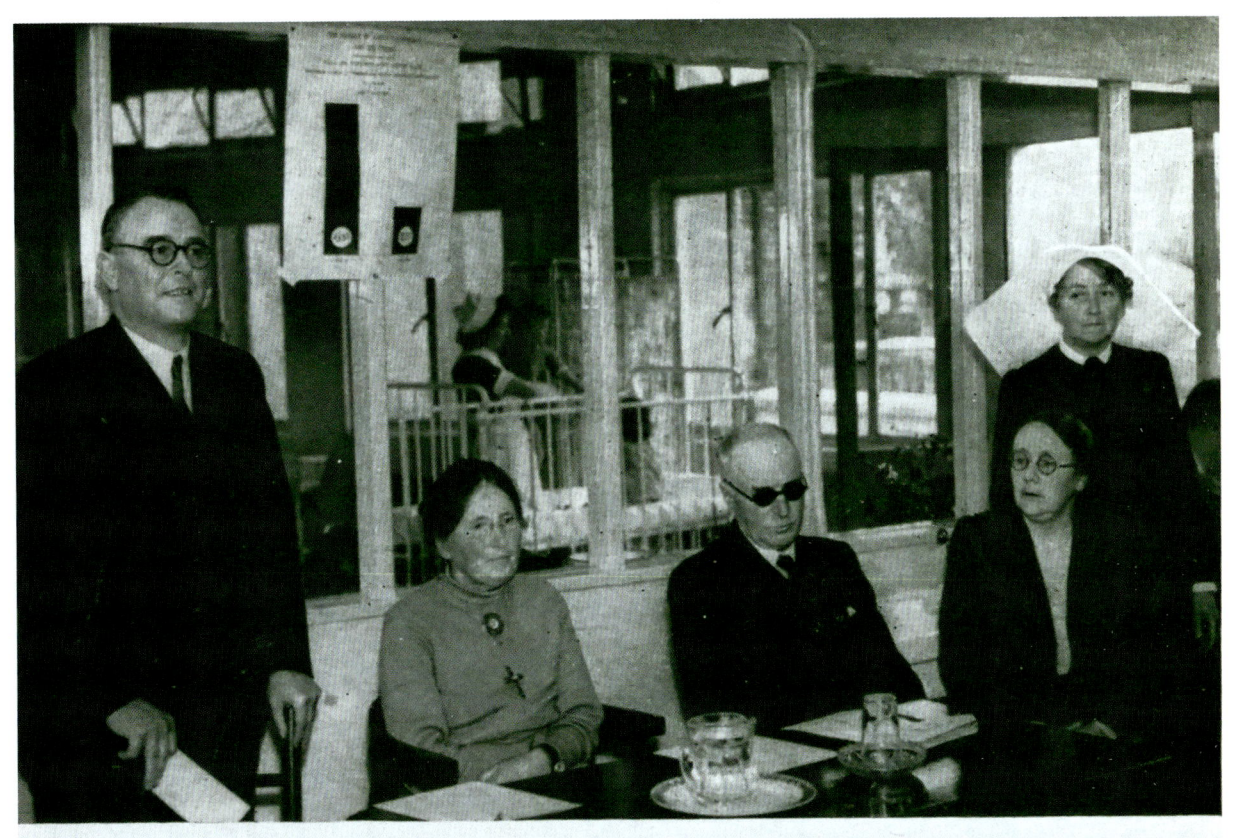

Dr. Ward addressing meeting at opening of
New T.B. Extension.

Also in picture left to right :
Dr. Lynn, Dr. Moorhead, Dr. Price and Matron.

Opening of the New TB Extension at St Ultan's Hospital, 1945. SU/7/3 Courtesy of the Royal College of Physicians of Ireland.

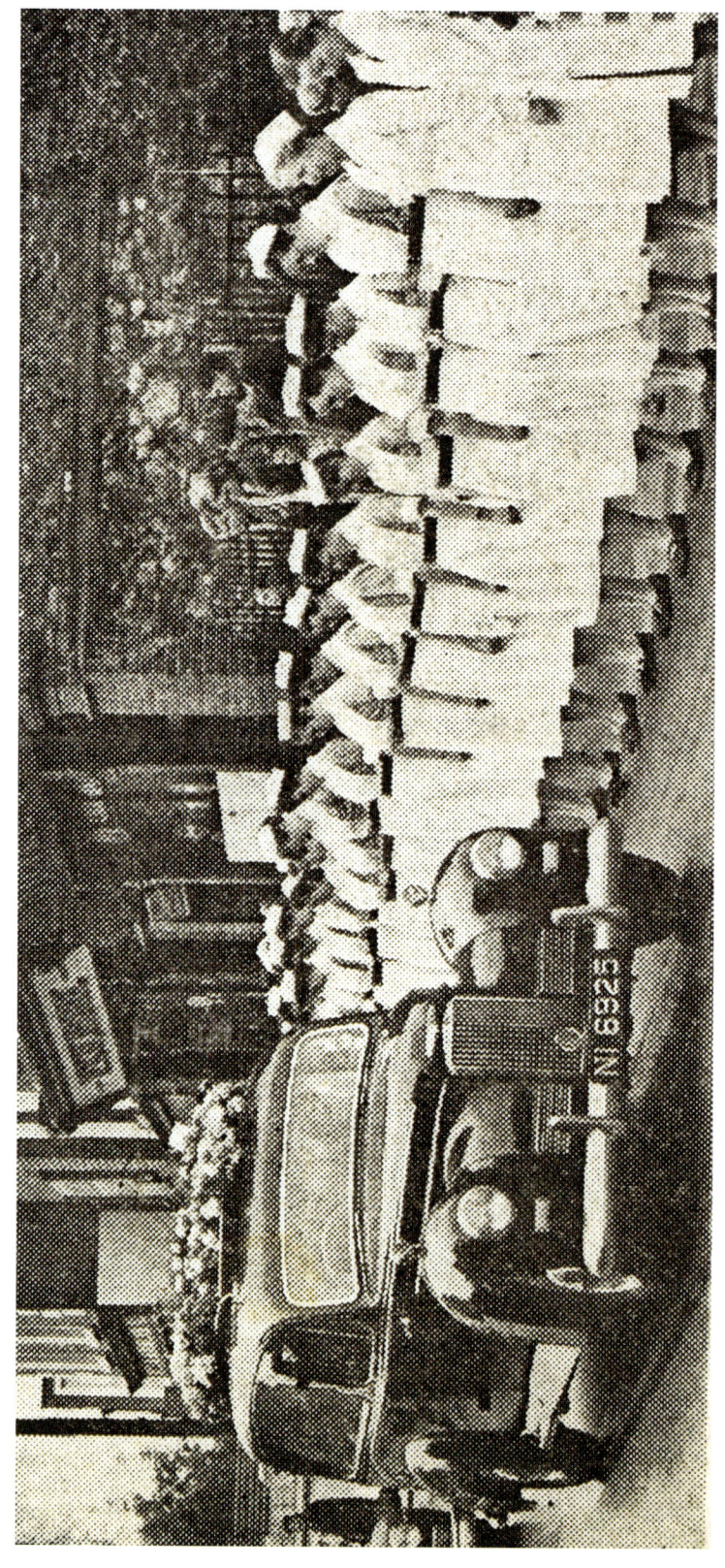

Nurses line the street as the remains of Kathleen Lynn pass St Ultan's Hospital, from the *Evening Press*, 16 September 1955. SU/7/4 Courtesy of the Royal College of Physicians of Ireland.

SECTION 3: 1933–44 POLITICAL AFTERLIFE

The early 1930s saw Fianna Fáil, under the leadership of de Valera, come to power. The decade 1922 to 1932 had seen the stabilising of the democratic principles of government in Ireland under a Cumann na nGaedhael-led government; and although there were anxieties, a smooth transfer of power occurred in 1932. Some political women, among them Lynn, had hopes that this would be reversed with de Valera in power, but they were soon disabused of that notion. Fianna Fáil continued what the first Irish Free State governments had begun and introduced further anti-women legislation, including the Criminal Law Amendment Act, 1935, the 1936 Conditions of Employment Act and the 1937 Constitution. Lynn was one of the many feminist and republican women who railed against the attacks on the rights of women workers and campaigned against the 1937 Constitution, particularly the 'women in the home' articles.

The second half of the 1930s saw a gradual decline in infant mortality rates in Ireland to 66 per 1000 in 1940. However, the start of the Emergency (as the Second World War was known as in Ireland) saw infant mortality rates increasing back to 83 per 1000 by 1943, considerably higher than in other areas of the UK. The hospital noted the hardships caused by shortages of fuel and food, especially the lack of vitamin C as no oranges were to be found in Dublin in 1941. As a result, death rates in the hospital were higher in 1944 than in 1933, although the rates of death from TB fell from 63 to 20 per cent.

For St Ultan's the 1930s were dominated by ambitious expansion plans for a purpose built 150-cot hospital on the site, amalgamating St Ultan's with the Harcourt St Children's Hospital. As the decade passes the annual reports show increasing frustration as these remained just plans, due to opposition from the Catholic hierarchy. They were more successful with the St Ultan's Utility Society which constructed 32 flats to provide social housing for the community. St Ultan's continued to develop international links, sending doctors and nurses to study across Europe and attend conferences. The hospital received visits from the BMA, Dr Maria Montessori and two TB experts Dr Water Pagel and Professor Wallgren of Gothenburg. TB became an increased focus from 1936 with the opening of a dedicated ten-bed TB ward, and the research of Dr Dorothy Stopford Price. A Montessori teacher was appointed to the hospital in 1936, and an Almoners Department opened in 1939 to provide social work support to the hospital. Despite the limitations of space, the hospital saw a 66 per cent increase in the number of in-patients treated over the decade, with 524 patients treated in 1944. Changes came to St Ultan's in 1944, as well as the death of the long-time Hospital Secretary Madeleine ffrench-Mullen, that year also saw the retirement of the Matron, Miss Dougan, who had been with the hospital since it opened in 1919.

Nothing Lynn did throughout her political and medical career was undertaken without ffrench-Mullen by her side. They shared the same political ideologies and experiences, from the Rising to their work in St Ultan's, and as local councillors on campaigns for women's and workers' rights, better social housing and help for the urban poor. They shared the same network of friends and colleagues, the same love of the outdoors and gardening; they spent time apart on holidays occasionally and always enjoyed their reunions. Their life together was one of domestic and public work. By the end of this decade Lynn would face into the following years without her life partner by her side.

1933

January

Sunday 1

8.30 Xt. Ch. 2 clergy. V. mild day. We had some cards. I had over 50, back to Teac by 11.30. S.O.S. Emer v. bad. Went with M ffM & fetched her here, she'll only kill herself. After Teac went back to Aunt F. Had fine dinner, turkey soup, goose, cauliflower, woodcock, plum pudding. Got more cards & letters. Home 11. Miss Sullivan fell, much shock. Dr Rice sent her to Adelaide.

Tuesday 3

Great news. Dail dissolved at midnight. Dev says country must give clear mandate to stop mouths of those who cry country is divided. Govt. liable to be thrown out at any time. Investors must feel security to put into 300 new factories etc. Dr Hill not coming till evg. alas! Dr O'Leary came 9.30, boils much the same. John offered to help in elect. work. Cupped small boil. V. hurting. Dr O'L says glyc.& Epsom good !!![395]

Monday 16

Last day Glencormac, gorgeous sunbath. John came about 2. All went well at Cosgrave's meeting. No serious casualties D.G. but many rushes. Cosgrave guarded by million police. Mrs Skeffington arrested in Newry y.day at prisoners' meeting but home to-day D.G. Mary Mac working for elections D.G. & v. disgusted at C na mB. Mulcahy has left Cosgrave, all say his last move has finished him. Signed Pension forms.[396]

Friday 27

Cold still. This evg. F.F. 65, C na G 37, C.P 8, Ind. 9, Lab. 7. I. Lab. 1, wh. is wonderful. Campbell of L.G.D. talking to Lady Aberdeen said "don't fear for Ireland, she has an honest man at top"! He is Scotch but has vision evidently. Sighle hears they will do their best to make

---

395. The 7th Dáil was dissolved on 2 January 1933 and a General Election called for 24 January.
396. *Mrs Skeffington arrested in Newry* – arrested in Newry for breaching an exclusion order, issued in 1926, banning her from Northern Ireland. On 15 January 1933 she accepted an invitation to speaker at Newry, was arrested and imprisoned.

it impossible to do business here & that we are in for a bad 6 mos. We must take high hand.[397]

Tuesday 7

Dev. appeals to Unionists to throw in lot with Ireland & try to understand her greatness, otherwise they have now nothing here. V. true. He opened Moydrum station last night & spoke of the ancient Irish nation not the new infant state of Cosgrave & Co. It is mild now this year too, but no primroses yet that I saw. Douglas played on the wireless Concert in Mansion Ho. & M ffM went.[398]

Thursday 16

Slept late, Teac Board v. important. We'll soon have all land required for building. D.G. Our plans are praised by Comt. of Reference. Mrs Cosgrave showed how Meath anyhow is so far much worse off for Sweep. D.G. we aren't. The Nurses' Pension Scheme advanced a bit. Matron does well D.G. Hear of people working & D.G. for it. John busy at Hills. We had long rounds D.condra way, bad pts. all.[399]

Tuesday 21

8 a.m. R.mines,v. cold wind at times & hail. Gt. news = Mrs Skeffington's return. A month in Armagh jail, she had welcomes in Dundalk & Drogheda & a fine one here in College Green. Procession, 3 bands, banners & so on. Peadar O'Donnell the one jarring note with his inciting against F.F. he is v. like agent provocateur. We bought flowers for Mrs S. & lily of the valley for bride & groom.[400]

Thursday 23

Gt. surprise. Eoin Duffy relieved of his post. Chief of Police, was offered another job, wouldn't take it. Broy to succeed him, he seems good. Mrs Skef in, long talk, she had fire & food as she fairly wished in

---

397. The final tally in the 1933 General Election was Fianna Fáil 77 seats, Cumann na nGaelheal 48 seats, National Centre Party (CP) 11 seats, Labour 8 seats and Independents 9 seats. *L. G.D.* – Local Government Department. *Lady Aberdeen* – Isabel Hamilton-Gordon, Marchioness of Aberdeen and Temair (1857–1939), British philanthropist and advocate of women's interest, former Vicereine of Ireland.
398. *Moydrum* – a town in Co. Westmeath.
399. *Mrs Cosgrave* – Mary Josephine Cosgrave (*c.*1877–1941), social worker, local politician, Chairman of the Meath Hospital committee, and a member of the Saint Ultan's Hospital Board.
400. *Mrs Skeffington's return* – After a short imprisonment in Armagh, Hanna Sheehy Skeffington was released, fined and ordered to keep the peace.

Armagh jail. Gov. & Matrons not bad. Head lady said she was "terrible astonished " at her, expected virago evidently. Matron had turn of V. but it wasn't serious. Scheme on to drain some of Mediterranean over hill into Jordan, fertile with J. [ ]southward to Dead Sea.[401]

March

Monday 6

Fine mg. after storm, J & I left at 9.30. M came with us to border. Maher there, nice drive home. Found all well, v. busy day. In Teac M has collected rents fr. cottages (1st time) Plans going ahead to rehouse them, build flats in Pemberton's yard, maybe. Roosefelt has made fine, manly statement & finished with "so help me God" wh. looks well D.G. Time says U.S.A. on brink of ruin, like them.[402]

Thursday 23

Special Teac Board, signed deed of purchase of Pemberton estate. Good. Matron going to Glencormac to-morrow at last D.G. Many we know drew horses, Nurse Hartnett, girl in Bray (share) etc. John got U.S.A. papers wh. show how mad Eng. is that Banks are to be State Controlled, quite private lending, won't be tolerated. J & I went to Xt. Ch., recital, Cathedral Quartette, good & more.[403]

Monday 27

8 a.m. S. B's, a most glorious day of sunshine, we had sunbaths for babies on flat roof, nearly too hot, took them out of their flannels & woollies & left them kicking naked. Jews everywhere protest against Germany & boycott it, say it's a ret. to barbarism wh. is true. John all on for going away & doesn't seem to feel it at all. Trial of secret document cases on again. Hope all will go well.[404]

---

401. *Eoin Duffy* (1890–1944), Revolutionary, Pro-Treaty, First Commissioner of the Civic Guard (Gardaí Síochána). *Ned Broy* – Eamon 'Ned' Broy, former member 'G' Intelligence Division' DMP, double agent for Michael Collins, member National Army, joined Gardaí Síochána in 1925. *Scheme on to drain some of Mediterranean* –A scheme devised by German engineer Herman Sörgel to build a dam across the Straits of Gibraltar, lower the water level in the Mediterranean bringing millions of kilometres of land back from the sea and connecting Europe with Africa, creating a new continent, Atlantropa.
402. *Roosefelt* – Franklin D. Roosevelt (1882–1945), was inaugurated as the 32nd president of the United States on Saturday, 4 March 1933. He actually ended the speech with the sentence 'May He guide me in the days to come'.
403. *purchase of Pemberton estate* – Purchase of a yard next to St Ultan's from the Pemberton estate.
404. Lynn was a strong believer in the benefits of fresh air and sunshine, the flat roof over part of St Ultan's was used as an outside ward for 'sunbaths'.

Friday 31

The rioters who broke up Connollys house & attacked Mrs Skeffington set on by A.C.A. & then Mulcahy has the effrontery to condemn F.F. for allowing it, how could they have known of it! All of a piece with priest led mob in 1913 agst. those who sent strikers & children to England. Found iodine dressings fr. 1916, sending them to Museum. C na mB Ard Feis quiet & small & saying usual absurd things, pro British to last.[405]

April

Thursday 13

Maundy Thurs. 8 a.m. R.mines. Not much cold wind & lovely sun. Read a bit of M ffM's lovely book on pool gardens. Revelations in Moscow trial of English engineers v. believable, bribed people to spoil machinery etc. & one of the men was on Shannon Scheme here. Yes, England has found her match at last. Teac does nicely D.G. Got Easter things & was busy here. John off to his friends, the Prices & Aunt & Emer came & Mrs Skeff. in mg. She's off Phoblacht.[406]

Saturday 22

Busy all day, much to see & do but got time in aft. to fix up pond with sand in bottom & to fill it. Garden very enticing. Cold wind & sharp frost in night. English Fascisti honoured in Rome, with Nazi, are they coming combined? Italy seems boss of Europe now. Mussolini asked to allow dual monarchy Austro-Hungary. They say Otto-[ ]Urlk = King of Hungary.[407]

---

405. *A.C.A.* – Army Comrades Association, founded in response to the victory of Fianna Fáil in the 1932 election and led by Eoin O'Duffy, popularly known as the Blueshirts. Later called the National Guard, provided protection for Cumann na nGaedheal candidates. *C na mB Ard Feis ... pro British to last* – Cumann na mBan dropped its commitment to the 2nd Dáil at their 1933 convention, which lead to a split and the formation of Mná na Poblachta, who continued to believe that the members of the 2nd Dáil were the legitimate government, a stance that Lynn supported.
406. *Six British subjects who were employees of Metropolitan* – Vickers was arrested and publicly tried in 1933 by the authorities in the Soviet Union on charges of economic 'wrecking' and espionage. *Mrs Skeff. in mg. She's off Phoblacht* – Hanna Sheehy Skeffington and left-wing republican Frank Ryan resigned as editors of the republican newspaper Poblacht na hÉireann because they felt it was under completely the control of the IRA and unsympathetic to left wing political views.
407. *English Fascisti honoured in Rome* – 21 April 1933, Sir Oswald Mosley (1896-1980), leader of the British fascists was honoured by Mussolini with a two-hour parade and reception, with Mosley making a speech paying tribute to the progress of fascism. Uniformed Nazis were present as well.

Friday 28

Busy day. M ffM on Report. We admitted 7 babies, perfect number, hope they'll do well after our long quarantine. Albina came to b.fast & was happy. We reassured her we weren't F.F. Bob de Coeur wants to start organization for Connolly & the nation. V. good. Saw Emer in mg. Grace Plunkett has drawn v. fine advt. for sweeps, bridal pair, inevitable & how calmly that risk taken.[408]

May

Friday 12

Connolly & MacDermott's anniversary & day of Budget, it must be good for I. Times is so mad over it & so self contradictory. All possible British goods are on tarriff & large amt. goes to relieve unemployment. Income tax 5/- in £. It will be hard on those who pay but will relieve distress. Gt. United Missionary meeting in Mansion Ho. Bps. Tinton Perside of Kilmore spoke well & liberally.[409]

Thursday 25

Ascension Day. 8 a.m. R.mines. Teac Annual Meeting the 15th. It was showery mg. Took photos of Sighle & Sally K. The meeting was gt. success. D.G. Vincent Kenny spoke so well of M ffM [ ] regarding her & rightly so as the Teac's mainspring. All went well & the cakes were lovely & also ices. v. busy after getting Douglas to Duns, throat again.

July

Wednesday 5

Saw Juliana Hosp. beautiful, v. complete. Got many tips. Then University Hosp. much older, new Nurses' school. Had excellent lunch there, people v. kind. Photo taken at Juliana Hosp. ready & for sale in aft. Peace Palace v. fine but alas! we know its efforts are not genuine. Presents fr. different lands interesting. Then Picture Gallery, v. fine Rembrandts etc. Then long & lovely drive to Warmond at Larger Lakes. Saw storks for 1 st time. Old home & furniture there v. fine, carriage &

---

408. *Albina* – Albina Broderick/Gobnait NíBhrudair. *Bob de Coeur* – Robert DeCoeur, member of the Irish Citizen Army, fought in 1916. Member of the Old Irish Citizen Army Comrades Association. *Grace Plunkett* – Grace Plunkett, née Gifford (1888–1955), cartoonist and republican, widow of executed 1916 signatory of the Proclamation, Joseph Plunkett.
409. *Connolly & MacDermott's anniversary* – anniversary of the execution, in 1916, of rebel leaders and signatories to the Proclamation, James Connolly and Seán MacDermott / Seán Mac Diarmada.

harness encrusted with [cowries] & old sleighs. More variety of cakes at the tea than I saw at Baden (Wien). D.G. for nice day.[410]

Thursday 6

Left beautiful Schvening, sorry. Leyden Univ. photo again. M ffM this time raced over hosp. 600 beds. 3 hrs. Nearly dead, couldn't remember half we saw. New, nice in gardens, no open windows [ ] V hot no time for bathe, round by sand dune pass = their Gap of Dunlo, then M. Mental Hosp., no barriers, all busy & fairly contented. V. lovely grounds lakes & trees. Plenty of Storks. Tea at Kent Hosp. Walked much there too. Then Amsterdam. M went to bed. Hear strike on Mail boat.

Wednesday 26

Another lovely day, all well, went to Pharmacology seat, v. good anaesthetics & [diurstics]. Bilbo of Italian Squadron to take Irish Mail to-day. A.C.A. has been out recruiting the army reserve, such cheek, O 'Duffy prime mover in it. To-day, army order forbids reserves to join A.C.A. or "hat" guard. Good party. V. good. M ffM went to Reception at Castle, lovely, all the Unionists there, they have no spunk. Dev. gave magt. welcome. D.G. for day.[411]

August

Wednesday 9

8 a.m. S. B's. John's last day. We packed early, then usu. round. Papers say "Nat. Guard" ball last night, Cosgrave's motor stoned, not safe for him to leave Metropole till 4.30. We heard much booing anyhow. Other cars of Ireland's enemies stoned too. Had nice dinner for John. We are sad at parting. I saw him off at Dun Laoghaire, committing him to God's care. We had our night prayer last thing.[412]

Wednesday 16

V. busy. Early Matron rang to say electricity in S. wing almost went on fire again at 4 a.m. became nearly red hot. D.G. it was turned off in time. We had consultation & now D.V. all will be well. Blue Shirts

---

410. *Juliana Hop.* – Lynn visited the Juliana Children's Hospital in The Hague, on a visit she and ffrench-Mullen took to the Netherlands and Germany.
411. *A.C.A.* – Army Comrades Association. *O'Duffy* – Eoin O'Duffy had become leader of the ACA in July 1933. *Reception at Castle* – held for delegates from the British Medical Association annual conference, over 2,000 people in attendance.
412. *'Nat Guard'* – National Guard, the ACA was renamed the National Guard.

have called off Sun. Church Parade, weakness. John Brennan said there were bluebottles buzzing round carcass of C na nGael! Emer & Douglas came, both v. well. Nice day.[413]

Monday 21

V. nice night, showery day, one v. heavy one, almost like cloudburst for few minutes. Ground well soaked now. F. Rhodes took Olga all day, Botanic Gardens, 1st, then drive with Miss Ethel, L McFanagin etc. Dev. says Blue Shirts = Fascisti & will not be tolerated. No Gen. Elect. nec. Gt. finds in Moate, Cranogue, ladies' leather shoes, amber & glass beads, 25 ft. canoe, bone dice, bronze knife.[414]

September

Wednesday 6

8 a.m. S. B's to pray for Ireland & Utility Soc. petition. V.V. busy all day, in aft. heard case was now listed o.k. for Wed. week. We must be thankful for even that. Wrote M ffM long letter. The Bass prosecutions cause much trouble, crowd tried to rush comt. house, cordon of military round it & all this because I.R.A. are so self centred they would ruin Ireland to assert themselves. Much colder, like rain D.V. D.V.[415]

Tuesday 19

8 a.m. R.mines, some rain at last esp. in evg but not much. Child Welf. 10.30. New milk scheme much better D.G. Many more eligible. Nice sunbath. I think Dev. all right tho' so many agst. him. Bass prisoners hungerstrike. If only they would let things alone & not start martyrising when there is no need! L Murphy came & liked balcon. We got in a lot of pears but Susie says not half yet.[416]

---

413. *Blue Shirts* – Blueshirts, nickname from their uniform of blue shirts, for members of the National Guard and previously the ACA. Female members were known as Blueblouses. *C na nGael* – Cumann na nGaedheal.
414. *Cranogue in Moate* – A Crannóg, ancient Irish lake dwelling, was excavated at Ballinderry bog, Moate, Co. Westmeath, in 1932 and report published in 1933.
415. *Utility Soc.* – St Ultan's Hospital Utility Society was established in 1933 to establish model tenements homes for Dublin's poorer citizens. The Society, led by ffrench-Mullen, build flats on Charlemont Street. The site is now occupied by Dublin City Council social housing flats, ffrench-Mullen House. *Bass prosecutions* – In 1932 the IRA began a boycott campaign of British goods. They imposed a boycott of Bass beer, brewed in Burton, England, selected because many Irish pubs served it. Several IRA men were arrested and tried for attempting to enforce this boycott.
416. *liked balcon* – Lynn believed deeply in the health benefits of fresh air and the sun, she had architect Michael Scott design a balcony outside her bedroom, where she sun-bathed and slept when she could.

Wednesday 27

Dense fog fr 4 a.m., had to land at Vlissingen thro' customs at Esschen, fog gone. Lots of lovely dahlias & rich black earth, not like usu. sand. Saw v. old fashioned looking baby here in Rosendal with white embroidered pellise & little cape such as we wore. Rain fr. Vlissingen to Antwerp. D.G. it went to Brussels. Changed no money in Holland. Red Strong's The Garden, Spa endlich, I halloed, dear M heard but didn't see me. Is well. Later drove to Barrisard, saw lots of gold fish & sizes, most tiny. Glorious evg. Bed early.[417]

October

Wednesday 4

We arr. Dun Laoghaire abt. 6, had lovely crossing & slept like tops. Saw Aunt F. a moment, v. well D.G. then home. Mary & animals v. glad to see us & all well D.G. Bed till 10, lovely sun, had short sun bath then rushing day of pts. Mrs Bennett has given M ffM lovely new green linoleum for office. V. kind. Seems report unfounded re Mulcahy & Eng. War minister Dev apologised. Others wouldn't accept. Just like them.[418]

Wednesday 11

8 a.m. S. B's. bright sun a bit, sunbath. Med. Board went well. We appointed Dr Scally H.S. Dr Price had 'mane' poor thing = adhesions, she says. I Times furious over farmers, gives such a biased a/c of storms of meteors wh. came because we got into umbra of Orion, our atmosphere smashes up meteors & renders them harmless. Got fragile 1st born son into Teac, such a mother! Colder now.[419]

Monday 23

8 a.m. S. B's. dark still day. Sweep prizes nearly all drawn. Many to see. M ffM well, thinking of starting the cycle again. Good. Evg. she & I went to Sinn Fein meeting in Parnell Sq., Fr O'Flanagan, new. President there. It was [ ] as futile as any before & degenerated into a squabble betwn. S.F. & the I.R.A. members present. Waste of time to go.[420]

---

417. Lynn was in Holland visiting children's hospitals.
418. *Seems report unfounded re Mulcahy* – de Valera accused Richard Mulcahy of having private meetings with the British Minister of War, Lord Hailsham, while on a visit to Glasgow.
419. *Dr Scally* – Dr Clara Scally, graduated NUI 1921.
420. *Fr O'Flanagan* – Michael O'Flanagan (1876–1942), Irish language scholar, inventor, and historian.

Thursday 26

8 a.m. Xt. Ch. V. cold day, N. wind. babies warm on S. roof all the same. V. full day. Hospitals' Commission at 11. We had gt. talk. Jack O'Carroll, Dr Madden & Dr Andy Cooney, Mr Doran. They think better have Central Trustee fund & pay out yearly for Hospital expenditure. Long Teac board, pts. then. Lecture in Harold's X. Sighle says in Cork I.R.A. & Blue Shirts were both fully armed & clash seemed inevitable. D.G. not.[421]

November

Thursday 9

8 a.m. Xt. Ch. Lovely sun in mg. F.F. Ard Feis seems to have been v. good. Dev said he must govern in interests of all, not only Republicans & must quell all lawbreakers & he was going straight for Republic D.G. New York has elected an anti [ ] Lord Mayor who promises to reduce rates etc. Hear Mr Scott gone on a terrible bend, alas, it it's true. Bulbs in Teac.[422]

Tuesday 14

8 a.m. R.mines. Gt. rejoicings over Hitler's victory. All Evangelic Church bells ringing. Hitler has commanded clergy to throw out all Jews but D.V. some pastors won't have this unXtianity.[423] Whole border of yellow auriculas in full bloom in Ormond Rd. Teac all well D.G. Child Welf. has new sub Comt. to consider scheme for replacing creches by nursery schools.

Saturday 18

Such showers, drenching. We inspected creche in Meath & Henrietta Sts. Meath St. one quite good, much improved since the pre 1916 times when I was its Dr. Nun in Henrietta St. greeted me so that she must be good rebel. Aft. S. John 's Ambulance sale, got snipe & venison & nice sweets. U.S.A. has recognised Russia, well done. More & more we must pray for whole world. M. v. neuralgic, must rest.[424]

---

421. *Hospitals' Commission* – A Hospitals' Commission was set up in 1933 to examine the resources and needs of various hospitals and to advise the Minister on how best to use the sweepstakes funds. *Jack O'Carroll, Dr Madden & Dr Andy Cooney, Mr Doran* – Joseph O'Carroll, John A Madden, A. F. Cooney and Michael W. Doran were all members of the first commission.
422. *New York Lord Mayor* – Republican candidate Fiorello La Gaurdia beat incumbent Democrat, John P. O'Brien, in the election on 7 November.
423. *unXtianity* – un-Christianity.
424. *U.S.A. has recognised Russia* – On 16 November 1933 US President Franklin Roosevelt ended almost 16 years of American non-recognition of the Soviet Union.

December

Tuesday 5

8 a.m. R.mines. After all, Thomas letter is just what one wld. expect, says since treaty Ireland has been contented & prosperous, does he forget Cosgrave's [77] murders & the Civil War & all the horrors of Kerry. We don't. He doesn't seem to want the question of a Republic to rise tho' saying before we could choose as we liked. M ffM had 3 terrible letters fr. Reddin, what is he up to? Cold day.[425]

Monday 11

8 a.m. S. B's, in time for once. Much to pray for. M ffM interviewed Sean T. re flats & he was sympathetic D.G. Now Cronin is arrested O'Duffy has gone on the run in the North, a strange place for an Irishman to save himself!! Old Dr Whiltlaw is dead, 84, I shld. have thought him much older, seemed old 35 yrs. ago Revolution in Spain is made most of to distract people here.[426]

Friday 29

1st night on balcon. for ages, felt v. fresh, frosty. I was quite warm. Emer has letter in "Press" re leader of 27th wh. she thinks shirked the Republic, to-day's leader answers her quite well. Let us be united for Freedom. At last at last Utility Society contract signed & all ready. It took 9 mos. We would have had flats built by now. Rain in evg. Hear a gt. plane smash. Teac big disp. Dr Scally's back.

---

425. *Thomas Letter* – communication between J. H. Thomas, Dominions Secretary, and de Valera. *Reddin* – Messers Reddin & Reddin, Westmoreland Street, were St Ultan's Hospital's solicitors.
426. *Sean T* – Seán T. O'Kelly (1882–1966), Fianna Fáil Minister for Local Government and Public Health. *Cronin arrested* – Edward 'Ned' Cronin (1897–1946), ex National Army, founding member of the ACA, Blueshirt organiser was arrested in December 1933 and imprisoned for three months on the charges of sedition and membership of an illegal organisation.

1934

January

Wednesday 10

V. windy night & now as bad again & wet. Emer just gone, is getting small house in Kimmage, v. happy about it. A London Surgeon flew thro' fog to Jersey & did [trephining] on boy, accident case. Poor Hanratty safe in Grangegorman D.G. He molested 12 women in a short walk. A v. busy day getting pts. to hosp. etc. Everyone says how much more money is circulating in country.[427]

Thursday 18

Storm still. Tram men belonging to Eng. Union not permitted to join Irish one & have come out on strike because some Irish did join Union. D.G. most trams running still. Project on for Union of Central European countries, leaving France & England out. Teac Board went well. D.G. Miss Griffin to ask Reddin to apologise to M ffM. All agog for Madam Montessori on Sat. Thumb much easier to-night D.G. Saw Derrig re Gaeltacht.[428]

Saturday 20

Busy day, so glad y.day went well & then to-day, busy mg. Saw tiny prem. in Donnycaney, 3 weeks old twin T. 92, could it ever do? All preps. went well but we feared bouquet would never come & my brath was left in taxi, both turned up D.G. Reception splendid, Madam Montessori so beautiful & gracious. We had lovely Irish music, Sighle Hallissey, Schofields. Madam thanked for recept. flowers, music & babies.

---

427. *[trephining]* – Probably trephination, a surgical procedure to where a hole is drilled, incised, or scraped into the skull. *Hanratty* – John Hanratty (1892–1965), senior member of the Irish Citizen Army. *Grangegorman* – Grangegorman, the oldest public psychiatric hospital in the State.

428. *Tram men belonging to Eng. Union not permitted to join Irish one & have come out on strike because some Irish did join Union* – Some Tram works (from the Dublin Tramway Company) belonged to the British based Amalgamated Transport and General Workers' Union (ATGWU) which complained that its members were being poached by the Irish union, the Irish Transport and General Workers Union (ITGWU). 600 ATGWU members did transfer to the ITGWU in January 1934. *Madam Montessori* – Dr Maria Montessori (1870–1952), Italian physician and educator, developer of the Montessori educational method. *Derrig* – Thomas Derrig, (1897–1956), Fianna Fáil politician.

Monday 22

Nice day. All 3 papers have photos of Dr Montessori in Teac, some quite good. Independent's a/c best. All went well to-day. 92 prem. is now 97 D.G. & looks v. comfortable. O'Duffy tries to downfall Govt. & does it badly. Sean T. v. emphatic that local bodies must build & not shilly shally & then blame Govt. for bad houses. Miss Rhodes back & not too bad D.G. We think of getting wireless for nurses in Teac.

Tuesday 23

8 a.m. R.mines, nice Spring-like day. Child Welf. 11.30, they won't listen to Louie Bennett asking for better wages for chars. We got electric iron for 4/11 v. cheap, & tea towel with greyhounds & electric hares on it. Thumb sorer. Seymour thought piece of bone shld. come away. Mr Pringle saw it & said no, keep it quiet, so I must, alas! M ffM has extension phone in D.G. Mother Goose in evg. Was gt. fun, goose lovely.[429]

February

Friday 2

8 a.m. R.mines. All Maternity Homes to be inspected & licensed, excellent. Nurse Weills has come back to us on staff. She has terrible English accent & is untidy looking & sister always such a model of neatness. All Utility Law business done D.G. Evg. Dr Hill rang, Annie in labour, we took her to Holles St. poor girl. Judgement deferred in O'Duffy case. Ch.of Ir. Gazette admits more employment.[430]

Wednesday 14

Ash Wed. 8 a.m. R.mines. Med. Board went well. Revolution going hard in Vienna, the war started in Austria. D.V. this isn't another. All going well with Govt. here if only they are firm with those who shrink at nothing to injure them. We appointed new H.S. & hope she will be as good as they say. Bazaj has sold shop in Moore St. so we got tea fr. himself. He is better. Frosty to-night & fresh.[431]

---

429. *better wages for chars* – better wages for cleaners.
430. *Judgement deferred in O'Duffy case* – the case was whether or not a Military Tribunal could hear charges against Eoin O'Duffy, ex Garda Commissioner and leader of National Guard and Young Ireland Association (now illegal organisations) on charges of sedition and membership of said illegal organisations.
431. *Revolution going hard in Vienna* – 1934 Austrian Civil War, ended after a few days with the defeat of Social Democratic organisations and the left.

Friday 23

To-day wearing blue shirts illegal, what harm O'Duffy has done in the year. D.V. the Govt. will go strong & show it is not to be trifled with. Young German came travelling for needles etc. V. good stainless ones. I ordered a doz. He knows v. little English. F.R. does well D.G. V. busy all day. Mrs Henchie massaged me in evg. the piece of bone is quite loose now, it was it & not the joint wh. I felt creaking. God send rain.[432]

March

Monday 5

M's birthday & I not there. F. Rhodes sent for me early, had v. bad night, nagging pain. Had morph. & was easy & slept, she was so tired, sent again at 6 p.m. Then moribund, clear to last & thinking of us all. She passed at 10, quite peacefully D.G. she is at rest with Him. & we are the losers. Rain. Roosvelt a year in office, he has done much & the people are with him. F.F. has increased 49%.[433]

Thursday 8

Our 1st day without dear F. Rhodes, how lonely all Teac is! Lovely sun. Labour has decided on organizing a one day strike as a protest against Fascism under guise of Blue Shirts & showing how Fascism has destroyed Liberty in every country. It is a splendid move. My thumb is really better D.G. D.G. Nurse Farrell nearly wept with joy when she found I was not a F.F. & still stood for Freedom.[434]

Saturday 17

9 a.m. S. Patrick's. We had Albina Broderick with us & back to b.fast. She is a gt. woman. I was at S. Andrew's at 11.30, fine congregation, Albina & M ffM went to S.F. Conference & did good work. I fetched M home at 5 & we had dinner & quiet aft. M just dead tired, slept a lot. Had old Gramophone favourites. Cold showers & crowds were earlier. Arr. Aunt F. abt. 8.45, she had no Service, alas![435]

---

432. *To-day wearing blue shirts illegal* – Wearing of Uniform (Restriction) Bill, 1934 which sought to ban political uniforms in Irish public life introduced to the Dáil.
433. *F Rhodes* – Fanny M. Rhodes, daughter of Samuel and Fanny Rhodes, long-time friend of Lynn's.
434. *Nurse Farrell* – Elizabeth O'Farrell (1884–1957), republican, anti-treaty, continued to reject the legitimacy of the Free State.
435. *S.F. Conference* – Sinn Féin meeting.

Friday 23

Hoped to be up but slept late. Dev. introduced bill to abolish Senate & v. rightly, they were terrible to obstruct Blue Shirt bill wh. was so obviously for general good. He says election now might mean bloodshed. The Blue Shirts are terrors. Golden Millar won Grand National. M ffM listened in to race for 1st time, v. thrilling. Evg. I went to Coll. Phys. Dr Price & Dr Hardiman on Mendel-Mantoux.[436]

May

Sunday 6

Rogation Sun. 9 a.m. S. P's Gaelic. Quite a good few there & new ones. It poured in night but was finer till after 12. Rain didn't spoil the monster Labour antifascist demonstration. M ffM, Mrs Bennett & Mrs Wilson saw fr. Gresham. I did usu. things. Saw Alice Wynne, who is much better D.G. It has blown a western gale all day & is hard at it now. We have all windows shut.

Friday 25

8 a.m. S. B's, it poured in night & on to 2 but was fine for Aunt F. at 3. Maher says she has had fine time & he drove her home by new sea road in gt. joy. Miss Gethings is leaving on 4th, too bad. Airmen have not left Wales yet. Dev. made fine speech on abolition of Senate wh. 3rd reading, had large majority. He says we have a right to complete freedom & England wouldn't stand restrictions she puts on us.

June

Monday 11

S. Barnabus, 8 a.m. R.mines, lovely day. They need rain. D.V. will have it now. I.Times v. troubled by scandalous behaviour of Blackshirts, as bad as any Irish but they're the only hope against Communism! Gt. letter fr. M ffM D.G. Had fine sunbath & shopped, got hat & having dress settled for street . Evg. went to Mick Donnelly's, he has fine place, if only he could get well.[437]

---

436. *Dev. introduced bill to abolish Senate* – De Valera successfully introduced an Act to amend Article XII of the Constitution and to abolish Seanad Éireann as a constituent House of the Legislature. *Dr Hardiman* – probably Dr Townley Hardman (*d.*1957), radiologist. *Mendel-Mantoux* – a test for screening for tuberculosis.
437. *Blackshirts* – paramilitary wing of the Italian National Fascist Party, known as the Squadrismo, also called after the black shirts they wore as part of their uniform.

Wednesday 20

8 a.m. S. B's, wind coldish, some sun. Muriel sent £1 for poor. Much better to her than L Wellwood her mistress & will have her in Aug. when Jane away. House of Commons refuse to take off import duties on our stuff. Abp. in Maynooth gave fine address to candidate priests on tolerance, much needed. Sent my Republican Proclamation to Museum. D.V. it will be safe. M ffM to join us in Glen on 5th.[438]

July

Wednesday 4

A most glorious day. Did usual things, saw moon at abt. 11.30 a.m. Papers say 46 executed in Deutchland, It's terrible. Charlie Byrne came with milk & veget. Mr Williams & Eoin here all day, doing sheep, turf etc. A motor & party here all day. Dear M ffM arr. in v. good time & so well & lively after travelling since Mon. She says 55 executed & that is end of Hitler, prob. true.[439]

Thursday 16

Board Day, went well D.V. Miss O Lloyd appointed permanently. We pray it's for the best. Saw Perolz. she is doing well. A nice day, bad babies better D.G. Hear Cork Examiner making for strike. We'll try to get it. Citizen Army seems def. linked with Congress & P. O'Donnell. Report McNeill dropped dead in mg.& Cosgrave in Eng. same day, such nonsense. Teac had many visitors–Sommerille-Ross's cousin.[440]

Friday 24

8 a.m. R.mines, a glorious day, lovely sun. M ffM & Olga went to Glendalough with 2 cousins & had lovely time. Hearst says there'll be no European war. D.V. that is true. In Germany Hitler has arrested over 100 & taken them to unknown destination, for 1 million voted against

438. *Republican Proclamation* – Proclamation of Independence 1916, printed at Liberty Hall, of which very few remain.

439. *executed in Deutchland* – Night of the Long Knives, a purge of political opponents carried out by Hitler between 30 June and 2 July 1934. Among those executed was Ernst Röhm, leader of the SA / Sturmabteilung, known as the Brownshirts.

440. *Miss O. Lloyd* – Miss Ormsby Lloyd was appointed Housekeeper at St Ultan's Hospital. *Perolz* – Márie Perolz (1874–1950), republican and trade unionist. *Congress & P. O'Donnell* – in 1934, having failed to influence the anti-treaty IRA towards a more left-wing stance, Peadar O'Donnell broke with the IRA and co-founded the Republican Congress with a group of fellow pro-communist republicans. *Sommerille-Ross's cousin* – most likely Ethel Penrose (1857–1938), children's writer.

him in Plebiscite. Brave people they were. Douglas photographed us with his bright bulb.[441]

September

Saturday 1

8 a.m. S. B's, many usual people back. Nice day D.G. Eng. paper says Prince George engaged to Greek princess, also that German woman made gt. anti war speech in London. Women must unite, why had they to rear children for gun fodder? Fascism unmasked. Germans work in Labour camp for keep, under military condit. & they call it "employment". All ready for to-morrow. D.V. it'll be fine.

October

Wednesday 3

Up early, v. wet. M came to sta. M ffM & Maher met me. All well & I got straight into it. Out to see Alice W. & Aunt F. 1st thing. All went well D.G. in Teac & No. 9. Herald gives a/c of Russia. The economy side is excellent but the political side, one can get no information about at all. Tyrannies seem to be universal now. Here unemployed are doing archaeological excavations. Have found much.

Sunday 14

20 A.T. 8 a.m. Xt. Ch. H.T. decorations nice, wind cold but I had lovely bath & didn't feel wind at all, it was lovely. I wrote plenty in mg. Psychology of the Soul v. good & helpful. Poor Alice Wynne had bad night but D.V. she will be better now. Home late. M ffM had long, & I say, wasted day at S. Fein Ard Feis. The whole thing is dead & shld. be buried.

Tuesday 16

8 a.m. R.mines, warmer to-day. Gt. gales thro' country & in Derry thunderbolt, snow in England. D. MacArdle agrees with us that Press is awful but says she can do nothing, then who can. Teac busy & happy. Alice Wynne not well last night, sent such a queer message. I

---

441. *Plebiscite* – 19 August 1934 the German public voted by large majority in favour of Hitler becoming Führer und Reichskanzler (merging the post of President and Chancellor), a new title created after the death of President Paul von Hindenburg earlier in the month.

only went on chance, had Dr Micks to see her, he agrees all possible is being done. Dinner Rhodes.[442]

November

Tuesday 20

8 a.m. R.mines, nice sun. Gt. fuss over £3,000 of notes stolen in P. Office. Japan won't play 2nd fiddle to U.S. & Britain. Maj W. Newell came to say M ffM's protegee had been elected to Incurable. Express gives gt. a/c of speech of Dr Crofton to opticians! [ ] lauding his methods & claiming too much for them, as always. Teac nicely. all preps. for Bermingham.[443]

December

Monday 3

8 a.m. S. B's. Dark & warm & v. busy day. Teac Board did what was wanted. We saw flats wh. are really v. nice & wonderfully planned. They shld. be happy in them. The U.T.P's incitements to violence continue. It is such nonsense to say they can't pay annuities when they can back horses etc. Butchers try to give inferior meat to poor against regulations.

Monday 17

8 a.m. S. B's. A nice day. New Holles St. hospital opened with gt. eclat. M ffM says it is nice but has many defects. The kitchen is after pattern of U.S.A. & Continent. Sean T. gone to U.S.A. for Xmas. We shopped some in mg. got cards ec. & I did pts. Had to go to Dun Laogh. 10 pm. D.G. Mrs Smithwick is getting a local Dr. V. stormier earlier.[444]

Monday 31

8 a.m. S. B's. hurried back, b.fast hasty, we were off to Lasernas (Elizabeth Somers) funeral Mass Blackrock, 10 o/c Dev. & most Ministers there & a crowd indeed. We took Mr Ernie O'Malley & Matron

---

442. *Press* – the *Irish Press* newspaper, founded in 1931. It represented the Fianna Fáil viewpoint. *Dr Micks* – Robert Henry Micks (*b.*1895), physician to Sir Patrick Dun's Hospital.
443. *Gt. fuss over £3,000 of notes stolen in P. Office* – a registered package with £3,000 enclosed went missing between Ballsbridge Post Office and Pearse St., sorting office. *elected to Incurable* – a new Board of Governors of the Royal Hospital of Incurables, Donnybrook.
444. *New Holles St. hospital opened* – Francis Walls, Assistant bishop of Dublin, opened the first section of the new Holles Street Hospital on 17 December 1934.

home. Then pts. & post cards & saw about things. Aft. the Independent rang up to say Dr O'Leary of the School Inspection was lost off a liner in Mediterranean & wanting her history, referred to Angela Russell. I fear she was mental.[445]

---

445. *Lasernas* – Elizabeth Somers (1881–1934), republican, journalist and industrial revivalist, also known as 'Lasarfhiona Ní Shamhraidin'. *Mr Ernie O'Malley* – Ernie O'Malley (1897–1957), Irish Republican and writer. *Dr O'Leary* – Dr Mary Margaret O'Leary (*d.*1934), Assistant Medical Officer of Health for Dublin, drowned while on a cruise in the Mediterranean, reports of her death referred to her having been in poor health. *Angela Russell* née Coyne, (1893–1991), physician and social reformer, wife of Dr Matthew Russell (1874–1956), Medical Officer of Health for Dublin.

1935

January

Saturday 5

8 a.m. S. B's. fine night but this aft. rain again & v. damp. More trade agreements with Britain. Dev. does well. D.V. Lady Lavery dead. She wasn't a very famous Irish woman. Mr Scott delighted with amalgamation proposal. D.V. it will work. Pts. nearly all day. Evg. tea F. Clarke much as usual. Farmers now miauling abt. agriculture, now they are insatiable. Have manifesto of 18 points.[446]

Thursday 9

Up latish. Med. Board discussed plans of amalgamation & approves of principle. D.V. we'll work out details satisfactorily. We confirmed appt. of Dr. Gordon as H.S. She is same standing as Dr Dougherty, looks younger in spite of her hard life. We went over flats, they're very nice & soon will be done D.V. Saw Keller at Island Bridge. River lovely, full, dark, silent. Sky beautiful.[447]

Wednesday 16

8 a.m Magdalen to thank for so much, Beatsy, Saar etc. Mild day. Special Med. Board re admitting children up to 2 & sending delegates to Hosp. Congress Rome. Beatsy wonderful, sitting up, taking Bovril, red bow in hair. M ffM so delighted. Saar settlement will bring Peace they say. Discussed Dr Addis with Moorhead, he doesn't think much of his like.[448]

February

Thursday 7

A v. cold day & night tho' I was warm on balcon. All went well. There are to be new Judges & a High Circuit Court as well as the lower one

---

446. *Lady Lavery* – Havel Lavery, née Martyn (1880–1935), painter. She was born in America which may be why Lynn did not consider her a famous Irish woman. *Miauling* – complaining.

447. *Amalgamation* – The proposed amalgamation between Harcourt Street Children's Hospital and St Ultan's to form a new, larger, better resourced Children's Hospital. *Dr Gordon* – Dr Kate Mary Gordon, graduated NUI 1935.

448. *Saar Settlement* –The Saarland was occupied by Britian and France from 1920–35 under a League of Nations mandate. In a plebiscite on 13 January 1935 a majority favoured reintegration with Germany, which took effect on 1 March 1935.

& District Judges are to be abolished. Now there may be some chance of fair play for us, impossible when all judges were English appointed per C. na nGaels. Poor Pat O'Connor dead, he was good in old times. Saw Ida with Aunt F. All well there.[449]

Monday 11

A v. busy day whole time, no word of Dr Hill, I miss her. Poor Moore O'Farrell & his son shot while at dinner in their house near Tullamore & Mr Scott happened to be there. He got awful shock. The boy has spinal column injured. It is an affair of evictions & I hear I.R.A. has something to say to it. Just hear that poor Nora O'Shea died this mg. She was ill so long, poor Nora.[450]

Tuesday 19

Had lovely mg. on balcony like summer feel much better to-day D.G. & on for food U.S.A. Courts have upheld Roosvelt & won't allow bond holders to demand more for Bonds than present dollar worth. M ffM played lovely records in evg. & we had happy time. Mrs Henchie pleased with her. She says my thumb is wonderful.

March

Monday 11

Strike goes on. V. busy day with many pts. & phones etc. Consult. with Mr Gunn re Miss Jellett in afternoon, he, no more than Dora, isn't forthcoming. V. doleful over pt. Evg. M ffM, Matron & I went to Bob's de Coeur's funeral fr. Mater to Church St. Saw so many old I.C.A. people who loved him. We had J. Shanaghan, M. Cavanagh & Mrs O'Hanlon in car.[451]

Friday 15

Lemass now advocates organising strike breaking squads to drive busses etc. alas! that it shld. come to that. Bill O'Brien says rightly

---

449. *C. na nGaels – Cumann na nGaedheal. Pat O'Connor –* Commandant Patrick O'Connor, 0/C No. 2 Battalion, Kerry No. 1 Brigade, died in Adelaide, March, 1934.

450. *More O'Farrell –* a local land agent in Longford, who secured eviction notices for eleven tenants. An intervention by the local IRA turned violent. They raided the Lissard House as a dinner party was ongoing and More O'Farrell and his son Richard were shot, with the elder man dying soon after. *Nora O'Shea –* Dublin Cumann na mBan, anti-treaty, imprisoned during the Civil War, assisted in the rescue of 19 Republican prisoners from Mountjoy Jail in 1925.

451. *Miss Jellett –* Mary Harriet 'Mainie' Jellett (1897–1944), artist.

that the Minister shld. hold balance even, not weighted to capitalist side. V. busy day. MffM & Mrs Cosgrave interviewed Mr Monks Rates Dept. & have got promise of 50% rebate on disputed rates. D.G. that is splendid.[452]

Wednesday 27

Might have been up early, but I fear, lazy. Most glorious day, perfect sun had 40 min. sunbath & a v. busy day all the time. Unions repudiates I.R.A's interference in strike. All I.R.A. leaders etc. arrested, Sean McBride not there, on run now. They say it is re shooting of police, Peadar O'Donnell, the great humbug, released unconditionally. Here carpenters' strike pending.

April

Tuesday 9

8 a.m. R.mines. A German leader says he is godless & proud of it. Alas! Strike same. Tram Co. are dismissing officials. Poor Susie is v. angry with the men & knows nothing of Labour & all it means. Peg Tyrell v. well D.G. Hear Iveagh Trust are looking for a large housing scheme. Perhaps they'll do Charlemont, Richmond St. D.V. Mr Scott has asked M ffM to be godmother to the baby. Lovely rain.[453]

May

Monday 13

1st sleep on balcon. for ages, it was lovely. Rebecca came before b.fast over to say row with Miss O. Lloyd & she & all staff leaving. It was a worry, had long talk with Matron & she has many complaints too. I had to remember "God never faileth" & now D.G. peace has come. V. busy day, hear they had to have curfew in Belfast to quell Loyalists & antis. No rain.

June

Friday 7

8 a.m. S. B's. D.G. I fasted this Fri. unlike last 1st. Terrible showers

---

452. *Strike goes on* – 1 March 1935 almost 3,000 transport workers, members of the ATGWU and the ITGWU, voted for strike action in support of a bus driver summarily dismissed from the Dublin United Tramway Company, accused of dangerous driving.

453. *Iveagh Trust* – Given a statutory legal basis by the Iveagh Trust Act 1903, the Iveagh Trust is a provider of affordable housing in Dublin.

D.G.& now W.wind after E. for months. A busy happy day, not v. exciting. They're getting v. busy for bye Election. Matron's niece came fr. Holles St. gt. excitement there, woman admitted, died in 2 hrs. fr. mening. & baby removed alive by Caesarian after her death. Garden v. enticing now, things grow well. Hear Margot Trench v. ill.[454]

Tuesday 11

8 a.m. R.mines. V. heavy showers. All came, had one race down garden. V. busy day. After dinner had long case wh. kept me going. Terrible storm y.day in England, floods of rain. Milch cows shot in Cork by Fine Gaels. horrid. Emer had fine letter in re not allowing women to work. Lemass new Bill.[455]

Saturday 21

8 a.m. S. B's. So nice to be warm Babies nearly all out on roof, nearly too hot. Hear Galway is winning for F.F. hands drawn. D.V. it is true. Meeting of Joint Comt. re Amalgamation. I think all well but we need more understanding. Sighle, Frank came, so nice to see them. Still good letters in papers re treatment of women. God helped thro' day.

July

Friday 19

We slept well. Last year there was no amalgamation question to give us care like now, but God helps. Rained much all mg. Aft. girl hikers came, drowned, got lost, Glendalough to Donard in mist, came down here instead. We fed & dried them & they left in sun for R.drum. No more hills for them to-day. We did some shucking. M ffM is wonderful Quite warm. D.G. for day.

August

Wednesday 7

Another hot day tho' little real sun. 1st day of pts. saw nice few. Hear we may get a senior student fr. Meath, would be a help now. The waxbills flourish D.G. & are fine under Rebecca's care. Teac has bad

---

454. *Margot Trench* – Margot Chenevix Trench (1889–1936), cultural nationalist and political activist.
455. *Lemass new Bill* – In 1935 the Conditions of Employment Bill was introduced by Seán Lemass, Minster for Industry and Commerce. Section 16 of the Bill dealt with restrictions on female employment, many feminists and women trade unionists objected to the Bill.

babies & we're full up. Emer phoned, glad to be congratulated on V. Presidency of Trades' Council. Hear Miss Chevinix & a laundry worker are going to Geneva re Women's Work.[456]

Friday 9

A v. busy day, enormous disp. Then 11 to 4.30 House pts. fairly D.G. Nice day & sun after all the rain y.day. The last 1/2 mil. Jews in Germany are in a terrible way, not allowed to flee, left absolutely boycotted & miserable in every way. Horse Show has done excellently, more sales than ever. Fr O'Shea in Teac, says Ireland has prospered since 1932 D.G.

Monday 19

8 a.m. S. B's. A v. nice day. 3rd big fire Sinn Fein House with lovely ceiling & chimney pieces gutted & alas! Annie Higgins & her mother burnt to death, she was with us in Mtjoy in 1916, a music teacher. War seems more than ever imminent but God can change everything. Evg. Olga, Mrs Bennett, Frau Grabish & we two went to John Bull's Other Island, Abbey, great.[457]

September

Monday 2

8 a.m. S. B's. Surely we must all pray for Peace. Miss Chevinix rang last night to ask M ffM to go to W.W.U. meeting on Tues. night re Geneva, says it shld. be spoken there. Nice sun. Many to see. MffM's friends came over Teac & were much pleased. They went then to Mr Moore's & heard old stories of Carantrilagh, Tuam, girls buried in garden orgies of 150 yrs. ago etc. I remember some of it fr. Tuam of yrs ago.[458]

October

Saturday 5

8 a.m. S. B's. F. Clarke there, Jim's birthday, nice & warm. V. busy mg. 2 letters fr. M ffM, one saying she'd be here 9th, the other that her

---

456. *V. Presidency of Trades' Council* – Molony was elected Vice President of the Irish Trade Union Congress (ITUC) in 1935. *Miss Chevinix* – Helen Chenevix (1886–1963), suffragist and trade unionist, worked in the Irish Women Workers Union with her partner Louie Bennett.
457. *Annie Higgins* – music teacher, Cumann na mBan, took part in the 1916 Rising, she and her mother lived in a flat over the Sinn Féin offices on Parnell Sq. *Frau Grabish* – Agatha Bullitt Grabisch (1875–1945), American born, married a German doctor, and during 1914–18 became involved in the Irish movement in Berlin, meeting Casement, later visiting Dublin often, and made friends with Lynn.
458. *W.W.U.* – Irish Women Workers' Union.

treat. wouldn't be finished for a week or so she won't come till 16th, a terrible blow to us who were counting on the 8th for sure. D.V. she'll come 16th. Nice aft. with F. Clarke in Bray, bathed in surf, fine. War news same as last night. Tea with Mrs Clarke.

Tuesday 15

8. a.m. R.mines. another v. warm day, T. 68. S. Nesbitt McQuaide came to dinner, she is v. well D.G. & Mr Pringle is v. pleased with her. She had benign growth beside Gall bladder, all removed D.G. R.mines Child Welf. good. We could draw up a good scheme. Dr Price & M ffM. consulted re more Nurses, to be housed in No. 35. One of our cacti looks bad, I say rot.

November

Friday 8

8 a.m. S. B's to thank for all God's goodness y.day. A. V. busy day. 62 in disp. Hear there is to be new amalgamated Womens' Soc. to see we get our rights & truly, the men were quite willing we shld share dangers of war but now withold fruits of it. The Women are sending a Peace Aeroplane to Abysinnia with all Red X stuff. Saw "Noah" Abbey.[459]

Tuesday 12

8 a.m. Magdalen, v. frosty night but lovely on balcon. Med Board went well. Dr Barry only objected to amalgamation because we hadn't beds enough! No word of Dr Byrne (Apb.) Dr P says Moorhead only approached by Stafford Johnston on subject, never by Abp. It is all mean, underhand work. Gt. fund started for Arranmore survivors. Hope it'll do well. Gt. floods in North, Coleraine etc. M ffM v .sore.[460]

Wednesday 13

8 a.m. R.mines. Child Welf. 11. V. frosty as usual. Mrs Maud Walsh has same story of R.C. Abp.s disapproval of our amalgamation. A v.

---

459. *'Noah' Abbey – Noah: a play* by Andre Obey was on in the Abbey Theatre.
460. *Dr Byrne (Apb.)* – Edward Joseph Byrne (1872–1940), Archbishop of Dublin, 1921–40, opposed the plan for amalgamation on religious grounds, as the proposed new hospital would not be under Catholic patronage. *Stafford Johnson* – Dr James Stafford Johnson (1889-1983), founder member of the Medical Guild of Sts Luke, Damian, and Cosmos which promoted solidarity among Catholic medical professionals, he opposed the amalgamation plan on sectarian grounds. *Arranmore tragedy* – On 9 November 1935 a boat left Burtonport for Arranmore Island, it sank en route with a loss of 20 lives, all Islanders.

well circulated lie it is. Oxford Group lunch at Hibernian at 1. My 1st experience of it. Seems v. good but does not have the depth of Fr FitzGerald & [Walter] Millocks, I think. Gt. account of Arranmore disaster.[461]

Wednesday 20

8 a.m. Magdalen, to get strength for the hard day. It went better than we thought D.G. & we were all sorry we had to ask Dr Barry to resign off Med. Board when she should not consciously represent us for she holds that her Abp. doesn't approve of amalg. so she can't. A terrible day of rain estp. in evg. & night. Had files etc. ready for Miss Griffin & she never came.

Thursday 21

8 a.m. Xt. Ch. as dark as y.day, but no rain. V. busy day. Teac Board full. Miss Griffin not there so I changed it. Med. Board deputation. Dr Webb read splendid statement out wh. told well, we got out the whole petty story of the C. Abp.'s disapproval no reason given but that of religion wh. doesn't come in at all. Whole thing to come up in a week.

December

Sunday 1

Advent Sun. 9 a.m. S. Patrick's, there we had Albina, she & M went to Sinn Fein Ard Feis, her Cuman was expelled, they had only a miserly few, 26 Cuman only in country. They won't have anyone in 2nd Dail but those elected in '21 so it must die out, won't have the '23ers or any abstentionist elected since. I had nice day with Aunt F. V. wet & cold.

Thursday 5

8 a.m. Xt. Ch. V. cold & frosty. Saw Mrs Cosgrave early, she will go to Miss Griffin, she did & not much result. We will go on in absolute trust for He can find a way. Had quite long talk with the Misses Lawrence, 1st time since 1916! or before. Went to inaugural meeting of Mna na hEireann, it shld. put Women 1st, for without them there can be no Freedom.[462]

---

461. *Oxford Group* – an evangelical bible study group.
462. *Mna na hEireann*– this is an error, Lynn likely means Mná na Poblachta, which was set up by disillusioned members of Cumann na mBan. They held fast to the belief that the only members of the 2nd Dáil were the legitimate government and reaffirmed the oath taken to the Republic in 1916.

Friday 20

Aunt F. wonderful D.G. Left fairly early. Miss Meggett better. M ffM & I went to Deputation to their Abp. with Belton, Dr Barry & Mrs Hackett. He gave long list of his 'reasons' against amalgamation, all the things we have never done & can easily say will never be done, he is terrible domineering without reason. We can well answer all he says. We know right will prevail D.G.[463]

---

463. In the statement Byrne 'opposes this amalgamation on religious ground solely', he saw the boards of the two hospitals as Protestant and feared the new hospital would attack Catholic morals, undermine the faith of patients, provide contraception, and sterilise children seen as 'unfit'. (SU/4/4 – Saint Ultan's Hospital Papers, RCPI Archive).

1936

January

Thursday 2

8.30 Xt. Ch., don't know why it was 1/2 hour later, nice in mg. & now v. cold again. The Swedes are mad with Mussolini for bombing of their Red Cross Unit in Abyssinia, it was an unheard of thing to do. The Senate is nearly defunct but did it's bit to hold up the Guarantee Fund bill, wh. is not fair, the bill, I mean. Dr Hennessey died suddenly in the street going to office, his heart has long been bad.[464]

Thursday 9

8 a.m. Xt. Ch. hurried back to b.fast & dentist 9.30, came on a Housing Comt. & aft. regular hurricane fr. S & torrents all the time. Lull abt. 9. Now wind rising again. Mrs Kettle thinks Abp.s objections futile. A pity he interferes outside his province. The measles children are bad enough, poor things. I wish we had the adult serum, former epidemics did so well.

Thursday 16

8 a.m. Xt. Ch. v. wet night. Sl. snow in mg. Didn't lie in. Teac Board. Dr Barry had to be at Peamount. Mr Bolton proposed that copies of Abp. statement be sent to Board members with skeleton reply, special meeting to be called, the hopeless muddle is clarifying D.G. We know God does all. Emer to dinner, not v well, but pleased. Nice letter fr. John

Tuesday 28

8 a.m R.mines, a lovely day with bright sun. M ffM gave red Azalia, Susie silk stockings & Flo. snowdrops & lovely cards, it was a dear Birthday, gladdened by excellent letter fr. Miss Griffin for Abp. Her sister must have talked sense to her. We said D.G. give trust to Him. M Cunningham says votes don't count, S. Ultan does. Aunt F well D.G. not depressed by funeral.

---

464. *Guarantee Fund bill* – Land Purchase (Guarantee Fund) Act, 1936. *Dr Hennessey* – Dr Thomas Hennessey (*c.*1871–1965), Cumann na nGaedheal politician and medical practitioner.

Wednesday 29

8 a.m. Magdalen, glad Mr Waring there. Teac Special Board, Belton was appalling but we carried sending of reply to Abp. by 1 vote D.G., that is done anyhow. It was great to have Miss Griffin's draft reply, for he produced nothing. Evg. v. tired & felt as if Mr Hanafin's hare didn't sit well in stomach, so early to bed while M typed letter.[465]

Friday 31

8 a.m. S. B's foggy & Birminghamlike as usual, much rain aft. Hear Stafford Johnstone lecture to National students on the danger to R.Cs of T.C.D. & all the R.C Abp. stunts we know so well. We must refute these. All non R.C. hospitals involved. Big Disp. nice. Dr Murison so good, Matron says best ever. Miss O Lloyd bad with chill got at King George's funeral Service.[466]

February

Friday 7

8 a.m. S. B's, fairly warm at 8, by 9 wicked cold S. wind wh. went thro' & thro', must be snow overhead. Terrible to have no heating in N. wing tho' babies seem quite warm D.G. Gt. a/cs of how Abysinnians come out of caves & happy. Italians, they have got gt. advantage of being at home. Dr Price read fine paper on T.B. in young children & case devel. in 6th week.

Friday 28

8 a.m. S. B's. V. hard to hear Mr Simpson. Nice sun in mg. but the smokey atmosphere tells. V. busy in Teac. M ffM wanted to bring whole correspondence with Abp.to Hosp. Commission, they'll be ready for it to-morrow. Cooks came in aft. both flourishing. Told them of old Jack Finn of Ballyinagibbon, his daughter was there in 1886 when we went to Cong. V.old.

---

465. A letter, with the Boards reply, was sent to the Archbishop by Madeleine ffrench-Mullen, as secretary to the Board. The letter indicated the Board were not unanimous in the approval of the amalgamation, Drs Lynn, Webb, Tennant, O'Doherty and Price in favour and Dr Barry against. Their main argument was that 'in the interests of sick children and for the saving of infant life the hospital shall expand into a larger more up to date unit, such as can be achieved by amalgamation'. (Archbishop Byrne Papers, Dublin Diocesan Achives, IE/DDA/AB7, Box 60).
466. *Dr Murison* – Dr Kathleen Duffus Murison, graduated Trinity 1925.

March

Wednesday 4

8 a.m. Magdalen. Mr Singleton prayed for. He died absolutely suddenly, playing Badminton. Mrs is terribly upset, poor thing. We polished up brasses for Muriel etc. I went to Fred Mangan & signed my will. D.G. it is done. I have been long threatening. All pray for Peace & D.V. it will come. M Comerford editor new editor of Press women's' page, wrote well of Teac. Got newborn twins in, mother v. ill in Rotunda.[467]

Wednesday 11

8 a.m. Magdalen. Poor Nurse McGonigal has Cebro Sp. Mening. Dr Micks took her into Duns, she is seriously ill. Med. board went well. Poor Dr Barry looks wretched. There are hopes of Peace tho' France wants all her own way & German troops removed fr. own territory. If Geneva can only stand on merits & not on treaties, unfair to vanquished. Milder day.

Friday 27

8 a.m. S. B's. Poured all night & most of mg. some v. welcome sun. Coal strike serious enough. They will make no concessions to Hospitals we hear, wh. is unfortunate, will make them unpopular. Interviewed 2 Oxford Group ladies, they were v. glad because we all decided [same] separately. Cathal O'Shannon came re Hist. of Citizen Army.[468]

April

Friday 3

8 a.m. S. B's We can't get coal fr. Guinnesses but D.G. we are promised a ton of coal on Wed. Teac does well on whole. Debate re Republic did all good, sensible arguments on our side. Sean MacBride & Mary Mac. Made mincemeat of Packenham & McDermott. I couldn't go but M ffM did. All the world were there Gt. a/c of impregnability of Abyssinia.[469]

Wednesday 8

7.30 R.mines, was v. tired in mg., up late writing cheques, all bills paid now, D.G. More revelations in Ball case, but I can't read it it is

467. *M Comerford* – Máire Comerford (1893–1982), Cumann na mBan member, journalist.
468. *Cathal O'Shannon* (1890–1969), revolutionary, trade unionist, writer, and journalist.
469. *Pakenham and McDermott* – Frank Pakenham, 7th Earl of Longford (1905–2001), and Frank MacDermott (1886–1975), Senator, barrister, soldier, politician, and historian.

so horrid & sordid. Med. Board all discussed plans for tinies. Place for T.B. babies, 10 Nurses, Service Room, cost £650, not dear. A nice day. Sally K charmed with her antique arm chair.[470]

May

Friday 1

8 a.m. R.mines, fasting day went v. well. Lovely sun early but wind cold. V. busy all day. Hear both Cork murders were by Cork I.R.A., wh. is a law to itself, every pt. of country I.R.A. only obeys local leaders. It is now a public danger, alas! how it has fallen fr. 1916 M ffM & I went to Miss Cunningham's At Home in evg. Met Dutch Consul & interesting people, nice time.[471]

Wednesday 6

10 hrs in bed & only fairly rested. Poured night & mg. thunderstorm Ballybrack 6 a.m. Has looked like it for days. Mussolini triumphs over his massacre of the poor Abyssinians & says it's a glorious conquest. Arrogant & foolish. All Church bells rang but S. Peter's. D.G. for that. Mary Mac laments imprisonment of Sean & young MacCurtain but how diff. they are fr. I.R.A. of 1916.[472]

Wednesday 13

Up late, did things in mg. Med. Board, we are to get Bassinet cots, letter fr. Hospital Commission, we may go ahead with our shanty for 10 babies & the Nurses. The babies in No. 10 are to come back to Teac to-morrow evg. V. big disp. Budget out to-day, nothing to write home about. Mussolini ordered British Red X out of Abyssinia.

June

Monday 22

8 a.m. S.B.'s. Another, 3rd night of thunder & lightening & long this time. Torrential rain. 2 killed in Lurgan & some trees etc. here. Mrs

---

470. *Ball Case* – Edward Francis Ball, of Booterstown, Co. Dublin. On 17 February 1936, after being refused £60 to go on a foreign tour with the Gate company, he killed his mother Lavena 'Vena' Ball, with a hatchet. He was found guilty but insane.
471. Retired Vice Admiral Henry Boyle Townshend Somerville (1863–1936), was killed by the IRA at his home in Castletownshend, Co. Cork on 24 March 1936.
472. *Sean & young MacCurtain* – Seán MacBride (1904–88), and Tomás Óg MacCurtain (1915–94), son of murdered Lord Mayor of Cork, Tomás MacCurtain.

S.S. got thro' to Bodenstown as Press & held impromptu meeting at X Roads, read M McSwiney's oration & messages fr. prisoners & sang Soldiers' Song all before police got up to stop them. Sorry I wasn't there. Brutal batoning of crowds here. Frau Grabish & she had dinner here. We had gt. talks. Warm day.[473]

Tuesday 23

8 a.m. R.mines, quiet night D.G. no thunder. Hear a possibility of joining New Repub. party by Sinn Fein & ret. of IR.A. to Allegiance to 2nd Dail, good. Strikes settled, we hear in Belgium. Child Welf. went well & I ordered things for Glen & got goldfish, big ones. Teac nicely D.G. Garden grows well. Hoardings have "Love, Joy, Peace", never saw that before, is it Oxford Group? V. rushy day.

July

Monday 6

A v. quiet day, saw no one but postman. News that Geneva has gone wallup as Matron would say, well anyhow the League of Nations was never any good. Had such nice time with Workman's book & realization of what Redemption means. It is all so wonderful and new, tho' so old. Pangar was much better, was quite like himself again. Tom came in evg. Liked papers better than gramophone.[474]

August

Thursday 13

8 a.m. Xt.Ch. Quite nice day. Much warmer in evg. Nearly 70 [degrees]. Leader in I times says Fine Gael & F. Fail's programmes nearly identical now. Hopes that F.Gael will renounce all idea of Republic be sensible & British & all will be well. Criticises Dev. for doing & saying what he used to denounce so heartily. A.G.O.W. here & in Teac. Amalgamation quiescent, not dead. Election Day.[475]

---

473. *read M McSwiney's oration* – The Press reported that despite the banning of the republican demonstrations at Bodenstown, Hanna Sheehy Skeffington managed to get to Sallins Cross Road and there read an address which was to have been delivered at the graveside by Mary MacSwiney.

474. *Geneva has gone wallup* – League of Nations meeting in Geneva Session of June–July 1936 heard an appeal from Emperor Majesty Haile Selassie of Ethiopia against the invasion of his country by Italy, but to no avail. *Pangar* – one of Lynn's pet cats.

475. *Election Day* – By-election in Galway, 13 August 1936, Martin Neilan, Fianna Fáil won, James Hogan, Fine Gael runner up and Count George Plunkett, National Centre Party, lost his deposit.

Friday 14

8 a.m. S.B's. Nice day. V. busy. Op. with Dr Hill 10 then Teac, hard 4 hrs, & pts. here etc. ending up with Sighle, Mrs Skeffington & Emer here. E. is now president of Trades Council D.V. she'll fill post well. Nothing in papers re election wh. looks v. hopeful. If they were cocksure, they'd let us know it. Duke of Sutherland having yachting cruise round Ireland, that's for no good.[476]

September

Thursday 3

8 a.m. Xt. Ch. Much rain in night, but lovely day, such sun! Had sunbath D.G. Got bulbs in Woolworths before they got too mixed. Man shot in Tipperary now dead. Mrs W Power v. worried over it. Was it another case like Conway? Teac v. busy indeed. Emer came & D.G. she is better. God grant His Grace to keep her so & of course He will. Another Turas to Cashel coming off.[477]

Monday 14

8 a.m. S. B's. Saw poster re tragedy in Arbour Hill. One of the poor lads has hanged himself, no wonder after that inhuman treatment! alas! that Dev. should have sunk so low. Haven't heard much abt. it. Went to Cumann na mB Office, Police & G. man there, saw girl in next office, she says had to communicate now at all. This poor lad had only ordered a lorry for Bodenstown, only 24.[478]

Tuesday 22

8 a.m. R.mines, nice aft. sun. M ffM & Mrs Bennett went to Trade Show, Pasteur, it was splendid. Mr O'Donnell & friend to Morgenrot . Child Welf. went well. More tales of fear of our proselytizing afterwards. D.G. some are more enlightened. In Teac Dr Price will talk to Rotunda people re special ward for T.B. mothers. Evg. Miss Sullivan gave advice re S. Brigid & S. Patrick for mosaics in S. Peter.[479]

---

476. *Duke of Sutherland* – George Sutherland-Leveson-Gower, 5th Duke of Sutherland (1888–1963), British courtier and politician.

477. *Man shot in Tipperary* – Daniel Gleeson, farmer, of Nenagh shot during a house raid. *Conway* – Michael Conway, a republican condemned to death in 1936 for the murder in Co. Waterford of John Egan, whom they believed had informed the authorities about IRA drilling. *Turas to Cashel* – Trip to Cashel, Co. Tipperary.

478. *tragedy in Arbour Hill* – Seán Glynn, 24, serving nine months imposed by Military Tribunal for unlawful association, was found dead in his cell on 13 September 1936.

479. *fear of our proselytizing* – if amalgamation with Harcourt St went ahead it was thought the new hospital would be more Protestant in ideology and there could be proselytise patients.

Saturday 26

8 a.m. S. B's quite nice day tho' cold. V. busy for hours & hours up & down. Gt. news. Moss Twomey & 3 others moved fr. Arbour Hill to Glass House & Moss to have visit D.G. & they say all the rest are to go to Mjoy. It's a victory. Gt. meeting in C. Brugha St. Plackards Dev the Hangman 78 etc. B Oman says a priest has said Ch. of Rome is Capitalist, always & will [therefore] go under, wasn't so before.[480]

October

Tuesday 6

8 a.m. R.mines, a glorious day D.G. A terrible fire in Pearse St., an exide factory & that in busy St. & in an old tenement house, 3 poor firemen were killed. I never remember any being killed before. I enquired at Station & saw Mrs Joe Connolly, she was feeding the 7 orphans of one fireman. Teac quite nicely. Saw Esther & I have got her into work for me D.G[481]

Wednesday 14

8 a.m. Magdalen, soft rain now 3 nights. V. busy mg. Teac Med. Board went well. Dr Barry v. keen we should protest against Dr English's treat. in being passed over & man fr. Enniscorthy asylum being put over her. It is a gt. wrong. Douglas here again, pleased with dinner, we had v. nice trifle of pears, raspberry, sponge cake, jelly with cream & custard. V. warm to-night 62.[482]

November

Wednesday 4

Up for b.fast. Had v. busy day but felt well D.G. The F.F. Ard Feis was terrible when questions asked about murder of Sean Glynn, Dev. said they were governing not playacting & that no one was in prison

---

480. *Moss Twomey* – Maurice 'Moss' Twomey (1897–1978), revolutionary, he had been sentenced by military tribunal to three years imprisonment for membership of an unlawful organisation.

481. *poor firemen* – Thomas Nugent, Peter McArdle and Robert Malone, Dublin firemen were killed when a series of explosions collapsed two buildings at Exide Batteries on Pearse Street on 5 October 1926. *Mrs Joe Connolly* – wife of Fianna Fáil politician, Joseph Connolly.

482. *Dr English's treat.* – In March 1936 Dr Mills the Resident Medical Superintendent (RMS) of Ballinasloe Hospital died, Dr Ada English had been acting RMS for some months during his illness and had worked in the hospital for 32 years. She was passed over for the RMS post in favour of Dr Bernard Lyons.

for Republicanism. Such appalling lies. M ffM in gt. form, thinks Joe McGrath will help to finance flats D.G. Some v. depressed. I'm not.[483]

Sunday 29

Advent. 1st. 8a.m. Xt.Ch.Much warmer. Could have bathed. Usu. day Marjorie, Ronald & Billie came abt. Ch. time. It was as good to be there again. Good Sermon. M ffM at Ard Feis, it was better. Now Sinn Fein, Mna na P & 2 more sets are united for elections etc. Sinn Fein calling us to order for signing 1916 Roll of Honour. Anyhow I.C.A. had no 'traitors'.[484]

Monday 30

8 a.m R.mines. Lir v. saturated moisture & walls wet, then in evg. quite dry & cold / sleety. Shopped a bit in mg. while I had a moment, re fur for Aunt F. & Xmas things. Dr Price has got license to import Tuberculin fr. Norway & is v. pleased. Also Dr O'Leary says our new T.B. ward is up to any foreign one. The children are better there. Missionary Service Xt. Ch.Bp of [Artic].[485]

December

Tuesday 1

8 a.m R.mines. Gt. excitement over McCarron, for 40 ins, head of the Local Govt. Dept. being fired at moment's notice & for no given reason. Sean T. was worried over all that was said about his scandalous treat. of Dr Ada English at Ballinasloe, they now seem to have some trouble in Grangegorman. Aonach now run by W.[ ]. As opened v. successfully, we saw many old friends there.[486]

Thursday 10

News came over wireless at 4, that King Edward has abdicated & hopes Duke of York will take on the job wh. he "feels too much for him". What

---

483. *murder of Sean Glynn* – the young IRA man found hanging in his cell in Arbour Hill on 13 September. *Joe McGrath* – Joseph McGrath (1888–1966), a director of the Irish Hospitals' Sweepstakes which was vital as a source of funds for St Ultan's Hospital.

484. *Ard Feis* – Sinn Féin Ard Fheis. *Mna na P* – Mná Na Poblachta. *I.C.A* – Irish Citizen Army.

485. *Dr Price has got license to import Tuberculin* – Dr Dorothy Stopford Price had visited Norway earlier in the year and met many of the pioneers of BCG vaccination in the country. On her return to Ireland, she requested permission to import BCG vaccine for testing in Ireland.

486. *excitement over McCarron* – Edward McCarron (1881–1970), civil servant, removed from his post as secretary of the Local Government Department in December 1936.

will happen now? God knows. It looks as if prophecy were coming true that George would be last King of England. Duke of York v. unpopular. Perhaps there will be a revolution. Our atmosphere unchanged.[487]

Tuesday 29

8 a.m R.mines, lovely sun. China getting united now agst. Japan. Heard abt. 2 that Jenny Shanaghan died this mg. We had thought her sl. better. She is the last of us women of Liberty Hall 1916 to go. Madam Markievicz was more C na mB. She is to have Republican funeral. Frank Robbins seeing to it. Our H.S. Dr Rogan at an unnecessary inquest, where she came out well.[488]

Thursday 31

8 a.m. Xt.Ch. nice sun, the T.Bs were out. J. Shanaghan's funeral fr. Mt. Argus was nice & Emer spoke well at grave, it was terrible ordeal for her, she is so sensitive, poor child. L. McGuinness, head of Carmelites came & had last prayers. I saw the old man & came home with Lizzie in car. Evg. we had M ffM's birthday party, Sighle & Douglas, roast pork leeks. Plum pudding. M. Pies.

---

487. *King Edward VIII* (1894–1972), abdicated on 10 December 1936 over his refusal to end his relationship with Wallis Simpson (1896–1986). He was replaced by his brother Albert, Duke of York (1895–1952), who took the regnal name King George VI.
488. *Frank Robbins* (1895-1979), ICA member, revolutionary and trade unionist. *Dr Rogan* – Dr Catherine Margaret Rogan, graduated RCSI 1936.

1937

January

Monday 4

8 a.m. S. B's, such a wet day fr. breakfast till aft. We all had hansels, M ffM gave mine in gold bag, signed paper for registration of Ballinagoreen. It has often changed hands since old Byrne's time. Dr Barry came with proposal to go ahead & build new hospital as Abp. won't have amalgamation. What's she up to now? M ffM will ask Hosp. Commission abt. it.

Wednesday 20

A frosty night, then rainstorm, now S.E. after W. for months. 'Flu rages & I was flying all day & all D.G, went well. M ffM came home tired & joyful at 10.40, the £5,000 promised anon. by lady has been allocated to the new S. Kevin's Soc. to start at once with, M had applied months ago for it. Fr Laborda's meeting brought in over £40, v good. In Teac, more 'Flu, alas![489]

Wednesday 27

Am grand to-day, no ill-effects, it was only reaction, not Flu. D.G. Fr Gannon wrote long letter re Basques, but Laborda shld. be able to answer v. well. Miss Griffin has died at Cognac, Mlle & Rollo will be v. sad D.G. to feel so well. M ffM v. tired & at night Mrs Mcelwaine has died before she got any pension & she had done so much for Ireland.[490]

February

Thursday 4

Usu. sort of day. M ffM is getting house next Teac slightly fixed for Caretaker to prevent its being burnt etc. by bad boys. Hopes to have Durkins there, fine for them. D.V. In Dail they got good carrying re McCarron, debate lasted 5 hrs. & he & family were in gallery. Hear they'll go up for city manager, he would do it well. We have aconites & snowdrops. Lovely sun.

---

489. *Fr. Laborda* – Ramon Laborda, pro-Republican Basque priest, he was hosted in Ireland by May Keating, socialist and feminist and wife of painter Seán Keating.
490. *Mrs Mcelwaine has died before she got any pension* – Cumann na mBan women were included in the Military Services Pensions Act 1934 but the process of applying was long and arduous.

Thursday 18

8 a.m. Xt. Ch. Teac Board went v. well D.G. No opposition now to building scheme. Le cunav De we'll get on quickly now. Busy all day & in evg. had Mrs Henchie & massage. D.V. it won't be long. Poor Norton suspended because he called Anthony a liar & it was true. Said Xtian front fascists & that's true.[491]

Monday 22

Never slept till [ ]. so up late. Poor Norgrove's funeral was to North Strand Ch. & to-morrow to Drumcondra Churchyard. The daughters looked v. pale & sad. Citizen Army abt. in force. Church welcomed them all. Alas it is a very bare barn, no flowers, nothing. V. cold all day & especially now. Rain over for the moment. Mr Scott says splendid act here re Town Planning.[492]

March

Tuesday 2

8 a.m. R.mines, v. heavy frost, had lovely night on balcon. M ffM did well at Hosp. Commissions & Library Comt. I had long round. Reading Connolly's Socialism, Nationalism & Religion, it is wonderful. He is so apt. & can refute the Jesuite with such ease. Dr Hill is fine again. Everyone much interested in her expectations. Hospital does well, no fresh measles.[493]

Thursday 4

8 a.m. Xt. Ch. It was cold in mg. & suddenly snow storm came on wh. didn't lie much for the ground was warm. Teac Special Board considered our Med. Report re new hospital. We are asking for 300 beds, little enough for our needs. They passed it all unanimously. Mary slipped in snow but was little hurt.

---

491. *Norton* – William Norton (1900–63), Leader of the Labour Party 1932 to 1960. *Anthony* – Richard Anthony (1875–1962), politician and trade unionist, TD, well known for his anti-communist views.
492. *Poor Norgrove* – George Norgrove (1876–1937), ICA member and father of Annie and Emily Norgrove who had both fought in City Hall during the Easter Rising 1916 with Lynn.
493. *Connolly's Socialism, Nationalism &* Religion – Lynn may mean Connolly's 1910 book 'Labour, Nationality and Religion', here.

April

Wednesday 14

Up late. M ffM off 9.30 off to City Manager who is v. encouraging re clearance of lane for new flats. Germans are having royal time here, say never so well entertained. v. rushed with seeing pros. & pts. & Med. Board etc. Crowds here aft. & evg. not done till 11 o/c A day one would like to garden!! Might have chance of smaller hosp. scheme.

Thursday 15

Called out 11.45 last night, back in 1/2 hour. Felt I had enough. Teac Board. Arr. for speakers at Ann. Meeting, put forward plan for smaller hosp. if we can't get the 300 cots. Matron poured forth all her household worries & isn't pleased abt. Nurses Thompson & Wills being Sisters, but we must advance. Dr Connolly says my eye is much better & so it is D.G. R. Jacob came, much interest in Cornwall.[494]

Friday 30

A v. busy day. 4 hrs. solid Dispensary & then many here. Moribund prem. Why won't they let us see them in time? This was 17 days old & had had no special care. Finished with accident case, then M ffM & I went to Reunion in Hotel Workers' Hall of all I.C.A. None such since 1916. Mrs Connolly there, anniversary of her wedding. May it be a start of better things.[495]

May

Saturday 1

8 a.m. R.mines. Another most beautiful, mg. dull. D McArdle is starting a fund for the poor Basques, v. good thing. The meeting to hear those come back fr. Spain, our lot, was v. good last night. They were refused several halls but got Court Laundry at last. Planted Kinlough primroses, v. nice ones Teac v. fair. Went with 2 Pension Board Drs to see poor Little, & he received them D.G.[496]

---

494. *Dr Connolly* – Probably Dr Mary Francis Connolly, graduated RCSI 1922, Assistant Surgeon Royal Eye and Ear Hospital, Dublin. *R. Jacob* – Rosamond Jacob.
495. *I.C.A.* – Irish Citizen Army. *Mrs Connolly* – Lillie Connolly, née Reynolds (*c.*1867–1938), married James Connolly, Irish socialist and trade union organiser, on 30 April 1890.
496. *D McArdle is starting a fund for the poor Basques* – In April 1937 the Basque town of Guernica was bombed by the German Luftwaffe in support of General Franco and his Nationalist army. It was destroyed and women, children and families were left destitute and homeless. Dorothy Macardle started fundraising for them.

Monday 10

Slept till 8.45, nice day, colder. Dev.'s lot are raising pensions all round & giving them to all & sundry, scandalous prep. for election. Children's Allowances raised fr. £25 to £100 or £200! & Bill man got £20 p.a.! Nurse. Comt. went v. well because He was there & felt. We will trust further. Susie brought little plants fr. Sat.'s Show, they look well, v. busy day.

Tuesday 18

8 a.m. R.mines. Another nice day D.G. Evg. meeting of Women Graduates to hear deputations' reports. Dev. much pained we shld. not think his Constitution perfect for women when there is discriminations in many sections. What could be expected fr. man made laws, however he said he approved of equal pay for equal work, wonderful, he doesn't apply it. Women will fight.[497]

June

Thursday 17

Slept late & had busy day, we are all working hard for Meeting of Protest against New Constitution & Women. Mrs Kettle had excellent R.C. paper where a priest said God made women to manage their own affairs, would any here dare to say so! Teac Board went well. Saw couple of election meetings, small & unenthusiastic affairs.

Monday 21

8 a.m. S. B's. Poor Bilbao taken at last & Franco congratulated by Hitler & Mussolini, Xtianity's gtst. enemies & the war is called Xtian. We had gt. meeting of Women in Mansion House It was full of Round Room & we had expected Supper Room. Most enthusiastic, speeches fine. We had all sorts of politics & religion. It was a fine spirit. Women are riz & rightly. Nice day.[498]

---

497. *Constitution* – The 1937 Constitution included articles which positioned women in the home. Many of the women's organisations, including the Women's Graduates Association, opposed the constitution because of these.
498. *Poor Bilbao* – The Basque city of Bilbao fell to Franco's Nationalist Army on 19 June 1937, it was the last part of the Basque country to be held by the Republicans. *gt. meeting of Women* – over 1,500 women attended to plan on how to oppose the draft Constitution.

Wednesday 23

Lovely early sun then dull till evg. Muriel sent £100 for house repairs, v. generous. I. Press poisonous to-day re Women's protest, said we were new protagonists for our sex & give it mostly 20 to 30 yrs. Sean T said I was only one with Nat. record. What of Sighle & Mrs Tom Dillon? Does he think that F. Fáil is Republican! sorry mistake. Owen may be T.B.[499]

Friday 25

8 a.m. S. B's. Warmer. Irish Press full of us women, many cheap sneers but they printed the graduates' reply to their jeers & also Mrs O'Callaghan's & Mrs Tom Clarke's letters in full & they put in mine. We have [ ] failed in impression. Big disp. in evg. Saw Mahers. Their place is beautiful, balcony & flowers & whole place so clean, don't look like poor relief at all.[500]

July

Thursday 1

Slept late, the nicest day yet, most like summer. Voted early. We put no for Constitution & Restore the Republic on voting paper. Front of Dublin Opinion lovely. De Valera wheels pram with Constitution for baby & all Ministers follow, whole family off to the country. Owen Skeffington more reconciled to a fear of work on hopes for French or Swiss Sanitorium. Sally K. has chill.[501]

Saturday 3

Slept later for y.day was tiring. Election results, Mulcahy out, 1st time since F.S. in, Belton too, D.G. so Xtian Front has got bad blow. Larkin in & only one Labour defeated so far D.G. Our Townships, R.mines & Pembroke, Cork, Sligo have thrown out Constitution, D.G. 61,000 have voted against it so far. Nice soft rain, so much wanted. Nice to have Albina here, she is so true & good.[502]

---

499. *Sighle & Mrs Tom Dillon* – Sighle Dowling and Geraldine Plunkett-Dillon, both involved in the revolutionary movement. *Owen* – Owen Sheehy Skeffington (1909–70), university lecturer and senator, son of Hanna Sheehy Skeffington.

500. *Mrs O'Callaghan's & Mrs Tom Clarke's* – Kathleen O'Callaghan and Kathleen Clarke, both former anti-treaty TDs, members of Cumann na mBan. Kathleen Clarke was also a former Senator who had always advocated for the rights of women workers in the Senate.

501. *Dublin Opinion* – a satirical magazine, published monthly from 1922 to 1968.

502. *Election results* – 1 July 1937 a general election and the referendum on the constitution was held in parallel. *Mulcahy out, 1st time since F.S. in, Belton too, D.G.* – Richard Mulcahy of Fine Gael lost his seat, as did Patrick Belton of Irish Christian Front (ICF).

Monday 5

Much rain in mg. Nice now & warmer. Desmond FitzGerald & Garoid O'Sullivan & another blue shirt defeated. Twelve Labour members now instead of 8, none defeated yet. Terrible pity 61,000 votes spoiled in Constitution ballot. Dr Hill can't work any more so I am v. busy. Saw Mr Scott, he promises to get move on with cottage.[503]

Tuesday 20

8 a.m. R.mines. Gt. rush to be off with Dr Price to Belfast British Med. Assoc. We drove in 3 hrs. easily & arr. Ulster Hall. Met Miss McDermott & her friend Miss Jordan. They gave me food & I saw Miss McD's sister, invalid, & she trying to support both, sad case, truly. Friends send in help D.G. Reception v. dull affair & feeding bad. Great crowd, fine night. Dr Thompson was nice = President. Saw Louise McIlroy & Jackson Smith.[504]

Wednesday 28

Great day for Belfast, King George & Elizabeth there early in mg. All the border Customs' huts were blown up, right across, in one place the Ulster police were made to fire their own hut & a bridge was blown up at Mt Pleant, 3 miles fr. Dundalk & all the trains held up till after 12 o/c, too late for Show. Big explosion in centre of Belfast, crowds panicked, thought it bomb.[505]

September

Wednesday 8

8 a.m. S. B's. Went to Magdalen but it was shut. V. rushing day. Evg. papers full of "gt. Naval battle in Mediterranean" God knows & can skill. . Med. Board went well. Appointed new Xray Operator R.C. of course. Christy's to go to R.mines school to-morrow D.G. I thought I was best person to go & yes D.G. M ffM safe in Dover train, so glad she was comfortable. Wrote to her & posted it in Westland Row at 8.5, just caught Mail.[506]

---

503. *Gearóid O'Sullivan* (1891–1948), Irish teacher, army officer and politician. *61,000 have voted against it so far* – the end result was acceptance of the Constitution by a majority.
504. 105th annual meeting of the British Medical Association was held in Belfast in 1937, Professor R. J. Johnstone, Professor of Gynaecology at Queen's University, was the President.
505. Assassination attempt on King George VI and Queen Elizabeth while on a visit to Belfast by the Irish Republican Army.
506. '*gt. Naval battle in Mediterranean*' – The Battle of Cape Cherchell, 7 September 1937, a naval battle during the Spanish Civil War between the Nationalist heavy cruiser *Balearic* and the Republican Navy light cruisers *Libertad* and *Méndez Núñez* several miles north of the Algerian city of Cherchell.

Thursday 16

8 a.m. Xt. Ch. much to do. All sorts of rumours of wars. They actually don't know who Mediterr. pirates are!! Teac Board all well, we postponed sealing of Deed of Nurses for it was sprung on us at last moment. Much warmer. Emer sl. better, had job with her last night. 10 poor harvesters fr. Achill Sound burnt to death in England. Saw Mrs Con Murphy, near her end.[507]

Monday 20

8 a.m. S. B's. Had long talk with Emer & not in vain I know. The poor Achill islanders, the accounts are heartrending, strange, the railway was opened in 1891 & that year a hooker was lost & 34 on her, now the railway is closed & the 10 corpses are last things carried on it. Irish Times hysterical over young harvesters & never realizes that when slums are far worse, they die of starvation by the score. Nice day.

Wednesday 22

Slept late & there. Letter fr. Dr Northridge saying he could see Emer to-night at 8, much coming & going to Sighle & John Brennan to see if we could keep her sober till then. Saw her, not too bad. Sighle went later & reported her fairly so I changed it in God's name & took him out at 8 & D.G. he helped her & she liked him & she asked him to pray with her. Muriel came, saw her for a little at N. Smith. God be praised for all.[508]

October

Tuesday 5

8 a.m. R.mines, rather foggy frosty night. Another lovely day. Sighle came. Emer told of woolpack ghost wh. haunts region of Marrowbone Lane, a huge ghostly shadow, v. terrifying. Strike settled D.G. D.G. after 7 mos. misery. The poor things must be much in debt. British boat torpedoed by mysterious submarine. Is it all a Financiers stunt to provoke war? M ffM wired fr. Dover, coming in mg. Hip hip D.G.[509]

---

507. *poor harvesters fr. Achill Sound* – The Kirkintilloch Tragedy when ten migrant workers from Achill Island, working on the potato harvest in Kirkintilloch, near Glasgow, burnt to death in their bothy (accommodation).
508. *Sighle & John Brennan* – Sheila Dowling and Sidney Czira (née Gifford), writer 'John Brennan'.
509. *Strike settled* – a strike for a pay claim by bricklayers (AGIBSL) and plasterers (OPATS1) unions began on 1 April 1937 and lasted until late September. It was the biggest strike ever in the history of the state.

Wednesday 13

Up 6 o/c just getting light, had gt. rush to get all done. Rising sun struck "Lug" & white mist crept over it fr. W. V. wonderful. shutters diff. at 1st but done, rush fr. train, all well. Left M at Ranelagh, she loved it. Pangur so glad to be home, in evg. he came & lay for hrs. on his bed. Mrs Clarke has spoken out at F.F. Ard Feis splendidly. We sent congratulatory flowers. Wonderful light on Sl. Cullenmore.[510]

Friday 15

8 a.m. S. B's, v. big Disp. Utility meeting. All well there. Evg. went to Assoc. Womens' Soc. meeting re Probation Officers, only 2 for all F.S. appalling. Mr Phelan U.S.A. spoke well & Mr Webb, hope they'll do something now. Picked up Sighle & M ffM. Dr Collis drove us home, he gave good criticism of new O.P.D. Mrs Cosgrave at both meetings.[511]

November

Thursday 11

8 a.m. Xt. Ch. Many poppies there of course. We heard big explosion at 8 a.m., it was some of old G. barracks, Dublin Castle, going up. No one hurt D.G. Recruiting Office went up in Belfast, they say ex soldiers did it, they are fed up with talk & poppies. Poor Ed. 8th publicly insulted by Eng. Canon in Paris who said he didn't want him in Church for Armistice.[512]

Sunday 21

Stirup Sun. 8 a.m. Xt. Ch. Lovely sunny day. I started for Town 12 o/c M ffM met me. We picked up Mrs Langan & got to Glasnevin long before procession. I unveiled memorial to Sean Connolly & spoke afterwards, saw so many old friends I hadn't seen for ages esp. of young boys & girls D.G. I told them to learn Ireland & Connolly.[513]

Wednesday 24

8 a.m. Magdalen, special Med. Board to consider changes in milk room. Matron back & giving good advice about it. M ffM & Sighle went

---

510. *Pangur* – Lynn's cat had been missing. *Mrs Clarke* – Kathleen Clarke.
511. *O.P.D.* – Outpatients Department.
512. *Ed. 8th* – Duke of Windsor, the former King Edward VIII.
513. *Sean Connolly* – Commandant, Irish Citizen Army, killed in 1916 at the City Hall Outpost with Lynn by his side.

to Women's' Meeting, it was good but they are making it political & want to put up women candidates instead of educating women voters. It won't work here, I paid off annuity on cottage £161.

December

Monday 13

8 a.m. S. B's to thank for safety in weekend & for lovely time in Glen. Allie Day, now Burke, came, she is not so v. different but needs attention & psychology. Had 3 to-day to comfort alone, D.V. they were helped. Evg. Paediatric meeting, v. interesting, Vaccine in Pneum. by Mobray of Temple St. Sighle here on ret., v. well. She thinks Women's Party won't do. Nation must be first.

Wednesday 29

Went to Magdalen but no Priest came, Mr Waring not well. However, had quiet time there. The day new Constitution comes into force, not a sign of rejoicing for it is all unreal & mockery & well Ireland knows it. Saw Aunt F. who is v. well. Seems as if France was getting the worst of it now in Spain. There are new trees planted all along canal at Portobello. M ffM overpersuaded to stay.

Thursday 30

8 a.m Ch. Joy of Joys, M ffM was back abt. 11 o/c & a great cloud rolled away. Got some letters with the foolish Constitution postmark wh. was only to be used y.day wh. will be much valued by stamp collectors. V. busy but got all done & we had v. nice Birthday Party. Mr O'Donnell, Sighle & ourselves & Douglas came in when we were 1/2 thro. We had nice evg. Fine day.

1938

January

Wednesday 12

Not out early. Nice day, lovely at Ballybrack, such a change to be clear. 1st meeting Nurses' Pension fund, decided on Corporate 5% Stock. Med. Board went well. Dr Micks appointed consultant unanimously. Dr Barry's opposition gone D.G. D.G. Read some of Lansbury's Peace address in Vienna, it is excellent & he goes straight for it & says belief in God & Xt. only thing to save the world.[514]

Thursday 20

Up late after late evg. Gen. opinion is that England knows War is near & wants contented Ireland & will pay good prices for it, even will let down North to end Partition. Teac Board went well. Matron v. creaght over nothing. Emer D.G. is better & more able to face things. Letter fr. D Reynolds, she says Fr FitzG. has had deep Xray wh. made femur brittle & it broke.

Monday 24

Mrs Connolly is to have gt. funeral to-morrow. Emer arranged for broadcast this evg. asking everyone in home, shop, office, field etc. to stop at 12 to-morrow & pray for her & her husband 3 mins while she is being laid to rest. We 1916 Women Prisoners are sending a cross. Mass 10 a.m. in mg. Stormy evg. tho' it was lovely day. Saw about things for Glen. D.V. we'll let cottage.[515]

February

Saturday 12

No call in night to Mrs C. O'Brien but as I was going, urgent message came. She was nearly gone & died in few minutes. Poor Mrs Kettle & Betty cried out so in grief, quite uncontrollable. D.G. the brother Judge Sheehy was there. I did my best. It wasn't much to comfort them. Then work, work till I got off by 8.30 to Aunt F. The Whist Drive

---

514. *Lansbury's Peace address* – George Lansbury (1859–1940), British Labour party leader, 1932–5, peace campaigner, social justice, and women's rights activist.
515. *Mrs Connolly* – Lillie Connolly (1868–1938), wife of James Connolly.

etc. made up £27 odd. A nice little sum to help the poor Schofields. It was a nice day.[516]

Thursday 24

8 a.m. Xt. Ch. Forgot S. Matthias till I heard Collect. Walked with F. Clarke afterwards. Saw something about new Welfare Centre of [ ] & with Elsons. Labour wants Gen. Election at once in England. Here it is boycotting Senate, rightly. Mrs. Hyland dead, we went to the Church with her, so many now going. We are always at funerals. Went to Stillorgan after 9.30.[517]

March

Wednesday 9

8 a.m. Magdalen, lovely to be there again. Windy but nice. Had gt. blow at Sandyford, country lovely with almond, copper, plum & Forsythia. 4 tons copper machinery missing fr. dockyard at Portsmouth. Many such things happen now. At Med. Board we decided to try & start Branch of Internat. Med. Womens' Assoc & also to have 2 new Wards for Isolation, if possible. Glass only 30 now.[518]

Monday 14

Mr Ferran has had detachment op. poor man, he must be in rundown state. Hitler going to Vienna with heavy Police Guard. Strange how one man, by all a/cs, not v. sane, can terrorise. Dev. would let no one snap him on ret. fr. London y.day mg. Even threatened to seize Pressmens' cameras.

Friday 18

Up late after late night. Hear Lemass & Aiken are quarreling with the rest & travelled home alone last time. Lemass wants his tariffs upheld. They are a poor lot & have spread misery everywhere. Child in Teac

---

516. *Mrs C. O'Brien* – Kathleen Cruise O'Brien, née Sheehy (1886-1938), sister of Hanna Sheehy Skeffington and Mary Kettle, mother of Conor Cruise O'Brien. *the brother Judge Sheehy* – Eugene Sheehy (1883–1958), brother of Hanna, Kathleen, and Mary, was a barrister and district court Judge.
517. *Mrs Hyland* – widow of Andrew Hyland, formerly of the 4th and 5th Battalion IRA, her daughters were in Cumann na mBan and she was elected President of the Dublin townships and Comhairle Dáil-Cheanntair of Fianna Fáil in 1937.
518. *Internat. Med. Womens' Assoc* – Medical Women's International Association was founded in 1919 with the purpose of representing female physicians worldwide. Dr Esther Lovejoy was its first president.

with G.C. Conj better D.G. Had v rushing day. Saw Mrs Cosgrave to-night, she is not v. well yet. Will go to Courtown Harbour for change.[519]

Wednesday 30

8 a.m. Magdalen. New Senate elected & we can't make out how the voting went or who voted. Anyhow, Fianna Fail has only got one more than other side & now they have 11 nominations & they will be all set for a docile, puppet Senate. Nice drive by Goatstown by D.drum to Stillorgan. M ffM & Mrs Cosgrave saw City Manager who is sympathetic to flats, so they hope to go ahead.

April

Friday 1

8 a.m. S. B's. So nice to have Mr Waring., many there. Lovely day Dub. Opinion lovely Dev. & Nev. = Neville Chamberlain. Commandant Kennedy nominated by Dev. for Senate, must be Louie, Command. of C na mB & out in 1916. Someone says it is reward for making C na mB vote for Dev. in Constitution. Hope not. Hear Ron's child a beauty. At '98 Celeb. meeting 8. They hope to have fresh Convention? Good. Nancy Heron cycle accident, went to her 12.30 a.m.[520]

Tuesday 5

8 a.m. R.mines. M sold old woman's gold watch for her for £2.7.6. bottle of gold fr. mine for £2.15, it was fair price, we think. Dr Lynch came & was glad to have chat, v. worried over Dev.'s arrogance & indifference to sufferings of poor. Surely we never thought our supposed own govt. would be so heartless. Saw wardrobes & little chests for Glen. V. nice evg. off to Balawley again, a Heron has 'Flu.

Wednesday 6

8 a.m. Magdalen. Emer better & went to work to face really unjust wrath of Miss Chevinix who wants to bring her before Comt., found whole staff riz at the idea & was gratified to find how they loved her, so the fear was turned to joy, thro' God D.G. I had a lovely round

---

519. *Lemass & Aiken* – Fianna Fáil TDs, Seán Lemass, Minister for Industry and Commerce and Frank Aiken, Minister for Defence.
520. *Neville Chamberlain* (1869–1940), British Prime Minister 1937–40. *Commandant Kennedy* – Margaret Loo Kennedy (1892–1953), Commandant Inghinidhe na hÉireann Branch, Cumann na mBan, Senator 1938–48.

Ticknock, Dundrum, Bride's Glen to B.brack. Fresh indictments of Dev.'s Govt. daily, the poor more & more oppressed. Lord, how long!

May

Tuesday 24

8 a.m. R.mines, nice day. We got clothes for M in mg. nice frock & hat. Child Welf. has at last taken in that dispensaries are being used as Welf. Centres, wh. is of course appalling. V. good a/c in paper of Dr Walters paper on Social conditions, he says be free 1st, then feed yourselves & so eliminate need for social service. Nice rain now D.G. Gt. Fairy Sweepstake Procession.

Monday 30

Joan of Arc's Day. 8 a.m. S. B's, v. quick Service, over in 20 mins. Nice day. All wonder why elections sprung so unwantedly. Peace work universal, we must make it felt at elections. Many people to do for. Poor Emer bad enough. M ffM's interview with Corporation re Flats went well D.G. & they may be allowed to build in 4 months, awful waste of time.

June

Tuesday 7

8 a.m. R.mines. Emer went out early about 7 & took Pledge for 3 mos. with God's help she'll keep it faithfully. I took her round with me & she was delighted with Beaumont, the sisters are most kind there & it is lovely. Road beyond Whitehall changed beyond recognition. The Thatch gone & a "Rond Point" there with shrubs & a wide, concrete road & heaps of new houses. Emer did well her 1st day.[521]

Wednesday 22

Late again. No word fr. travellers. mg. aft or evg. I wired at 7 & D.G. by 11 had reply, all well, they wrote 3 cards. How bad the posts are! Japs. reply to British that they are only acting as Brits did in Palestine to Arabs, wh. is true enough. Heard woman announcer on wireless much better & more distinct than the men with their 'beautiful' Winchester

---

521. *took Pledge for 3 mos* – The Pioneer Pledge of total abstinence through the Pioneer Total Abstinence Association of the Sacred Heart. Founded in Dublin in 1898. The Pledge can be taken for differing periods of time or could be lifelong.

accents! Called to Emer, she is here now & bad enough. Day ends well D.G.

July

Thursday 21

Up at 6 b.fast. All ready 7.20. M ffM, Sr. Helen, Frank & I all started for Town by 5.45, good journey even with ill pulling car. Found Teac well, but much for M ffM to clear up, she got nearly no food & started back abt. 6.30. It was Nurse Cadden's home where garden was all up, she is now in jail & her accomplice for doing away with poor illeg. babies, has long been watched, drives a wanky red racing car & has bluffed so far. Aunt F. all well & v. glad to see me.[522]

August

Thursday 18

Didn't get up in time, alas! Nice day tho' dark. Teac Board went all right, but only 4 at it. Now we have house full of bad babies, some gast. ent. V. severe & pneum. Long interview with Maher in mg. & evg. Maureen was to come here, but I went & found her, Mother being, I thought, too hard. We tried to show her that she must bear her punishment & really repent D.V.

Sunday 28

8 a.m. Xt. Ch. I had a v. usual day. M ffm was at Glen. Imeal at the 1798 Celebrations, she & Florrie Salkeld, crowds went fr. Dublin train fr. Antrim, bringing a stone fr. Sam McAlister's home to place on the monument to be erected to him at Dernamuck, the cottage where McAlister rushed out & so saved Michael Dwyer is to be rebuilt & used as museum of 98. It was a great day & fine spirit.[523]

---

522. *Nurse Cadden's* – Mary Anne 'Mamie' Cadden (1891–1959), was a midwife and backstreet abortionist in Dublin. She was convicted of child abandonment in 1939, she continued to provide abortions, one lead to the death of Helen O'Reilly in 1956. She was sentenced to death, but this was commuted to life imprisonment.

523. *Florrie Salkeld* – Blanaid Salkeld, born Florence ffrench-Mullen (1880–1958), poet and actor, cousin of Madeleine. *museum of 98* – Michael Dwyer is one of the most famous United Irishman leaders of the 1798 Rebellion. His cottage was located in Wicklow. In 1799 it was from this cottage that he fought the encircling British troops and escaped. Sam McAlister died on 15 February 1799 at the siege of Derrynamuck, Co. Wicklow, so Michael Dwyer (1772–1825), could escape.

September

Wednesday 7

8 a.m Magdalen. M. much better D.G. ht. steady. However, we kept her in bed. Med. Board went well & Montessori is D.G. to begin in Teac. Mrs Skeffington's pear tree is in blossom. I got some things for Glen. Teac nicely. We are getting new Swedish sedimentation apparatus. Mrs Cosgrave v. well, was asking abt. Nursery Schools, that Comt. has gone asleep!

Saturday 24

8 a.m S. B's. Nice sun. I Times says Peace & war are on knife edge. Hitler won't talk to Chamberlaine anymore. An 1842 map shows Prussia & Germany just about what Hitler wants now & has [Berechts] garden marked on it. Strange. Aunt F. v. well, but face all colours. Went to see Baby Jarret, Jack & Geoff drove me to Bray, they all adore their small niece.[524]

Thursday 29

8 a.m. R.mines. How we rejoice in the news of the 4 power conference at Munich. Evg. papers full of the German enthusiasm for Chamberlain etc. Anyhow we feel God is answering all our prayers for Peace. I saw Mrs Derrig & asked her to distribute Neutrality papers & she did. Wireless gives a/c of all precautions for evacuating of London, they seem good D.V. won't be necessary.[525]

Friday 30

8 a.m. S. B's. we are all so rejoiced that there is to be a commission tho' it seems terribly hard on the Czechs. I feel if all people were so willing to suffer for the general good, then the world wld. be v. different. Sighle says this is all wrong & that Germany wouldn't have fought, couldn't & that it is a triumph for fascism all along the line. Maybe so.

October

Tuesday 4

8 a.m. R.mines. Gt. storm last night, but we didn't see much harm done, boys & young men were cutting up the old elms on canal betw.

---

524. *Geoff* – George Geoffrey Wynne, Bank Official, and relation to Lynn on her mother's side.
525. *power conference at Munich* – Germany, UK, France, and Italy concluded the Munich Agreement on 30 September 1938, allowing for the German annexation of the Sudetenland.

Charlemont St. & Leeson St. Perh. the canal people let them, poor old women & children carried off all they could. M ffM hadn't even yet got leave fr. Corporation to start flats. It's monstrous. It was in Palestine poor Jews were killed.

Friday 21

8 a.m. S. B's. gt rush afterwards, for M ffM wanted to be off at 9.30, it was 10 & the Sweep Draw looked fine, it's Silver Jubilee, V. gorgeous. Lord Powerscourt said Chamberlain had done nobler deed than ever in the world before & an unprecedented one. We can hardly endorse all that. Emer none too well, but says she is taking pledge to-day. Hear the Pope has done some fine things.[526]

November

Friday 11

8 a.m. S. B's. v. mild all day. Jews pogrome continues in Germany & Nazis describe it as 'gentle' say they will settle the Jewish question once & for all, poor, poor Jews. Rained a lot Edythe came & her sister & were v. pleased with Teac & surprised at it's size & growth. Could not get to Fr O'Flanagan's meeting, pts. prevented all the time. Got bulbs at last & planted some.[527]

Wednesday 16

8 a.m. Magdalen. Mrs S.S. came in early & we discussed Jews. We must have a meeting of, at least sympathy. I went to Mansion Ho. after & saw Lord Mayor, but didn't tell him, now I'm sorry. Had unexpected lunch with Emer, came in on her & Iseult & Child. Iseult v. anti semitic. Hear there have been 3-4 more sacrilegious doings. Statue broken at Mt. Argus, row in a Church at 40 hrs Adoration. I'm sure it's agents provocateurs. Reddin gets worse & worse.

December

Friday 16

Another sleepy mg.after late night. Nice day D.G. Busy with pts. Poor Emer on a bend, alas! I found her dead asleep both times. Sighle

---

526. *Lord Powerscourt* – Mervyn Richard Wingfield, 8th Viscount Powerscourt (1880–1947), Irish Peer. *The Pope* – Pius XI, born Ambrogio Ratti (1857–1939), Lynn is presumably referring to his stance against racism and antisemitic laws.
527. *Jews pogrome* – Kristallnacht (Night of Broken Glass) a pogrom against Jews carried out by the Nazi Party across Germany on 9–10 November 1938.

came with me late, she promised to come here to-morrow D.V she will Teac v. fairly D.G. Mrs Wyse Power v. sad over Dr Gogarty's going to London, he alone can Politzer her properly. Heard of Poppy's sister, she is worse than I thought.[528]

Wednesday 21

8 a.m. R.mines, the shortest day was v. cold, fair amt. of snow lay. Many poor men out cleaning it a way. A Godsend for them, poor things. Had v. busy day & got a lot done. Sat Matron, after days. She seems well. Emer v. well. D.G. They say Fianna Fail riding hard for a fall. They do nothing until they are shamed into it. Joe McGrath's right hand man dead.

---

528. *Dr Gogarty's going to London* – Oliver St John Gogarty (1878–1957), surgeon and man of letters, friend of James Joyce, relocated to London in 1938.

1939

January

Monday 9

Aunt & I had good night, only up twice. She is fairly this mg. Went off by 11 & busy day. Did as many pts. as possible. Papers full of Chamberlain's visit to Rome & I. Times tries to bluff Italy afraid of England, says Eng. France & U.S. took [ ] for Fascist nations. Teac v. fairly D.G. Mary glad to see me I glad to be at home. Pediatric Club Cork St. v. good on Mening. & giving serum not into [Cereb].[529]

Wednesday 18

There have been 9 explosions in England, most connected with electric lighting. They blame I.R.A. & say that these forever stop ending of Partition, how often have we heard same story & now we know only such things make any impression on the tyrants. Fr. O'Flanagan speaking to-night on his visit to Spain, sorry we couldn't go. So delightful to be home for dinner.

Saturday 28

A v. nice Birthday, got off fr. Aunt F. & was here by 11. Sighle & M ffM & I went down town, shopped & had mg. coffee & cakes for a spree & drank health in coffee. Got nice things, cards, biscuits, sweets, silk stockings. Nice sun. Ripped top of my old skirt as birthday treat & now it's ready for M ffM. Reddin more hopeless than usual. Teac well. Letter fr. Tony Becker, all well with them in Berlin, D.G.

February

Thursday 2

Purific. 8 a.m. R.mines. V. hard black frost, then nice sun. Cold & frosty now. Hear Germany v. irate because Roosevelt says he'll help France in case of war. Hitler's speech speaks of long peace while they arm feverishly. The McCabe Pantomime party was a great success. Jimmy O'Dea surpassed himself & the marionettes were wonderful. Nothing Springlike about to-day.

---

529. *Cork St.* – Cork Street Fever Hospital, Dublin.

Thursday 16

8 a.m. Xt. Ch. Much colder all day. Defence of Ring case goes on not very convincing to us anyhow. Teac Board went well & we have instructed Reddin to make McDonald estate carry out its contract. This precious Govt. goes fr. bad to worse, now votes millions for defence & for enlarging the army. They are so terribly crooked & have in action denied all they stood for before they were in power.[530]

Monday 20

8 a.m. S. B's. A lovely day & v. busy. Poor Don MacDonagh's wife died v. suddenly, drowned in her bath in a fit, she has had them so long. I was worried when I found she had married, so she's gone like Don's mother, & his father was executed in 1916. M ffM & I celebrated carnival by seeing "Sixty Glorious Years" = Vic's reign, first all colour photography film, very beautiful & on whole prob. true to life.[531]

March

Thursday 2

8 a.m. Xt. Ch. V. set, stormy night, but fair day till evg. Storm some hours. Aunt F. gave book, Jew or Arab in Palestine, v. interesting, showing fulfilment of prophesy. Albina came & is well D.G. & v. pleased to be here. M ffM in bed all day, reaction fr. Antigen. Two young Teac maids knocked down by motor, but not seriously injured D.G. I. Med. Assoc. warns us re Treason bill & treating Republicans.[532]

Monday 20

8 a.m. S. B's. M ffM & Emer off early to Sweep. I got finished up & met M & Mrs Bennett at 1 for lunch at Gresham. Saw good many & talked. Labour meeting in Foster Pl. denouncing Banks & Govt. for not providing money for building. It is terrible to have 150,000 workless

---

530. *Defence of Ring case* – an action arising out of the anti-diphtheria inoculation of children at the Irish College in Ring, Co. Waterford, in 1936; afterwards 24 children showed signs of serious infection, which later proved to be tubercular in character and one of the children (a girl) died. An action was against Dr Daniel McCarthy, Dungarvan and the Wellcome Foundation in the death of the girl and the illness of her three brothers.
531. *Don MacDonagh's wife* – Maura MacDonagh, née Smyth, died 18 February 1939. Donagh MacDonagh was the son of Thomas MacDonagh one of the executed signatories of 1916 and Muriel MacDonagh, née Gifford, who drowned in 1917.
532. *I. Med. Assoc.* – Irish Medical Association. *Treason bill* – In 1939 the Oireachtas enacted a new Treason Act (which defined treason as an act of treachery against this State). Doctors worried that treating republicans who were committed to the overthrow of the State would get them in legal trouble.

in one small community. Hitler seems to have paused. At 3 we went to Art Academy Show. Many pictures inc. mine by L. Williams.[533]

Thursday 23

8 a.m. Xt. Ch., frost last night Hitler gone to Mernel & gt. talk of war. 3-4 more explosions in England, one poor car was blown sky high, but no loss of life mentioned. It was at Edgebaston, perh. on its way to arrange more electric blow ups. M ffM & I visited back lane behind Charlemont Mall = Kinehan estate where O.P.D & Nurses quarters are to be. It will be gt. improvement.

April

Wednesday 26

So late last night, wasn't up early. Conscription passed for England. We'll have fly boys over now, I suppose. Bright sun & v. cold wind. Teac nicely. Dr O'Reilly has asked to be kept on another 6 mos. & she is so improved we'll keep her. Evg. we had v. nice I.C.A. reunion, saw many there & lots of young ones. I spoke of single mindedness. D.V. to some effect. Christy Crothers child played pipes.[534]

May

Thursday 4

It was a busy day. Sighle came in with news Moira Deegan dead. In paper we saw how Comdt. Kennedy voted for capital punishment in new Treason Bill. How could she when she has been thro' so much herself for Ireland? In evg. when M Deegan being taken to Clarendon St. she was in command of old C na mB's. How could she![535]

Saturday 6

A nice Spring day. Hear Britain has made Alliance with Turkey & Pope pleads much for Peace. Dr Solomons wants us to take poor refugee Jewish girls to train as Nurses in Teac. I think we should. Went to Show with Susie & Sylvie & had v. nice time, things were beautiful & it

---

533. *L. Williams* – Lily Williams.
534. *Conscription passed for England* – the Military Training Act 1939. *Dr O'Reilly* – Dr Harriet Teresa Maud O'Reilly, graduated NUI 1939.
535. *Moira Deegan* – Maire Deegan (1891–1939), from Wexford, was a member of the central branch of Cumann na mBan, carried despatches in 1916.

was fine. They say war fears kept people from buying, how foolish they are. Sorry didn't see Workman.[536]

Monday 22

8 a.m. S. B's, glorious Summer day. Met Prof Wallgren in Teac, he is fine, we gave him a S. Ultan's book & he liked it. Later I went to Dr Price's to meet him & then heard him at Coll. of Physicians, it was a wonderful lecture on T.B. in Sweden, room packed, gt. enthusiasm, many spoke after & all to point. He was v. pleased. It was a long nice day.[537]

June

Monday 19

8 a.m. S. B's. Nice day, sunny, cold wind. V. lonely in empty house, b.fast in waiting room & dinner, cats don't know why. Outbreak of Typhoid not really bad at all in Kerry, letter in paper says to-day. King & Queen of England let go in launch in v. rough weather & got all wet, strange such risks. Gt. fuss over Jap. blockade, another warmongering scare. D.V. D.V. M ffM is safe in bed in Spa & resting.

Wednesday 28

Emer never came, hear she isn't well. Mr Stack must see to her D.V. Mrs Tom Clarke is Lord Mayor but Alfie's casting vote. I wish she were more suitable when she is first woman to be Lord Mayor. D.V. she will be given grace for her high office. Packed & arranged all mg. V. heavy showers. Saw Margt. & Mrs Doyle, both v. well D.G. Had easy evg. but many in aft. M ffM sent cards to Teac. Hope to see Poppy to-morrow.[538]

August

Friday 11

Late as usual, alas! my 1st night on balcon. since June! rather cold. Disp. fairly big & nice. Meeting of Utility, no quorum, but did routine business. No rain D.G. but one wee shower. Madam McBride had

---

536. *Dr Solomons* – Bethel Solomons (1885–1965), doctor, international rugby player, member of the Jewish Refugee Aid Committee of Éire.
537. *Prof Wallgren* – Professor Arvid Wallgren (1889–1973), Swedish paediatrician, Professor of Paediatrics at Karolinska University, famous for his work on tuberculosis, especially BCG vaccination.
538. *Mrs Tom Clarke* – In 1939, Kathleen Clarke was elected Lord Mayor of Dublin, the first woman to hold the office.

ceremony of presenting Irish flag fr. S. African Brigade to Museum. Emer enjoyed it. Sighle came late, old Mr Dowling dying of Pneumonia fr. sheer neglect & S & Frank cld get nothing done.

Friday 18

Another lovely day, Disp. & all went well. Hear Sighle doesn't like next door because stairs look shabby, she is hard to please. Roosevelt has new peace plan. Evg. we had Pearl & Emer for dinner & then Rosie Hackett & Mrs Kelly to meet Mr Fox who is writing hist. of citizen Army & wanted women's part of it. It was a gt. recalling of old times & people.[539]

September

Saturday 2

Off to Moira Schoffield's wedding at Dundrum Chapel at 9 o/c. It was so pretty & she made a lovely, slender bride in soft white satin. The young men friends gave the cake, lots of presents & nice party. Paddy seems such a nice boy & so fond of her, he gave her away. Wars & rumours of wars all day but latest is that Hitler is asking Poles to make peace. Aunt F. in good form D.G.

Thursday 7

8 a.m. Xt. Ch. Mr Hamilton there, v. heavy rain nearly all day. Had Board Meeting & decided on sandbags & cellophaning windows. People are v. skeptical war, think British & French have done nothing yet & that Hitler's announcement that there will be conference in 3 wks & then he has taken Poland is not true. M ffM much better & Olga will be off on Sat. D.V. only British blackout now.

Monday 18

8 a.m. S. B's. Early to pts. dark day. Russia invades Poland, poor Poles, hard pushed on every side. All kinds of rumours here, of mutinies in Portobello & Mallow, of losses of large amts of arms fr. Curragh & here & last of all that Fitz[ ] & Aiken are arrested, they seem fantastic. Went to Brugha's in evg., they were same as ever but children grown up & Rory, poor boy on the run.[540]

---

539. *Rosie Hackett* (1893–1976), Irish revolutionary and trade union leader. *Mr Fox* – Richard Michael 'R. M.' Fox (1891–1969), writer and trade unionist. He published *The History of the Irish Citizen Army* in 1943.
540. *Rory* – Ruairí Brugha (1917–2006), son of Cathal and Caitlín Brugha, republican, politician, member of Clann na Poblachta and then Fianna Fáil.

October

Wednesday 4

8 a.m. Magdalen, v. windy fr. East all day & in evg. & now pouring rain, it is v. long since we had any. They are talking over peace moves & nothing much happens. Dev. received the new British representative here, Maffey, queer name is it. Mahaffy? The change like that at times. M ffM was v. well & now is tired & pins & needles in foot & arm, not serious D.V.[541]

Monday 16

8 a.m. S. B's, much colder & much rain now & now much lightening & some thunder. British have lost 2 more important boats, Royal Oak & Repulse. They say coast of Scotland air raided U boat let load of timber thro' for Ireland. We fear Emer not v. well. Latest Oman has come into Teac, poor Prem. frozen by being baptized, shld. not have been kept out so long. V. busy all day & late.[542]

Tuesday 17

8 a.m. R.mines. such rain in night & cold mg. Later glorious sun. Kathy Barry, now Molony came early to say Con Lehane had been 4 days on hunger & thirst strike, couldn't live more than a day or so. So Dev has forgotten Thomas Ashe, how could he! We all worked our best & have got Alfie & the present Lord Mayor & Norton & Bill O'Brien & D.V. they will show the thing is known D.V. D.V. he will be spared.[543]

Friday 27

8 a.m. S. B's, cold mg. & nice sun then. Sighle went to Red X inauguration meeting, packed out. Dev. didn't turn up, afraid we suppose. Poor Con Lehane tricked off hunger strike. Jerry Boland promised his immediate release if he went off & Dev. wouldn't have it, raged & stormed when the Priest & Harry went to him about it. How terribly he has sunk. They are to have mass meeting for the Prisoners soon, I hear.[544]

---

541. *Maffey* – John Loader Maffey, 1st Baron Rugby (1877–1969), Career civil servant, appointed the British representative to Ireland on 3 October 1939.
542. *Royal Oak and Repulse* – British battleships. A German U-boat sank the British battleship Royal Oak in the middle of Scapa Flow, the Repulse was not sunk.
543. *Kathy Barry now Molony* – Kathleen 'Kathy' Barry Moloney (1896–1969), anti-treaty republican, member of Cumann na mBan, sister of Kevin Barry who was hanged in 1920 for IRA activities. *Con Lehane* (1912–83), republican, socialist, in the 1930s he was a member of the IRA Army Council.
544. *Red X inauguration meeting* – Irish branch of the Red Cross founded in 1939. *Jerry Boland* – Gerald Boland (1885–1973), Minister for Justice 1939–48.

November

Thursday 23

8 a.m. Xt Ch. so diff. fr. last Thurs. Rather raw & cold, took Bran out in mg.& he had gt. time. Minister of Defence sent 2 v. doubtful looking creatures to inspect us, asked how many of our pts. could run to shelter, said Nurses shld. wear masks in shelter, but not babys Why? Gift sale seems to have done well D.G. Emer wonderful. Had letter fr. Australia & snap of Peter John. I am glad he is John. Sent money off to India.[545]

December

Saturday 2

A v. nice sunny day, gt. news After Sean McBride's masterly treatment of Burke's case proving illegal detention Burke was released & now all the prisoners are out & Con Lehane is taking action agst. Gov. of Mtjoy for wrongful detention. It is well to show them there is a limit to their aggression. Poor Dr Donnelly hardly knew me, for N gone. Addio v. ill indeed.[546]

Monday 4

A v. cold, sleety, haily rainy day. My leg much better D.G. I rested all day & read Madam Gonne's autobiography, she shows herself v. well, doesn't seem to mind saying she lied etc. Poor thing, her standards are not high tho' she's a wonderful woman. The poor English deportees have bad time, many were well off there & lost all, now have only what we can spare them.

Thursday 14

Teac Special Board to offer Re. Huband £3,000 for his interest in new hosp. site. (Board approved D.G.) & also passed Nurses' cheques a week earlier for Xmas. Many pts. Rev. Mother in Beaumont v. old & not hurrying she decides to keep my pt. with a Nurse for present. We pity those 2 men condemned to death for explosion in wh. perhaps had no part. It was a terrible thing for defenceless people.[547]

---

545. *Bran* – Lynn's dog from 1939 to 1948.
546. *Burke's case* –The Offences Against the State Act enabled the Government to intern without trial members of the IRA. Seán MacBride was one of the internees in the case of *Burke v. Lennon* which led to the striking down part of the legislation as repugnant to the new constitution.
547. *Two men condemned to death* – Peter Barnes and James McCormack condemned for the 1939 Coventry bombing; Barnes protested his innocence.

Wednesday 27

We left by 8.15 train, nice mg. Saw M & Jane off at Amiens' St. It was good they came. Was in No. 9 by 9.30. M ffM at b.fast. We settled & tidied up a bit & heard news. Went long round, pts. not so bad. Much joy over raid on arsenal wh. was v. cleverly carried out There were 4 hrs there & cleared the whole place, they say, over million rounds ammunition. We hope it will be destroyed. Poor M fM v. tired. Frosty & nice.[548]

---

548. *raid on arsenal* –The Christmas Raid on the Magazine Fort in the Phoenix Park, 23 December 1939, by the IRA, some of whom were prisoners just released from internment. They stole a lot of weapons and ammunition from the Irish Army.

1940

January

Tuesday 9

8 a.m. R.mines. Child Welf. discussed new arrangements for our payment with Dr. Reddin, he is as destroyed with it as we are & he has Harcourt St, Temple St. & Sunshine Home as well to check. It is terribly exacting & quite useless. On Sun. I saw some big black backed Gulls about Merrion, never saw them here before. Sir Ed. Coey Biggar gave M ffM useful advice re finance.[549]

Thursday 18

Frost came, nice sun. Teac Board, we are hard set to raise £3,000 for Huband Estate. D.V. we'll do it. Meantime we have instructed Mr Scott to proceed with measurements. Dr Micks says nowhere else do babies get nursed as in Teac, the "mother love" is there & D.G. it's true & will be always. Hear of eggs frozen through & man's false teeth in tumbler in bedroom, he couldn't get them out till wife came.

February

Wednesday 7

Ash Wed. 8 a.m. R.mines, Alas!, after all the protests, they hanged poor Barnes & McCormick this mg. & last night Emer brought news of every party in British Parliament joining for their reprieve & Abps. of Canterbury & York & all kinds of Labour people. No news came till midday & fr. silence we hoped now nothing may happen, all Cinema & theatres here are closed & Mansion House has blinds down & whole city mourns. All are united in sorrow.[550]

Friday 23

Lovely sun, later showers. Babies out on roof a bit. M ffM recovered D.G. Big disp. & many pts. Evening went to reading of Citizen Army history

---

549. *Dr Reddin* – Dr Thomas Kerry Reddin, ran Dublin's Child Welfare Centre, son of Teresa Reddin one of the founders of St Ultan's Hospital. *Sir Ed Coey Biggar* – Edward Coey Bigger (1861–1942), medical doctor and politician, Irish General Nursing Council President, and Irish Free State Senator.
550. *poor Barnes & McCormick* – IRA men Peter Barnes (1907–40), and James McCormick (1910–40), were hanged in Winson Green Prison, Birmingham, 7 February 1940. They had been convicted of participating in the 1939 Coventry bombing, which was part of the IRA's sabotage campaign in England.

by Fox. He has finished the History, it is good but a bit disconnected. U.S. Peace Emissary goes first to Italy, then Berlin, evidently England is of 3rd or 4th rate importance. They have practically signed contract for Charlemont Utility Flats. Emer not well.[551]

March

Wednesday 13

8 a m Magdalen, v. cold again & trying to sleet. Saw new moon, not thro' glass. Sighle came in at 10, had just heard over wireless that Sir Michael O'Dwyer shot dead in Indian meeting in London to-night, a Cabinet Minister & another former governor of India shot too. The downfall of British Empire comes on fast. D.G. Finland has made Peace with Russia. Fair terms.[552]

April

Monday 1

A nice blowy, sunny day. Hear there are 6 on hunger strike for 37 days in S. Bricin's & Mtjoy, including Jack Plunkett. It is such a mistake now for no one cares whether they die or not, alas! the H. Strike is played out. We all realize how helpless we are with muzzled censored Press etc. V. good Paediatric meeting in Teac on tonsils & good discussion.[553]

Tuesday 9

8 a.m. R.mines. Mr Perdue's voice v small, has had laryngitis. Went to the fateful Child. Welf. meeting & found the whole thing quite incomprehensible. They have done something v. queer, for they say order was made on Feb. 27th when I certainly never heard of it till Mar.12th. We must try to clear muddle. Dinner McElwaine's, v. nice & friendly, hear Hitler has invaded Denmark, Norway & Sweden but Britain made them not neutral.

---

551. *Charlemont Utility Flats* – The Charlemont Utility Society was formed in 1936 to improve housing conditions in the area between Charlemont Street and Richmond Street.
552. *Sir Michael O'Dwyer* (1864–1940), Irish born colonial officer was assassinated by Indian revolutionary Udham Singh (1899–1940), in revenge for the Jallianwala Bagh massacre in Amritsar on 13 April 1919.
553. *S. Bricin's & Mtjoy* – St Bricin's Military Hospital, and Mountjoy Jail. *Jack Plunkett* (1897–1960), younger brother of Joseph Plunkett.

Tuesday 16

8 a.m. R.mines, frost last night & some hail to-day. News that poor D'Arcy the H. Striker has died, he had done nothing but attend that meeting in Jan. The swoop was made & couldn't give his name & had nearly finished his 3 mos. He leaves a wife & 3 small boys. It is terrible that any govt. would let a man die for such a small offence. There is much sympathy everywhere with the poor men.[554]

Wednesday 17

8 a.m. Magdalen, so glad to be there. Lovely mg. sun, not so much later. We got old boiler out in laundry. New one (2nd hand) £130 v. cheap. Went to poor Darcy's funeral, never saw so large a one since Madam's, everyone went. At inquest jury expressed much sympathy & added a rider that steps must be taken to ensure no further loss of life. Funeral started abt. 8.30 from S. Bricin's & wasn't over till 10.30. Crowds lined streets. We had Miss O'Daly & Sighle.

Friday 26

Another lovely day. The more one hears of explosion in Castle, the worse it seems. It is so terrible to have priceless glass gone & the gem Chapel Royal destroyed. So strange that Broy's Harriers never heard mine being laid. Dev. visited site himself. More autocratic actions of Govt. Talk about Hitler! A wee cabbage with 4 small leaves costs 1 1/2 now, it would take 6 to feed one person. 8 cauliflowers better value.[555]

May

Tuesday 7

8 a.m. R.mines, after b.fast raid, 4 detectives said there had been shooting down town & had I attended any wounded, were quite civil & only looked into study. Heard later 2 detectives shot by IRA trying to get Maffey's mail bag wh. they didn't do. One G. man v. seriously wounded. When I got back fr. Aunt F. at about 11, 3 more came looking for arms & went all over house. Quite like old times.[556]

---

554. *poor D'Arcy* – Tony D'Arcy a senior IRA leader died after a 52-day hunger-strike in Mountjoy Gaol.

555. *explosion in Castle* – an explosion caused by a bomb or landmine which caused much damage to the Francis Johnston designed 19th-century Gothic revival style Chapel Royal. *Broy's Harriers* – In 1934 Garda Commissioner Éamonn Broy oversaw the creation of the Auxiliary Special Branch of the Garda Síochána, they were nicknamed the 'Broy Harriers'.

556. *Raid* – her home in Belgrave Rd was raided by police, Lynn was obviously still a suspect republican. Reminiscent of the days it was raided by the Black and Tans.

Friday 10

Now Holland & Belgium are invaded & they say Leopold has asked Allies help, not v. likely, Sighle, Emer, Mrs Skeff came in & all are fairly sure Britain is done & surely her power was not for good in the world. We had cordon round us & every house in place searched for arms, they said, but it was for wounded man. F. Fail disgusted for Cosgrave won't fight them.[557]

Thursday 30

8 a.m. Xt.Ch. rather dark mg., cleared beautifully for our 21st anniversary. I wore summer frock & M yellow coat & skirt. We had crowds & Dr Micks spoke v. well. Matron was so very surprised at her presentation, Tara brooch, with inscription. All were happy & sun was splendid. Rumour that Westminster bombed. Duff Cooper says Hitler is no man, he doesn't drink.[558]

June

Thursday 6

Didn't go to Church, alas! Lovely day, our 21st Birthday dinner for the Nurses was a great success, all were very pleased & happy. M's pretty little menu cards were signed & resigned & they enjoyed cold salmon, lettuce salad, mashed potatoe, ices, coffee & cake, then they took photos. I made a wee speech, wh. M says was good. Big new German offensive, which has pierced French line again. People panic.

Tuesday 25

8 a.m. R.mines, v. cold showers, one good hail shower tho' French have signed armistice, irregulars continue fighting & English back them up & here "irregulars" are shot. We are trying to get signatures for MacCurtain's reprieve. We are laying in all we can in way of coal etc. wh. they say won't interfere with the poor. Dr Hill back 5 days, had fine time.[559]

---

557. *Leopold* – King of Belgium, Leopold III (1901–83).

558. *21st anniversary* – of the founding of St Ultan's. *Duff Cooper* – Alfred Duff Cooper, 1st Viscount Norwich (1890–1954), British Conservative politician.

559. *MacCurtain's* – Tomás Óg MacCurtain was sentenced to death for mortally wounding Garda Síochána Detective John Roche. He was granted a reprieve and served seven years in prison.

July

Friday 12

It blew & poured in night, river over big stone, took photos of it & Sally. Fair day on whole, hear Med. Board have decided to virtually close Teac, I wrote Dr Price that they have no authority to do so, it must come before Board on 13th. Such panicky nonsense. I think babies more likely to die of gastent. than bombing. Sighle & S.K. had to walk to ford, river high.

August

Monday 12

8 a.m. X. B's. 1st day of work & it was a busy one, nice. Pts. glad to see me wh. of course I liked. U.S. Foynes air mail to run weekly now. More air battles & many planes lost. Saw Reids & they say all the A.R.P. in Jersey collapsed at 1st sign of danger, a place left derelict. Horrid how they bombed Gurnsey, their own place.[560]

Wednesday 21

8 a.m. S. B's. V. stormy fr. N.W. but nice. All went v. fairly. M ffM worked hard at my dress. Rosslare boat attacked again by machine guns. One man dead. The 2 who were caught in Rathgar Rd. are sentenced to be shot by new Court. Floor not finished yet, no B.black came so we are doing in front room is rather cramped. They say Trotsky was attempted to be assassinated in Mexico, what's he there for? [561]

September

Thursday 5

Slept late. Alas the appeal has failed & poor McGrath & the others are to be executed to-morrow but McCurtain was reprieved at the last minute! They are trying for a truce between Dev. & I.R.A. & D.V. it will succeed. Germany's speech to-day was v. good. The idea of a few manufacturers causing such a war is awful. Then Germans are all trained, all fed so different from us, alas!

---

560. *A.R.P.* – Air Raid Precautions.
561. *The 2 who were caught in Rathgar Rd* – Detective Sergeant Patrick McKeown and Detective Garda Richard Hyland were killed during a raid on 97A Rathgar Road, an IRA 'safe house' on 16 August 1940. IRA men Patrick McGrath (1894–1940), and Thomas Harte (1915–40), who were present in the house, were arrested, tried by military court, sentenced to death, and executed, despite campaigns for clemency, four days later. These were the first executions of IRA members since the Civil War.

Monday 9

8 a.m. S B's. Cold mg., warmer then. Terrible raid over London admits to 400 dead & thousands wounded & late on they have had more & 1,000 dead, it is terrible, but Churchill asked for it & is surely getting it. It is terrible to think of, if only they would make peace. The S. Ultan's Aeridacht only just cleared expenses. Glad it did, even that. They want 16/- for covering eiderdown!!![562]

October

Monday 7

8 a.m. S. B's. Lovely clean air after all the rain. They are talking of bringing English children over here, chiefly sick ones & in same breath of evacuating Dublin children wh. is hardly like people endowed with reason. So far as we can see, things are much the same. Paediatric Meeting good. Miss Candon dissuaded nervous child & was very nervy herself. Clinics starting.

Thursday 17

8 a.m. Xt. Ch. foggy & grey. Busy with pts. Trustees meeting to invest £113 in 3 1/2 Corporation Stock at 90. Then Teac Board, no quorum for 2nd time, dreadful. Hosp Commission wrote they will be responsible for our overdrafts, want a/cs sent in soon as possible. Poor Henry v. bad, has become violent, had to get him to Union. M ffM not home yet 9.30, working at invites to Foundation Stone of new flats in Charlemont St. Epidemic of Smallpox feared.

Friday 25

8 a.m. S. B's, nice sun N.E. wind, nice busy day. Teac does well. Our 2 new staff Nurses have come & seem nice. Olga writes fr. Guilford, they have raids there constantly & haven't been in bed for 8 wks. tho' little damage there. Complains can't write, postage so dear. How thankful we shld. be here. God keep us so. Petain & Hitler confer re Peace & Britain deny any likelihood of it.[563]

---

562. *Aeridacht* – Aeridheacht, open air Festival.
563. *Petain* – Marshal Philippe Pétain (1856-1951), Word War One French General, Head of collaborationist regime of Vichy France from 1940.

November

Friday 1

8 a.m. Xt. Ch. lovely mg. Hurried back here & had lots to do, settled abt.pts, with Dr Hill, M & I collected stoves, kettles etc. & went to Flats & saw all in train there. Did Disp. We all went to Flats by 39. Mrs Clarke, Lord Mayor laid stone her 1st. Sally K presented bouquet, silver trowel. Was lovely. Speeches good, we got abt. £40 at show & £140 before. Poor old Mrs McBirney was so delighted to be helping. Mary excellent. D.G. for day.[564]

Wednesday 6

8 a.m. Magdalen, just in time. Churchill laments loss of Irish ports & makes unfounded accusations of West re fueling German boats. It sounds v. sinister, but D.G. Roosvelt is re-elected! President & he D.G. can be trusted not to permit tampering with our ports as he did in July. Another pouring day, one woman said, what matter about rain when it can't bombs.[565]

December

Wednesday 4

8 a.m. Magdalen. V. dark. More poor refugees with pitiful tales. One of our Teac trained Nurses, Nurse Casey, who with her friend, Nurse Maguire, got full training in England & were Jubilee Nurses, was killed while visiting cases in Watford in air raid, we are all so grieved. Mrs O'Connor gave M ffM some good ideas re new hospital. John Brennan was received into Roman Church to-day, she couldn't be persuaded we weren't political.

Friday 20

Had a night out but 1st for very long. Cottage Home willing to take children. Wired Muriel so she replied, impossible, so we must face a lonely Xmas. Nelly rang to say bomb had dropped near Sandycove St. Aunt F. quite unruffled D.G. I rang afterwards & heard all well, the plane was chasing Mail boat. Hear Kennedy says there will be civil war in U.S. if British interfere with our Ports, so we are [ ].[566]

---

564. *all went to Flats* – foundation stone of the Charlemont Flats laid by the Lord Mayor of Dublin, Kathleen Clarke.

565. *Churchill laments loss of Irish ports* – The treaty ports, Bearhaven and Spile Island in Cork and Lough Swilly in Donegal, which would have been very useful to the Royal Navy, and the British war effort, had been returned to the Irish Free State in 1938. Churchill had objected at the time.

566. *Kennedy* – Joseph Patrick Kennedy (1888–1969), US Ambassador to the United Kingdom.

Tuesday 31

8 a.m. R.mines. Fire seems to have wrought much havoc in London, they have had to dynamite many historic buildings. Was trying to get round in taxi, but they fear no more petrol to be had. Hear a petrol boat went down that caused shortage & they sent a boat away in Autumn instead of letting people have all they wld. take. With Aunt F. by 8. All well. V. cold E. wind.

1941

January

Friday 3

8 a.m. S. B's. At 4 a.m waked by big explosion wh. shook the house, it was a bomb wh. fell on S.C. Road & demolished 2 houses, no one killed by God's mercy. It was terrifying & was an hour awake in Teac they all rushed to passage & stayed there till mg. We have arr. now that all babies will be rushed down in evg & all will sleep in safest places. God grant no more bombs.[567]

Sunday 5

2 A.E. 9 a.m. Gaelic S. Patrick's, very cold, hear 2 below freezing, in room it was 38. Quiet night & day, D.G. Aunt F. v. well, had dressed crab for dinner & loved it, she's great for 97. Miss Phelan rang this mg. Poor Mrs Wyse Power passed over at 2 a.m. I am so sorry for Nancy & she only over op. on 2nd. She is v. brave. Still frosty to-night. M ffM rested all day.[568]

Wednesday 29

Was v. late last night & not up early. Wet & rather windy, esp. now. I Times leader stresses the vast resources of Germany & all her advantages & says clearly that unless help is forth coming at once Britain can't carry on. God grant she may not be helped to continue the old regime of tyranny & spoil action. Sighle, M ffM had another grand supper of mushrooms & brown bread. Colder.

February

Saturday 1

S. Brigid. 9 a.m. Gaelic, 6 again. D.G. Nice & mild & a little sun & many birds. Barry of Cork says he has evidence that the 2 boys had nothing to do with Coventry affair. Gt. meeting in Oak Room to try to save them. It was heartening to have so many of all shades drawn together. D.G. for it. S. Brigid helps on her day. They are all agog to

---

567. *it was a bomb wh. fell on S.C. Road* – bombs from German planes fell on Donore Avenue, South Circular Road destroying two houses and injuring twenty people.
568. *Nancy* – Nancy Wyse Power (1889–1963), Cumann na mBan, Celtic scholar, civil servant, diplomat and nationalist and daughter of Jennie Wyse Power.

work & a sub comt. is now working. Alas! that the Chief Rabbi was the only priest there.[569]

Thursday 20

We hurried for M ffM, had Comdt. Delaney, Mr Doran etc. coming to see our A.R.P. arrangements. They see we can't do adults, only as clearing station. Delaney was delighted with the place & the babies. Dr Moore v. mad indeed over the way the Govt. has misappropriated our Sweep stake funds & now refuse to give us our money while they finance their own schemes. In Papers the new Crumlin Hosp. for children is going ahead to blot us out!![570]

March

Thursday 20

8 a.m. Xt. Ch. Such a hard frost, temp down 10 to 40 [degrees]. Was a bit cold on balcon. then lovely warm sunny day. V. busy. Teac Board decided to approach Govt. again in face of crying need for employment to let us start new hosp. Perhaps with Judge Wylie's scheme on the way. England v. severely bombed again. Oh for Peace. We were at Book Fair, 1st & v. good.[571]

April

Saturday 5

V. cold & raw, just one sun gleam. Tea ration was 1/2 oz. last night, this mg. 1 oz. senseless, says plainly England has plenty but punishes us by not letting it over here. How bad they were not to get it & lots else fr. U.S.! Hear Haw Haw is always stressing how England will be bankrupt & starving. Had Poppy & her mother to dinner & heard much of Atlantis & it's country stores, [ ] goats etc.[572]

---

569. *Barry of Cork* – Tom Barry (1897–1980), IRA leader. *Coventry affair* – 1939 Coventry bombing, which was part of the IRA's sabotage campaign in England, two Irish men arrested and tried.

570. *A.R.P* – Air Raid Precautions. *the new Crumlin Hosp* – the new Crumlin Children's Hospital. Built on land donated by the Archbishop of Dublin, opened in 1956.

571. *Judge Wylie* – William Evelyn Wylie (1881–1964), created the Guild of Goodwill in 1941 to establish outlets for additional produce, thereby enabling farmers to employ more men. The company, through two subsidiaries, established restaurants supplied with produce grown in Ireland and brought food and fuel to Dublin.

572. *Haw Haw* – Lord Haw Haw was the nickname for William Joyce (1906–46), a fascist and propagandist, he broadcast Nazi propaganda over the radio from Germany during the war.

Friday 18

Another wet day but not so bad, wind down Glen. News of bad raids in Belfast, much damage along river where factories etc. are. Hear 30 new planes destroyed in factory. Hundreds of refugees fr. B'fast crowding into Dublin. Muriel said they had raids, they heard planes passing over. Aft. M ffM went to well, 1st time for years, we planted watercress. Mick fixed clock.

Tuesday 29

8 a.m. R.mines, F. Clarke v. anxious for news & then wouldn't listen to it! Emer went off just after we went out & ret. fairly drunk. S & I were v. angry when she had to go to Council Meeting to decide her fate. However, she went, all went well, but S. went for her & she got v. drunk & S & I had trouble to get her home. Alas! she is never really off now.

May

Tuesday 6

8 a.m. R.mines, bad raid on Belfast, they leave the City now at night & sleep in field round it, it is so thickly built on. Poor things have come here. Bridges all being blocked with concrete by military, why? Emer came back so disheartened. Miss Bennett was horrid to her & quite unjustifiably so for last thing didn't happen when she was on duty with her till 1 a.m.[573]

Tuesday 13

8 a.m. R.mines, looks like rain. Gt. excitement over Herr Hess coming down in plane near Glasgow unhurt, but of ankle. German reports say he is insane. English say not, people think it was not unpremeditated. House of Parliament wrecked, all Commons, anyhow. Emer didn't come home, gardened a bit & did many pts. Oranges & lemons come in.[574]

Thursday 29

A lovely day for annual meeting, all thro', there were planes last night, several, we hear & antiaircraft guns, wh. made soft explosions we heard. They say one down in Brittas Bay. Had meeting in garden.

573. *Miss Bennett* – Louie Bennett (1870–1956), head of the Irish Women Workers' Union (IWWU).
574. *Herr Hess* – Rudolf Hess (1894–1987), deputy Führer to Hitler, Hess landed in Scotland on 10 May 1941 while on an attempted peace mission.

Lord Mahon said MffM, Matron & I made the hospital, true, in many ways. He gave £20 for us & Util. Soc. We got more money than ever D.G. Raids there & much shaken, say nearly all Belfast in ruins, alas. U.S.A. said to be in war now.

June

Tuesday 17

8 a.m. R.mines. Child Welf. 10.30 Arranged for some Nursing lectures & subs. to Mobile kitchen for distress bad in Crumlin area. Emer had conference all day & M ffM 3 meetings. U.S.A. has closed all German Consulates & papers would make out it is only matter of time to be at war for "Freedom" wh. = Capitalism. We worked in garden wh. does v. well. Sighle brought trout fr. West.

Sunday 22

2 A.T. 8 a.m. Xt. Ch. lovely day, had nice bathe. Hear Germany has declared war on Russia, why in the world, it seems so foolish to attempt so much more & when she has just made peace betw. Russia & Japan. We had nice day & all went well. Emer tried to escape twice y.day fr. Coolock, she is so terrible when the drink is on her, poor child.

Friday 27

8 a.m. S.B's. Felt v. much about Emer's state, rang Dr Taylor, who recom. Dr Dunne, Grangegorman & he is to see her to-morrow. D.V. some good will come. Had fairly hectic day so many to attend to. War reports indefinite. Pessimists say famine comes, but there is prospect of a good harvest, so there. Curry planted out my little lettuces & thinned the turnips. Hospital went well D.G.[575]

August

Wednesday 6

8 a.m. R.mines, warmer, was v. tired but glad to have Celeb. D.G. resting all day. Teac left house surgeonless & with no visiting Dr for Dr Webb has been holding fort & is off now, so I had to get Dr Murphy to sleep in & help in mg. & I must go every day. Sally K has sl. Jaundice. Emer is bad, v. weak & unstrung. Could do no housework at all. Mary v. well D.G. Aunt F. looks frail. I have to find senior maid.[576]

---

575. *Dr Taylor* – Dr Richard Hamilton Taylor, graduated UCD 1924, psychiatrist. *Dr Dunne* – Dr John Dunne, graduated NUI 1922, Chief Medical Superintendent at Grangegorman Hospital.
576. *Dr Murphy* – Dr Kathleen Eva Murphy, graduated NUI 1931.

Friday 8

A v. busy day in Teac for hrs. & consultation with Dr O'Brien over Emer, she says she shld be certified at once & I must see to that. Ah! it is the only chance for her. Posters about Berlin bombings, but we heard no particulars. Mary & Mrs Nedham worked well & house cleaning is nearly done so I may start work on Mon. 11th D.V.[577]

Thursday 21

My 1st night out since June, it was fine till mg. & then rained a bit. Teac Board, we decided on Publicity campaign like Cork St. wh. has so got hosp. started. We say if Govt. transfers the Sweep money, then let us borrow on their security till they get free. M & I saw "Remembered For Ever" new play, absolutely true, showing how Republicans are let starve & politicians make capital out of those who died.[578]

September

Wednesday 3

Slept late. Lovely night & day. We had special Med. Board to appoint House Physicians. Dr Price's star one failed us, is going to England at higher pay. We hope she won't lose her life there. They are to build 600 more shelters here, it wld. be more to the point to provide food & fuel. Germans are at Leningrad. Labour makes fuss over Brit. Govt. saying let Germans & Russians fight while we consolidate.

Tuesday 9

8 a.m. R.mines, little sun, but not bad on whole. Leningrad cut off completely. Had long interview with Wyse Power & Mrs Skeffington re new scheme to use locked up Sinn Fein funds. It seems quite good but inevitably leaves much in Dev.'s hands. Evg. at Owen Skeffington's, gt. revelations re injustice & incompetence of Govt. re turf & oil. Sighle strangely stands up for Govt., so anti social.[579]

---

577. *Dr O'Brien* – Dr Eveleen O'Brien (1901–81), psychiatrist, was then practicing at Grangegorman Psychiatric Hospital in Dublin.
578. '*Remembered For Ever*' – *Remembered For Ever* (1941) by Bernard McGinn, Abbey Theatre.
579. *locked up Sinn Fein funds* – In 1924 two trustees Eammon Duggan (*d.*1936), and Jennie Wyse Power (*d.*1941), on legal advice, lodged the balance of the central fund of Sinn Féin in a Trust in the High Court. On his mother's death, remaining trustee Charles Stewart Power suggested to de Valera that the money be used to support needy revolutionary veterans. Lynn and Sheehy Skeffington supported this.

Friday 12

It was a great day, the opening of the Flats went off splendidly as M ffM's shows always do. There were crowds & everyone was delighted with the size of the rooms, the airy brightness, the individual balconies in wh. Mr Scott had got geraniums etc. put. They looked lovely & all speeches etc. Went well. Much talk of peace fr. many sources. One is that Hitler, when all Europe under him will just ignore Britain, let her sink or swim.

Tuesday 23

Miss Watson & Aunt F. had good night. I had 5 nights in succession & could not continue it. Mrs Lamb sent in chicken. A.F. wonderful, lies exhausted & then rouses up & gives orders as usual. Was in Teac & No. 9. all well. Poor Kiev. reduced to ruins before Russians left it & it was their oldest, most beautiful city & had been taken in 1914-18 & was unharmed then![580]

October

Thursday 9

Went early to W.Point to phone to M ffM. had to wait 1/2 hr, then had satisfactory talk, she'll send on passport, rain started & it poured all day, as a year ago. We had my mushrooms for b.fast & they were v. nice. The place fill of disreputable looking soldiers. I wouldn't like to be here always. Communal feeding progresses in Dublin & Germans are v near Moscow now. Had a lazy day.[581]

Thursday 16

Was lazy, all went well. Teac Board to see Minster & insist on being allowed to start building to save babies. Hear news of Moscow is very grave this evening. If only they would make peace sensibly! Went to N. Smith after dinner, such a lonely, desolate place now. Got all water glass eggs out & brought home bucket, w. is large & heavy. Bus v. crowded tho' not the last.

Tuesday 21

8 a.m. R.mines. beautiful sun. Govt. has [removed] fr. Moscow. Saw Dr Dunne & had long talk re Emer, ret. here to find house had been

---

580. *Aunt F* – Florence Wynne died on 28 September 1941, aged 97.
581. *W.Point* – Warrenpoint, town in Co. Down, home of Lynn's sister Muriel.

raided when only Kitty here, for Emer apparently. The questioned poor little K up & down. Evelyn Wynne will take a good many things of Aunt F's. Had Child Welf. meeting re Xmas party, quite good. L.G.D. has written that that they will receive deput. re new Teac on Fri. good.

November

Tuesday 11

8 a.m. R.mines, at last, in aft. rain stopped & sun came out. Child Welf. wants to open up new clinics, 2 a week instead of one. Crowds are so great. They discussed breast feeding & dried milk. Poor O'Grady may get well, they think the Guard was mad. Gt. floods in South. A boat comes with wheat & a coal boat for Navy was chased in here with much coal D.G.

Thursday 27

8 a.m. Xt.Ch. & M ffM went off with all the packages, the full of the taxi to Mansion Ho. I went in evg. Prisoners' Sale doing v. well indeed. Good crowd. Things dear enough, sheepskin rug £5, & whole sheep 30/-, seems a lot. Madam McBride greatly failed, there against Drs orders, & v. frail. Hear Peace not far off. 3 million rosaries in U.S. for Peace. It was wonderfully warm all day.

December

Monday 1

B. busy day, Child Welf. 10.30 Arranged for Xmas party, went v. well, then pts., hosp. Crumlin 3.30, talk to Mothers. Dr Toher will give out tickets for Party. Home, pts. then to Portobello to see Muriel, Sighle met her all right & she looks ever so much better, then dinner, then Paediatrics at Rotunda, new nurseries are quite marvelous, such lovely prems. so diff. fr. what we get. They keep cots at 80 & room 65 about, back to Muriel & home after 12 & tired.[582]

Wednesday 17

8 a.m. Magdalen, thought I would have been too tired to go. To day's news shows England in gter. & gter. difficulties, the Japs are almost in India, how the Empire is crumbling! & the Soviet leader kowtowing

---

582. *Dr Toher* – Dr Margaret Toher, graduated RCSI 1920, Medical Officer South Earl St. Dispensary, Dublin.

to King George. Nice sun, cold. Did much on cycle. Brenda Brugha brought 4 nice old steel engravings, 3 of Ireland, Narrowater, Delphi & Cormax's Chapel, they were 1/- each & [Thustira] 2/-, v. cheap. Gave last talk to Child Welf.[583]

Tuesday 30

8 a.m. R.mines, v. hard frost & cold D.G. no wind. Mary insisted on stove at b.fast. Nice day, M ffM 61 now & v. well D.G. Did things for party & fixed up a bit, got small present for M ffM. Evg. we had Sighle, Roisin Jacob & Douglas to dinner, wh. went v. well, tho' M ffM & D. very late for it. There are great tales of Germans being frozen to ground where they sleep, poor things & of how well British treat prisoners.

---

583. *Brenda Brugha* (*b*.1916), daughter of Cathal and Caitlín Brugha.

1942

January

Friday 2

8 a.m. S. B's, our Party day, so D.V. I'll have next Fri. for fast. At Town Hall at 10.30 all worked well & heaps of cakes & provisions came & milk & all sorts D.G. All went v. well, they fitted in & were v. content, Cinema beautiful, then plentiful tea & then prize drawing. Every Mother got a present. We had 30 money prizes & some tea & sugar & corned beef & clothes, [ ] & brawn.

Monday 12

Slept till 8.50. Busy enough, went for meal & flour. No shortage of flour, hear oats was bought in by farmers & held to get 42/- a barrell later sold at 12/-. All mills had to stop, now farmers have been made disgorge & mills work again D.G. How grasping people are! got butter beans at 10 per lb. used to be 4. Cable fr. Singapore took a month to come to Mrs McElwaine fr. Percy. She is v. anxious of course. Japs see to do very well. D.V. Peace soon.[584]

Thursday 22

Slept late, v. droughty day indeed. M still in bed but better. Britain in v. bad way. Singapore in gt. danger & they say can't afford to lose it like Hong Kong. They lament that U.S. hasn't sent help, but it has other fish to fry. Australia can be got at thro' New Guinea. Saw Emer in Richmond v. well. Poor Lorna Smith is very mashed up & her brain [oedematous] = had lumbar puncture done.

Thursday 29

Nice sunny day D.G. Reports of debate in Dail "on new order for condemning political offenders" v. scathing for Dev. The document wh. he holds as enough for death sentence might have been written by him in 1920 or so & both F.F. & F.G. have been 'guilty' of such orders. War goes on & Northern Govt. sees no reason to apologise to Dev. for arrival of U.S. troops. F. Clarke had her party here about 7 & it was v. nice & she was happy.

---

584. *Mrs McElwaine fr. Percy* – Edith Margaret McElwaine and her son, Sir Percy McElwaine, KC, (1884–1969), Chief Justice of the Straits Settlements (Penang, Malacca, and Singapore), 1936–46.

February

Friday 27

Up at 7 for Barney Mellowe's Mass in Hospice at 9.30. Got off in good time. Tint Murphy drove us & Frank Dowling. V. large funeral, all sides went. Dev. & co. who mostly look a bit thinner than formerly. Walked back here & fixed dinner etc. then call to pt. It was near 12 before Teac, v. big disp. Aft. Hosp. Commission discussed accommodation for gast. but decided on central place for 100, all hospitals to do what they can.[585]

March

Thursday 5

Mg. not bad, then v. cold & small snow, Dev. had the poor man shot in cold blood to-day. Plant was his name. It was an awful thing to do, alas! for renegades. The weather suited the deed & yesterday they had gt. hopes that his clergyman might have succeeded in saving him. He was not R.C. There was a huge meeting outside Mountjoy last night. The first man ever acquitted & then condemned & shot.[586]

Monday 9

8 a.m. S. B's. Glad to be there once more. Poor Mary Mac is gone. She lasted v. short after Sen. Can't hear of anything being done about her here but people have gone to Cork for funeral. Hear Rangoon gone & Java & an. M.P. says they must give India liberty at once or she'll take it. How the Empire crumbles! Margt. did well to-day.[587]

Sunday 15

4 in L. 8 a.m. R.mines. M ffM went to 9. I rushed after fixing up here to try to be at Wicklow Hotel at 9.45, didn't arrive till 10.10, no bus before 10. She met me there & we had b.fast & went to Mary MacSwiney's Mass at 11 & George Plant's 11.30, music nice, heard 2 sermons & a bit. Talked to E. Taffe who says people in North v. dissatisfied at food & everything. News of big naval defeat for Allies, situation of Australia serious! Glorious day. At S.Cove, cool for everyone.[588]

585. *Barney Mellows* (1896–1942), Sinn Féin politician.
586. *Plant* – George Plant, republican, IRA, convicted by Military Court in February 1942 of the murder of the alleged IRA informer Michael Deveraux, executed by firing squad at Portlaoise Prison on 5 March 1942.
587. *Mary Mac* – Mary MacSwiney (1872–1942).
588. *E. Taffee* – Aoife 'Effie' Taaffe, republican.

Friday 27

Up late after late night, another nice day, tho' wind cold. Neru announced his plans for a free India, busy in dispensary & Utility meeting after. M ffM, Dr Price & Mr Scott all conferred re new T.B. place, it may be started in 6 weeks. Dr Price spoke at Academy on the earliest case of primary T.B. on record in lungs, pretubercle. Sections showed organisms in situ.[589]

April

Friday 24

Slept late, nice day but such cold wind. Had v. troublesome mother fr. Arklow, but fixed her by sending her straight to Dr Micks, who said he would do all necessary. War news good. Evg. we had a great 1916 rally, Citizen Army, C na mB. A youth 'squad', many bands, practically length of O'Connell St. They read the Republican Proclamation in Irish & English & laid a wreath on memorial in G P.O., fine.

Thursday 30

Went to 8 Xt. Ch. & found it was 7.45 & just almost over, too bad. Much warmer & wind changing. D.V. we hope now for rain for crops & gardens. Got in some most welcome money D.G. Evg. we went to Commemoration dinner in Gresham 1916-1921, about 500 there. It was a wonderful re-union & a fine aura, things are improving & we are coming together at last. Soldiers' Song splendid.

May

Wednesday 13

8 a.m. Magdalen, thought I was in excellent time, but no, warmer, some sun. Went to T.C.D. meeting re feeding of school children, they & U.C.D. are feeding 800 daily since before Xmas, very fine it is. Speeches good. Dr Collis said his 200 were 5" below average height & 5 lb. in wt. & they made up on one balanced meal daily costs. Families on assistance get same amt. whether or 10 children. They never had proper food & improve gradually.

---

589. *Neru* – Jawaharlal Nehru (1889–1964), Indian anti-colonial nationalist, principal leader of the Indian nationalist movement in the 1930s and 1940s and became India's first post-Independence Prime Minister.

Thursday 28

Slept late after hard day, Poppy Wilson lost in mg. but she turned up at night D.G. Showers & sun. Annual meeting went v. well D.G.D.G. All were pleased & happy & speeches good & short. British out of Burma & now desert fighting in Libya. Japs are sinking U.S. boats off U.S. now. We had crowds D.G. Evg. went to hear the Editor of Dublin Opinion & Mrs Skeffington debating womens' use of vote. He said they hadn't done well, she opposite. V. good & amusing, gt. crowds.

June

Thursday 18

Was lazy in mg & sorry for it later. Rushed to pt. before Board meeting at 11. We are to have Baby Aga for milk room & Mr Moylette says we must take our claim for anthracite at once. He is not a day older. Sean McEntee has cheek to warn hospitals against expenditure & says Govt. is trustee of Sweep millions. Truth is they seized them & they are gone west now with much more.

Friday 19

8 a.m. S. B's. a good many there. Lovely warm day D.G. Sebastopol is gone & 2 retreats in Tobruk area. Things go well with our Allies. Gahndi & Nereu both say they will accept nothing else than complete freedom for India. How much wiser than we were 1922. We gardened & I planted out the pot of Delphiniums, they were v. crowded & I took care of all the smallest ones, prob. the best kinds.[590]

Sunday 21

3 A.t. 8 a.m. S. B's. most glorious day, we started for Bodenstown abt. 11.30. Mrs S. Skeffington, Miss Hughes, Ann Devlin & I, passed constant stream of cyclists, met F.S. troops & a few gen public coming fr. their show. Nice lunch on grass, splendid crowd, all young, good statement, it was a memorable function. Tea in Kill with Mrs FitzSimons, gt. Republican, safe home. Evensong 7.15. British are out of Libya D.G. & D.V. soon the powers of evil will be quelled.

Monday 29

8 a.m. R.mines, quite cool day & little sun. M ffM had b.fast in Teac. Got legacy fr. Aunt Julia of £13, v. unexpected, she was always just.

---

590. *Gahndi* – Mahatma Gandhi (1869–1948), Indian lawyer and anti-colonial nationalist.

10.30 Child Welf. We have a move on about site for Centre & D.V. it will go thro'. Hear Egypt is gone. Germans advance so rapidly. A terribly busy day. Saw crowds & have nothing done for Glen. We'll have Sr. Helen M. Cummins, Miss Hughes & S.K., a lot.

July

Friday 17

Up at 9, worked hard, they arrived abt. 1 o/c Sylvie & all, gt. work then fixing beds etc. Gretta came as we sat down to dinner & Maura before we finished. We teased them both & Maura was so helpful. M ffM v. dead, slept for hours. All well in hosp. but she had gt work about coal. Hear Germans do v. well in Russia & Libya. Stormy all day & now. M ffM says we have enough, 4 doz. buns & cakes.

August

Friday 7

8 a.m. S. B's. worked hard all day. M ffM's things were a problem. All done now but waiting room & hall. Poor Fr O'Flanagan died at 4 a.m., he lasted v. short after going in to Home, only a few days. Hear it was cancer of liver. Mrs Skeffington in about Reprieve for the Belfast boys. Hear the R.C. clergy are working hard in North where religion counts for persecution. R.C. shops put out of bounds for U.S. troops. Germans have done all they want in S. Russia, D.G.[591]

Thursday 20

Eventful day. British raid on Dieppe a terrible fiasco & they used mostly Canadians, lost 800 & many planes. They say Russians demanded help wh. Britain can't give. Appeal for Belfast boys will be turned down, Sean says, but we'll have to work Heaven & earth. Money & sympathy pour in D.G. & America is roused & all sorts everywhere here. U.S. troops in Belfast are in bad way, bored, too much money, immorality rampant.

Monday 31

8 a.m. S. B's. busy day, huge meeting in Mansion House, overflow much larger fr. the Green to Moleswoth St. a dense throng, a fine spirit, a Unity not seen for many a day & speeches fearless for 32

591. *Reprieve for the Belfast boys* – six Belfast republicans under sentence to death.

county republic & D.V. we'll have it & D.V. poor Williams will be saved. He takes all the blame, tho' it is proved he was unconscious when the policeman was firing hard. They collected about £100 I think.[592]

September

Monday 7

Up late going all day, planted out lettuces & radishes. Warmer D.G. Stalingrad not quite gone yet. Those poor foolish boys in North have had scraps & 2 more police are dead & F.S. troops rushed to Border. Why I can't think, for they wouldn't be siding with the boys & shldn't be necessary to quell those few lads surely. Read reports of 3 maternity hospitals with interest. Results excellent with starved women.

Friday 11

8 a.m. S. B's, dark till aft. Had early meeting. Cosgrave Memorial. We arranged draft appeal, few at meeting. Had great big disp. & busy day. Dr Brille there, her father was Deutch & because of that she was asked at once to resign fr. post in Cork Hosp. town. She hadn't been appointed. They said they wld. lose all subscribers, so much for largemindedness of "Protestant Cork". She will do deputy with us while Dr Alston is away, got down Home [ ]peers/pears.[593]

Monday 5

8 a.m. S. B's. a lovely day & nice sun D.G. Was v. busy up & down on cycle all day. Went with Dr Webb to Crumlin & she started her lectures there, good crowd of women & babies & in fair condition. They talk of fight for ruins = Stalingrad. Poor Jane v. bad, they thought she would die last night = malignant disease of stomach. Chilblains are coming in already, people have them & it isn't cold yet.

---

592. *Williams* – Thomas Williams (1923–42), IRA, Belfast. Easter 1942 the Northern Irish Government banned parades to commemorate the Easter Rising. IRA unit staged a diversionary action against the RUC to allow three parades to take place in West Belfast; during this an RUC officer was killed and six IRA men were captured. All six sentenced to death, five commuted, but that of Williams, who stated he was the leader of the IRA unit involved, was not commuted. He was hanged on 2 September 1942, in Crumlin Road Jail.
593. *Dr Brille* – Franziska Gertrude Brill, graduated NUI 1942. *Dr Alston* – Dr Patricia 'Pat' Alston (*d*.1977), paediatrician at St Ultan's Hospital, worked with Dr Stopford Price on introducing the BCG vaccination to Ireland.

November

Friday 6

8 a.m. S. B's, got thro' 1st Friday v. well D.G. U.S. Elections have gone agst Roosevelt = agst. the war & D.G. for that. It is hard for them to have solidarity & such a mixed crew they are, they send in "American Letter" round rather on plan of 'Devil of the Deep' specially produced for Irish consumption. Saw Mr Downey & bought 250 Carroll's Tobacco shares for £400 not bad = D.U.T. money & Aunt F's & M's.

Friday 13

8 a.m. S.B's frosty & on the way an old man said "It's a fine mg. God bless it" v. unEnglish. The poor O'Neill boy was done in y.day mg. & no one can make any protest, but God will recompense. Germans in all France now. The Gift Sale does v. well, crowds there this evg. & all pleased. Got leather work & old engraving, saw pr. bellows for 12/6 & a lovely crystal vase perh. I may get them later on. Saw L.W. again.[594]

Tuesday 24

8 a.m. R.mines. Erskine Childers is not forgotten. Took M ffM to see Dr Micks, he can find nothing wrong D.G. Says the loss of weight is prob. due to the old thyroid trouble. H.t & B.P. all N but how often she has had v. irreg. ht. & exhaustion. We are only to have 6 ozs. butter now, I hear & eggs are 5/- a doz, & inprocurable at that. What will the poor do? who are starving. Fell over grate on dark path. Unhurt.

December

Friday 11

8 a.m. S. B's. sun to-day D.G. Fear we aren't to fore with Xmas Party this year. U.S. won't extend. Roosevelt's powers, as he asked them, so there, they don't want war. Allies' position & precautions on all fronts & British people want plain statement re whole situation, will they get it? We had a very sympathetic Dr Fannin fr. LG.B. in the Dept. was as nice as he, perhaps we might get on. 'Saor an Leanb' made nearly £70 to-day.[595]

---

594. *poor O'Neill boy* – Maurice O'Neill republican, IRA member, arrested on 24 October1942, after a police raid on a safe house in Donneycarney, Dublin, in which Garda Detective George Mordant was shot and killed. Tried by Military Court and executed in Mountjoy Jail on 12 November 1942.
595. *Saor an Leanbh* – the Irish Save the Children fund.

1943

January

Friday 8

8 a.m. S. B's, another dark, raw mg. I Times leader doubtful re war, the reports say great things for Allies. Roosevelt appeared heavily guarded & many U.S. are not slow to say that home comes 1st that Britain & Russia shld. only get surplus stuff, wh. seems sense. How Roosevelt has changed! Women's Social League going to put up Mrs Skeffington as women's card date for Dail.[596]

February

Wednesday 3

8 a.m. Magdalen, was in time for wonder, nice sun but cold, hear snow in Tipperary. Med. Board only 3 attended. Dr Brill still runs temp. sent to Baggot St. poor child, she hasn't happy home, with grandaunts. They say last German out of Stalingrad. A little girl of 6 has discovered over 1000 silver coins of John's reign, minted in Carlingford mostly, at Corofin Clare, the largest find ever in Ireland, were under a stone in old laneway.

Wednesday 17

8 a.m. Magdalen, mild day. Hear Mr Grady of Gas Co. has been embezzling for yrs, has made away with £40,000 has escaped to England. He gave his daughter a beautiful house & furnished it when she married last year. M ffM admits to being. v. tired & may go to Bally later on. D.V. Hosp Commission object to our "Establishment" wh. = houses on Mall [ ] inexpensive & they are all we have to make a little money! Susie prepared ground for fig tree.

Monday 22

8 a.m. S. B's. A perfectly beautiful day, warm & sunny, dug trenches for runner beans & sowed radishes over it, sowed mustard & cress. Poor Gandhi very weak they say & they won't release him tho' he is nearly dead. M & I are on biscuit fast for him. Got 3 daffodills in

---

596. *Women's Social League* –The Women's Social and Progressive League founded in 1937 by Hanna Sheehy Skeffington to oppose the anti-women articles in the Irish Constitution. It ran women candidates in the 1938 and 1943 General Elections.

garden a mg. before last year. Saw Mrs Noble & she isn't nursing her baby, such a pity, poor baby, he is a fine child. Saw Peg for 1st time for ages, she agrees Sally is most lovely child.[597]

Thursday 25

Nice day, tho hail showers. Alas! the Cavan fire was terrible, 36 dead. The poor children were locked in dormitories over Laundry, where fire started, had got well away before noticed. Took time to break open doors & then no proper ladders or hose etc. Bigger girls heroically tried to save little ones, only one old woman of 80 with the girls. The worst fire since Drumcollagher. Was at meeting describing possible Women's Party.[598]

March

Monday 8

Off by usual train M v. nice all thro', couldn't do enough. She is fairly well D.G. colder but nice sun. Knitted hard all way up train v. full. Teac all fairly well & happy. Here ditto. Great excitement over appointment recommended of non-Gaelic speaker to oversee Celtic studies in U.C.D. I fear Abp. McQuaid is following in steps of predecessor forbids secret societies & education in any but R.C. schools & colleges. Permanent officialdom.[599]

Tuesday 9

8 a.m. R.mines. Nice day. M ffM not coming till 11th.I somehow felt she wldn't come to-day & I am lonely but glad for her. School burnt down in Bray, no one hurt D.G. How do the fires occur! Gt accounts of all the Allies but Russia doesn't please U.S.A. doesn't acknowledge all the help she gets, says U.S.A. who fear later on Germany & Russia will unite. Heard that before. Planted beans & shalotts.

Monday 29

8 a.m. S. B's nice & sunny, but v. blustery. M ffM destroyed for firing & none to be had but D.G. got 4 ton wood before night. In evg. went to

---

597. *Gandhi* – February 1943, Gandhi undertook fasting for a period of 21 days to protest his detention for six months.

598. *the Cavan fire* – On the night of 23 February 1943, 35 girls and one adult died in a fire at St Joseph's Orphanage, Main St., Cavan.

599. *Abp. McQuaid* – John Charles McQuaid was appointed to the Archdiocese of Dublin in 1940.

Maeve Cavanaghs "In the time of the Tans". New, is really v. good, on the whole, tho' parts very stilted & unreal, other parts just lifelike. The Town Hall was full, mostly young. Nurse O'Toole & 6 pros. went. We were 9 coming home in tram.[600]

April

Monday 12

Up in good time, a glorious day, warm, sunny, had gt. bathe in river. Michael late, Susie & I put up lower back shutters, no hurry after all. Esther's boy came with us to R.drum, all eggs etc. safe, all well here D.G. & M ffM had good time with Sylvie at concert Sat. Dev. is now saying he wants women's help in country when up to this he ignored & despised us! Things have grown well even in the few days.[601]

Friday 16

8 a.m. S. B's. Colder mg. but lovely day. Larkin & Hannigan calling each other names in Labour meeting. L. said he founded party & H said Connolly did. Of course, Connolly was the genius. Govt. have lost their case re education, judges unanimously say Constitution leaves parents free to choose school etc. All things grow rapidly D.V. rain will soon[602] come.

May

Tuesday 11

8 a.m R.mines to thank for lovely holiday, sun bright & warm. Franco begs belligerents to make peace for there is no hope of one conquering the other & why continue useless slaughter! V. true & it looks as if with God's help, it would come. Teac well but they gave the back ward for T.B. while I was away, shld. not have been done without more consideration. To-day dear Bessie is ever so much better & D.V. will live a good while yet.

Wednesday 12

Nice Day, tho' some warm rain, had Bessie to lunch at Bewley's, she is v. much better D.G. We got an inditement of Childers by members of

---

600. *Maeve Cavanaghs 'In the time of the Tans'* – 'In the Time of the Tans; a Play in Three Acts' by Maeve Cavanagh MacDowell (1878–1960).
601. *R.Drum* – Rathdrum a village in Co. Wicklow.
602. *Larkin and Hannigan* – James Larkin (1874–1947), labour leader and Joseph Hannigan (1904–57), Labour politician and medical practitioner.

Indust. Develop Assoc., he acted scandalously to favour the Jews. How terrible that they do such things & the Hitlers retaliate & one know why. We shld strive and strive to convert the Jews. Mrs Skeffington is fairly hopeful of her election.[603]

Friday 21

Up late, another nice day, papers have little news of war. D.V. it means Peace is near. Our temp. House Physician is married & has 5 children, she doesn't look 34, eldest 10, youngest 1 1/2, she is very competent D.G. Teac busy. Nurses Maguire & McCarthy gone & a gt. dearth of lately qualified pros. so many gone to England. We must keep all we have to carry on Alex. Coll. [Coole] Playground.

June

Saturday 5

Nice day, some showers, did usu. shopping, discussed new nurses with Dr Price & Matron who was wonderfully reasonable D.G. Aft. we went to tea with the Heilters, saw the bride. M ffM says she is Welsh, not English anyhow. Frau is nicest, they have fine garden & plenty of veget. Now they say De Galle is to be arrested. Anyhow France hasn't united on Allies side. Mrs Skeffington makes good show.[604]

Sunday 20

Trinity Sun. 7.30 R.mines. Wolfe Tone's Birthday 1643 (I think) Mrs Ginnell, Miss Hughes, ourselves & Sally went. We took her as Ann Devlin didn't turn up, it was wet part of time but cleared for oration, fine crowd there for us, no one for F.F. but Military. Simon Donnelly spoke v. well of how unfree we are still & of Tone's great Republicanism. Nice lunch there & we all came back here to tea. Country lovely.

Monday 28

8 a.m. S. B's. & then such a rushing day but got thro' somehow. Lovely & warm & settled -looking. Did what I could for Glen. Aft. here was one frantic rush & Bill Oman came & said he was staying for tea & wld.

---

603. *Childers* – Erskine H. Childers (1905–74), Fianna Fáil politician, secretary of the Federation of Irish Manufacturers (1939–44), latterly the Confederation of Irish Industry. *Indust. Develop Assoc.*– National Agricultural and Industrial Development Association.
604. *De Galle* – Charles de Gaulle (1890–1970), French soldier, writer, statesman, and architect of France's Fifth Republic.

escort me to meeting later. Pts. not gone till 7 & then v. sl. dinner, then IC.A. presentation to me of lovely copy of new I.C.A. History. They were so nice about it. I was quite overcome, they are dears.

August

Saturday 14

A lovely day, early to pts. & then Fint. Murphy re Income Tax, he settled it all so nicely & quickly I needn't have been worrying over it & I did in spite of all I say. Churchill is somewhere unknown & we all do feel Peace is near. Nice mg. shopping & aft. F. Clarke & I went to tea at K Darden's & it was v. nice, they are so kind & nice & garden v. nice too. M ffM saw cousins.

Friday 27

Slept late & it was uneventful day till aft. when phone message came. Douglas ffM had been found dead in his bungalow just then. It was a great shock. I went at once & saw him & arranged about laying him out. No inquest nec. for I had examined him 3 days ago. He was here y.day in gt. form, but he had had several [ ]c/syncopal attacks lately. God knows best. M ffM brave, dear child.[605]

Monday 30

B.fast early & off to 10 o/c Mass for Douglas & funeral after. M was v. good. So many there & all sympathetic & nice. They fired 3 volleys over him & had Last Post. Bugler not v. good. The flowers lasted well. Then M & I went & had coffee & settled we shld go to Solrs. Later he came while M rested, she is sole heir so will clear bungalow at once. Piano here, Alsatian to get good home. She howled & howled after funeral, one faithful creature. D.G. day over.

September

Sunday 19

13 A.T. R.mines, much warmer & quite nice day. Had sunbath. Gt. searching of heart over Dorothy Crisp's article on Ireland in Sn. Despatch, an English paper. She thinks Ireland is loyal to Britain, poor dear & that we are longing to wave Union Jacks. Tea with Miss

---

605. *Douglas ffM* – Douglas ffrench-Mullen (1892–1943), Irish Volunteer, fought in 1916, musician, brother of Madeleine ffrench-Mullen.

McFeran & saw dear Billy. He has had a hard time. M ffM tired all day, poor thing. Had nice ride to D.L. & back.[606]

October

Tuesday 12

8 a.m. R.mines, nice & warm. Child Welf. 11.30 Arr. re. lectures for Crumlin, we are to have new Nurse there D.G. Tried to get back my garden. D.V. on Thurs. We'll have a field day in garden & Curry & get things reconstructed a bit. Many say Peace near & D.V. it is so. M ffM spoke of Teac to Wom. Suff. Assoc. & had a great success D.G. She is less tired.

Tuesday 26

8 a.m. R.mines, nice, warm day, Child Welf. heard from Dr Murphy that the Corporation will pay for no child who wasn't sent by Child Welf. & it only touches fringe of the families who come to us, so all the rest may die for all they care. Oman child got suddenly v. ill in Steeven's. Either pulm infarct. or spontaneous collapse, she is a little better now D.G. Is the war over?

November

Friday 5

8 a.m. S.B's. V. wet night & dark day, got thro' 1st Fri. v. fairly well D.G. Our new H.S. seems nice. Dr Murphy rather burdened with responsibility of seniority. Poor Victor Emanuel getting nothing for himself. How the capitalists can wangle things to their own ends! Saw piece of soap brought back by prisoner fr. Germany. It was not bad at all, fair size & smelt quite good. They got a meal daily, so did we.[607]

Wednesday 10

8 a.m. Magdalen, lovely till aft. then pours & fine again. Called to pt. who had colonic lavage & was better, to Barnacuillia boy, better D.G. & Peter too. M ffM had much to do & decide. She sent letter to McEntee. D.V. he will be impressed. Pt. who seemed featherheaded has read Hist.of Citizen Army & was surprised I was in it.[608]

---

606. *Dorothy Crisp* (1906–87), right-wing English political figure, writer, and publisher.
607. *Victor Emanuel* – King of Italy Victor Emmanuel III (1869–1947).
608. *McEntee* – Seán McEntee, (1889–1984), Fianna Fáil politician, Minister for Industry and Commerce.

December

Wednesday 1

Poor M ffM had terrible asthmatic attack soon after I had gone to bed & was gassing & livid & cold persp. Gave adrenalin & got Dr Murphy & she got better & slept but I was v. anxious & got Dr Micks at 9 a.m. who said her heart was all right & it was going everyway last night. However, she is to rest. Teac boiler being taken down but all fairly well D.G Butter 2/4 a lb.

Thursday 9

V. dark mg. Comt. for Party, we are no forwarder than last year but D.V. we'll be all right. I have so much to think of now. M ffM is off duty but God will help me thro'. M ffM is much better D.G. & can do more. We are hoping to get nicer cakes than last year, if we have money enough. The laundry is to be out of action to-morrow to have valves finally fitted. L.G.D. won't hurry with Nurses' quarters & T.Bs part is nearly done.

1944

January

Wednesday 5

8 a.m. Magdalen, 1st night on balcon. for ages, it was lovely. To night is too windy, alas! Had good day. We discovered cost of T.B. extension before L.G.D. messed it up = £1500 instead of £5,500 & little to show for extra money. Dr Murphy here & very washy after 'Flu. All well in Teac D.G. It was a nice day & all went v. fairly well. Had long letter fr. Waller Young, saying Mervyn Wynne is dead 1 1/2 years in Singapore.

Tuesday 18

Mary up at 7, thought it was 8. I wondered at early sounds. M ffM had good night. When packing midwife fell, call came for Mary & off she had to go then, man came to have hand dressed. Ambulance came 12 sharp. We left at 12.30 had v. good journey & M seems better & had good dinner. Dr Hill brought lovely soup & we had woodcock Lily had cooked & nice parsnip & potatoes. No news of Mary. Nurse Maher came for a little. All well D.G.

Monday 31

M had a v. good night & spent day on balcon. in sun, she is better D.G. I think Dr Taylor imagines he is better than Dr Moorhead but I don't. Nurse came & stayed with me all day wh. was good. Now le cunabh De M will get better. Tried to get Mrs Kettle to help in Teac but she says she cannot undertake more responsibility. I must wait for God to raise up helpers for us. I don't see where to turn no one seems of use.[609]

February

Wednesday 16

8 a.m. Magdalen, v. cold mg. & then lovely sun. Dr Price came & saw M on balcon. & thinks she looks v. well, true. Settled things for Board as well as I could. Hear first Dali Llama & just lately new Llama have died of mysterious disease wh. is v. unaccountable. Except by foul play prob. British so now Thibet is left leaderless for present Llama, who has all the stigmata, is a child & must be educated up.

---

609. *le cunabh De* – Le Cunamh Dè (Irish), with the help of God.

Thursday 17

It was a hard day, 10 o/c Meeting with Mr Scott & McGinley re heating of T.B. wing. It will have to be by boiler alas! Then Board 11 & long & tiring discussion on financial position . Dr O'Connor seems to think we are being maneuvered into hopeless position by L.G.D. who will disown us & support Abp's new Hosp. in Drimnagh, but God will help us as heretofore we know. M ffM nicely. Sylvie & Susie gone to Glen.[610]

Saturday 26

Only waked at 8.45. V. cold in aft, started sleeting & it goes on still N.E. wind. Got shopping done before wet came. Gt. rumours of clashes on border, ultimatum to Dev. re Ports but they'd take them if they really wanted them. Soldiers called up at 3.00 a.m. & head of Red X told to be ready. We don't somehow feel it in the atmosphere. Mrs S.S. says she heard rumours y.day. Nothing fr. Haw Haw on wireless.

March

Thursday 9

A notable day, M ffM came in taxi to Teac but first to Whitefriar St. for a moment. All in Teac overjoyed to see her & D.G. she was none the worse. Many v. glad too, for Christy has got work, she is so thankful & so are we all. I went to Barnacullia etc. & found all well. Many miners on strike in England, they get no look in, poor men. Poor Emer bad. Dr says she must be put up.

Saturday 11

8 a.m. S. B's. I. Times says Dev. refused U.S. request for removal of German & Jap. embassies wh. was what we heard last week. Of course they are raging because we are not suffering as badly as other poor countries. The barbarity of attacks on Rome & Florence is just like ancient Goths & Huns. Poor Miss Willis got faint in hospital & had to lie down on H. Surgeon's bed. M ffM rested, she was overtired.

Tuesday 28

8 a.m. R.mines, fog, then nice sun. Busy day, now no coke to be had for Teac, but we ordered anthracite & [ ]breaze wh. must do for 70,000 miners on strike & we'll get no coal, so we may as well work our own

---

610. *Abp's new Hosp. in Drimnagh* – National Children's Hospital.

coal. Hear a tanker in. D.G. Vaccination not being enforced now at all I hear. We have written Dr Russell about it. I fear M ffM's rheumatism is a paresis, with no loss of sensation, God help us.[611]

April

Sunday April 16

8 a.m. Xt. Ch. Nice to be there after so long away. We had a bad night. Poor M up twice trying for a motion, succeeded at last, but v. exhausted. Tried all day & only a little. I did report for her to try & save her worry. V. quiet day & warm. Evenson 7.30. Mr. Cross gave forth on horrors Jews suffer in Nazi lands. Stuffed into trains & left till dead, packed into cells & steam turned on till dead etc.[612]

Tuesday 18

It was a nice day & we were entertaining most of it. We just had M ffM in the chair when the Reids arrived. I had them to dinner while M. had her's in drawing room. They were nice & didn't tire her, they took her to the Church, then we went to pier & there found Mary & Bran, who almost eat us for joy. Reids left, Mary & I took M home to bed after 4. Mary & I talked things over. We agree it'll be long before pt. can do much. D.G. she isn't too dead to-night.

May

Tuesday 9

8 a.m. R.mines, a month since I was there F. Clarke says . Interviewed Dr Moorhead re new Sec. for Teac & he certainly thinks we shld. get young energetic person & D.V. we will, tho' now Mr O'Connor says his person would want over £300 a year & dear M ffM had only £250 & nothing at all for years. Nurse not well, so I am taking night. Went to National Planning Exhibition & it is a revelation & for all Ireland.[613]

---

611. *Dr Matthew Russell* (1874–1956), Medical Officer of Health for Dublin.
612. *Mr Cross–* probably Canon A. Cross of the Church of Ireland Jews' Society. *Horrors Jews suffer in Nazi lands* – this entry reveals an awareness of the genocidal killing which was happening in concentration camps.
613. *National Planning Exhibition* – held in the Mansion House between 26 April and 5 May. It was held to publicise the issue of national planning. The centrepiece of the Exhibition was a huge, contoured map of Ireland on which visitors could see, with the aid of cameras, how plans might appear.

Thursday 11

V. warm day, put on lighter vest. M ffM nicely. Brought her to Miss O'Reilly's Home at 6 in ambulance & went again at 9.30 & stayed till she was almost asleep. D.V. the change will be good for her. All sides are surprised at Dev.'s callousness in precipitating an election at such a time. But he has no thought but for himself & Party. Saw Bessie & the Sean & both well. D.G. & good a/cs of Mary & Allie Burke. She's gone to Cong.[614]

Friday 12

Slept on balcon. Nice. 18 days to election & everyone v. angry. Meath suggests return of same members sensible idea. G.S.R. enquiry stopped till after election. Govt. stops nothing. M ffM nicely, saw her 3 times. Interviewed Mr O'Connor, he advocates younger person for Sec. & he seemed more reasonable about it when I told her so. Poor M. I arranged to see Dr Barry, Mrs. Kettle, Mrs Ceannt. Teac v. fairly D.G.[615]

Friday 19

M ffM not well, v. breathy & coughing.= misses her Thyroid, in Teac all v. pleased. We liked our presentation. Settled about grass cutting etc. They rang fr. Nursing Home. M breathless again & wanting the [Thepoid], got some fr. Sister & went & found M very "mangey" & low, but she improved wonderfully when comforted & petted a bit, later I rang them & she was better & D.G. now she is D.V sleeping on her side.

Friday 26

They rang fr. Nursing Home when I was in bath, dear M dying, but she had gone quite suddenly a few moments before. Nurse saw a change, put her arm round her & she was gone D.G.D.G. she was so happy & spoke of y.day a moment before. Tom Kelly came & was so nice, we rang all we could & how the news spread, rings & callers all day. The laid her out beautifully, such nice flowrs & she looks lovely at rest, happy.[616]

---

614. *Miss O'Reilly's Home* – the intention was for ffrench-Mullen to have a rest in Miss O'Reilly's while Lynn prepared for the St Ultan's AGM.

615. *days to election* – The general election was called for Wednesday, 23 June. *G.S.R.* – Great Southern Railways.

616. *dear M dying* – Madeleine ffrench-Mullen (1880–1944), died aged 64.

Saturday 27

8 a.m. S. B's, a day of 'phones, wires, messages, interviews, but I got away & did Teac & some messages & saw my darling M surrounded with lovely flowers & looking so serenely happy D.G. Was a bit worried for fear funeral would arrive soon after 3 instead of 4 at Whitefriar St. but fixed it up D.G. all right. V. nice appreciation in papers & not too terrible picture. It looks like rain. Saw Lily Kelly & she was v. nice & kind, asked me to Bally.

Sunday 28

Whitsunday, 7.30 R.mines, a beautiful day, got some wee flowers in garden & bunch of yellow roses & went & said good bye to the earthly M ffM & sat there a while in the stillness, the yellow roses make the coffin so sweet. Later they all came & Mary just in time to see the last of her & then crowds at Whitefriar St. All knew me & not the family. My hand was tired shaking. Back & tea with Sighle & Emer came & later Poppy here.

Tuesday 30

8 a.m. R.mines The funeral day, we were down early with the flowers we had & left them in the Mortuary Chapel, the others were wonderfully fresh D.G. Fr Devlin said Mass & looked old & feeble & said he was fond of her. Crowd there. At the Cemetery too & Bill Oman spoke of her so naturally & spontaneously, it was a lovely sunny day. So many, many mourn her & are kind to me. Emer & Sighle & Nugents with me.[617]

Wednesday 31

8 a.m. Magdalen, found myself in Clyde Rd unconsciously & then hurried to Leeson St. not v. late, talked with many sympathisers in mg. Mrs Skeffington, who has written a beautiful little a/c of dear M for the Press. So busy all day had no time to think but had good few letters to read. Papers seem to say Allies have nearly won the war, how I miss M ffM's grasp of the news! Lily Reilly said they were relations but she belonged to me.

---

617. *At the cemetery* – Madeleine ffrench-Mullen was buried in her family grave in Glasnevin Cemetery.

June

Monday 5

Hadn't to leave W.P till 10.10 D.G. & I had been v. nice with M.[618] but the loneliness coming back, with no M ffM to greet me & say what barren wilderness it had been while I was away! All had gone well D.G. & I was glad to be back. Saw Geoff & he thinks well of going ahead with bungalow. Later Joe Kelly rang & says the other Joe is willing to act executor too when we heard he wouldn't they're getting Carton & O'Meara solrs. to act.

Tuesday 6

8 a.m. R.mines, v. cold. Hear Invasion at last going on & little resistance. Rome taken, Germans did not defend it, not wishing its destruction. A unique pottery bowl excavated in Carlow may be a missing link betw. bronze ages? Rode out to Mrs Ceannt & had long talk. D.V. she will be a great help on Board. Mrs. Kettle rather broken reed now. So so lonely for dearest M ffM.

Friday 16

S.B's to thank for God's goodness y.day. Pilotless 'planes have worked fearful havoc in London, a/c over wireless says glow of its burning seen plainly on continent. It is appalling that war shld. be like this. Worked hard all day at clearing out with Irma & Susie helping but went with pension to see poor Peter Little, they were most kind & he is to have full pension while he lives, perh. not long.[619]

Saturday 17

Only up at 8.30, quite nice, sunny day. Roisin Jacob came in mg. About Mrs McGinley & then says she'll sort all M's political papers, some job, about 5 pillowcasesful. Irma & Susie & I worked hard all aft. & Mary & I all mg. We have got out all M's stuff now. Sighle & I [ ] at night. The gt. excitement is arrest of Dr K Murphy & Fergus.[620] They say that they had someone on the run. Poor Isolde, it is hard on her.

---

618. *v. nice with M* – visiting her sister Muriel in Warrenpoint.
619. *Pilotless 'planes* – The V1 and V2 flying bombs were pilotless winged bombs powered by a jet engine.
620. *arrest of Dr K Murphy & Fergus* – Charlie Kerins (1918–44), was arrested on 16 June 1943 at the house of Dr Kathleen Eva Murphy, later O'Farrell, who graduated NUI 1931, daughter of Dr Cornelius Murphy, republican activist. Kerins was tried, convicted, and executed for the shooting of Garda Detective Sergeant Denis O'Brien in September 1942.

Thursday 22

Up late, the 1st really hot day. I have no one to tell me now how war is really going on, alas! She was so clear headed. Teac all right so far tho' Mrs Russell says she'll have to go to England if her nephew can't get work here. Cleared out my own stuff all day & there is plenty more to do, it will take time, but I must do it by degrees. The 1916 letters are so interesting & the Suffrage ones & my speaking in the Park.

July

Monday 3

8 a.m. S.B's 1st day of Miss Gilmartin's work. I was sure she was Kilmartin, she is gentle, but can hold her own. I think. Nice day, interviewed Elsie [Reeves] & she was helpful but a bit inclined to be on the side of Matron wh. was natural. We are seeing what can be done about getting stock of turf, like other hospitals. Annie McSwiney came in evg. & we had great talk, she was so sorry she hadn't heard about M ffM.[621]

Thursday 6

8 a.m. S. B's, soft day. They say Hitler says in the end the Germans must win, the complete cycle will = their victory. The robots seem to be doing terrible damage in England & the people are demanding statement. Here Minister says rise in prices unavoidable, but how do they manage it elsewhere? Long talk with Dr Barry & also with Miss Fletcher. Mr Scott's office & all satisfactory D.G. Gently reprimanded Bridie who had locked up Aga, felt dear M. helping all the time.

August

Tuesday 15

8 a.m. R.mines. Another beautiful day. F. Clarke v. glad to see me & hear news. Child Welf. 10.30 no quorum. Settled for next time. Teac goes fr. new office progresses. New T.B. place ideal for this weather. Sally & I got cycles & all the other things arr. before we were back. We unpacked & divided spoils of Glen. Saw about char, wrote several letters about Ardbraccan. Birch tree better of watering. Lovely apples for eating, such treat after so long.

---

621. *Miss Gilmartin* – Matilda Gilmartin appointed St Ultan's Hospital Secretary in 1944 to replace Madeleine ffrench-Mullen.

September

Tuesday 5

8 a.m. R.mines, V. stormy, & wintry & wet. Allies go on. Heard for 1st time that King of Belgians is prisoner & removed to Germany Govt. or pseudo Govt. seems to be in London. Queen of Holland prepares to return. Barrel of fermented blackberries exploded in South & killed a man. Miss Gilmartin has made out scheme to present the Corp. re payment for Interns. Saw Mrs Morrison re Nurse.

Tuesday 12

8 a.m. R.mines, another beautiful day. Had Child Welf. & then Florrie Salkeld & I went to Mr Broe's to see the bust he has done of Madam. It is very well done but not her at all, too stylised & affected. I am to get Mrs S Skeffington to see it. Teac v. fair D.G. Mary let me back into our balcon room, the floor is well dried & we have dear M ffM's Indian rugs down.[622]

Friday 22

Slept on, it poured in the night & I thought it was a drip in the roof at 1st but bundled in quick. V. heavy showers later. The Dail reports are sad reading, recriminations & the people suffer alas! We are worse than when British here. Poor T.B. people live in filthy rooms in yards with flooding, then the Corporation pumps itself a new Chief Medical Adviser appointed for L.G.Dept.[623]

October

Monday 2

8 a.m. S. B's. V. Autumnal day tho' nice. F.F. Ard Feis has many quite good resolutions about language Republican proclamation to be hung up in schools etc. D.G. for it, for the old spirit had seemed quite dead so far as Govt. is concerned. A pilotless plane escaped fr. U.S. soldiers in Wash & headed for Liverpool, crossed Ireland & fell into Atlantic when petrol exhausted. D.G did no harm.

Tuesday 17

8 a.m. R.mines, Child Welf. 10.30, arranging about Xmas party. Then long discussions with Miss Gilmartin about running of Teac, of course

---

622. *Mr Broe* – Desmond Broe (1921–68), Sculptor.
623. *new Chief Medical Adviser* – Dr James Deeny (1906–94).

it is in a muddle & for long & long M ffM wanted to change it but it wasn't done, however, with God's help it will be now. Mr Scott wrote lovely appreciation of dear M ffM & her work in Charlemont flats & her marvellous way of overcoming insuperable things.

November

Thursday 9

8 a.m. S. B's that poor queer man lies prostrate on ground in prayer it looks so extraordinary somehow. Bright & cold. Pts till after 6 so no chance of being at Mrs Oman's removal fr. Rotunda to Corpus Christi. Went at 7.30 to Womens Social & Political meeting. Madam McBride's paper on Inighni na hEirin read by Rose Jacob, such a thrilling a/c of their counterblast & [ ] Party of Victories one in the Park. I vaguely remembered about of it, unionist then.[624]

Monday 27

8 a.m such a frost, roofs white, soon went. V. cold then & after dinner v. warm again, such weather. I write with my dear black pen. Man rang this mg. he had found it in his porch. I had asked way there on 19th, a fairly good day. Albina goes to-morrow. How last year comes back to me. The dear one, if we had realised how bad she was but it was all in God's Hands & He knew. Dr Lowe, who killed Thomas Ashe, dead.[625]

December

Thursday 7

Slept till 8.45. Mary was tiring last night. Now Britain & U.S. disagree, may it be true about rogues falling out, for the poor honest, do want their own. Labour approves of Dr Dignan's proposals for better Public Health services. Very cold & windy day, not so wet. Saw Nurse Maguire

---

624. *Inighni na hEirin* – Inghinidhe na hÉireann, radical separatist nationalist women's organisation founded by Maud Gonne (Madam) in 1900. *Party of Victories one in the Park* – Inghinidhe na hÉireann organised a 'Patriotic Children's Treat' in the Phoenix Park, in protest at the visit to Dublin of Queen Victoria in April 1900.
625. *Dr Lowe* – Dr William Henry Lowe (*d.*1944), a local doctor, with no prior experience in artificial feeding, brought in to help feed the hunger strikers in Mountjoy Jail in 1917. Lowe botched the force feeding of Thomas Ashe leading to Ashe's death.

& her little son & she was pleased. Was at Ch. Home Sale, v. nice & evg went to Mrs S. Skeffington's but it was over & did well.[626]

Monday 11

Up late after late night. Did Xmas things & pts. Much phoning these days. Evg. we had a great Paediatric meeting in Temple St. where the nuns were & met Dr Collis & Dr Price. They showed cases of deformity, club hands, spina bifida, congen. dislocation of hip & gave early diagnosis = widening of perinaeum. Showed girl of 12 who was almost 6 ft. & can grow still. Assoc. didn't approve of trying Stilibosterol.[627]

Monday 25

8.30. W.Point, we all 3 went. Nice day & a little sun. We had presents in middle of b.fast for I was hungry. M is v. pleased with cycle-bag I brought & Jane with her prayer book & hymnbook combined. We had fine turkey this year & celery & v. good plum pudding. Aft. we all went to the Sanatorium to see same girl as 2 yrs ago & we greeted many there. A lovely quiet Xmas.

Sunday 31

1 A. Christmas 7.30 R.mines, very dark mg. but nice day. Sent N.Year's cards hard, to Geoff's for dinner, saw Mrs Good D.G. she does well. Such a nice time with the children at Geoff's. Aft saw Madam McBride, she looks so old & wrinkled & worn, but v. much alive. Back to tea at Geoffs, then here, wrote more. Evensong. at Magdalen, nice carols. Then home, supper, more cards & bed.[628]

626. *Dr Dignan's proposals for better Public Health services* – John Dignan (1880–1950), Bishop of Clonfert, published *Social Security: Outlines of a Scheme of National Health Insurance* in 1944, sparking a debate about public health provision in Ireland.
627. *Stilibosterol* – Diethylstilbestrol a nonsteroidal oestrogen medication, discovered in 1938 and used for a variety of purposes including prevention of tall stature in adolescent girls.
628. *Geoff's* – The Geoffrey Wynne family, wife Stella (née Phipps), children Beresford 'Berry', Robin, and Beryl, Clonskeagh, Co. Dublin.

SECTION 4: 1945-55 LIFE WITHOUT MADELEINE

In 1945, a post-war Ireland was inward looking, poor, underdeveloped and marked by economic stagnation and emigration, in particular the rate of emigration remained high among single women. The years saw the reconstruction of Europe under the Marshall Plan, however, as Ireland had been neutral, this did not impact on the country or its economy. Despite this there were several agencies which offered aid, especially to children who had been impacted by war in Europe. Lynn was heavily involved in one group, Save the German Children Society (SGCS), which brought German children for periods of one to three years to live with Irish families. Women's activism and campaigns were channelled through new organisations such as the Irish Housewives Association, who campaigned unsuccessfully for Hanna Sheehy Skeffington in the 1943 General Election. They continued, in coming decades, to seek real equality for women, and lessen the impact of inflation, high prices, bad housing, and lack of access to proper education for women and children.

In 1948, De Valera and Fianna Fáil, after 16 years in power, lost the general election amid continuing unrest due to the economic difficulties. John A. Costello of Fine Gael became Taoiseach of a broad inter-party coalition including Clann na Poblachta, Labour, Clann na Talmhan, and National Labour. Appointed Minister for Health, Dr Noël Browne, whose parents had died of the disease, was determined to eradicate TB. Once his TB eradication campaign was successfully underway, in 1947, he proposed a 'Mother and Child Scheme' under which all mothers, and children up to the age of 16, would be eligible for free health care. However, this scheme was undone by a combination of opposition from the Catholic Church and the medical profession. Browne was eventually forced to resign, and the scheme lapsed. The economy began to recover somewhat, especially the agricultural sector; new social housing was built to help clear the tenements; and investment on healthcare continued, especially in work on TB.

Following the spike in infant mortality in the early 1940s, rates began to fall sharply from 1947, reaching a record low of 38 per 1000 by 1955. Part of this reduction was due to the wider availability of antibiotics: St Ultan's Hospital recorded first using the 'wonder drug' Streptomycin in 1947. St Ultan's saw a similar decline in death rates, by 1955 just 3 per cent of the patients admitted to the hospital died. During this period the vaccination against, and treatment of, TB became an increasingly important part of the hospital's work, not always to the delight of Lynn. In 1945 a new 30-bed TB unit, with large balconies, was opened. It treated children up to five years of age, and Montessori teaching was reintroduced. BCG vaccinations were carried out on a large scale from 1947 with 100 vaccines administered that year, the number would rise to 1,446 per year by 1955. The hospital's part in the roll out of the vaccine in Ireland was recognised in 1949 when the newly established National BCG Committee was based in the hospital. The same year a new BCG unit was opened with 12 beds.

Outside of the BCG work, the hospital continued to develop their outpatients and almoner (social work) service. International visits and training for staff was re-established, including regular attendance at the International Hospital Federation. Locally the hospital developed links with the Rathmines Junior Red Cross Branch, who raised funds for new equipment. The Utility Society was dissolved in 1948, as Dublin Corporation took over the responsibility for the flats.

Lynn's diaries during this last decade of her life are often philosophical. She was among those surviving 1916 rebels who gave a witness statement on her deeds to the Bureau of Military History. She also collected artefacts and papers together and deposited them with Cork-born Christian Brother, William Allen, who assembled, over many years, an impressive archive of the revolutionary period. She often reflected on what the rebels of 1916 had fought for, and a sense of disappointment at what was lost – the socialist republic and equality for women – pervades her later years. But, ever the pragmatic person, she continued working in St Ultan's until shortly before she died.

1945

January

Wednesday 3

8 a.m. Magdalen, v. stormy, going = centre of cyclone, even worse, coming back & then at b.fast snow & no wind but then raw and miserable. Med. Board want to give testimonial to Matron, we all must join. They & we all are worried over laundry & heating off B. wing. Much antiChurchill news in "Peace news", they put no tooth in their condemnation of all he has done to destroy the world. God grant Peace.

Saturday 6

8 a.m. R.mines, fairly busy. All so delighted Sister will be Matron. We are to have visit fr. Dr Craig, Brit. Ministry of Health on Mon. aft. He is inspecting Paediatrics here & is to talk on it at Paed. Assoc. on Mon. night & I have to go to dinner for him at Hibernian at 6.30. Miss Cantwell lent me jacket to wear. Our wee dinner here went well. J. Lynch's fowl excellent & Nugents & Miss Tighe of Claremorris, B.robe enjoyed it much.[629]

Monday 8

A colder day. T.40, busy enough. Pts & Dr Craig came to Teac at 5. Dr Barry etc. came too, he is v. nice & approachable & saw as much as possible & was pleased to get S. Ultan's book, rushed back to change & then to Hibernian, a v. nice dinner indeed. I was next Dr Craig & Dr Moorehead, only woman there. Paediatric meeting was v. large & interesting. Future of Paediatrics by Dr Craig. They say Teac is unique.

Friday 19

8 a.m. S. B's. sl. snow, white gardens, roads like glass but got on well. Gt. news. Mrs Hornidge has left us £100, she always was a dear & £100 to Katherine Maguire Memorial fund. Is there such a thing? Churchill said how marvellously they had saved Greece!!! McEntee says there will be v. little Sweep money, where has it gone? & that Hospitals will be municipal & voluntary ones will be of no account, won't they?[630]

---

629. *Dr Craig* – Professor William Stuart Mcrae Craig (1903–75).
630. *MacEntee* – Seán MacEntee (1889–1984), Fianna Fáil Minister for Local Government and Public Health 1941–8.

Sunday 28

Septuag. 7.30 R.mines, weather same. F. Clarke v. pleased to have me on Birthday. I do miss dear M ffM. All v. kind. Sighle gave eggs & Mary Cummins cake. F Clarke little towels. People are so kind. I went to dinner with Susie, she was alone. V. nice there. Then opening of our new Ch Adelaide Rd. for Irish Services. It was packed & nearly all young. All in Irish, even Blessing by Abp. he must have learnt it off.

February

Wednesday 7

8 a.m. Magdalen, v. stormy, but I managed it. V. busy all day, saw Dr Moorhead, he says we can do nothing abt. Sweep Funds. Govt. just rides roughshod thro' all rules of honesty etc. but he says hospitals must go on & they must find some way to finance them. Med. Board went well. They approved of my suggestion of inscription for dear M's photo. Poor Germans! I do feel for them, they will fight to the end & will have no "unconditional surrender" brave souls.[631]

Tuesday 27

8 a.m. R.mines, nice day. Miss Clarke says weekend was appalling, others don't. News & Views gives terrible a/cs of starvation in Germany & France, newborn babies wrapped in paper, no supplies at all & England has large reserves of all necessities & troops want luxuries etc. sent for themselves & wont give space for what might well go. God look down on all the misery. How great must be our sin to need such Christianity. Mrs Bennett came to Teac, 1st time.

March

Thursday 15

8 a.m. S. B's to pray all might go well at Board & D.G. it did. Miss Lavery appointed on month's trial & Miss Fletcher given notice. Mrs Burns applied to Board for rise in pay & was mad because they didn't give it at once. We are to find out how other hospitals do. Alas! she is a firebrand, one can understand why Arnotts didn't keep her. Told Sr Kearns we wished her to stay on Top landing, she seemed to take it well. Mr Scott to supply new sketch of new hosp. for report.

---

631. *inscription for dear M's photo* – the photo was displayed in St Ultan's with the following inscription: 'Madeleine ffrench-Mullen, F.C.C.S., whose indomitable courage and energy as Secretary guided this hospital successfully through its first 25 years. Obit 26th May 1944.'

Tuesday 20

8 a.m. R.mines, some nice sun & no rain All say war will soon be over D.V. I had a letter fr. Boston fr. lady who wishes to leave us endowment for a cot, kind person. How M ffM's helping us! Had Child Welf. & did Teac things. Now Dr Price is rather inclined to think Rebecca is not the infector, but she must go. Paediatric Comt. interesting Post Graduate course ignores Paediatrics & they are a good half of Medicine & the most important half.

April

Monday 16

8 a.m. S. B's D.G. things better in Teac. As I was going there on bridge, dray on wrong side. I couldn't avoid, struck it gently & came down on back D.G. motor behind could stop in time, not hurt but left leg not comfortable now. Fear we must have Dr Ward to open T.B. wing, McEntee has passed on all such functions to him. Dr Price disappointed, but we must not antagonise Ward. V. busy all day. Crowds of pts. Lovely & warm.[632]

Saturday 21

8 a.m. S. B's, cold & harsh, but nicer later, the 8 M.Ps etc have gone to see German prison camps 1st hand & all the horrors, when one thinks of what they did to us & the U.S. to the natives, one knows their insincerity. Poor Germany almost squeezed in betw. enemies & surely they are no worse than the Allies. Teac seems all right. Saw Miss Jackson who is much better D.G. Gardened a bit & felt lovely all day.

Monday 30

8 a.m. S. B's, bitter wind & hail & lovely sun in shelter, poor Mussolini & others shot & hanged to petrol pumps head down, surely barbarism is rampant again & no wonder, with God forgotten & then they pretend the United Nations are working for righteousness. The Russians are v. determined to have all their own way. All say Hitler is dead. Himmler seems chief now. Teac nicely D.G.[633]

---

632. *Dr Ward* – Francis Constantine 'Conn' Ward (1891–1966), physician and Fianna Fáil politician, MacEnteer's Parliamentary Secretary for Public Health.
633. *Mussolini & others shot* – Mussolini, his mistress Calra Petacci, and several of his supporters were shot on 26 April 1945; on 29 April their corpses were hung upside down in Rome. *All say Hitler is dead* – Adolf Hitler committed suicide on 30 April 1945.

May

Wednesday 2

8 a.m. Magdalen. Dearest M. How often I thought she couldn't last & she rallied, but it is so well she went when she did. Hitler's death in action announced today. It is well he is gone. Poor man, for he was great in many ways. Tonight they say peace is declared, but no fuss of any kind here. In Teac Dr. Egan giving trouble again, so I told her she would have to go at once. We could not have her upsetting everything.

Friday 11

8 a.m. S. B's, lovely day. Anniversary of the dear One's last journey. How we hoped till the last for her recovery! Now we see it was all for the best. She was not able to guide things as she used. In Teac, Matron's 1st & 2nd & Nurse O'Toole going for weekend to a new holy place near Burton Point, where "apparitions" have lately been seen. D.V.it will improve Matron 2nd. All goes fairly well there. A v. persistent rumour that Hitler is alive, in one way I hope not.

Tuesday 15

8 a.m. R.mines. I Times very false & mean about neutrality, as of before. Peace, everyone was agreed that Neutrality was the only good thing Dev. ever did! K. O'Brennan says "it's Smilies inferiority" complex. Geoff & Stella came in evg. & saw over house & garden & were pleased. They'll take piano any day now. In Teac all seems well. They were greatly thrilled with gooseberries I brought them. Got new sphygmomanometer with dear M ffM's money.[634]

June

Tuesday 5

8 a.m. R.mines, much rain in night, day dark & cloudy, warmer. Dr O'Doherty heard that Teac will likely be made entirely a T.B. hospital but D.V. D.V. no we never started with that idea & the L.G.D, must be let get away with everything. More subscriptions D.G. Churchill now is quite gone over to politics & slates his late comrades. Saw the T.B. exhibition, it is quite good. Dr Dillon recommended potatoes & herrings.[635]

---

634. *K. O'Brennan* – Kathleen O'Brennan (1876–1948), journalist and playwright. *Sphygmomanometer* – an instrument for measuring blood pressure. *Smillies inferiority complex* – Robert Smyllie (1893–1954), editor of the *Irish Times* from 1934 to 1854.
635. *Dr O'Doherty* – Rose O'Doherty, graduated NUI 1921, Honorary Visiting Physician to St Ultan's. *TB Exhibition* – a TB Exhibition ran in the Mansion House from 28 May to 8 June 1945.

Tuesday 12

8 a.m. S. B's, no rain to-day but some in night. F.F. is very uncertain about Sean T. & they try all they're worth to win votes. Reports of crops are good. That new slug stuff is splendid, but M's little larkspurs were drowned in a slug mucus. I had to lift it off in layers. Mrs S.S. says there was a fine lecture on Davis in T.C.D. & Dev. there comparison betw. Davis & O'Connell, who was vanity personified & surrounded by little men, just as Dev. is now.[636]

Tuesday 19

8 a.m. R.mines. The 4th really hot day, tho' cool breeze. I was roasting on ret at 4 & by 6.30 I was chilly, nothing cools me like aft. pts. Sean T. in of course but with no sweeping majority & on McEoin's 2nd prefs. All very uncertain in war & peace news. Japan will be tough. Had sunbath. At 3 went to Mr Scotts re the £525 wh. he had taken off a/c & then claimed. I spoke to him like a mother & when I said this would discredit M ffM he gave in at once D.G. for we had nothing in kitty.[637]

Friday 22

Late again. San Francisco conference says they have agreed on a basis for a better League of Nations. One hopes so. Sean T. is to have a triumphal entry to the Viceregal Lodge, coach & 4, silver harness & livried coachman etc. thro' decorated streets. All in such bad taste for Plebians like him & Phyllis Ryan, perhaps she'll want coronet next & then money squandered on that & Europe starves. Horrible.[638]

July

Friday 20

It is so long since I had H.D. nearly a fortnight. D.V. Sunday will bring it. Quite nice sun, but drenching showers. Had 1/2 hrs. sunbath. We made v. nice fish dish with tinned mackerel, parsley sauce & broad beans & had shape & sugar & cinnamon for 2nd course, hadn't that since Dusseldorf. Got 3 papers, Wed. Thurs. Fri., report that Hitler & his wife are in Argentine, this later denied. Dev. made real Devish

---

636. *Davis & O'Connell* – Thomas Davis (1814–45), writer and Daniel O'Connell (1775–1847), politician.
637. *Sean T. in of course* – Seán T. O'Kelly was elected President of Ireland on the second count.
638. *San Francisco conference* – United Nations Conference on International Organization held 25 April to 26 June 1945, resulted in the creation of the United Nations Charter. *Phyllis Ryan* (1895–1983), Irish chemist and nationalist, second wife of Seán T. O'Kelly.

statement about F.S. being a Republic, on all fours with Document No. 2. He has such a crooked mind.

August

Tuesday 7

8 a.m. R.mines. V. nice day, mg. cold. The U.S.& Britain have discovered a new "atomic" explosive, made by splitting the atom with uranium & have used it on Japan, result = a severe earthquake, so now there is nothing to prevent the whole world being blown up. Wonderful how God allows men to be so mad in destruction. It will never be worth while to build anything permanent or beautiful now unless God intervenes.[639]

Thursday 9

Up late again, these days are tiring. Met Emer, who is much upset over atomic bombs & says it must be the end of the age & says how frightful it is for people to say it will lead to universal peace. God's ways are beyond us, but we trust. Cleaning v. nearly finished only study & hall to do. All China is washed & places turned out I got a little done in garden.

Thursday 16

8 a.m. S. B's, busy. Canon Stringer here before I was back fr. Church, much upset, poor man. Didn't like Elpis, so I got Portobello D.G. Teac Board went well, we are to have Mr Nix & Mrs O Shea Leamy as Corp. Representatives Rained here, put quite dry up at Sandyford, saw May McMahon in her new house. D. M McArdle threw her out on July 1st & she couldn't get into new house till 4th, so had to store furniture for 3 days & baby 14 days old. D. is inhuman. Mrs Brennan got thro' Martin's ordination well on Jy. 4th Milltown.[640]

Friday 25

Poor Britain faced by serious financial crisis, for U.S. has stopped Lease-Land agreement, wh. she says was plainly stated to be only for the war. Britain says, not so. Australia v. mad not to be let into negotiations, so there's another snag. This peace business is really

---

639. *a new 'atomic' explosive* – the atomic bomb detonated over the Japanese city of Hiroshima on 6 August 1945.
640. *May McMahon*, née Coghlan, was a member of the Ranelagh branch of Cumann na mBan and had been in Kilmainham with Macardle during the Civil War.

as bad as war. What a mess the world is in. Nice day & all well here. Cement strike ended D.G

September

Monday 3

Didn't wake till 15 to 9, another nice day. The Peace all signed & delivered. The Russians coming into warmth. Japan at very end have nabbed the islands taken fr. Russia in v. old days, 40 yrs ago. They are good grabbers. MacArthur says there can never be another war, too destructive, but will anyone inclined to grab mind that? All well in Teac D.G. & Matron v. pleased things went well D.G.[641]

Tuesday 4

8 a.m. R.mines, sorry I was not in S. B's, couldn't be helped. 12 million Germans wander about starving & sick & dying & there is no provision for them, while Allied troops buy up any food there is to supplement their rations & Poles rob refugees of anything they have. England owes U.S. 50 billion 560 million & unless she can export, will be beggared & her markets are gone now & she has no raw stuff.

Thursday 6

8 a.m, a lovely day. Mrs S.S. & I went to Sean T. at the Vice Regal, the avenue has tilled fields now each side, old Polo Ground I think. He was v. nice, has promised to work things so that Madam's bust will be repaired & put into a good position. Afterwards as we saw reception rooms wh. are fine & lovely Bossi chimney pieces, old brass mounted grates as we had in Shrule ages ago. Most of evg. spent quelling reporters publishing visit.[642]

Thursday 27

Slept on. Nice day, interviewed Senator Douglas & he has promised to come on Board, but can't be v. regular. He told of Norway, where all municip. Flats have laundry attached & washing is compulsory & in Summer Municipality sends all children to the country. Oh that we could do that too. A F.F. T.D. in Galway harboured 2 of the German

641. *MacArthur* – Douglas MacArthur (1880–1964), General of the Army of the United States.
642. *Mrs S.S. & I went to Sean T. at the Vice Regal* – Seán T. O'Kelly, President of Ireland, living in the Vice Regal Lodge in the Phoenix Park, later renamed Áras an Uachtaráin. *Madam's bust will be repaired* – the bust of Countess Markievicz in St Stephen's Green had been damaged.

internees who were ordered home, poor boys, hard luck for them. Bigger & faster 'planes come daily to Collinstown.[643]

October

Sunday 7

19 A.T. 8 a.m. R.mines. The North has taken off Summer Time to-day & we are going on with it for spite, it seems. Gazette v. good on attributing bad motives to good actions = sin agst. H.G. that is true. We must not judge. John Brennan has excellent letter in it re starving German children. Many are feeling that way now D.G. Nice day, saw Miss McFerran & had long chat.[644]

Tuesday 16

8 a.m. R.mines, dull till aft. then short sunshine. Child Welf 10.30. Arrangements for Xmas Party invites to be on attendances. Eoin McNeill dead now, was same age as Madam. All are agreed that U.S & British in Deutchland are well fed & clothed & the poor Germans die of hunger. Mrs Russell says she decided to go when Miss Gilmartin restricted the fuel. She will be a v. great loss. There are always troubles in Teac.[645]

Thursday 18

8 a.m. R.mines, colder. Teac Board went well. Our financial position better D.G. We appointed Miss Hurley of Baggot St. Almoner. She was best, & Senator Douglas on Board. Board room looks so nice, a credit to Duff. Evg. went to Peace meeting on atrocities. Greenings says always were & will be while the old man is uppermost. They are keen to back up the "Save the German Child" idea D.G. One man wld take 6.[646]

Saturday 20

8 a.m. S. B's, turning to rain, Dr Murphy's letter in Times to-day. I had long talk with her. She is under Dr Mary Andrews, a new psychologist

---

643. *Senator Douglas* – James Green Douglas (1887–1954), businessman and politician. *A F.F. T.D. in Galway* – two escaped German internees from the Curragh were found in the home of Mark Killilea, Fianna Fáil TD for Galway East. *Collinstown* – now Dublin Airport.
644. *John Brennan* – Sidney Czira (née Gifford).
645. *Eoin McNeill* (1867–1945), Irish language enthusiast, Gaelic revivalist, nationalist and politician.
646. *Almoner* – Almoner was a precursor to the modern social worker. *'Save the German Child'* – the Save the German Children Society was founded on 16 October 1945 by Dr Kathleen Murphy to find foster homes for German children in Ireland.

lately come to Dublin. I hear she is excellent. D.V. the Save German Children will weather the storms & avoid pitfalls. Muriel never came & Susie & I went to concert alone, it was marvellous. Solomon is a great pianist, the music was grand. M came at 5, says I never said to come Fri, she thought concert evening.[647]

Wednesday 31

8 a.m. Magdalen, v. warm & muggy. Sean T. at Trinity & apologizing for being there! Priest in North spoke well for Unity on Dev.'s lines. Mad rush for car licences now. Russia almost has atomic secret & is happy. They say 200 German children have been sent to England. Albina in gt. form but has failed a lot. Saw Nurse O'Toole, her op. was not a complete clearing, will require X Ray. Dr O'Driscoll v. meek but responsible.[648]

November

Thursday 8

Rested in mg. Long talk with Poppy. D.G. she will stay on in Teac, she is touchy & Miss Gilmartin not like dear M ffM. How we miss her. Now some lecturer says atomic energy can blow up not only the world, but the whole solar system. I suppose in bygone times people thought & said the same about new discoveries but now surely "Men's Hearts are failing them for fear".

Thursday 15

Rested in mg. Teac Board had little of interest. Jews calling for violence to obtain what they were promised i.e. full return to Palestine, is it their time at last? Same story over & over that secret of atom energy must be shared by Allies & only used for Peace. Will US. consent to let Russia know. Had v. busy day & forgot Comt. for German Children, so sorry.

Thursday 29

Slept on, v. busy day, ending up with packed Save German Children meeting in Broadway. Many branches formed. I had charge of N. Dublin but they so scattered only individual effort possible. Certainly

---

647. *Dr Mary Andrews* – probably Dr Mary Frances Andrews, graduated NUI 1942.
648. *Sean T. at Trinity* – President Seán T. O'Kelly at Trinity College Dublin.

it has aroused gt. enthusiasm. Felt like dear M ffM after it, as if "all the stuffing was gone out of the puppy". Churchill is slating the Labour Govt. for not having done more to restore industry etc in Britain. Surely war has brought no gain.

December

Friday 14

Late after late night, hurried along & did a good deal. Hear Mrs Skeffington was overwhelmed with astonishment when she saw the acct. of her presentation, now D.V. she will be able to get a good rest & write her memoirs in peace. Tried to get Xmas things done, but there were many pts. etc. Saw Dr Webb., she has failed greatly & given up all her work but Hospital, better so.

1946

January

Saturday 5

8 a.m. S. B's, quite warm all day. Searching U.S.A. for suitable home for United Nations Soc. May it be honester than League of Nations! Miss Gilmartin says pawn shop is being sold for £5000 to another pawnbroker, but we won't despair tho' corporation won't take the flats either, we must keep aim ever before us of New Hospital. Poor little McGlynn girl has got osteomyelitis & pyremia & is terribly ill, penicillin & everything given.

Wednesday 9

How the years fly! V. wet & stormy all day & again now. In Teac long Nursing Comt. at wh. we settled all the Nurses' pay satisfactorily, I think. What a blessing it is Matron Mulligan not Dougan! Miss Cantwell gave £2 & I am giving it to Teac & the other for the Xmas Party. In News & Views I see the Palestine Police are recruited fr. Black & Tans & R.U. Constabulary & also an a/c of the luxury & plenty of the occupiers in Germany & starvation of the occupied.[649]

Saturday 19

8 a.m. S. B's, snowy like last year & hard frost all day Prof. Engel came & saw Teac & he is very nice & a truly babies Dr & so sensible. He was much pleased like Dr Kerry long ago. Evg. we had dinner for him at Shelbourne, I took Dr Murphy. It was v. nice, but Dr Mowbray, Chairman, dumb, foundered me by saying I was the person who started Paediatrics here.[650]

February

Wednesday 13

8 a.m. Magdalen, busy day. Utility meeting, deputation fr. "Charlemont Labour Council" re damp flats. Mrs Green spokesman, Grant there.

---

649. *Palestine Police are recruited fr. Black & Tans* – British Gendarmerie in Palestine began recruitment in January 1922 and most recruits came from disbanded members of the RIC and Black and Tans.
650. *Prof Engel* –Stefan Engel (1878–1968), expert in paediatric tuberculosis, joint author with Walter Pagel, of *Handbuch der Kindertuberlose,* was introduced by Pagel to Dr Stopford Price and visited St Ultan's. *Mowbray* – John Mowbray, graduated UCD 1926, Visiting Physician Children's Hospital Dublin.

Mrs Walker spoke sensibly to them. We would do what was possible & they had always alternative of getting other accommodation. Poor little Anette v. bad, nothing will take her temp. down. Many plane crashes daily now. Flu not much better. Billy here, & v. nice as usual, dear boy.

Thursday 28

A v. cold night but was all right on balcon. lovely sun. 25 Jew children flown to Belfast to Jewish settlement. In evg. heard revolution in Russia & Stalin has taken over control of army. What an uneasy world & the Peace of God over all. Libelous statements in news of the World re Hemple & our Save German Children Soc. Dr O'Sullivan will take action, he says. The unfortunate Germans must live.[651]

March

Saturday 16

Late this mg. for y.day was tiring. Teachers striking on 20th. Derrig is scandalous, such false insinuations. V. busy. Matron is wonderful now she stands up to things. She says Miss G. had letter fr. Corp. P.H. Dept about infectious certif. sent in, improperly filled & that was what Miss G spoke to Dr Breen about. How Dr B twisted that for her own purpose. Evg. talked to Pros. abt. Teac & their duty. Got one inferior 4 leaf shamrock.[652]

Thursday 21

Slept on after late night, Teac Board 11, nothing much, glad to see Mrs Nix back, she helped over bonus question. Derrig says he won't even give in to teachers tho gold wouldn't repay them for important work. Hear large altar vase stolen fr. Church here, such sacrilege. Young Sinclairs are having fireworks, thought 1st it was a shot in the lane. Interview with Dr Moorhead & Dr Murphy who had much gone off the boil fr. what she was. All amiable.

---

651. *Jewish settlement* – a group of Jewish child concentration camp survivors were brought to Millisle Farm in Co. Down. *Hemple* – Dr Eduard Hempel (1887-1972) was German Minister in Dublin, 1937–45.
652. *Derrig* – Thomas Derrig (1897–1956), Fianna Fáil Minister for Education during a bitter strike by the Irish National Teachers' Organisation lasting from 20 March to 30 October 1946. *Dr Breen* – Dr Victoria Irene Maud Breen, graduated RCSI 1943.

Thursday 28

Nice day & v. rushing. Dear Mrs Skeff. much worse I don't think she'll last too long, v. somnolent, anneuric. Did much on cycle all day. In U.N.O. the "Russian man" outvoted, left council chamber at once. Russia says she has secret of atomic energy, so they will all now be able mutually to destroy each other. Truly the world is mad, mad. S. Peter was right, 2nd Epistle 11 10-12, Then come the new heavens & earth & righteousness.[653]

April

Monday 8

Up 7.30 misty mg. We were well ready when Michael came & left our dear Glen to take up burden again. Constantia Maxwell, whom I remember as a child, back with us to R.drum. We were laden with eggs, milk, butter, all so kind. Here all had gone v. fair. Mrs Skeff. & Mrs Dowling with us still. V. busy & gt. rush to get to S. Kevin's for Paediatric meeting. Really the hosp is v. nice & children well cared for. Saw bad spina bifida etc.[654]

Tuesday 23

Nice day, M & I went for milk & then I saw Miss Lennon, we had dinner & then it was train time, good journey, found Mrs Skeffington had passed on Sat. 29th at 7 a.m. (before I left), v. busy evg. packing & seeing people. Now it is 1.30 a.m. & all is practically done D.G.

May

Wednesday 22

8 a.m. Magdalen. Warmer at long last. D.G. some sun. Derrig won't give in. I Times says v. foolish, teachers so v. important & they spend so lavishly on much less necessary things. They will have no enquiry abt. prisons either. For I.R.A. are "criminals" & mustn't dictate. Have recreation in large airy room, looking out on farm, in fact luxuriously treated! In North same holds good. Warnock says that malicious are to say prisoner beaten.

---

653. *U.N.O.* – United Nations Organisation.
654. *Constantia Maxwell* (1886–1962), historian, first woman appointed Professor at Trinity College Dublin.

Saturday 25

8 a.m. S. B's, yes dearest M & I were & are near together all day. It was a nice day, quiet rain in night, then fine & windy. The Sunshine Home meeting was very successful, they had tent & grand tea. Dr Collis just back fr. Sweden spoke v. well, aid so truly we all could do with 1/2 our amt. bread & so more cld. go to Europe. He is getting some children over, so D.V. more will come. All babies & up to 1 yr. are dying there.[655]

Friday 31

Rode cycle to-day & all well. Splendid reports in papers ect. I Times. Dr Price's B.C.G. vaccination has had a fine set off, other speakers well reported too D.G. It is a great day for Teac Ultain & we are all so proud & pleased. It was a nice day. I got brown shoes but only polishing leather to be had, no lighter make. The Aughrim twins are dears. I hope they will do well, a boy & girl & very like. Times remarks on Dev's anxity about election.

July

Friday 26

8 a.m. S. B's, G.B. Shaw is 90 to-day, paper very full of it. F. State is to join U.N.O. if it can. I Times has such a false leader, said 90 per cent of us were proBritish!!! Had taxi & got tickets etc. for Glen Jack seems weak to-day, he has had a hard time of it, not a bit anxious to get up but D.G. he is where he is. Long talk with Dr Andrews, she is a wonderful woman, so absolutely devoted to her patient's good. V. heavy rain since 6 o/c.[656]

August

Thursday 22

Nice day, didn't go out early after y.day. Jack in gt. form & down on steps as I went out D.V. he does well. Busy in mg & in aft., had such a crowd, 7 of one family, 3 babies, twins & a younger one. Evg. Save German Children. The a/c of our treat. by Red X is not nice, they want to thwart us all along. We must do some reorganising of Teac, I fear. How M ffM's influence is missed, she made all work for love.

---

655. *Dr Collis* – Robert Collis (1900–75), had worked for the Red Cross and seen the liberation of the Bergan-Belsen concentration camp. He was instrumental in bringing five orphans from the camp to Ireland in 1947 and adopted two of them.
656. *G.B. Shaw* – George Bernard Shaw (1856–1950), playwright and critic.

September

Thursday 12

Op. in mg. Dr Hill & I, Jack wanting me, had to wait till after it. He does v. well D.G. Letters fr. R.dun to him & me. Anniversary of 1st mention of "Save the German Children" & now D.G. it goes ahead & D.V. we'll have them soon. I got back my dear black pen. I felt I should, & later Bran's lost muzzel & also hairnets I had mislaid. Had to cycle, no getting into busses. Sean T & Dev to entertain the English Mr Morrison, we're "all wan" now it seems.[657]

October

Wednesday 30

8 a.m. Magdalen. Great news. Teachers' Strike over. R.C. Abp. begged them to go back for sake of the Children & they are nobly doing it. Will the mean Govt. be generous to them now? I do hope so. Machinery in laundry broken down, they work on cheerfully, a temp. motor is to be put in till our's ready. Lovely aft. Saw Frau Grabish. She is very thin but in good heart. Herr, she says, is better, but it's malig. I hear.

November

Thursday 21

8 a.m. S.B's. Had to hurry away to Teac Board at 11. We are to see about dissolving the Utility Soc. & taking over flats. Mrs McGloughlin says we must make tenants pay rates when they can. Would it be practicable? A v. busy day with all. Dr Barry has left Peamount, resigned & can now have more time for us. Evg. Save German Children Council. Went well. It has been gt. encouragement that convention.[658]

December

Tuesday 10

8 a.m. R.mines, milder & foggy late mg. No further news of Sugar strike. Child Welf. 11. An assistant for Dr Reddin advertised for she knows nothing of it. The Corporation are as autocratic as the Govt. News & Views says Spain is the last stronghold of Xtianity & France it's saviour according to Jesuits. England, U.S. etc = Freemason wh. = Communism wh. = negation of all religion. Matron & Nurse O'Toole back fr. Kellystown, they had terrible weekend, out 2 nights in rain, praying.

---

657. *English Mr Morrison* – Herbert Morrison (1888–1965), British Labour politician.
658. *Peamount* – Peamount TB Sanatorium.

1947

January

Tuesday 14

8 a.m. R.mines, v busy, couldn't do Child Welf. Scotts v. contented & happy D.G. They are eating horseflesh & swans in England. Here turf ration cut by half, trains only 4 days a week. Milk to be rationed, cream only for butter. Sugar 6d a lb. At Miss Jackson's funeral Mt. Jerome at 2 o/c. Many hotel guests there. We all liked her so Dear Jackson looks v. old & bad. Poor Charlie was so sad, dear boy, it was his 1st day to work. V. stormy now again.

Friday 17

Late again, when will I be a bit frisky in mgs! I have been at it so hard ever since Xmas. To-day busy too. Churchill launching a new United States of Europe v, good if it will work Many good people on the Committee. It didn't rain all day & there was sun. Such a relief! Taxi man asked if I'd be long, he had had no dinner. Geoff came said Pat & Ronald with them at 7 p.m. she only out of Nursing Home this aft. & they left new baby & other 2 alone in house.

February

Saturday 1

Another bitter day, wind S.E. & very cold, thawing slowly. Going all day in taxi, costing 46/- Went to Larkin's lying in state. He had a tumour they say. The R.C. Abp. visited him, so glad he returned to religious observances after lapse of years. Saw young Jim, not much of a man. I remember Emer fetching him Maundy Thurs 1916 fr. S. Enda's & sending him North for safety. Very stormy now.[659]

Friday 21

More & more snow, but not colder. V. hard to travel. Robin D.G. better. In Teac a spate of dying prems. born on Districts, no fires in poor houses, one dead on admission on 19th, another twin on 20th & it's little brother just dead now. 2 more sets still (one pair born 3 a.m.

---

659. *Larkin's lying in state* – James Larkin died on 30 January 1947. *Young Jim* – Larkin's son, James Larkin Junior (1904–69), labour politician and trade union activist.

to-day) are almost gone. It is terrible for v. old & v. young. Jack quite upset over them all. Poor Poppy in bad way too, the 27th day of cold.

Monday 24

S. Mathias. 8 a.m. R.mines. V. slippery, fetched F. Clarke, she is v. brave. Fuel situation same. Lemass blathered to-night of turf, turf & never mentioned that there was such a thing as Irish coal, imported coal can't be counted on he says. Concentrate on turf. Teac has had 11 twins in last week. 2 dead on arrival & 5 of the 9 dead now. Worse & worse a/cs of Germany & in London 2 old women found frozen in bed & women & children wait for coke fr. 7 a.m. to 7.30 a.m.

April

Wednesday 16

This day month was blizzard of floods. To-day nice & no rain. I put out my n. dress on balcon. & in a moment or 2 it was gone, no trace of it, sudden strong gust. Found it other side of road later. Michael came & we went to Cullentra to tea, all v. nice there & they are well. Gt. a/cs of all the snow & hardship but they had fuel. They are hard hit with bread rationing, some people are days without bread, ration not nearly enough. Happy day.

Thursday 24

8 a.m. S. B's after weeks of absence, only Sr. Mary & I there, lovely sun. Thinking much of this day 31 yrs ago. Went to Ceilidh in Mansion Ho. in evg. felt like a ghost fr. the Past, so few there I knew. Many young folk wh. is good. Lately released prisoners there, someone made quite a good speech, stressing our want of freedom but is there any freedom now in this distracted world? At Save German Children earlier, quite good.[660]

May

Friday 2

8 a.m. R.mines, nice sun, strong cold E. wind. 1st Fri. went well. Poor little scrap in Teac we all say acute obstruction, but Mr Stokes says not surgical & there we are! D.V. she will recover. Running a temp too. Went to T.B. Assoc. Meeting, it was v. good. Drs Todd & McPhail over

660. *Ceilidh* – Irish dance.

fr. England, were excellent. McPhail started in Gaelic & we all clapped. We spoke of Rehabilitation & was v. good & human, insisted Drs must gain confidence of pt to do any good.

Monday 19

8 a.m. S. B's, another lovely day, had to fetch meat, butcher has no messenger now. Nothing doing, plenty to do, in Teac good news. Hosp. Commis. practically promises expenses of Dr Steen & Dr Alston to Paediatric Congress New York. God & S. Ultan did that. Evg. met Mrs Mangan & Mrs McCarron to settle up Cosgrave Memorial & D.V. it will soon be audited & finished. Curry did gt. job on Sighle's garden & got manure for us wh. I knew not of.

Friday 23

Dear MffM's Memorial Mass was at 9 in Whitefriar St. Fr Devlin, a good many old friends there. Emer I was glad to see & Mrs Bennett, she gave me a copy of Ruth's novel on Mrs Siddons, v. readable, so far. Many more old friends too. Hear Temple St. v. mad because they were not told we were applying for funds to send Delegates to N. York. D.V. it will smooth but Miss Hopton Scott here. She is nice old thing of 83. A lovely sunny day D.G.

June

Wednesday 25

8 a.m. Magdalen, another v. full day. Med Board 10.30 we discussed Dr Collis ideas & say we are competent to diagn. Diarrh. as well or better than he. Then Utility at 11.30. We appointed a Mr Bennett sec.& Molloy caretaker by the week. D.V. both will work well, the sec. seems competent. About 3 went to Lett & signed Will, so glad to have that off my mind. Planted Tagetes & hope they do well. V. busy here aft. & evg. Had interview about Kent baby.

July

Tuesday 8

Up abt. 7, to get Cury's b.fast. It rained plenty in night & to-day warmer, tho' drenching showers & some thunder. In many parts of U.S. & Canada saucerlike object seen in sky, going at 300 to 1300 miles an hour & 10,000 ft. high, no one knows what they are. Prob some Russian new thing invented by their German prisoners. Baked all mg. & made biscuits wh. are good. Willie came in evg. & is v. nice.

August

Wednesday 13

Waked 8 o/c, another lovely, hot day. Utility Soc. 11.30, Young Mr Walker there, he is a pup & very fond of making difficulties in the way of winding up the Society & I don't believe it amounts to so much after all. Then pts. etc. Hear poor Mr Taylor our nice A & D man is v. bad in Baggot St. The world goes on in its godless futility. When will they learn sense? Dr Grabish dead, must have turned R.C. Frau doesn't realise it at all.

Friday 15

8 a.m. S. B's, a Feast there = Repose of B.V.M weather lasts D.G. Did Dispensary, 1st time since June 27th India passed to Indians at 12 o/c y.day. Marvellous rejoicings Hindus & Mohamadans rejoice together D.G. Egypt will be next. Saw Gertie Haughey & the Dr. He looks old. She v. well. They're off to England to-morrow. Jack had letter fr. Raymond wh. he didn't show me. Perhaps Geoff read it for him.[661]

Wednesday 20

Another grand day. Paper full of appalling explosion in Lisbon, whole poor quarter of town near docks wiped out. Dead & dying everywhere. I rode to see Mrs Hamilton at Temple Hill & she had sent message y.day to ask me not to come. Went on to Dean's Grange. It must be ages since I was there, the grass was in seed & so dry, pulled it up easily. Grannia's & Aunt F's graves quite tidy.

Thursday 21

8 a.m. Xt. Ch the sexton welcomed me back not so warm. Teac Board went well. Dr Russell there, he will be helpful D.G. knows the LG.D. inside out & is cautious Save German Children did much. Dr Murphy & I are to send circular to Drs & hospitals for the appalling need in German Childrens hospitals. Saw old I.C.A. friend, Mrs [Chaney] who insisted on my going to see her husband who lives near my pt.

---

661. India and Pakistan were given independence from British rule at midnight on 15 August 1947.

September

Tuesday 30

8 a.m. R.mines. It was cold in night & only 50 in mg. Warmed after. Hear big shops are to dismiss their hands on Sat are not taking in £5 a week. The Oslo Dr says Dr Price must have her B.C.G inject. & will send prefabricated house for it. D.V. he'll succeed. Long visit to Dr Murphy who is suffering from nicotine poisoning abt. 40 cigs a day for 33 yrs. Lovely warm sun.[662]

October

Monday 6

8 a.m. S. B's, so good to be there & D.G. We managed Dr O'Doherty & had her car put safe under Coffeys & so God showed us the way to keep M ffM's garden in front of Teac & not have it car park & other things went well too. Evg. supper in Harrison's to meet Sec of Reconciliation Fellowship. He works on Save Europe now princples & is good. Then to Cadram Protestunach. We had good meeting & had done much. Told then babies must hear Irish fr.very start.

Saturday 11

Rested in mg. another beautiful warm day. Many to go to. All well in Teac, how I miss dear M ffM on a Sat. Office closed, all gone by 1 o/c so diff. MffM always stayed & worked in peace Sat. aft. & was as late as usual for dinner. Banks have settled back. Geoff much relieved but overwrought & nervy still. John came in aft. & said good bye & after dinner I went & saw Geoff & brought [Passcorine] for him.

Thursday 30

Rested & felt so to-day. Cold but nice sun. So many accidents & loss of life on all sides & accounts of further horrors & starvation & missing in Germany & Cent. Europe Really the bombing of Germany seems as bad as Hiroshima in its thoroughness. Poor Nurse Connolly sent off with Diphth. It is too bad & one of the Immune Globalin babies has measles now, so that doesn't protect either.[663]

---

662. *The Oslo Dr* – Johannes Heimbeck (1892–1976), Norwegian physician who introduced BCG vaccination programme in 1926.
663. *Immune Globalin babies* – Immunoglobulin (antibodies) given to babies in an attempt to protect them from measles.

Friday 31

8 a.m. S. B's. Nice, cold day, some sun. Sean McBride got in & Tipp. man too & F.F. lost heaps of 1st preferences, it's well they should be a bit shook!! Of course, Dev. always thought no one could do anything but himself. They think if Clann cld get enough to hold the balance it wld. be excellent. Geoff & Stella voted for Sean. G. thinks him honest. D.V. it is so. Hallow Eve children everywhere.[664]

November

Wednesday 5

8 a.m. Magdalen. Mr Waring back at last D.G. nice day. Met B & we did a lot, are to see about teaching for D.C. & P. Drs Alston & O'D we appointed Dr Barbara Stokes, Clinical Asst. & are to [beard] Dr Deeney to B.C.G. again. Saw pts. Another letter fr. John saying he is cared for well D.G. & Muriel wrote back still bad, afraid of hurting it. I fear Jane is not pleased John is coming but D.G. Mary is charmed.[665]

Tuesday 11

8 a.m. R.mines, v. stormy night & day & pouring now & wild but warm. Nursing Comt.went well. We accepted Sr Kearn's resignation & made Nurse Hogan T.B. sister & Sr Houlihan in Sr Kearn's place & a new Night Sr. to be got. I went to Dr Taylor who says waterlogging of my legs esp. left fr. standing, capilliary stasis of ankles. I am to have much Benerva (of course) & Thyroid later.

Thursday 19

Rested. Wrote etc. saw pts. In Teac by 12.30, finished up there & was off to Bureau of Mil. History at 2.30, saw v. unimposing oldish man there, v. prosy. Didn't get far but he lent questionaire with many caveats. I am to show it to Emer. I didn't feel called on to make statement. Evg. Trades Council. T.B. meeting Proposal is to make levy on workers & build sanatoria & support them.[666]

---

664. two by-elections were held in October 1947, Seán MacBride (1904–88), won in Dublin County and Patrick Kinane (1892–1957), won in Tipperary both for Clann na Poblachta.

665. *Dr Barbara Stokes* (1922–2009), paediatrician and disability campaigner, Stokes remained at St Ultan's until it closed in 1984 and was responsible for the transfer of the archives to RCPI. *Dr Deeney* – James Deeny (1906–94), Chief Medical Adviser for Ireland.

666. *Bureau of Mil. History* – Bureau of Military History was established in January 1947 to allow individuals record their own experiences of the fight for Irish independence.

December

Friday 12

Jack better, off to Sale & pts. Jews & Arabs at it hard, no Peace there in partition. Sale, stalls good but tea room nothing done. I brought urn & cups & saucers, the head lady was useless. At 3 urn not even on. 2 rings with teapots to boil water! Lord Mayor v. good. Gave me money for Teac. Any amt. of stuff & no room to show it. Crowds there D.V. it will make well. Jack nicely this evg. [667]

Thursday 18

Late again, after late night. All distant parcels off but one. Teac Board, Dr Russell there & most useful D.G., we have him. 4.15 interview with Dept. re B.C.G hut. Dr Price v. pleased. We think they will do what we ask. They are quite nice. Mr Scott there, he says Anthony & baby 1 1/2 so they grow. The T.Bs painted Xmas cards for us & gave me 2. I fear they will miss poor Bran. Sally home & v. big & fine. Saè G. Children, we told off Mrs Rapple a bit.

---

667. *Lord Mayor* – John McCann (1905–80), Lord Mayor of Dublin.

1948

January

Wednesday 7

The day of the Gift Party, I was 1st there, then Min. Mulcahy, saw about handcart to bring things down. All v. well under weight, then Med. Board went v. well D.G. then back to R.mines, a fine young McCulloch there minding things, all went smoothly D.G. & we got thro' by 4.30, almost all were pleased. Then many were in evg. Cold day but dry D.G. & D.G. to have party safely over.[668]

Tuesday 27

8 a.m. R.mines, F.Clarke had many tales of wind & rain. Mlle Faurer wrote for my Birthday & Susie & F.C. brought presents, so kind. Sean McB had v. good letter in I. Times re how when free, we might be very friendly with Britain, but like Canada etc. must be free fr. sterling. English have bought £10,000 worth of land fr. us, then not pleased, we with inflation as result. All set for McCabes' coming on 29th.

Saturday 31

Wld have liked to be early but so stormy, managed later to ride a bit. Poor Gandhi was shot at close range by a Hindu of 35 when going to Prayer Meeting, supported by his arms on shoulders of 2 grand daughters. Whole world grief stricken. The Friends are to have Commemoration Service in Eustace St. on 3rd. Made chaircover for study & did many other things.[669]

February

Wednesday 4

The Election day & I can't go voting. They sent for me before time & I was reading & not quite ready. It wasn't bad at all. The [ ] hurt but not much. There was bony growth just below skin, he removed piece fr. both phalinges & left toe so Mary will be happy. Not much pain all

---

668. *Min Mulcahy* – Mary 'Min' Mulcahy, née Ryan (1884–1977), member of Cumann na mBan, wife of Richard Mulcahy.
669. *Poor Gandhi* – Gandhi was assassinated on 30 January 1948 by Hindu Nationalist Nathuram Godse (1910–49).

day, often worse going about. Quite comfortable & ready for food. D.G. D.G. for all.

Saturday 14

This anniversary was like this day 46 yrs ago, yellow crocuses etc. gt. growth, grand sun. They say Sean McBride all right if he can control his followers, who, like the rest, will be out for soft jobs & forget their country, v. true. We were out on Navan Rd. on verge of country, lovely. All well in Teac. Hope Lord Mayor may be able to do something to get us leave to send help to Germany.

Monday 23

Snow almost gone in mg. quite now. Not much news. New Gov. busy Nat. Health Insurance Strike settled by Norton. Some nice sun. Evg. Paediatric meeting discussed teaching & left us out altogether. I shld have spoken but alas, [ ] me. Ideas quite good, a joint teaching Comt. to arrange for all those seeking instruction.[670]

March

Tuesday 2

8 a.m. R.mines. My 1st night on balcon. for ages & ages. Had a most mixed & uncomfortable dream. Mg. was lovely, then fog, then warm rain. Nice busy day. Albina wants me to join some staunch Republican Cuman & alas! it seems now that the West must unite & fight (by trusting God, we say) against the [Russian] if the Papers say true, wh. is v doubtful. Made pillowcases.

Wednesday 3

8 a.m. Magdalen, took specimen for Dr Taylor first. A most lovely mg. in Teac, babies out by 9 o/c D.G. Med. Board 12. We arranged to have a Session for Postgraduates for short term after Easter D.G. D.G. we are making a start at teaching. God arranged for us to have Dr Stokes on Board. She has all teaching requirements at her finger tips. Letter fr. John in great heart starting D.V. to-day so rejoiced his long waiting times is over.

---

670. *Nat. Health Insurance* – the 1948 Social Welfare Act. *Norton* – William Norton (1900–63), Minister for Social Welfare.

Thursday 18

John not up to much all day, v. restless & cold etc. Teac Board went well D.G. & Dr Russell so glad we are to teach. Letter fr Cowan Solr. for Sinn Fein funds case, wanting me to go to a conference at Four Courts at 11. I rang & said I couldn't, then had to go at 2.30 was brought in to the Court by a porter who had been at Dr McNabb's gunrunning when stuff was dumped here delighted to see me.[671]

April

Tuesday 20

Rainy mg. John better D.G. wrote in mg. After dinner went to Dublin by bus fr. Jameson's corner. Saw Teac & got butter, they have no maids now but Kitty, but they're coming. Rushed to No. 9, found I had forgotten my keys & couldn't get all I wanted, gave primroses to Mrs Burns. Jack, Miss White & F. Clarke & caught 6 bus back. John all right. Dev.'s evidence quite good in S.F. case. He can't deny his letters etc.

Saturday 24

This day 32 yrs ago! It was beautiful like this. I went by 12.20 bus to Town for Alex. Coll Guild Conference. Mrs Davidson, who is here, is an old Alexandra girl, of 20 yrs ago & would have come if she had thought about it. She says her invitation went to Australia. Her husband is Australian & is only over here about 10 days, she & the children longer. Saw plenty of old friends & had nice time. Frances Woodside etc.

May

Friday 7

8 a.m. S. B's, 1st Friday. In Four Courts all day, tried to do my fast, but felt so faint had to have chocs. & then lunch in Teac, it was very tiring. D.V. I'm done with it now. The new (1934) constitution is ridiculous saying S.F. must not associate with any but Republicans as if one could live without associating with them! The membership is now about 100, the Sec said. I was there till 3.30. I was very tired, but got through D.G.

---

671. *Sinn Féin Funds case* – Sinn Féin President Margaret Buckley took legal action against the State in 1941, to recover the funds that had been lodged in the Free State Courts two decades earlier in 1925. *Dr McNabb* – probably Dr Hugh John McNabb, graduated UCD 1899.

Thursday 13

Nice day, my new jumper came, it is beautifully knit & smart. Dr Barry says we must have Mass for dear M ffM, nice of her. Got aft. pts. done in good time & went with K. O'Brennan's funeral to Beechwood. Met Bob Henry who is very keen on getting Broe's statue of Madam for the Green. John came back fr. R.mines more dead than alive, took an hour to walk it. temp. 11.4, better with bed & whiskey.

Thursday 20

Teac Board 11. D.G. went well. We sealed a resolution calling on members of Utility Soc. to dissolve who will force their hand i.e. Solrs, Mrs O'Shea = [ ]Leamy there, v. delighted with our Report. Project to make a balcon. for South Wing wh. has no sunshine roof now. Nice letter fr. Lal & snaps of christening of Elizabeth. They are off to a farm now. John v. well & Jack but in front again. Lovely sun, coldish N wind.

Thursday 27

The Annual meeting day. All went very smoothly & everyone did their best & I never was so little tired after one. The speakers all came & spoke v. well, Dr Catharine O'Brien, Senator Douglas, Dr Ite Brady (whom dear M ffM couldn't stand) the Lord Mayor & Dr Alston. Dr Barry chaired it very well indeed & spoke nicely of the Staff. It all went with a swing D.G The new jet propelled plane circled Dublin at 10 miles a minue.[672]

June

Thursday 17

Rested this mg. Teac Board went well, sealed Utility Soc. deed of surrender. Went to Cerise's op. Mr Stokes did colostomy but so far nothing has come through wh. to me is very disquieting. Dr O'Doherty rang Drs Price & Alston v. insistent that all waiting T.Bs should be admitted at once. I must consult Dr Moorehead about it. These days are very unrestful but God sends trials & we must face them.[673]

---

672. *Dr Catharine O'Brien,* Chief Schools Medical Officer County Borough Dublin. *Dr Ite Brady* – Dr Ita Dymphna Brady, graduated NUI 1923.
673. *Utility Soc. Deed of surrender* – the social housing built and operated by the St Ultan's Hospital Utility Society were transferred to Dublin Corporation.

Friday 18

8 a.m. S. B's, went for strength for much perturbed by Dr O'Doherty's a/c of Dr Price & Dr Alston, says they threaten us unless we give in about T.B. pts. & have Teac exclusively for them–am seeing Dr Moorhead about it on Mon. Evg. went with Susie to "The best years of our lives" it was good & true to life, the men in it are v. like John, unreasonable often & pettish & then v. nice.[674]

Wednesday 23

8 a.m. Magdalen. Hear Mr Waring better D.G. bad breakdown this time. It was good to be in Church with the Med. Board before me & difficulties to face. We arranged all amicably. If T.Bs come in the Dr in whose cots they are will be responsible for them & Drs Murphy & Alston must stick to their 3 each. I was so thankful all went well. Dr Stokes is v. valuable, she is a gogetter, a pusher perhaps. Everyone seems pleased with new Trade agreement.

August

Thursday 19

Walked dear Bran down to Teac, took 40 mins, alas! The Board went well, no quorum, but we did all necessary. Took Bran round garden & he tried to get over low wall but couldn't. Took him to Lamberts & had to leave home after 4. Lambert says malig. somewhere & he shld. be put to sleep. I felt I couldn't part with him so soon & then, what's the use of prolonging it! So I saw him & said good bye & he'll go to sleep to-morrow.

September

Monday 13

8 a.m. S. B's longed that dear F. Clarke shld. be at rest & she is. Matron rang, she passed on abt. 12 o/c last night D.G. She was brought to the Church abt. 5 o/c & I begged the coffin might be at Chancel steps & the Canon allowed it D.G. Teac sent flowers & I sent a Cross. Funeral to be on Wed. to Dean's Grange. A fairly busy day. Teac nicely tho' short of staff now. D.V. all will go well to-morow with Dr Brown's visit.[675]

---

674. *'The best years of our lives'* – 1946 film directed by William Wyler, about three US Servicemen re-adjusting to societal changes and civilian life after World War 2.
675. *Dr Brown* – Noël Browne (1915–97), physician and politician, as Minister for Health 1948–51 he waged a war against tuberculosis in Ireland.

October

Friday 8

A nice busy day. County Council Elections' results in. Mrs Mulvey headed the poll & Dockrell in in D.L. Talk of War of course. Poor John lost for something to do. If only I could keep him busy out! Mary & he don't get on & she talks of leaving, but D.V. I have persuaded her not to mind him.[676]

Wednesday 20

Rested in mg. Busy day, out & some in. Some poor girl found dead in the Green, murdered or suicide, found by keepers in mg. Horrors multiply. So glad to hear dear Miss Scarlett left £100 to our Irish Church & S. Finians. A nice tho. breezy day. Got a good blow at Balally D.G. John went to Dr McConnell, Ely Place, he seems a bit of a quack. He had never heard of me or Teac, so goes fame. Muriel getting electric light.

Friday 29

8 a.m. S B's wind not so cold D.G.D.G. Dr Barry & I interviewed Mr Doran 10.95 re Miss Gilmartin's salary. They think increment of £25 to £500 wld. be all right & she is pleased now. Mr Doran said they knew nothing of 7 yr or 10 yr plan & he didn't think Archepiscopal influence was accountable for our not being mentioned. Says International Hosp. Congresses are being revived & I am to write to him saying how useful they are.

November

Thursday 4

8 a.m. Xt. Ch. v. stormy night & windy day. Trueman in & with good majority. John came with me around. Nice sun.Evg. Save German Children convention went well. Dr O'Sullivan & I are made Vice Presidents & new Lord Mayor President. Matron wonders where Dr Murphy got money to send Fergus & Isolde abroad.[677]

---

676. *Mulvey headed the poll & Dockrell in in D.L.* – M. Mulvey, Fine Gael and H. P. Dockrell, Fine Gael.
677. *Trueman* – Harry S. Truman (1884–1972), was re-elected President of the United States in November 1948.

Monday 8

8 a.m. S. B's beautifully sunny day. Dr Browne is really unfair to Med. Profession & blames us for high death rate & because all have not v. best attention & really we have always done all possible for poor in hospitals etc.& only in govt. controlled places were they neglected. Dr Abrahamson said truly we weren't responsible for housing, feeding, resting the people. At Avoca Sale & saw all 3 v. well D.G. John's pleased.[678]

Friday 12

Up late, full day enough. Big Dispensary. Eight poor souls lost in fog landing at Liverpool, had been here & in I of Man, visitors. Matron off to see sick sister, long weekend. Teac nicely. Papers are so full of fighting & unrest, that it is horrid to read them. Town decorated. The man fr. Bureau of Military History came & was delighted to get file of 1916 Catholic Bulletins. He is to see Mr Mahon & hear War News Sheets.

Saturday 27

The Republic bill goes on. McEntee seems determined to throw all the mud he can at those who stole F.F. thunder. Lodged money in Bank, hurried to Teac, had lunch early & got the 1.30 bus to Firhouse, had long visit to Pearl who looks fat & well & really had little to say about her health. Poppy came to dinner & to talk about her friends & spirituality. D.V. I helped her a bit.

December

Saturday 4

Rested in mg. Then long round fr. 10.30 till 5. Saw Mrs Mellows & heard graphic account of raids, esp. the one before Liam was done in when British officer held pistol to her chest & gave her so long till he fired, 3 chances. She said Damn you! Shoot & he said you're a brave woman. We have white robed Nun now learning Almonering in Teac, the scalded baby progresses D.G. It was lovely bracing day. Poppy planting bulbs in Teac. I felt I'd love to garden too. Gossiped with Dr Hill in evg.[679]

---

678. *Dr Abrahamson* – Dr Leonard Abrahamson (1896–1961), Cardiologist, leader of the Jewish community in Dublin.
679. *Mrs Mellows* – Sarah Mellows née Jordan (1865–1952), mother of Liam Mellows (1892–1922), revolutionary, socialist and anti-treaty republican.

Thursday 16

Lovely day, no rain now 2 days. Teac Board, read many letters & passed cheques, over £2,000 this month & our overdraft is £10,000 odd. All the same we go on fearlessly, many tinies, little Michael's temp is now 96.4 up over 8 degrees D.G. How did he lie with so low a temp? Nurse Knox has given notice, she is over anxious & so many others the reverse. Save German Children all full of arrangements for Sale.

1949

January

Friday 7

8 a.m. S. B's. D.G. got thro 1st Friday v. well indeed. Was so tired last night went to bed & not to Save German Children Comt. Hear the Carol singers brought in over £80, excellent. Big dispensary & then round of visits. V. wet. Mrs Dillon is starting the work on Mon. & Mary has cleared out all almost fr. bird's room & caboosh, mostly only fit for jumble. Wet in aft. I do feel my back so tired but D.G. leg is better tho' still I walk badly, getting old.

Wednesday 26

A v. full day, E.S.B. inspector came early & says we are to wire up & he'll pass it or not Things are nearly finished now in kitchen. Pts. to see & shopping for W.Point etc. Quite forgot I was to meet Dr Price at Teac till too late, but she came later & says there may be a scheme for having us [seat] of H.Q. for B.C.G in Ireland if we approve. I think it would be good for us & them. V. busy here aft. & evg. & Dean Kelly came & painted dresser.[680]

Thursday 27

A full day, long round in mg. Early dinner, fairly busy aft. Save German Children evg. Dr Price told how Govt. can grant money to float companies but could not give it for financing B.C.G. vaccination here. How many concerns are financed by Govt. money, I wonder. At Save G.C. meeting some were v. worried because money given to Salvation Army in Berlin & were convinced it would be used for proselytising, Rome never did so!!!!

February

Monday 14

8 a.m. S. B's. felt I must go. Not v. lovely, 47th anniversary. V. mild T. 56 & crocuses etc in blow. Insurance people surprised we hadn't

---

680. *E.S.B.* – Electricity Supply Board. *H.Q. for B.C.G in Ireland* – The National BCG Committee was established by Noël Brown in 1949 to expand BCG Vaccination in Ireland, it was based in St Ultan's Hospital.

dismissed Nurse Mangan at once. Should we? The kitchen done at last. Dr Taylor says all Govt. rotten. Where are the Sweep funds? If Govt. has them, where is interest on the? Where did Dev. get that sum of money he gave British in '39 or so, it never appeared in Budget.

Tuesday 15

Teac Board went well. We appointed Sean O'hUadaigh solr. & that was well done, I think. Our Audit shows our deficit down to about £900 a great drop due to more paid for pts. & a full house all the year. No epidemics D.G, Poor Dr Alston's coat stolen fr. rack on stairs & a Nurse had one taken fr. her room lately. Thieving rampant. Sean McBride seems to be taking the lead in his sect. of small nations. He is so [ ], God keep him straight.

March

Wednesday 2

Ash Wed. 8 a.m. R.mines, Very few people had ashes on foreheads today, hear Priests won't let be taken fr. Chapel & people never could all wait to get it = reason. Bright but v. cold. Med. Board went well. Dr Murphy's not been in since Jan. so we must let Dr O'D act instead. Dr Stokes wants to do minor surgery, good. Had long talk with Dr Moorhead. he says we were right not to dismiss Nurse Mangan, a gt. relief to Matron. Miss G & me. Sr Farrell troublesome.

Wednesday 23

A busy day. J & I got chair for Ann 37/6 but strong & shabby. Then Sandyford etc. In Teac nothing but accounts of how trained Nurses won't work, even those we thought well of. God does give us hard time & no M ffM to cheer us thro & Dr O'Doherty says she won't lecture Post Graduates! What's coming over them all! Ernest Guinness dead at Knockmaroon, he was 71 & a generous man.

Thursday 31

A v. full day. Brought my black case full of Easter Week & after mementoes to The Xtian Brother Superior in N. Richmond St. Schools. He is very keen on such & was delighted with all I brought. Many pts. too. In Teac Sr Farrell has left, she was heartbroken at the last & wept copiously. If only she had shown us some consideration which she when she was here, but Matron says she found fault to the last.

April

Monday 11

7.30 a.m. R.mines, busy blustery day. Saw Herr Kohling, he is wonderful, considering but they don't want him to know his condition. Hear the Meath Election was surely planned, so many got 38 votes, they must have had arranged. Our Dr Stokes says her uncle is so depressed over it & it was dreadful for him to be turned down by a parcel who had just bought votes to oust him & his tradition, but such things bring their own punishment.[681]

Monday 18

Easter Monday., The day of the Declaration of the Republic & except for a few flags & some wearing the colours, there were only the official celebrations. I went to nothing & Sally said there were crowds but no excitement at all. How differently we pictured it in 1916. I thought something like the Eucharistic Congress with crowds in the Park, all in Gaelic costumes & singing last verse of Breastplate

Monday 25

A cold, bright, showery day. In mg. sl. sleet on high part but nice, it was. I got washing done & dry. Later showers were worse. A nice, glennish day. Cold now. Dr Price wrote Mr Sheehan of L.G.D. has scheme on that Teac shall be national Centre for B.C.G. sounds good & D.V. it is so. Certainly, Dr Price is pioneer & shld have running of it. Off at 9. D.V. to wedding.

May

Monday 9

8 a.m. S. B's 1st time I was there on a Mon. for ages but wanted help for Teac. Dr Price, Miss Gilmartin & I went & saw Minister at 11.30, had to wait 1/2 hr. Things went well but Teac Board will have to be responsible for working of Scheme. Dr Price thought the Comt. shld be but no. We'll have to see Sean O'Huey about it. Fine day but we long for rain Marjorie here & had tea with John in kitchen.

---

681. *Meath Election* – Election at the Meath Hospital Joint Committee on 4 April 1949, many Protestant members of the former Joint Committee lost their seats, including Henry Stokes ('our Dr Stokes' uncle'). It was generally considered that a takeover had been planned for some time, originating with the Knights of St Columbanus. The Hospital, although listed as non-denominational, had been Protestant administered and had a reputation for discriminating against Catholics for appointments.

Thursday 19

8 a.m. Xt. Ch. to pray all might do well at Board & it did. We passed resolution agreeing to carry out Ministers' wishes & sponsor B.C.G Project for Ireland. D.V. we'll do our duty. Matron's resignation accepted with much regret. Things do seem to be advancing & we know & feel how dear M ffM is helping us. Now for my lecture, Annual Meeting & Sunshine Home Annual Meeting.

June

Wednesday 1

A much more restful day D.G.& I am not so "dead" to-night. Dr Browne has announced his new B.C.G. plan already, he was to have kept it for our opening of new wing. Med. Board went well. Dr Murphy there & so thin, poor creature, she says things are no easier even yet. We are to have old Xray room for Drs room & coffee provided in mgs. There was some thunder & lightening this aft. & big showers. Saw Miss Gilmartin much better.

Monday 20

The day of the opening of the new B.C.G. Unit, it was a lovely day & I more or less forgot about it & had to settle up as well as I could . None of those I expected came. Meeting went with great eclat, lots there & all very pleased. Dr Browne spoke so well & nicely about Dr Price & her European fame. It was a day to be proud of & Mr Doran so nice & pleasant & all seemed propitious D.G.

Wednesday 29

S. Peter 8 a.m. R.mines, back to sun & N.E. wind, alas for crops. We are getting a man cook in Teac. I think it will be quite good, he was in the Army, that is 3 men now employed. Got things done by degrees, lorry came & took heavy things. Man came & lifted linoleum in kitchen. John arr. safe & I had never said he was going. Trains changed, we go by 10.30 fr. Harcourt St. not 9 a.m. W.R. much better.

July

Thursday 21

8 a.m. Xt. Ch. D.G to be there, a v. full day. Board went well & we had all arranged as we thought about Miss Hurley being Sec. of B.C.G. Comt. & Dr Price agreed & then the B.C.G. Comt. at 2.15 wouldn't

agree at all & wants separate sec, tho under Miss Gilmartin. It is all hard to arrange, I felt nearly addled. Went to No. 9 & got things, lovely peas & spinach in garden. Saw Jack, Poppy, talking to him happily. Then rush for train back.

August

Monday 8

A nice day, my 1st pt. day, all went well & John is in gt. form seeing after wire for outside steps etc. He seems v. well & talked a lot over 4,000 dead in earthquake S. America, a whole mountain removed into a river. In Teac Miss Gilmartin on my advice, is to advt. for Assist. Sec. She must get her holiday, she has had such a hard time with Mother's illness & extra work. Matron leaving very soon, alas!

September

Saturday 10

In I. Times Dr Chisholm, a Canadian, said at Conference of World Peace Organizations that there is a new Biological product, 7 oz of wh. is sufficient to wipe out the whole of mankind & that it will happen unless we stop aggression i.e. turn to God for one war would kill 90% of life on the earth. A nice, quiet day, got a lot of clothes for Germany. Nurse Brophy, an old Teac girl came, wanting comfort & help.[682]

Thursday 15

Busy day. Teac Board 11, went well, they approve of Miss Rynne, new under Sec & Dr Stumpf who has worked wonders in her domain. B.C.G. Comt. 2.15 only Dr Price fr. Corp. & myself at it, they discussed technique etc. Save German Children v. thrilling, German ship Captain, 1st officer & Mate came, such nice men & told of shops full of stuff & no money to buy it. We allowed them £10 for food for their children. I gave 1 st. sugar & butter.[683]

October

Monday 10

They came early to fix roof & found cracked slate. D.V, it'll be all right now. Dr Edith Somerville of Somerville & Martin Ross dead, she was

---

682. *Dr Chisholm* – George Brock Chisholm (1896–1971), psychiatrist, World War 1 veteran and first director-general of the World Health Organisation.
683. *Dr Stumpf* – Dr Robert Stumpf, graduated Apothecaries Hall 1924.

an artist too & horse breeder. Got Mrs Berry into Portobello this evg. D.V., she'll do better away fr. Elsie & she'll get a rest. Didn't get parcel off to Berlin yet but it is ready now. Soft, mild day.[684]

November

Tuesday 8

8 a.m. R.mines, not so cold. Child Welf. 11, stayed till after 12, then to Bank & lodged a good deal D.G. to get it out of here, shopped, did Teac quickly but had to have taxi to Military Hist. interview. I stayed over an hour but didn't get v. far. Miss Kissane is interested in little anecdotes etc. I am to go to her in a week & I have more to do than she. Evg. Ted came v. pleased with Glendalough & that he & I are in Burke's landed gentry & we have no land!

Monday 14

A very rushing day many to see in mg.& things to do for dinner this evg. Got out by 11 & got all done. Mrs Berry does well D.G. Dr Price v. het up about B.C.G. & says there are machinations on to take B.C.G. fr. us. We say let position be made clear once & for all. The dinner was a great success, the food beautifully cooked & all else. We had a nice time. Mrs Moran wants her flat let & Billy & Ceciul want one nearer the Church, so there.

December

Tuesday 6

8 a.m. R.mines, Billy not there. Mr Doran & Hosp. Commission 11 o/.c We discussed Miss Gilmartin's salary & she is to be raised at once to £500 & increments to £600. the best we could do. Elsie not bad D.G. A nice mild day. Hear Dr Spain has case on, where he left in placenta in Caeserian sect. but he saved mother & child. Mater has case too. Did some card buying etc. It is so hard to do Xmas things this year. Another Pro. fr. R.drum.[685]

---

684. *Edith Somerville* died 8 October 1949; with her cousin Violet Martin she published under the pseudonym Somerville and Ross.
685. *Dr Spain* – Dr Alex William Spain, obstetrician, and later Master of the National Maternity Hospital.

Thursday 15

Such a rushing day! Teac Board 11, we settled a lot, letter to Hosp. Commission re Miss G.M's salary, she is the worst paid sec. in Dublin. Getting new Venetian aluminum blinds for T.B. Matron Mulligan's presentation now reaches £70 almost. Many cheques to sign & things to arrange in Teac, then to see pts, then home, settled things. Pts. till 4.45, taxi to Dr Price's long & wearisome discussion re our not being responsible for B.C.G., imported by others. Long Abbey St. meeting too.

1950

January

Wednesday 18

Up a bit late, consultation with Seymour at 10, then Bank & looked at frocks. Pim's most likely. Dr Alston waiting for me in Teac to say Dr Price has had stroke, left side paralysed, she was giddy y.day & sl. pale 11 p.m. she is much the same. What a loss she will be, at best she'll be only half herself I fear. John v. busy & happy helping B & C with new flat.

February

Saturday 4

Not v. busy day, but did things for John. Dr Stokes rang, wanted to see me at once. I feared trouble with Dr Alston over dispensary, but no, it was only a testimonial for her application as assist. to Dr Dunlevy, hope she'll get it. Saw Mrs Danesfield installed in new B.C.G. rooms, she is much pleased. Dr Brown never answered Dr Price's letter, written day of her stroke, telling him. Strange.[686]

Thursday 16

A hard day, car to pts. Teac Board 11. It went well, but afterwards Dr Barry & I interviewed Sr D'Arcy about her objecting to Miss Gilmartin entering her room. We pointed out that Miss G.M as officer of Board, has entry everywhere, she said she had never been submitted to such an indignity & that she'd leave, but we pointed out that it wouldn't happen again & what a loss she'd be & we hope it will blow over. B.C.G. went v. well indeed.[687]

March

Saturday 4

A lovely day, warm & bright. Went 1st to Bureau of Military Hist. & D.G. finished my statement wh. only goes to 1921 so the Civil War doesn't come into it. Teac nicely, then pts. Saw old Curry who D.V.

---

686. *Dr Dunlevy* – Dr Pearl Dunlevy (1909–2002), physician and epidemiologist of TB, Dublin Corporation TB office.
687. *Miss G.M* –Matilda Gilmartin, secretary at St Ultan's.

will come next week. Back here, then to D.cdra to German Child, after dinner Eric & Marjorie came, still in [ ]switters about the baby, I am to look after it. Then May Cummins, now D.V. bed at 11.30.

Sunday 5

1 in L. 8 a.m. R.mines. A perfectly lovely day, brilliant warm sunshine. What a different Birthday fr. last year. Now M doesn't want us anymore & is quite content to be separated from us all. In fact, she seems to revel in it. Well, she doesn't know how it hurts. We went to Berry's Confirmation in Donnybrook Ch., it was a beautiful, solemn Service. I was at his baptism.[688]

Thursday 23

V. nice day, tried to get out early & managed to be ready for Mr Scott in Teac at 12 to see what could be done for the old back ward. Out to T.B. sect. It is so insecure that it would be better to rebuild it & have good milk room & small tea room for Nurses & passage into the Cross ward, could be nice, but New hospital recedes ever further back. B.C.G. went well & Save German Children.

Saturday 25

Lovely day, v. busy all the time. Pts. not too bad Evg. went to Peace Meeting of all those interested to start a live campaign for Peace. They say this Govt. & all Govts. do things without consulting the people & when. they know they wouldn't approve, i.e. letting U.S. & British officers measure all our air fields, they sold off end of Partition as a reward for ending Neutrality. We shld be like Switzerland & Sweden.

May

Saturday 20

Nice soft rain & plenty in night & abt. 2 o/c cleared for Sunshine Home Meeting I hope. . Had busy mg. & had Curry in Teac & he planted all Caufield sent. & D.V. they'll do well. Went to Magdalen at 3. Somehow I find the Missioners hard to follow, says v. well known things but he is good & earnest. Winnipeg in great danger from flooding & Bessie's stepbrother Rex is there, she is so fond of him. A lovely Spring day.

---

688. *M* – sister Muriel Lynn. *Berry* – Beresford 'Berry' Wynne, son of Lynn's relation Geoffrey Wynne.

Thursday 25

Our 31st annual meeting & a cold N.E.wind, no hanging ivy in the garden as so often in bygone days. It went with a great swing D.G. & everyone was pleased & happy, tea & decorations lovely. B.C.G. sect. much admired. 1st thing in mg. a ring fr. Nursing Home. Bessie breaking her heart over Dean being certified, hadn't realised it. I said then wait a few days & leave Jack down, agreed. In evg. he was restless & she wld. pet him.

June

Friday 9

S. Columba's Day, I didn't go to S. Bs or anywhere, alas, too tired. Tried to go to Disp. but too much else to get thro'. M very well & seems contented. Jane wrote, wanting to come to-morrow, so wired her to come. Did Teac, wh. is well, but v. dry, all are pleased about M. Did pts. in aft & tried to get on with letters but head too tired. M is the show. pt. in Hosp. All delighted with her. D.G.[689]

Friday 23

Not hot this year but pleasant. M on balcon. & enjoying it most of day. In Teac a 3rd B.C.G. baby has collapsed. I talked to Nurses, Dr Alston & Matron & then Dr Barry & I went into all the details of the milk room. Gave special warning about hands. Not admitting any new ones for a week. With God's help even little Ann will pull thro'. Muriel in gt. form, was down the garden with me in evg.

August

Monday 7

Bank holiday, nice & fine & sunny. We packed & cleaned all day. Glen crawling with trippers. Willie came about 6 & Mattie Toomey a little before him with lovely lettuce & eggs. Former was a gt. treat for us. Willie brought Michael to help & put all in van & D.G. got across ford safely. Willie Junior sent for fr. Cullentra to help the sheep dipping. Mr Whelan had beautiful pony foal, such spindly legs.

Wednesday 16

A day of terrific showers. In Teac the B.C.G. Nurse being appointed. One prepared to go with Drs to Country to be appointed. Teac not in

---

689. *M* – reconciliation with sister Muriel who needed treatment in St Ultan's.

good way. Staff expenses have gone up greatly & bed occupancy has gone down. What will happen with the new hospitals being built. We'll be snuffed out if we don't buck up.

Saturday 19

I worked at clearing Bureau bottom drawer & burnt lots of old suffrage papers etc. Kept a few Republican ones for Xtian Brothers' School & card fr. Mr Ginnell to me. I am giving them the German Internee model boat too. Spent aft. with Margery & Eric & Melanie, she is a fine child & they are a happy trio. Eric so good & thoughtful. The garden gets nicer & nicer.[690]

September

Monday 18

Hurried up in Teac to be ready for lunch Dr Price's at 1.30 Miss G.m. takes Dr Alston's side strongly. Dr Price much better & hopes to ret. to us. She talked of Drs A.M & S says Dr A too valuable to be treated so, but quite realises her stubbornness. Why oh why didn't she make some overture to us as a Board. In evg. had gt. talk with Dr Barry. She thinks the same & I must try to fix all up. God & He alone can help me.

Wednesday 20

V. cold mg. & evg. Had radiators part of time. Didn't rain so much. Hear Mr Scott is near the end also Titia Scott. Voting day for Corporation. I voted for Andree Skeffington & another woman. Brigid voted but didn't say for whom. Sally enrolled in Univ. Coll. Maura Grant came & was nice as usual. Had a lot of evg. pts. Got my new glasses & they seem good.[691]

Friday 29

8 a.m. R.mines, only Miss Colson & I there, where was Billy. The angels again helped Dr Barry & me with Dr Alston, she won't admit any excuse for our giving away her dispensary & it was all due to her not letting us know by word or letter that she had thought of it at all. She is stubborn. Then we talked to Dr O'Doherty & made her see that Dr A really does work for us in Teac.

---

690. *Xtian Brothers' School* – Christian Brothers, O'Connell School, North Richmond St, Dublin, Brother W. P. Allen's Collection is now in the Military Archives. *Margery & Eric & Melanie* – Eric Craigen, his wife Margery (née Wynne) and daughter Marjorie (born 25 January 1950), Dundrum, Dublin.
691. *Andree Skefington* – Andrée Sheehy Skeffington, née Denis (1910–98), feminist, wife of Owen Sheehy Skeffington.

October

Wednesday 4

It was an arduous day, but all went well D.G. 1st at Med. Board, they agreed to nullify decision re Dr Alston's O.P. She is reinstated & Dr Stokes gets Dr Barry's & all is amicable once more. D.G. for the relief. Then spoke to Sr Hogan about ret. to O.T.Bs & she agreed. Spoke to Sr D'Arcy about Sr Hogan. Home, v. tired. Good bye to Ted, giving him eggs & porksteak.

Thursday 5

Up early & off to Mrs Stack's funeral at 10, Our Lady of Peace, Merrion Rd. so many there I hadn't seen for ages, funerals are reunions of ancient friends. Dev. looked well, Mrs S O'Rahillys, Bob Brennan, Ria McBride, Cathal Brughas etc. Fr Alston came when Sighle, Sally & I were starting with carnations as a token of gratitude. I was much touched D.G. D.G. evg. saw Billy, his cold better.[692]

Tuesday 31

8 a.m. R.mines, nice sunny day. Dr Pringle & I interviewed radiogaphers. Dr Barry turned up when we had finished & chose Miss Murphy from Gardiner St. who has best qualifications by far. Sorry about Miss FitzGerald, but she took it well. Got Hallow Eve things, we had colcannon & early dinner. I got the ring. Evg. Sally came to tell she was happy, went at 8 to join her faction. She loves College.

November

Monday 6

Nice day, tired in mg. A day of meetings. B.C.G. 5.30, re deputation to Minister, just back for dinner & then off to Paediatric at 8 in Teac. They arranged to have Honorary Members of people to be honoured & made me 1st because I was oldest Paediatrician. Long discussion on Mother & Child Act some v. much opposed. Comt. to be formed at once.[693]

---

692. *Mrs Stack's funeral* – Winifred 'Una' Stack, née Cassidy, (1878–1950), Cumann na mBan, wife of Austin Stack (1879–1929), revolutionary and Sinn Féin TD.
693. *Mother & Child Act* – Act proposed by Dr Noël Browne to modernise the Irish healthcare system and make it free for mothers and their children up to 16. The scheme was opposed by many doctors, and the Catholic Church.

Monday 13

V. cold day tho' some mg. sun. Early to Teac where Dr Connell took me to Custom House on Deputation to Dr Browne, he launched on us, that he thinks it time to make B.C.G. a national thing, paid for by rates & taxes, it would be an enormous task & Dr C & I fear, would not be carefully done as we have done it so far. Better go slow, but that's not Dr Browne. Busy day.

Friday 17

Busy day, nice sun. Med. Assoc. & Dr Browne bandy words. When things like that go on it becomes infra dig & does no good. Disp. went well, good many there in dribs & drabs. John thinks the Pregenonole is doing good. D.V. it is so. Went to cinema show in Eustace St. A Quaker thing, v. interesting of cycle racing & trick riding & then Switzerland.

December

Monday 18

Frost gone D.G. but dark enough. Sent off parcels but on a/c of the strike only to Wicklow, not Kildare. Teac fairly. Gt. rush for Writers' Club Dinner & Cecil brought little J. Plaster left too long on vaccination & scab smelly, but child all right. Dinner v. nice. Miss Dargan guest of honour & D. MacArdle runner up. She wrote of European children. I can't get over how she treated May Coughlan when pregnant.[694]

Tuesday 26

Another bright, cold day. M & I walked to the Lockharts new bungalow, abt.1/2 way to Rostrevor. It is very nice & roomey & has many new gadgets. We walked home too. Radio says Lia Fall stolen fr. W.minster. It is long since we thought of it. I wonder who accomplished it. Emer will be thrilled. V. hard frost now. M not overtired D.G.[695]

---

694. *Miss Dargan* – Ena Dargan's book *The Road to Cuzco: A Journey from Argentina to Peru* published in 1950. *Treated May Coughlan* – May McMahon, nèe Coglan, anti-treaty Cumann na mBan and friend of Lynn's was lodging with Macardle, who evicted her, a few weeks before McMahon moved into her marital home.
695. *Lia Fall* – An Lia Fáil (Stone of Scone) used in the coronation of Scottish Kings before being removed by King Edward I to England in 1296. It was stolen from Westminster Abbey on 25 December 1950 by a group of Scottish students.

1951

January

Wednesday 10

Did round in mg. Flu increasing rapidly, quite busy with it. Well after 2 when I got to Teac, there Matron & Miss G.M. much distressed for Miss Long's accounts are not right & she has told lies about them. We agreed she must go, but later Miss G.M. relented & is giving her another chance, for her mother ill & her brother idle. Connie Murphy the latest 'Flu victim. We have got in a good lot to day D.G.

February

Wednesday 14

Med. Board, we discussed Mr Scott's report on Back ward & for 1st time I realised that the maids were sleeping in an unsafe building. I always only thought of ward above. Dr Murphy still undecided about T.B. dispensary when I thought it was all settled. She is difficile.

Thursday 15

Teac Board 11 went well, a good attendance. We are taking steps about unsafe back ward & putting maids in another room, seeing to new boiler house etc. The scurrilous pamphlet sounds as if it was a speech of Dr Browne's, alas if this is so, for it is so false & low. Mr McPhail came & says Derek is child of mixed marriage C of I & R.C. I never knew it, so it is all right if he goes to Hospice.

March

Thursday 1

A mild, lovely day, tho' not so sunny, old lady came as I was just going out, hurt her wrist. I took her at once to Meath & left her & it was a fracture & she was set & all satisfactorily. Met Dr Stokes at Teac, she saw all the Meath Med. Board have had a v. bad time & have aged much. How can they stand it with Board against them. Saw Dr Taylor & Dr Price, she is well & says we must sit on Dr Murphy.

Wednesday 7

The day of the Med. Board Meeting & final settlement of moving of T.B.

Dispensary back to Miss Wall's rooms. Dr Murphy was so stubborn & futile in her objections one felt sorry for her, it was a long meeting but worth it to have things peacefully settled. Snowed all day, such slush & cold wind, frost a while, now snowing again. Paper full of rumoured changes in Ministry, Meath Hosp. bill & Met & C.Welf. Scheme.[696]

Thursday 15

Teac Board 11. Mrs Kettle gave great dissertation on all the benefits wh. have come since women got votes. It is true, but for my part I had thought it would have transformed the world & it didn't. I thought the same wld. be when the British were gone, but that was a much greater disappointment. Save German Children are fixing up fisher's family in house in R.farnham.

April

Thursday 12

Papers full Dr Browne resigns & Mr Costello takes over as stop gap. All the correspondence published & it isn't nice reading. Dr B. tells McBride v. clearly what he is. I am not surprised for he is Madam's child & then Gen. MacArthur deprived of all his commands & he will dispute Truman's right & they say whole U.S. will split well it may avert war & be God's plan. Everyone on tip toe of expectancy.[697]

Friday 13

Alas! to-day is v. unlike '47 when we sat out in the sun, how we had some sun in mg. then bitter cold & sleet & now will it never stop! A lot more about the Govt. Sean McB says Dr B not normal for a year & someone else said Sean abnormal 3 yrs. So undignified, one feels ashamed of being Irish. MacArthur flying home, they will take no criticism or correction. Nannie says no single day fine this year.[698]

---

696. *Meath Hosp. bill* – A private members' bill brought in in 1950 to reconstitute the governing body of the Meath Hospital following the events of the previous year.
697. Noël Browne resigned as Minister for Health on 11 April 1951, due to opposition to the Mother and Child Scheme. *Mr Costello* – John A. Costello (1891–1976), Taoiseach 1948–51. *McBride* – Seán MacBride (1904–88), son of Maud Gonne, referred to here by Lynn as 'Madam'.
698. *MacArthur* – American General Douglas MacArthur relieved of his command by President Harry S. Truman on 11 April 1951. The official reason was that he had overstepped his authority and defied Presidential policies aimed at ending the Korean War.

Thursday 19

Teac Board 11, at 11.30 we had deputation fr. B.C.G. Prof. O'Mara
& Dr Cowell, they were v. pleased with our suggestions, wh. can now
go before the Dept. Busy in Teac till 3, then to Dean's Grange & Kill,
cost 19/- for taxi. Hear only one train to Rathdrum in mg. at 7.25 so
we'll have an early start on 23 D.V. & D.V. it will be fine & warm. Save
German Children v. full of the Prauses, they must leave house & perh.
Ireland altogether, alas![699]

Friday 20

Lovely sun, wind a bit coldish but more Springlike, no more will be
said about Dr Browne we hear. Teac all very fair D.G. Did all I could for
Mon. but much still to do. Emer missing fr. morning till after 8, came
back very drunk, she will have to be put in again. It was Isulte who
took her out & in a week Mrs Clements got stroke & Emer has to leave
& ret to Dr O'Brien who had refused to keep her any longer.[700]

May

Monday 7

8 a.m. R.mines, bright & cold, some sleet. Had gt. hunt for Shamrock
St. it is off Mt.joy St. & they said it was off Berkley Rd. Was in time
for Med. Board at 12 to ascertain our views on the new Mother &
Child Scheme, we don't want to give up our being an Infant Hospital
& become like the other Children's hosps. We don't want Drs on Staff
that we didn't chose ourselves. B.C.G. at 5.30 went well too tho' we are
uncertain abt. progress.

Thursday 17

My 3rd night on balcon. Sometime in Oct. I think was last. Teac Board
11, was short to point. Had letter fr. Trades' Council wanting me to
advise on Mother & Child memorandum they are sending in, I'll do it
I think. Dr Barry says it is an honour to be asked, a nice sunny day.
Evg. Save German Children. Poor Prauses must leave & no reason
given. Mrs is much better D.G.

---

699. *Prof. O'Mara* – Professor Robert Allen Quain O'Meara (1903–74), professor of medicine and
medical scientist. *Dr Cowell* – John Cowell (1912–2008), physician and medical administrator, director
of the National BCG Committee.
700. *Isulte* – Iseult Stuart, née Gonne, (1895–1952). *Dr O'Brien* – Eveleen O'Brien (1901–81),
psychiatrist at Grangegorman and Helena Molony's partner.

Friday 25

A fine day tho' wind cold. Nan is no trouble in the house. Amused herself downtown. We had v. nice plaice for dinner. No dripping to be got. Another sign of war. Fat being witheld. Evg. went to meeting of Neo Natal Paediatric Club in Rotunda. Prof. of Paediatrics in Welsh Univ. spoke not too much new except that they don't wash or dress babies till they leave hosp. They are starting milk bank & Coombe has electric breast pump. We had one 25 yrs ago.

June

Tuesday 5

8 a.m. R.mines. Another perfectly lovely day. A lady reporter of I.Times interviewed me in Teac re writing up Teac, motif to be what Republican women did after being out in 1916. I hope she got it right. It will be a bit of publicity. Nan had early dinner & tea at 5 & left before 6 for Liverpool boat. She had nice time here. Evg. Infant Aid meeting. V. good speeches, tho' Dr Reddin was too outspoken. They had good crowd. Have bed on balcon with own mattress.

Wednesday 13

The day of meeting of new Dail, they sat all day till about 9 o/c, news came that Dev. was in with maj. of 5. Dr Ryan Minister for Health & a bad one he'll make. Got tomato plants & Bill Oman & I planted them. He is invited to Kathleen's convent in U.S. by Rev. Mother & all expenses paid, lucky Bill. Windy but warm. Teac quite good D.G. B & C go to Timoleague for July. We remember it as children.[701]

Thursday 14

A day with warm wind, many enervated, but it was balmy D.G. Went about pendant, but couldn't get it done. Dev. has all his old crowd back & an inept lot they are except Lemass. Childers may be better than some but Derrig etc. hopeless. There couldn't be a greater contrast. Farmers lament Dillon. We planted the tomatoes same time last year. I thought we were late this time.[702]

---

701. *Dr Ryan* – Dr James Ryan (1892–1970), was Fianna Fáil Minister for Health 1951 to 1954.
702. *Childers* – Erskine Hamilton Childers (1905–74), appointed Minister for Posts and Telegraphs. *Dillon* – James Dillon (1902–86), former Fine Gael Minister for Agriculture.

Friday 15

Nice day, Teac & usual things. Reporter in I. Times, Irish woman's Diary, gave nice a/c of Teac & it's origin, except that she said MffM was Chairman of Board. A Mr Toner fr. U.S. rang. I am to see him & wife to-morrow. Evg. very excellent a/c of Danish T.B. scheme in Coll. of Physicians by Dr [Winge] who has been organising here for 3 mos. We really have done a lot tho' we say so ourselves.[703]

August

Thursday 9

Nursing Comt.10.15. We heard Sr D'Arcy 1st. She denied there was any trouble at all, didn't remember her outbursts with Dr Stumpf & Matron, we ragged a few things out of her & she said she wld. resign & we accepted it. The other sisters all said they were happy in everything but Sr D'Arcy's treat. of 2 new ones. Later she denied having resigned & told Matron she had no intention of leaving & wld. not wait to see Sec. when told to. Many pts. Save German Children in evg. Got eyedrops for Frau Kohling, to post in Germany to-morrow.

September

Wednesday 5

Prices are to be up & down as Lemass fancies so we'll less than ever know where we are. I walked a lot to-day & D.G.it doesn't hurt, but I am tired now & dropping asleep. Med. Board went well D.G.& they took Sr D'Arcy's going v. sensibly. Quite warm & less rain & it was fine longer. Trueman says he has means to wipe out civilization & it is suicide not to provide then.

Friday 7

Weather holds. The Padraig Colums have lost their vaccination certifs. & said they must be redone. When I had got the lymph. they found only a cert to say successful marks visible, necessary, so there. I am always getting lifts now. D.G. latest = Susie, Ruth & husband. Teac all right. D.G. all amicable there D.G. Hear harvest quite good in the West D.G. Sighle told how Tom Barry was missing 2 days D.G. he has turned up. Childish fears.[704]

---

703. *Dr [Winge]* – Dr Kund Wing, Danish physician, chief physician in Copenhagen Central Municipal Dispensary, and tuberculosis expert whom Dr Stopford Price had met in 1936.
704. *Padraig Colums* – Padraic Colum (1881–1972), writer, and his wife Mary, née Maguire (1884–1957), Cumann na mBan, teacher, writer.

Monday 17

Phone went at 7, a call to Kill O'Grange, went as quick as I could & the pt. opened the door!! She had had pain & was better, but she won't last long. Lovely mg. but day cold. Was at Bank but forgot some cheques. At 6 meeting at German Embassy new German-Irish Soc. to be started at once. Very late for dinner. Poor John hungry. I sewed sheet in evg. Now to bed.[705]

October

Wednesday 3

Another dull, warm day. The British are taking their dismissal fr. Persia meekly. How low they have sunk. King George does well. Med. Board went well. I got cheques fr. Dr Murphy for £50 of the £100 I lent her. D.V. she'll stump up the other half soon. Sr Hogan does Matron's duties quite well D.G.[706]

Wednesday 24

Lovely sun early, not so cold. Dr Price was in Teac y.day & was v. pleased with her welcome, she is better, but such a wreck of what she was. Liam is very devoted to her. I was at Balally so lovely there & peaceful. Mary at 85 out digging potatoes. Evg. inaugural meeting of the Irish German Soc., supper room packed. Minister & Frau Patrons. Dr O'Sullivan President. Liddle & I & another V.Ps met the Telfords there, they have been changed.[707]

November

Friday 9

No rain till late aft. D.G. Reporter Times would look at nothing but B.C.G & we hoped the gen. Hosp would interest him. They are all on for B.C.G. now. In evg. Eric came & took me over to Margery. D.G. she is in better for to-day & with God's help she will get on now. Planted Fire King wallflowers in a few minutes before aft. pts.

---

705. *German-Irish Soc* – 24 October 1951 the German Irish Society was inaugurated at the Mansion House. Its aim was to strengthen the cultural ties between Ireland and Germany, Lynn elected one of the Vice Presidents. *Dr O'Sullivan* – Professor P. O'Sullivan /Proinsias O'Suilleabhainn. *Minister & Frau Patrons* – Dr A. Katzenberger, German Minister to Ireland.

706. *The British are taking their dismissal fr. Persia meekly* – the agreement between Iranian Prime Minister Mohammad Mossadegh and the USA to nationalise the Anglo-Persian Oil Company.

707. *Liam* – Liam Price (1891–1967), judge and antiquary, husband of Dr Dorothy Stopford Price.

Thursday 15

Teac Board 11 went well, we did many things. Mrs McGloughlin had drawing of Bronze for Mrs Cosgrave's Memorial, it is very handsome & a good size D.G. Busy all day. Evg. Save German Children Convention, we are winding up, can get no support now but we hope to be able to help while our little money lasts. We defeated the resolution to give ourselves Certificates of merit.[708]

Monday 26

A nice sunny day, frost last night. I put on all my best for the Minister's coming at 12, at 10.30 we had Child Welf. wh. was quickly finished, Mrs Mulvey is a fine business person. Dr Ryan is very much himself, but older & seemed impressed with all he saw & heard. They were glad of tea & biscuits, tho' Matron made a fuss over getting it. We have hopes of our Xray waiting room.

December

Thursday 13

A nice sunny day & now fog. Did a good lot. No much news at least I can't remember. New Nurses' Home in Meath is a tremendous affair, 150 Nurses & rooms & sitting rooms & kitchens galore. The old home, wh. is comparatively new, will be extra hospital beds. Have nearly all parcels ready D.G.

Thursday 20

A bright, shining mg. D.G Called to pt. before b.fast & it out the mg. I quite forgot Teac Board till 11.30 then rushed to it & found only 2, a Miss G.m. they were leaving when I arrived. I made them come back & we did the necessary routine things. Evg. went to Irish German Xmas Party. Dressed & found hardly anyone had done so. Singing beautiful, old German & Irish carols & harp & violin. It was a treat.

---

708. Elizabeth McLaughlin, sculptor, her best-known works are the Countess Markievicz and Poppet statues in Dublin.

1952

January

Thursday 3

Cold & frost go on but wind less D.G. That Captain still sticks to his listed ship tho' all the rest have been taken off. It is to save owners salvage charges he says. Blaskets seem cut off, no Christmas candles seen fr. mainland. D.V they are all right. Went to Save German Children, they are now getting out raffle tickets for £1,000 worth of prizes from Germany.[709]

Saturday 12

So we had our earthquake last year & it was prophesied for 1952. Evidently didn't make much impression. Full list now of y.day's Aer Lingus crash in Wales. So many Dublin people, 2 Drs & one Medical student, one dietitian. They say the plane tore a crater in the boggy ground. All were instantly killed. Susie took me to Alice in Wonderland & Beaver Valley. Latter interesting. Frosty now.[710]

February

Monday 4

Lovely sun, but frosty night & now freezing hard. A full day but got thro' all right. Poor little Johanna still there but only for new incubator she wld. be gone. Sean McEntee gone to London to consult with British over austerities. Couldn't we arrange for ourselves? North & South consult over Tourist arrangements, good.

Wednesday 6

Dampish day. Med. Board. Dr Murphy put in Minutes what I had said not to be taken seriously about her not having sent in her report of Congress last July. She is really vindictive where Miss G.M. is concerned & I wasn't quick enough to say it, must be deleted, so I have written my protest. Poor King George passed away in his sleep last night. He might have lasted longer if there had been no op.[711]

---

709. *Blaskets* – The Blasket Island off the coast of Kerry. It was finally evacuated in November 1953.
710. *Aer Lingus crash in Wales* – An Aer Lingus C-47 was en route from London to Dublin, suddenly went into a dive and crashed near Llyn Gwynant, Wales. All 20 passengers and three crew were killed.
711. King George VI died on 6 February 1952; in September 1951 he underwent an operation which removed his entire left lung.

Friday 22

Hear poor Emer is in Grangegorman again & speaking to no one. Alas for her. Lovely Springlike day. Poor Mary Jordan in Dun's again by gt. kindness of Dr Micks & Dr Hill is a brick too. Busy all day & was v. tired. To-day we got sack of potatoes cake, butter, sugar, snowdrops. On 20th I dropped a packet cont. £7.6 in Donnybrook Crescent & this evg. an old pt. brought it back. She traced it thro' Teac. I never expected to get it.

March

Wednesday 12

A day of many ups & downs with the Geoghegan household. Finally they have gone back to 1st plan, Miss G. to Nursing Home, Katie to hosp. Dr Hill let her maid stay at Miss G's the whole day, but that can't go on. In Teac we had a contretemps, Miss G.M & Matron, strongly disapproved of Dr Murphy's sister as locum for Miss Leavy & then Dr Micks says Miss L all right, so no locum necessary. Dr Cowell's Mother better D.G.

Thursday 27

We did great work in the garden, Susie & Curry there. I only gave orders. S. pruned roses & planted Jerusalem artichokes. Curry cut grass & renovated back & front & whole place looks tidy. We interviewed Dr Doreen Murphy whom we hope to put on the Staff. She seems very nice & we got good recommendations. Saw Dr Price, she disapproves of playroom, unsuitable for our cases.

April

Wednesday 16

Foggy mg. felt overwhelmed with things to do, took a Benzedine & had a headache & dry mouth, but later felt frisky. Got thro' a lot & had nice driver. Interviewing candidates was much easier than y.day. We appointed the woman, Dr Eithne Fox, she was the best by far. D.V. she will get on well, for I said all I could for her. Deidre Byrne gave us biggest box of chocs. I ever saw 6 1/2 yrs. A lovely thing D.G. a good lot done.[712]

---

712. *Dr Eithne Fox* – Dr Ethna Constance Fox, graduated NUI 1943.

Friday 18

Up quite early, a lovely day. B.fast at 8, we had time afterwards for me to plant out some bulbs. We never were in such good time or had so little luggage & no fuss. Glorious to be away. Glen perfect D.G. & taxi man so good. Plenty of sun & breeze & grateful heat. I was singing in my heart like the river for joy. We did a lot but of course there is plenty more to be done. Willie came when we were going to bed. I'm off now 9.30.

May

Saturday 3

A mildish soft day settled in. Susie left after b.fast. I went to Teac & found all well there D.G. then to Alex. Guild Conference & it was good. Dr Noelle Davies of Denmark was brimming over with her subject & carried us all along, raptured, would Ireland were so. Mrs Oliver Hughes on Back to the Land, showed what Countrywomen's Assoc. had & were doing. Alas! we are in a backwater there too, as well as politically.[713]

Thursday 15

Teac Board 11, we are getting sunblinds for T.Bs & new 2nd hand boiler. wh. may be good enough. V. warm day. I am always tired now, in aft. & want to lie down & rest. Evg. S.P.G. & Save German Children both interesting., Ireland, India both partitioned, both self-governed. both diff. religions. Abbey St. to be given up at end of month.

Thursday 29

Went early to Teac with greenery & flowers, all goes well there D.G. Came back here & spent long time phoning about John's box of tools. They are not in Dublin. D.V. they're not lost! Annual Meeting at 3. Went with great eclat D.G. & Mrs Sean T. was really very nice. & had no side on. Told of Teac in 1918 when she helped. Evg. had to go to Save German Children wh. is winding up, office given up. They gave me China figure.[714]

---

713. *Dr Noëlle Davies* (1889–1983), educationalist, litterateur and political activist in Ireland, Wales, and Denmark. *Countrywomen's Assoc* – Irish Countrywomen's Association (ICA).
714. *Mrs Sean T.* – Phyllis O'Kelly, née Ryan (1895–1983), wife of President Seán T. O'Kelly.

June

Friday 13

Dr Ryan is not so bad after all. The rain came at last after such lovely soft, warm rain D.G. May Cummins is to have her operation at 9 tomorrow so I'll have an early start. Nice, busy day. Wrote to Nan Lawlor & asked her to come here for a rest & to see what could be done, poor Nan.[715]

Saturday 14

May's op. at 9, b.fast before 8. Mr Meade found fair sized ov. cyst r.side & small one left. Nothing else D.G. She was v. frightened the last moment. Busy all mg. Much colder & overcast. Aft. went to Bray & saw the old ladies there who are wonderful considering all things & so pleased I came. John tinkering still at cistern. Now says it must be taken down. It has wasted a terrible lot of water.[716]

Saturday 21

A nice soft day. This year all Dublin is full of the Cong film, The Quiet Man. Frank Dowling says he can get us in whenever we arrange. Elsie Berry took me to Matron Mulligan for tea & we had a nice time. They were very full of the Quiet Man & say it is very amusing. Seems rather to ridicule the C.of I. clergyman, but we'll see.[717]

Friday 27

Did many Friday things. Evg. Susie & I went to "The Quiet Man" it was very disappointing. The scenery might be anywhere, only the bit of a cross in Cong recognisable & to have Abbey players making such boofoons of themselves seemed to me degrading. V. kind of Frank to get us in of course. It was very long & wearisome.

Saturday 28

Did usu. Sat. mg. things. Miss Molloy brought gooseberries & I made 12lb jam, v. good it is. Aft. Miss G.M & Matron went by 1.50 train to Sunshine Home. Dr Barry got me a seat with Dr Thornton & we were there in good time. Dr Ryan laid stone of new Sunshine Home v. nicely.

---

715. *May Cummins* – grew up next door to Lynn and ffrench-Mullen.
716. *Mr Meade* – Dr Henry Meade, graduated RCSI 1909, surgeon.
717. *The Quiet Man* – 1952 film directed by John Ford and filmed in Mayo.

We had nice time, spacious ground, tea good. Saw many incl. old Mrs Beveridge & her brother, v. friendly. Mrs Dr Ryan ditto & Sean Brady & many more.

July

Friday 11

Much colder got last I.Times for Printers' strike is on. Heard Evg. News over wireless. Eisenhauer has beaten Taft. Weather forecast good. Nice busy day. Lorry came & took all, a big load for it had much porter in it. Curry doing Teac garden. I planted canariensis. Saw Scientific exhibition. B.C.G. looks v. well. Got some primulas there. Many in aft. & v. tired.[718]

August

Monday 18

Rained all night & this mg. & blew fr. East again, colder, cleared later. Went to Bank & found I wasn't on the rocks after all. D.G. tho' I thought I was. Mrs Strickland Hurley came to Teac & was very nice & pleased, hadn't been since Eucharistic Congress D.G. Heard much Teac news bad & good. Aft. here busy too & people to see later. Terrible floods in Somerset & Devon, whole towns washed away when mad river altered course.

September

Tuesday 16

8 a.m. R.mines, Billy celebrated, 4-5 there, overcast all day as it so often is. Mrs Kettle a bit better, spent much of day trying to fix her up. Betty is no earthly use, Owen Skeffington is in France, consulted Dr Barry & she approves of asking Fr Devlin so went to him & he agrees a nurse the only thing & Mr Kettle agrees, so one is coming to-morrow. D.V. D.V. all will go well. It has been a real hectic day.[719]

Wednesday 17

Mother's Day passes almost unnoticed now but she is near. Mrs Kettle's Nurse seems suitable. D.G. & she is better, taxi then to Xtian

---

718. *Eisenhauer has beaten Taft* – American Presidential election, Eisenhower was elected.
719. *Betty* – Elizabeth Kettle (*d.*1966), solicitor, daughter of Tom and Mary Kettle, née Sheehy.

Brothers School, N.Richmond St. with more things for Brother Allen, he is an enthusiast & the collection wonderful. I am so glad to have helped him. Then to Mater Sr Donnelly is better D.G. & Cecil's uncle & Aunt who had serious smash up, car ran into them. D.G. they're better.

Monday 22

A v. busy tiring day, saw to Josie Cummins & gave Benzedrien for exam. Dr Mulcahy very insistent that Mrs Kettle shall go to S. Patrick's tho' she is perfectly sane but for depression wh. is all due to her not casting her burden on the Lord, if only she would. However, she is content to go there. Judge Sheehy says Betty shld be permanently certified & it wld be well. Evg. very dead tired.[720]

Saturday 27

Bright & cold, taxi to Roebuck Rd. & S. Patrick's. They have taken down the spire of S James's & I couldn't make out what thre new building as I thought was. Mrs K having shock treatment & v. boorish young Dr. told me. He didn't even know who the statue was at the end of the corridor waiting room. Aft. potted all the big geraniums & planted the bulbs. Saw Dr Hill in end.

October

Thursday 16

Nice day. Teac Board 11, new Corp.member, Mr Barron, went all right. Many cheques to sign, got all done & saw Florrie, who is much better. John complains of stomach but eats everything. Dinner at 6 & resuscitated Markievicz Comt. Meeting 7.30. Emer has gt. ideas if she only holds out to carry them through. At Chelsea Hospital for old Irish Pensioners. Many very bad & tiny babies in Teac.[721]

Friday 17

Soft & warm T. 59 degrees now. V. busy, met Emer at bus & we went down as far as Teac together, she is fine. In Teac the very dehydrated twins are a bit better D.G. & no one else v. bad. Many here in aft. Evg.

---

720. *Judge Sheehy* – Eugene Sheehy (1883–1958), barrister and circuit court judge, brother of Mary Kettle and Hanna Sheehy Skeffington.
721. *John* – John Lynn, Lynn's brother, returned to Ireland from Australia in 1948 and lived with her until his death in 1954.

went to hear Mrs Kingston's a/c of International Women's Conference at Naples, they did useful work, I think for Peace & Equality. Miss Rhodes & Miss Harrington took me home.[722]

November

Monday 10

A fine, bright day for a change. Nothing unusual. Curry, Teac. Evg. went to Fabian Soc. T.C.D. a woman read paper on 'Must we Perish', v. good. Peace propaganda. Frank Robbins proposed vote of Thanks & launched into a tirade against Russia & Communism & the next speaker put him nicely in his place. Frank never was in Russia, other was 8 times & knew his facts. It was v. enthusiastic meeting.[723]

Thursday 20

V. dark all day, lights on. Teac Board went well D.G. & we did much business. Such a lot of cheques to sign. Took me 1/2 hr. Evg. Elsie Berry took me to Peace Meeting in Miss Cantwell's old House, basement & hall rooms, now seems to be a Labour place. G. Jeffers gave an a/c of China & says they have done amazing work since their freedom. All have land, landlords just have their share.

Friday 21

Poured all night & day till about 10. Cold & miserable. Dr O'Doherty is to do lumbar puncture again on my cerebritis child, who is still very unconscious. The Whiteabbey case is looking for a man with a scar on his cheek. It seems the girl had taken to fencing, were the wounds inflicted with a sword? Evg. T.B. soc meeting Dr Crofton's son gave paper on chemotherapy. He looks well.[724]

---

722. *International Women's Conference at Naples* – International Alliance of Women, Sixteenth Congress, Naples, September 11–19, 1952. Three members of the Irish Housewives' Association, Lucy Kingston, Helen Chenevix and Andrée Sheehy Skeffington attended the conference in Naples.
723. *Frank Robbins* (1895–1979), trade unionist and old comrade of Lynn's from the Irish Citizen Army.
724. *The Whiteabbey case* – the body of Patricia Curran, aged 19, daughter of Lancelot Curran, a Northern Ireland high court judge, was discovered in the driveway of her family home in Whiteabbey, Co. Antrim on 12 November 1952. She had been stabbed 37 times. *Dr Crofton's son* – Sir John Wehman Crofton (1912–2009), physician and public health campaigner, son of Dr William Mervyn Crofton.

December

Monday 15

Slight snow & much frost. John came with me to the Bank & found he had over £400 in it, he was amazed & took out £50 as a loan to Billy, who moved to-day & B says he'll keep it & use it if he has to. He & C lunched at the Rectory. C.I.E. moved them nicely. I never got an Xmas thing done. Banked dear M ffm's money to-day this year too. We are lonely for her.

Wednesday 31

Fine & cold, usu. things. Little Margaret who has been 2 yrs with us, top landing, was moved to B.C.G. she was terrified at being in strange place but got quite reconciled when Nurse May & Sr Buckley & those she knew came over & talked to her, poor little unwanted child & she is so fragile but is grand now. Just waiting for 1953.

1953

January

Friday 2

Frosty & cold. Elsie took John & the clock early to Delgany & they were back by 7. John says he'll have to make new bracket for clock. Old one won't do on modern frail walls. All seems well there. Paper has wonderful a/c of an Aer Lingus plane wh. had to make a forced landing in a field, plane wrecked, everyone landed safely. Air hostess praised for her calmness told all to pray.[725]

Wednesday 14

A lovely sunny mg. & the sunrise was wonderful rosy sight, birds singing & busy, obeyed urge to go & see Madam Gonne McBride, she was pleased. What a mass of coarse wrinkles her face is. Hard to imagine her a beautiful young thing. Some pilfering in Teac, Matron to see police about it. Attacks on women daily in Belfast. Evg. went to Billy's presentation, it was nice, women sang beautifully. We hope he got good lot.

Wednesday 28

Now I'm in my 80th year & going hard, but D.V. I'll have a proper rest with Muriel. That poor lion tamer mauled to death by one of his lions. He had several times been mauled but recovered. How was he allowed to keep lions in an unsafe way! Milk situation gets worse. V. busy with pts.up to late. All nearly done now 12.25.[726]

February

Friday 6

A full day. Dispensary over early, did rounds before lunch & pts. after, was a bit late at Peace Meeting. wh. was v. good but reports too long. My speech v. short & then I came home. Little John only a little better. Curran murder case seems horrible, that Ian Gordon must be quite

---

725. *Aer Lingus plane* – An Aer Lingus DC 3 Dakota, 'The St Kieran', airplane from Dublin to Birmingham crash landed in a field 14 miles south of Birmingham Airport. The air hostess was Philomena McCloskey, aged 23.
726. *Lion tamer* – Dubliner Bill Stephens was mauled by his own lion 'Pasha' at the Fossett's Circus winter quarters at Finglas, Co. Dublin.

abnormal. He complained when his comrades refused to lie to help him out. It rained a bit to-night.[727]

Friday 20

V. mild but no sun. T. up to 56 degrees, things growing well, crocuses in front of Teac quite showy D.G. Dispensary busy & Teac & a Pro & pts. to see & late for here non stop till about 6.30–45. Evg. much too tired to go to Peace Comt. meeting, leg not good all day. I was very bocity. Muriel coming next week. Hope she'll stay & come to Delgany. Pearl sent lovely snowdrops. We had Baby Boyd here while they at pictures.

March

Tuesday 17

8 a.m. R.mines. John slept well & wasn't down till I was finishing b.fast, he did go to 11.30. I had to leave him for S. Finian's 11. Mrs Ruth there & v. glad to see us all. Lovely sun. I did the roses & a little more & then mended J's shirts etc. It was a dear S. Patrick's Day & I had MffM's 4 leafed shamrock in broche.

April

Sunday 19

2 A.E. 12, Rathdrum. Fr Lillis is now P.P. of Aughrim & there was a grand Pipers' Band fr.Aughrim to welcome him at Greanane, wh. is a Chapel of Ease. He was there for 5-6 yrs. fr. 1922. Lovely warm sunny day. Mts. happy & wind E. We were J & I the only communicants & it was a wonderful D.G. joyful Service, where our hearts were truly lifted up. Aft. J. got a bad fall, slipped on a round stone at Whelan's, such a crash, he has a lovely black eye. Not bad.

May

Monday 4

Another perfect Summer day. Went to Teac as early as I could to hear about Nurse Cosgrove who has been missing since evg. of Sat. 2nd. She was said to be with an Aunt in Bray but why no message? & then

727. *Ian Gordon* – Iain Hay Gordon, a 20-year-old RAF technician, was convicted of the murder of Patricia Curran. His sentence was overturned in 2000 after the Court of Appeals found his conviction to be unsafe.

she & her Father turned up, she had been with Aunt on Quays. He wanted us to take her back, impossible. Got Dr O'D to see Katrina [ ] Yeats. She agrees it is teething & new baby & Mother's absence. It is now 10.45 & balcon next.

Friday 15

Sr Hogan left y.day, a man rang in mg. said she was gone & did I know she had forcibly fed a child y.day. I told Matron & Miss G.M. Later Sr Donnelly told Matron Sr H. had not only forcibly fed but had made the child swallow its vomit 3 times. She must have been possessed to do it, for surely she had never done it before. Anyhow it's well she's gone. Curry made garden fair. I did a bit & it rested me. Saw lovely new moon outside.

Tuesday 26

Whit Tues 8 a.m. R.mines, had some porridge & then 9 a.m. Fr Doolin's Mass for dear M ffM, he said it was for S Ultan's too, v. nice, straight back to Nursing Comt. We had tea & bis., chose 3 for interview for T.B. Phyllis McCabe. Back here, did house things & brought [ ] to Mac Geough for sale. Back to Teac, then aft. here, busy enough. Terrible floods & storm & thunder etc. in North & S. y.day.

Thursday 28

Annual Meeting. Glorious warm day, went early with greenery & flowers & was besieged for them tho' we got so much y.day. B.C.G & T.B. got some. It all looks very nice & fresh. Wore my blue (light) frock. Dr Reddin & Dr Alston spoke first, re report, then Mrs Tom Barry (Leslie Price) now head of Red X spoke & said how Dr Price, Dr Barry & I had helped in the fight. Lady Goulding seconded, she is very nice & practical & said how happy our children were D.G. D.G.[728]

June

Wednesday 3

The bitterest N.E. wind for long & long, little sun, we all have gone back to Winter clothes & they are hardly enough. D.G. Queen Elizabeth is

---

728. *Mrs Tom Barry (Leslie Price)* – Leslie Mary de Barra, née Price (1893–1984), was an Irish nationalist, member of Cumann na mBan and chairperson and president of the Irish Red Cross. *Lady Goulding* – Lady Valerie Goulding, née Monckton (1918–2003), disability rights campaigner, senator, and founder of the Central Remedial Clinic.

safely crowned & no one killed. A marvellous thing that was. She looks as if she could hardly bear wt. of crown. Now betw.11 & 12 rain has come D.G. It will perhaps take the cold away. The photos of Annual Meeting were very good.[729]

Saturday 20

Went early to Teac to see Madam Montessori's stepson & his wife. He remembered me, they are both nice & interested in Teac. At last Dept. sanctions new boilerhouse D.G. Did a little in garden. It is very dry. After dinner who appeared but Chevasse like a dream fr. a past distance. He looks very badly & worn but he talked & talked & talked till I was moidered & at last could enquire for Cecil, o.k.[730]

July

Tuesday 7

8 a.m. R.mines, only woke 7.30, such a rush & I was so tired but the busy day got done somehow & I had things & things to do J's letter came so we are off in mg. by car all the way & D.V. it will go off well. Such a lot to be packed & seen to. Phyllis McCabe's 1st day as T.B. Sister. She looks very well in uniform & D.V. will do well. Now it is after 12.30 & I must go to bed.

August

Friday 21

Saw Mrs Kettle in bus but she didn't see me. Betty is now in the best possible Mental Home in Scotland, got there by influence. She is not much better yet. Such a tragedy. Muriel came in aft. & was here before me, for I was delayed in Teac by interviewing Pro & talking to Lady Wicklow. M is fine & is glad to be here. It is a bit of a change for her. Such drenching showers!![731]

---

729. Coronation of Queen Elizabeth II took place on 2 June 1953.
730. *Madam Montessori's stepson & his wife* – Mario Montessori (1898–1982), was the son of Maria Montessori, born out of wedlock, and his second wife Ada Pierson. *Chavasse* – Claude Chavasse (1886–1971), English, immersed in Irish cultural nationalism, member of the Gaelic League, commonly wore a saffron kilt.
731. *Lady Wicklow* – Eleanor Howard, née Butler (1914–97), labour politician and architect.

September

Thursday 17

I didn't forget dear Mother all day. 38 years now since she passed on. Teac Board was all right. A beautiful day & night, a lovely 1/2 moon. I. Times very sarcastic at the way Dev. is lunching with British Cabinet. What villiany is he up to now? Walked to Annsley Park after dinner & am not too tired. It was a very full day but so nice to do things.

Tuesday 29

S. Michael & All Angels. 8 a.m. R.mines, cold & sunny. Did quite a lot, 12 House Comt. sorted out over 30 applications for housekeeper & chose 7 for interview. We have. v. bad congen. heart case, they are getting commoner. Evg. I.M.A meeting at 8 re = Health bill & after nearly 2 hrs discussion & many points of view were told it had passed & won't be altered. Minister out to suppress voluntary hosp.[732]

October

Thursday 15

Teac Board 11, Mrs Kettle has resigned, such a pity. Why will she let herself be overwhelmed by Betty's illness? So many have to be around & aren't submerged like her. John had another bad night but when I mentioned Dr Micks, he promptly got better. D.G. & has remained so. Meeting of Haven, refugee home, interesting & in it all sects. are [ ] one to help our suffering brothers & sisters.

Friday 16

Much warmer, John better all day & in better spirits, such a comfort after so many days complaining Dr Rose Barry's a darling, disp. is a real joy with her beside me. Did hosp. & all & interviewed, a Pro. fine girl, 5 ft. 8 1/2 & 11 st & 16. then Dene's & I planted 5 shrubs in back. Saw dear Margery. Evg. splendid paper by man who has studied all Eastern religions & recognises the good in all. Tagore must be v. old now.[733]

---

732. *I.M.A* – Irish Medical Association. *Health bill* – Health Act 1953.
733. *Dr Rose Barry's* – Dr Rosarie Barry, graduated NUI 1947.

Friday 30

Nice sun, coldish. Rather dreaded Disp. but new Dr very good & does what she is told D.G. Teac v. fairly. No rest all day. Saw Seumus Robinson last night, v. changed but voice the same. Protestant real Black & Tan, treat. of poor Mau Maus, I'll sign it D.V. Had to patch J's combinations. Mrs Moran had put in old blanket & it went 1st wash, so I put on patch. I had asked her to.[734]

November

Wednesday 4

Nice sun, cold. John says he didn't sleep all night & was in bathroom 4 times, Brigid says 10 p.m & 7 a.m. Cold is better, but he is cranky, poor fellow. Med. Board 12, long & tiring, we appointed Dr Rose Barry Junior Assis. Physician & are asking Dr Alston to resign fr. Sat. Disp. Wish Dr Barry had been there, Stokes is so difficle. Muriel's house was burgled by some local boy it seems & rings taken, but all 3 returned by boy's Mother.

December

Wednesday 2

Such a warm day T. 60 all thro', The Lords v. concerned about Mau Mau. Asked was it true there were 'humane' killings & were not natives shot down if they attempted to help their bombed villages & it was not denied or affirmed, of course it is so & well we know fr. our treat. here. Med. Board went v. well. Dr Doreen Murphy at once agreed to lecture Nurses, when Dr Stokes said she was too tired. All well here.

Thursday 10

A lovely summerlike day, with sun & no cold. Pts. & did some more shopping & spent a lot of money. Matron says gloves not worn now at receptions, well. Dinner early & Moire Ogue = Terry McSwiney's daughter & I went to the German reception. It was packed & I saw a lot I knew, several of the old Save German Children Comt. inc. Sean McKenna, Sean McBride, Dr & Mrs O'Sullivan, a Prince Ernest of Saxony, Erskine Childers etc. etc.[735]

---

734. *Seumus Robinson* (1890–1961), old Irish Citizen Army comrade. *Mau Maus* – The Mau Mau Rebellion (1952–60), also known as the 'Mau Mau Uprising' in Kenya. They were treated with extreme violence and terror by the British forces.
735. *Moire Ogue* – Maire Brugha, née Og MacSwiney (1918–2012), daughter of Lord Mayor of Cork, Terence MacSwiney, married to Ruairí Brugha (1917–2006). *Prince Ernest of Saxony* – Prince Ernst Heinrich of Saxony (1896–1971), he had moved to Ireland in 1947.

1954

January

Friday 1

8 a.m. R.mines, was late for John came down to warm himself in diningroom, said he couldn't sleep with the cold. I rushed back after receiving. He had porridge & said he wanted it at 7.30 a.m. Did an hour in Teac & was back for Dr Micks at 12.30. He recom. [mersabyl] wh. started working vigorously. At 3.30 he was afraid to walk. Rang Dr Micks & now D.G. he is in Dun's. Poor J, he is bad enough I fear.

Saturday 30

Snow gone, milder, lovely sun. Dr Connell came early, dear Dr Price passed on this mg. about 7, she had 2nd stroke & was 2 days unconscious, D.G. she wasn't left too long. Dr Cowell like a son to Mr P. Funeral Mon at 12 o/c. Tallaght. Dr C is sending spray of freesias & Med. Board a wreath. Such a lot of phoning & arranging. John very sorry for himself & breathless. Much better now D.G.[736]

February

Thursday 4

Snow almost gone. Taxi came about 9.30 & I had a scramble. All the 1916ers that are left were there. Emer & I were together. She is very well D.G. Couldn't find my note book, thought I hadn't brought it, but it was not here so back to Dundrum & there it was under the kneeling board. Dev. was there & Sean T & Mrs & Alfie Byrne, Mrs Tom Clarke & heaps more. Much warmer. John not so well after dinner but D.V. he has settled down now for night.[737]

Saturday 6

Such a beautiful sunny day, tho' hard frost, white in mg. Got some things done. Miss Gallagher, Kill-o-Grange going to Roebuck Home end of Feb. A threatening letter to kill Queen in Australia. Dr Ryan, a lumbering inept, makes a mess of Health regulations. I told Dr Cowell

---

736. *Dr Price* – Dr Dorothy Stopford Price died aged 64.
737. *All the 1916ers that are left were there* – at the funeral of Áine Ceannt, widow of executed signatory of the 1916 Proclamation, Éamonn Ceannt.

of Dr Price's picture, would it do in B.C.G. Comt. room. Mr Price thinking of a memorial there too.

March

Thursday 4

We were having early dinner & a nice one, for M's birthday is to-morrow when dear John had a bad fall in the hall, made a pretense of eating, got up to bed, fainted in trying to get out & was gone in an hour or so. Eva was a brick & stayed with him. He seemed to doze & so passed without a struggle. How thankful I am I was able to mind him to the last.[738]

Tuesday 30

Bright sun & hail showers, like last year. B.C.G. 5.30. Our Swan song. Prof O'Meara & most agreed there was no alternative but to wind up. Poor Dr Cowell looks so sad after all the untiring work he has done there for years & with one blow the Govt. ends it all. They put everything on the rates so they have more to squander & the Rates are overburdened already.[739]

April

Thursday 1

Milder & some sun. D.V. the worst is over. All papers now full of the H. bomb & it's unlimited powers of destruction, so now we are all set for S. Peter's prophesy of the end of the age. Miss G.Martin thinks Prof. O'Meara is only delighted to wind up B.C.G. He hasn't time to spend time over it. All well in Teac.

Friday 2

A real April day, soft rain & then sun. Even Brigid didn't shut windows or light stove in dining room. One wld. have loved to be in the garden. Had great massage & heat. My arm feels sore since. They say U.S. is going to use atomic energy for industrial purposes. Dr Cowell says the Dept. will say they never intended to close down B.C.G. & will ask us to reopen work.

---

738. John Lynn, Kathleen's brother died on 4 March 1954.
739. *B.C.G. 5.30. Our Swan song* – Minister for Health informed the National BCG Committee that they should recoup its expenditure by charging Local Authorities quarterly for the cost of services from April 1954.

Thursday 15

7.30 R.mines, many there. Teac Board 11. We thrashed & thrashed out the B.C.G. situation & so they had asked our advice, we said the Minister shl.d be interviewed by us & them & Prof. O'Meara has agreed to that, but we are to arrange it. It was a busy day. I got S. Patrick's flag for Teac D.G. Evg. R.mines, Archd. good, but too long. Service v. nice & many there. Lovely spring day D.G. I'm off duty now.

May

Saturday 22

Pts. in mg. Went by 3.20 to Sunshine Home, they had an enormous marquee, packed, sunny & cold wind. Home in full swing now. Dr [Weaverstroke], I remember the day he was born. Lord Wicklow in Chair & excellent he was. Saw very few I knew till the end & as I was going to ring a taxi Dr K O'Breen & Angela Russell gave me a lift & I was most thankful. The grounds are getting into shape & the Nurses' Home is in occupation.[740]

Wednesday 26

This wasn't a rushing day, tho' full. We'll have Costello again. I wish now Dr Brown hadn't changed his coat & he'd be Minister for Health again. All press for to-morrow but I take things easy, best of my play. Dear M ffM's day, she was so happy annual meeting had gone well & our quite time afterwards is good to think on.[741]

June

Wednesday 2

I had hoped I'd be able to get thro' a full day & I was. Med. Board 12. Dr Stokes asked last meeting to apologise & she replied she didn't know for what so we wisely have let the matter drop, she is hopeless. Did Teac, got arm massaged & it is much worse since. Walked to [ ] Home nearly 4, rested, a bit good few pts. Dinner a bit later, evg. pts. till nearly 11. I'm ready for bed now. Cold wind & some sun. New Dail to-day, will it last.[742]

---

740. *Lord Wicklow* – William Howard, 8th Earl of Wicklow (1902–78), Anglo-Irish peer.
741. John Costello was elected Taoiseach for the second time after the 1954 General Election. *Dr Brown* – Nöel Browne had left Clann na Poblachta and ran as a Fianna Fáil candidate in the 1954 General Election, so he was in opposition rather than in Government.
742. *New Dail to-day, will it last* – Fine Gael, the Labour Party and Clann na Talmhan formed the Second Inter-Party Government, a minority government, dependent on the support of Clann na Poblachta.

Wednesday 30

> Eclipse of sun at 12, it was cloudy, so D.V. no one blinded themselves. Dr Flynn did disp. for Dr Murphy & then retired. I sent for her when I was doing my rounds but she didn't come. I saw her & she said she had done quite enough, she is determined to rest & of course she has been overworked. Very hard to know what can be done unless dear little Rose Barry could come in in afternoon.[743]

July

Thursday 1

> Seorsias Irvine's funeral at 10. Full military honours, Republican flag, volleys over grave & last post. Such a lot were late for 10.30 was said first. I saw many old friends & they were glad to see me. Ernest Blyth & Childers there. In Teac Dr Flynn remains the same. Dr Broderick took this aft., Dr Murphy to-morrow & Dr Rose Barry Sat. Sun & will keep an eye. Packed for Glen some & am not too tired. We were grateful for temp 65 to-day.[744]

August

Saturday 7

> We are back a week to-day, it has seemed long. New Dr seems nice & helpful. Dr O'Doherty so good, does all she can. Susie & I went to Dr in the House. It is very good, but my deafness prevents me catching the jokes. It was a long sitting for me, 2 1/2 hrs. Then tea, then met Miss Farin & she is her old self, not much changed. Now at 11 I am v. tired. No rest this aft. D.G. for bed.

Friday 27

> Early to pt. & then Teac. Had big disp. all alone, tho' Nurse O'Toole helped. a Mrs Fitzmaurice, friend of Winsome's rang when I was out & again at 8, she seems nice but I had later news than she for she left home in May. We thought she was coming here & were to give tea but she hadn't time. Had to come in off balcon. at 8 but had 4 hrs out Letter fr. P. Hughes, he was here in July & I ever knew it

---

743. *Dr Flynn* – possibly Dr Mary Elizabeth Flynn, née Mansfield, graduated Trinity 1934.
744. *Seorsias Irvine* – George Irvine (1877–1954), republican, language activist and campaigner.

September

Friday 10

Nice day, tho' showers. Teac took considerable time & then I went to see Mrs Kettle, a more miserable person would be hard to find, but it is not all Betty D.G. & neighbours are good to her & D.G. for that. Then Mrs Taylor here, her child Annie has left her brute of a husband & is safe wherever she is for wh. D.G. Mothers have much to bear, poor things. Nothing now about Tinahinch at all.

October

Tuesday 12

8 a.m. R.mines, lovely mild day, stormy now. Did a lot of walking & am tired enough now, our new H.S. is very unsatisfactory, otherwise Teac well. B.C.G. went well. Prof. O'Meara is excellent, we welcomed Dr Barry on Comt. Poor Dr Cowell looks terrible with rigid neck, sprinted up for his disc, but he says he is better. Has to wear contraption Day & night.

Saturday 16

Had good long round & shopped for Muriel's coming & good long round. Annie McSweeny is dead, another link of 1916 gone. Saw a bee just now on my pillow, must have thought it was day with elect. light, put it gently out in a towel. Not so warm to-day & very damp.[745]

November

Wednesday 3

Slept till 8, bright sun & brisk coldish wind. Med Board 12. We appointed Dr Rose Barry our Sec & all were pleased. A good mg's. work. Had lunch at Y.M.C.A. Sale, such a babel of tongues, I was quite overpowered by the noise & the clergy seemed the greatest talkers. Aft. & evg. busy. Only going to bed at 10.40. Nice moon now.[746]

---

745. *Annie McSweeny* – Annie MacSwiney, Cumann na mBan, teacher, sister of Terence MacSwiney and Mary MacSwiney.
746. *Y.M.C.A.* – Young Men's Christian Association.

December

Wednesday 1

Lovely sunny mg. Pts. Med Board 12. Dr R. Barry seems tired. Papers full of wrecks of small schooners etc. Many lost. Irish boat saved 14 D.G. Now it is raining & blowing again. Eisenhauer says if U.S. sends ships to China it will mean war. God grant Peace.[747]

Saturday 11

A warmer day. Gt. pictures of the floods. Shannon 6 miles wide at Athlone & still rising, higher places drying out I suppose. Susie has laryngeal cold now, laid up for days & never told me. Teac all right. Had hoped to get things done but no. Saw Margery & Melanie, she has grown a lot.[748]

Wednesday 29

V. busy day, Puss on doorstep in mg. & v. glad to see me. Haven't seen him since. Pts., Teac, B.C.G. 3, interviewing Drs. I stayed for 3 & came a way after 4, room full when I got back, v. busy till 6.30 but 8.10, not many. Nice mild day.

747. *Eisenhauer* – Dwight David 'Ike' Eisenhower (1890–1969), President of the United States.
748. *Gt. pictures of the floods* – Gale-force winds ripped across Ireland on 8 December 1954 bringing torrential rain and widespread flooding.

1955

January

Saturday 15

Very wet & uncomfortable, stayed in bed till 12, went to Teac. Margery never came, so I lazed in aft. & then made list of cards & wrote long letter to Lorna. Cat most affectionate all day. Came for walk with me round Church & back.

Thursday 20

Up for b.fast. Teac Board 11. We got unanimity at last when Dr Barry very nicely explained situation of B.C.G. Had practically no rest all day. Only 15 min. when I came in, even tho' pts here & waiting. Frost all gone, much warmer out of the wind.

February

Tuesday 8

8 a.m. R.mines, such a restless night. I was awake every hour I think. Served me right for shirking Paediatric meeting wh. went very well & Dr R Barry read her paper on Jimmy & he behaved very well D.G. I saw Mrs Woods & spent an hr. there. Tired when back here. B.C.G. went well, soon over D.G. & now bed at about 9 o/c

March

Saturday 12

V. cold day, more snow promised. D.V. won't come. Yesterday went to C. O'Loughlin's & saw him & a friend & we had a great pow wow over old times. Refreshing to all someone who remembers dear M ffM. A lazy day on whole.[749]

Tuesday 29

Busy with Flu pts. Maureen Chevasse rang at dinner time, wanted me to drive with her at Standared, but I said I'd go after dinner, we had a great talk & I was glad I went, she leaves Thurs. I was back about 9. She is writing life of Terry McSweeney, but Muriel won't allow her to

---

749. *C. O'Loughlin* – Colm Ó Lochlainn (1892–1972), printer, publisher and Gaelic scholar.

publish. Eve Grania is studying Philosophy at Louvaine & is to take her doctor's degree.[750]

Thursday 31

A lovely sunny day, tho' frost last night & I'm sure now. Went to Balally, all better there. They let off 2 H. Bombs y.day, so we may expect more unpleasant weather. It they only be done with them. Spent much time trying to get Miss Colson & Miss Johnstone into Dun's. It is all settled now for to-morrow aft. D.G. I find it expensive having to go to S. Mary's instead of phoning.[751]

April

Wednesday 6

7.30 a.m. R.mines, had shorter rest for Med. Board at 12 wh. discussed much, we hope to have follow up. Montessori for those who have left the T.B. A beautiful, warm day. After Teac had to go to Kill-o-Grange, no aft. rest & evg. went on till after 10.30 I was so tired. Took an Omnopon.

Thursday 14

Saw pts.outside & did Hosp. Dr Thornton brought Lady Prof. Paediatric Columbian Univ. to see Teac. She was very pleasing & seemed interested.

Thursday 21

Sun later & wind colder fr. East. Teac Board 11. Went all right but Flats giving trouble esp. No. 19. When Connolly prevaricated so badly at former meeting. We'll have to bring the case to Court or have all the others doing same & inheriting their flats.

Sunday 24

2 A.E. 8 a.m. R.mines. Then 11.30 Commemoration Service. S. Mary's very nice, tho' not over many there., A beautiful day like 1916 was.

---

750. *Maureen Chevasse* née Fox, wife of Claude Chavasse (1886–1971), Maureen would publish her biography of Terence MacSwiney in 1961.
751. *Exploded two H Bombs* – Operation Teapot was a series of 14 nuclear test explosions conducted by the USA at its Nevada Test Site in the first half of 1955. Two of the bombs were exploded on 29 March 1955.

Packed last things & think all fairly well done now. I think I got 4 or 5 boxes of sweets so we shld.n't be short in the Glen. D.V. all will go well to-morrow.

Monday 25

Up in good time & had no fuss at W. Row. Mrs Campbell brought me up & porter got parcel fr. cloak room. Good journey down & Mackey met us, got us bread, potatoes much better than Dublin. Ford so wide now floods would make no difference. Rained all day since we came & blew, quiet now & now braineen annuas when storm went down.[752]

This is the last entry in the diary.

Dr Kathleen Lynn died on 14 September 1955.

She was buried in her family plot in Deansgrange Cemetery with full military honours.

Crowds lined the streets of Dublin on the day of her funeral as a mark of respect.

---

752. *braineen annuas* – anaus (Irish for down), Lynn may be referring to something that had happen in her brain/head.

SELECT BIBLIOGRAPHY

Atwal, Jyoti, Breathnach, Ciara and Buckley, Sarah-Anne, *Gender and History: Ireland, 1852–1922* (London, 2023)

Crookes, Gearoid, *Dublin's Eye & Ear: The Making of a Monument* (Dublin, 1993)

Cullen, Mary and Luddy, Maria, *Female Activists: Irish Women and Change, 1900–1960* (Dublin, 2001)

Farmer, Tony, *Holles Street 1894–1994: The National Maternity Hospital: A Centenary History* (Dublin, 1994)

Foster, Roy, *Vivid Faces: The Revolutionary Generation in Ireland, 1890–1923* (London, 2013)

Frawley, Oona (ed.), *Women and the Decade of Commemorations* (Indiana, 2021)

Gialanella Valuilis, Maryann and O'Dowd, Mary (eds), *Women and Irish History* (Dublin, 1997)

Gatenby, Peter, *Dublin's Meath Hospital 1753–1996* (Dublin, 1996)

Jones, Mary, *These Obstreperous Lassies: History of the Irish Women Workers' Union* (Dublin, 1988)

Knirck, Jason K., *Women of the Dáil: Gender, Republicanism and the Anglo-Irish Treaty* (Dublin, 2006)

Kelly, Brendan, *Hearing Voices: The History of Psychiatry in Ireland* (Dublin, 2016)

Kelly, Brendan, *Ada English: Patriot and Psychiatrist* (Dublin, 2014)

Kelly, Laura, *Irish Women in Medicine, c.1880s–1920s: Origins, Education and Careers* (Manchester, 2017)

Kelly, Laura, *Irish Medical Education and Student Culture c.1850–1950* (Liverpool, 2017)

Lane, Leeann, *Rosamond Jacob: Third Person Singular* (Dublin, 2010)

MacCurtain, Margaret, *Ariadne's Thread: Writing Women into Irish History* (Dublin, 2008)

MacLellan, Anne, *Dorothy Stopford Price: Rebel Doctor* (Dublin, 2014)

McAuliffe, Mary and Gilles, Liz, *Richmond Barracks: WE were There, 77 Women of the Easter Rising* (Dublin, 2016)

McAuliffe, Mary, *Margaret Skinnider* (Dublin, 2020)

McLelland, Gillian and Hadden, Diana, *Pioneering Women: Riddel Hall and Queen's University* (Belfast, 2005)

Milne, Ida, *Stacking the Coffins: Influenza, War and Revolution in Ireland, 1918–1919* (Manchester, 2018)

Mitchell, David, *A 'Peculiar' Place: The Adelaide Hospital, Dublin: Its Times, Places and Personalities, 1839 to 1989* (Dublin, 1989)

Mulholland, Marie, *The Politics and Relationships of Kathleen Lynn* (Dublin, 2002)

Murphy, William, *Political Imprisonment and the Irish, 1912–1921* (Oxford, 2014)

O'Connor, Anne and Parkes, Susan M., *Gladly Learn and Gladly Teach: A History of Alexandra College and School Dublin 1866–1966* (Dublin, 1984)

Ó Fathartaigh, Mícheál and Weeks, Liam (eds), *The Treaty: Debating and Establishing the Irish State* (Dublin, 2018)

Ó hÓgartaigh, Margaret, *Kathleen Lynn: Irishwoman, Patriot, Doctor* (Dublin, 2006)

Pašeta, Senia, *Irish Nationalist Women, 1900–1918* (Cambridge, 2013)

Quinlan, Carmel, *Genteel Revolutionaries: Anna and Thomas Haslam and Irish Women's Movement* (Cork, 2005)

Quinn, James and White, Lawrence William (eds), *1916: Portraits and Lives* (Dublin 2016)

Regan, Nell, *Helena Molony: A Radical Life, 1883–1967* (Dublin, 2017)

Ryan, Louise and Ward, Margaret (eds), *Irish Women and the Vote: Becoming Citizens* (Dublin, 2018)

Swanton, Daisy Lawrenson, *Emerging from the Shadow: The Lives of Sarah Anne Lawrenson and Lucy Olive Kingston Based on Personal Diaries, 1883–1969* (Dublin, 1994)

Tiernan, Sonja, *Eva Gore-Booth: An Image of Such Politics* (Manchester, 2012)

Ward, Margaret, *Hanna Sheehy Skeffington: Suffragette and Sinn Féiner: Her Memoirs and Political Writings* (Dublin, 2017)

Ward, Margaret, *Fearless Woman: Hanna Sheehy Skeffington, Feminism and the Irish Revolution* (Dublin, 2019)

Ward, Margaret, *Unmanageable Revolutionaries: Women and Irish Nationalism* (Dublin, 2022)

Archives

Archbishop Edward Byrne Papers, Dublin Diocesan Archives
Bureau of Military History, Irish Military Archives
Brother Allen Archival Collection, Irish Military Archives
Chronology of Irish History 1919–23 http://irishhistory1919-1923chronology.ie/index.htm
Irish Newspapers Archives
Radical Newspapers Archives
Kathleen Lynn Diaries, Royal College of Physicians of Ireland Archive, Dublin
Kathleen Lynn Papers, Irish Military Archives
Kirkpatrick Index, Royal College of Physicians of Ireland Archive, Dublin
National University of Ireland Archive
Royal College of Science in Ireland Archive, University College Dublin, Dublin
Saint Ultan's Hospital Papers, Royal College of Physicians of Ireland Archive, Dublin

Annual Publications

Annual Reports of St Ultan's Hospital for Infants
Annual Reports of the Registrar General of Birth, Marriages and Death
Medical Directories
Medical Registers
Medical and Dental Student Registers

Index